T0251238

ACTIVE PERCEPTION

Edited by

YIANNIS ALOIMONOS
University of Maryland at College Park

COMPUTER VISION

A Series of Books Edited by Yiannis Aloimonos

Aloimonos, *Active Perception*

ACTIVE PERCEPTION

Edited by

YIANNIS ALOIMONOS
University of Maryland at College Park

Psychology Press
Taylor & Francis Group
New York London

First Published by
Lawrence Erlbaum Associates, Inc., Publishers
10 Industrial Avenue
Mahwah, New Jersey 07430

Transferred to Digital Printing 2009 by Psychology Press
270 Madison Ave, New York NY 10016
27 Church Road, Hove, East Sussex, BN3 2FA

Library of Congress Cataloging-in-Publication Data

Active perception / edited by Yiannis Aloimonos.
     p.   cm.
   Includes bibliographical references and index.
   ISBN 0-8058-1290-3
   1. Computer vision.   2. Visual perception.   3. Vision.
   I. Aloimonos, John.
   TA1634.A27 1993
   006.3'7--dc20   93-11667
                          CIP

Publisher's Note
The publisher has gone to great lengths to ensure the quality of this reprint
but points out that some imperfections in the original may be apparent.

CONTENTS

CONTRIBUTORS

☐ **Yiannis Aloimonos** Computer Vision Laboratory, Center for Automation Research and Computer Science Department and Institute for Advanced Computer Studies, University of Maryland, College Park, MD 20742

☐ **Dana H. Ballard** Department of Computer Science, University of Rochester, Rochester, NY 14627-0226

☐ **Andrew Blake** Department of Engineering Science, University of Oxford, Parks Rd., Oxford OX1 3PJ, UK

☐ **Christopher M. Brown** Department of Computer Science, University of Rochester, Rochester, NY 14627-0226

☐ **Jan-Olof Eklundh** Department of Numerical Analysis and Computing Science, Royal Institute of Technology, Stockholm, S-100 44, Sweden

☐ **Cornelia Fermüller** Computer Vision Laboratory, Center for Automation Research, University of Maryland, College Park, MD 20742 and Department for Pattern Recognition and Image Processing, Institute for Automation, Technical University of Vienna, Treitlstrasse 3, A-1040 Vienna, Austria

☐ **Francesca Gandolfo** Department of Communication, Computer and Systems Science, LIRA - Lab (Laboratory for Integrated Advanced Robotics), Via Opera Pia 11A - I16145 Genoa, Italy

☐ **Enrico Grosso** Department of Communication, Computer and Systems Science, LIRA - Lab (Laboratory for Integrated Advanced Robotics), Via Opera Pia 11A - I16145 Genoa, Italy

☐ **Liuqing Huang** Computer Vision Laboratory, Center for Automation Research, University of Maryland, College Park, MD 20742

☐ **Martin Herman** Robot Systems Division, National Institute of Standards and Technology (NIST), Bldg 220, Room B124, Gaithersburg, MD 20899

☐ **Kourosh Pahlavan** Department of Numerical Analysis and Computing Science, Royal Institute of Technology, Stockholm, S-100 44, Sweden

☐ **Daniel Raviv** Robotics Center and Electrical Engineering Department, Florida Atlantic University, Boca Raton, FL 33431 and Robot Systems Division, National Institute of Standards and Technology (NIST), Bldg 220, Room B124, Gaithersburg, MD 20899

☐ **Ehud Rivlin** Computer Vision Laboratory, Center for Automation Research, University of Maryland, College Park, MD 20742 and Department of Computer Science, Technion Israel Institute of Technology, Haifa, Israel

☐ **Giulio Sandini** Department of Communication, Computer and Systems Science, LIRA - Lab (Laboratory for Integrated Advanced Robotics), Via Opera Pia 11A - I16145 Genoa, Italy

☐ **Massimo Tistarelli** Department of Communication, Computer and Systems Science, LIRA - Lab (Laboratory for Integrated Advanced Robotics), Via Opera Pia 11A - I16145 Genoa, Italy

☐ **Tomas Uhlin** Department of Numerical Analysis and Computing Science, Royal Institute of Technology, Stockholm, S-100 44, Sweden

INTRODUCTION: ACTIVE VISION REVISITED

Y. Aloimonos.
University of Maryland

> *What is, is identical with the thoughts*
> *of the one who recognizes what it is.*
>
> *–Parmenides*

ABSTRACT

This book is devoted to technical problems related to the design and analysis of intelligent systems possessing perception, like the existing biological organisms and the "seeing" machines of the future. Since the appearance of the first technical results on Active Vision [2, 5], researchers are beginning to realize that perception (and intelligence in general) is not transcendental and disembodied, as Parmenides noted more than 2,000 years ago. To be more precise, it is becoming clear that in our effort to build intelligent visual systems we must consider the fact that perception is intimately related to the physiology of the perceiver and the tasks that it performs. This viewpoint, known as Purposive, Qualitative or Animate Vision, is the natural evolution of the principles of Active Vision and in this introductory chapter some fundamental questions about vision are examined under the light of this new framework. A discussion of the ideas and research efforts that contributed to the development of the new paradigm of Active Vision, along with a short description of the rest of the book, is provided. Finally, the principles underlying purposive recognition are described and various topics including intentionality, functionality, behavior and visual categories are discussed in some detail.

1. WHAT IS VISION?

"Rose is a rose is a rose is a rose," Gertrude Stein said [32]. In her later days she went around asking: What is the answer? Getting no reply, she then started asking:

This work was funded in part by ARPA, ONR and NSF (under a Presidential Young Investigator Award)

What is the question? Finding the question to ask is the most important problem in any intellectual endeavor. So, what is vision? Or, to be more precise, what are the questions we should ask in order to both understand the vision of living organisms and equip machines with visual capabilities? Let us first ask a few such questions [29]. When reference is made to a visual system, it could be a biological or machine system; no distinction is made.

What kind of information should a visual system derive from images? Should the information be described in some kind of language? Should this information be in a single, general purpose form, leaving it to other cognitive modules (planning, reasoning, memory, learning, language, etc.) to transform it to suit their needs, or could a visual system directly produce forms of information suited to specific cognitive processes? Are descriptions of 3-D location, shape and material properties the only descriptions that should be produced, or can a visual system directly produce "high level" information (about qualities like edibility, for example)? Are there sharply distinguished modules for vision, reasoning, learning, planning, memory, etc., or are the boundaries blurred and different subsystems closely integrated with one another?

In simpler terms, can we examine an intelligent system possessing vision and say that this part is engaged in visual processing, this other part is performing planning, this other part is doing reasoning, these cables (or connections) are for vision to communicate with planning, these cables for planning to communicate with learning, etc.? In still other words, is an intelligent visual system designed in a very clean modular manner where the different modules correspond to the different cognitive modalities, or is the design more complicated than that? Is visual perception a passive process or an active process in space-time? Are visual systems entities that just "see" and do nothing else, or are they designed in such a way that they use their vision to do something, i.e., take an action? An action is anything that changes the state of the system or the environment; it could be a motion or a decision or the building of a representation, for example.

2. WHAT IS GENERAL VISION?

There are many researchers working in the "field of vision." There are psychologists, psychophysicists, neurobiologists, neuroanatomists, zoologists, neuroethologists, computer scientists, engineers, mathematicians, physicists and cognitive scientists. Are they all trying to answer the same question? Of course not [29]. There are those who ask *the empirical question* (what is), i.e., they are trying to find out how existing visual systems are designed; those who ask *the normative question* (what should be), i.e., they are trying to find out what classes of animals or robots would be desirable (good, best, optimal) for a set of tasks; and finally there are those who address the *theoretical question* (what could be), i.e., what range of possible mechanisms could exist in intelligent visual systems. It is obvious that these three questions, all of them very important, do not necessarily have the same answer, although they are related. Marr [23] dealt with both the first and the third question, but most of his work was on the theoretical question. He obviously mixed them up because he took the human visual system to be general. But a general vision system is a theoretical concept; it does not exist in nature and cannot be designed for many reasons, some of which are explained later.

Let us now return to the initial question. What is vision? To avoid philosophizing, let us take, as a working answer, Marr's answer: "Vision is the process that creates, given a set of images, a complete and accurate representation of the scene and its properties." We can now notice several things. This is a purposeless definition, i.e., it does not consider what is vision going to be used for. As a consequence, the extracted representation is as general as possible.[1] This is of course what researchers refer to, correctly, as general vision. However, general vision addresses the *theoretical question*, and it exists only in theory! The goal of research on the "theoretical questions" is not to create the most "general" observer, because the "general" observer exists only in theory; it is nothing but a concept. In nature, nothing is general. There is no general athlete, no general warrior, no general scientist. Research on the theoretical question will uncover general principles behind the miracle of perception. Such research will determine what is theoretically possible, or impossible, to derive using vision. It will provide the geometrical and physical constraints relating the data (images) to properties of the 3-D world. It will give the capabilities and limitations of general visual recovery techniques. For example, it will show that if models for the reflectance of surfaces or for their texture are available, then shading and texture may be used to infer properties about shape [16]. To give another example, the theoretical approach will prove that from a series of images taken by a moving camera we may be able to recover, in principle, the structure of the scene and the 3-D motion involved if we have some way of solving the correspondence problem [21]. It will also show that the correspondence problem cannot be solved, unless we employ a specific model of the scene.

Research on the "theoretical question" of general vision will not tell us how to best build a visual system. It will give hints, but it will not give a solution, because this is not what its goal is. It is research on the normative question that, using results of general vision, will propose ways of building intelligent, sophisticated and flexible visual systems. Human visual systems are just one example in the spectrum of biological vision systems; they are not general. The thousands of visual tasks that they cannot perform—while other animals can—and the many celebrated illusions to which they are subject are just trivial proofs of this simple fact. Adrian Horridge [17], a vision researcher who has been studying bees for the past thirty years or

---

[1] Of course Marr followed the general AI methodology of his times. The main emphasis in AI research has been the finding of general purpose methodologies and general purpose representations that preserve as much information as possible. A three step approach for solving any problem has been taken for granted. The conversion of sensor data into an internal representation and vice versa (i.e., signals to actuators, or decisions, that is all together actions) has been separated from the phase of developing algorithms to perform computations on internal data. Most research has been devoted to processing the internal data and as a consequence different subfields such as planning, learning, reasoning, vision and many more have appeared. Therefore, it is not surprising that the first influential theory of vision mainly concentrated on the computational and representational aspects. Vision was described as a reconstruction process, that is a problem of creating representations for increasingly growing levels of abstraction leading from 2-D images through the primal sketch through the $2\frac{1}{2}$-D sketch to object descriptions ("from pixels to predicates" [24]).

so writes that humans and bees are not that different in their visual systems regarding visuomotor control tasks. Of course humans have very large brains, nearly the largest one can find on earth. As a result, they have large amounts of memory and various other cognitive capabilities (for example, they can play chess, which elephants cannot). The human visual system interacts with all these cognitive abilities, hence its performance may appear spectacular, amazing and general. Spectacular it is, amazing it is, but general it is not. The simple fact that the spectacular abilities of the bee or the fly seem, to many researchers, to have little to do with higher-level human abilities reflects how little we understand the fundamental processes involved in vision.

3. What Is Active Vision?

Marr's contributions set the foundations for vision as a scientific discipline. His theories about early vision led neurobiologists to find in the monkey cortex interesting retinotopic maps. However, Marr left out of his theory a very important issue: the fact that all existing visual systems, from insects and frogs, to fish, snakes, birds and humans, are active. Being active, they control the image acquisition process and thus introduce constraints that greatly facilitate the recovery of information about the 3-D scene. "I move, therefore I see" [13] is a fundamentally true statement. And if we manage to make the human eye stationary, humans start losing perception!

The first technical developments in active vision [2] considered the problem in the context of the general methodological paradigm at the time, namely the one that treats vision as the process of *general recovery* [23]. An active observer was defined as one who is capable of engaging in some kind of activity whose purpose is to control the geometric parameters of its sensory apparatus. The superiority of an active observer vs. a passive one was clearly established by the fact that an active observer can perform classical general recovery tasks (like shape from x) in a more efficient way than a passive observer can. General recovery problems that are ill posed and nonlinear for a passive observer become well posed and linear for an active observer. However, it slowly started becoming clear that not only are the observer's geometric parameters relevant, but a whole set of other visual parameters as well. The ability to manipulate them in a controlled manner, as both an action and a reaction, started building the concept of active vision. However, the way the manipulation is done, to what extent and what kind of manipulation appeared to be task-dependent. The typical property of passive vision is that the observer is not capable of choosing how to view the scene, but is instead limited to what is offered, determined by the preset visual parameters and environmental conditions, including time sampling. The active observer, on the other hand, utilizes its capability to change its visual parameters to acquire favorable data from the scene in solving the specific task it has at the time. A passive system has to extract all the information needed from the given images, possibly engaging in complicated reasoning and computations, but cannot acquire more data which could facilitate the interpretation of the scene in view in order to achieve the task it is engaged in. Researchers started realizing that an active vision system is a system able to manipulate its visual parameters in a controlled manner in order to extract useful data about the scene in space and time that would allow it to best perform a set of tasks. Since vision is trivially active, it became apparent that the design of a vision system depends critically on the tasks it has to perform. At the same time, the fallacy of general vision started becoming clearer. An important observation was that vision does not function in isolation, but as a part of a system that interacts with the world in highly specific ways. In addition, researchers started realizing that vision systems do not have to compute all things at all times, but only what they need. These observarions led to the next natural development or evolution of active vision, namely the paradigm of purposive [1] (or animate) vision [6].

4. ACTIVE VISION LEADS TO PURPOSIVE VISION

An active observer that wants to reconstruct an accurate and complete representation of its extrapersonal space needs an unrealistically large amount of computational power. To give an example from human vision: one of its special features is the fovea. Humans look at the world using a small window that they move around using a very elaborate gaze control system. If the resolution of the human eye were everywhere equal to its resolution near the optical axis, then humans would have a brain weighing approximately 30,000 pounds! [30]

For reasons such as this one and several others [1] related to the inherent difficulties of complete visual reconstruction, the platonic view of vision as a general reconstruction process started fading away. A perceptual system and the world it lives in cannot be separated. They need each other in order to be complete, in order to make sense. The perceptual system has a relationship with the world it lives in; thus the system itself is a particular embodiment of that relationship. To have a "general" relationship with the world that obeys the laws of physics is something beyond any comprehension.[2]

There is simply too much that can be known about the world for a vision system to construct a general-purpose complete description. The information contained in the visual signal is much more than the system actually needs or can cope with. Thus the fundamental problem of a vision system is to determine what information from the image should be used and what representation of it needs to be built so that the relationship of the system with its world can best be implemented. In other words, the system needs to recover partial information about the scene. Knowing what kind of partial recovery needs to be performed depends on the relationship of the system to its world; to put it differently, it depends on the tasks that the system has to carry out, i.e., on its purpose. Purposive vision does not consider vision in isolation, but as part of a complex system that interacts in specific ways with the world. It is important to note that if the visual system knows what kind of information is needed and what it will be used for, this permits the system to alter its interaction with the world dynamically in order to make this information more easily available. Finally, since the relationship of the visual system to the world consists of perceptual capabilities and actions, its implementation (i.e., the

---

[2] One might be able to achieve such a general relationship in Plato's world of ideas.

design of the visual system) can be achieved through a reduced instruction set of perceptions and actions (behaviors) that does not require an elaborate categorical representation of the world (qualitative vision). The visual categories a visual system uses, and consequently the algorithms it needs to develop or learn in order to derive them, and the meaning of the symbols representing these categories, depend totally on two things:

(a) the characteristics of the system itself (its physiology, its mobility—is it flying, crawling, walking, etc.—and its computational capacity); and
(b) the tasks it needs to accomplish.

To summarize, purposive vision calls for partial and opportunistic visual reconstruction and for the development of new, flexible representations related to action.

5. Theoretical, Normative and Empirical Vision

If we want to use images in order to accomplish a task, we obviously need to recover something from them. However, there are many dimensions along which we can move when we perform visual recovery. The recovery can be partial or complete, the problem can be general or specific, and the assumptions used can be general or specific. The kind of research we perform depends on our position in this 3–D space. For the readers' benefit, some dimensionality reduction is performed and two 2-D spaces are presented which convey the message and improve the clarity of the pictorial description. Tables 1 and 2 describe this, if one examines the labeling of the axes. The concept of complete vs. partial recovery is clear. How "partial" partial is depends on the task (or purpose). What is a general or specific problem? A general problem is a problem of general vision, a module of Marr's theory (like optic flow estimation, shape from X, and the like)—a problem whose goal is to obtain complete recovery. A specific problem is one that answers a specific question about the scene. Usually, specific problems are simple applications of general problems. An example here will help clarify matters: The module of structure from motion (from a series of dynamic images, recover the shape and 3-D motion of the observer relative to parts of the scene) is a general problem. The following problems are specific: Is there anything moving in the scene as seen by a moving observer? Is it moving closer to the observer or is it going away? Is it going to hit the observer? How should the observe move in order to intercept it? etc. Obviously, specific problems require partial recovery of the visible world. In the sequel the difference between general and specific assumptions is explained. First of all, assumptions are constraints on space-time, the visual system and their relationship. An assumption is general when it holds universally, under any circumstances. A specific assumption is one that holds only for a subset of the world (or for a subset of visual systems and their relationships to the world).

When we assume that the world is piecewise planar, that is a general assumption, because indeed the world satisfies it (it is actually a theorem in differential geometry). However, in order to utilize this assumption for visual recovery we must make an additional assumption regarding the number of planar patches; and then

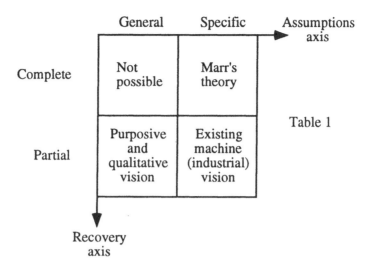

Table 1

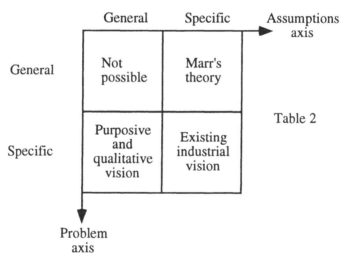

Table 2

our assumption has become specific. Similarly, we may assume that the world is smooth between discontinuities; that is general. Again, however, in order to utilize this assumption we must make some assumption regarding the discontinuities, and then our assumption becomes specific. We may assume that an observer only translates. If indeed the physiology of the observer is such that it only translates, then we have made a general assumption. If we assume that the motion of an observer in a long sequence of frames is the same between any two consecutive frames, we have made a specific assumption. If we assume that the noise in our system is Gaussian or uniform, again we have made a specific assumption.

Tables 1 and 2 show how general vision, purposive vision and industrial vision fit together in a continuum of completeness and partialness, generality and specificity. Purposive vision and general vision work together, with general vision providing hints and ideas and purposive vision designing the whole spectrum of visual systems. We can always formulate general vision problems as optimization problems. But global optimization is, in general, impossible and it requires specific assumptions in order to determine the coefficients involved in the global functionals (or to determine the priors in various general probabilistic approaches). Through such studies, however, we can learn aspects of the problem space that make it difficult and formulate ideas for robust partial recovery, under general assumptions. The fact that we can solve partial recovery problems under general assumptions should not be surprising; it is because this requires much less of the visual computation.

6. THE BIG PICTURE

Purposive vision is the vision of any visual system, including the human. Researchers are uncomfortable when they do not immediately see the big picture, how different cognitive mechanisms fit together, i.e., the brain. How can we view the brain as an intelligent, flexible, purposive perceptual system?

This problem is easier if we study vision in isolation [23]. The dominant view regarding the brain has been that it is modular. Each cognitive process is assigned a module; each of these "big" modules is broken down into submodules, and so on. It is becoming increasingly clear that this is not true. It is, of course, important to view the brain in a modular way. Modularity is a general principle that we follow when we design or analyze large, complex information systems. However, purposive vision (or purposive perception) suggests that these modules are behaviors!

A behavior is a sequence of cognitive events and actions, a set of visual, planning, memory, and reasoning processes working in a cooperative manner and "acting" on the system itself or its environment.

Is there a formal theory of behaviors? How do we describe them in a formal manner? How do we learn new ones and how do we build complex behaviors using a synthesis of existing, simpler ones? Is there a behavioral calculus? Several chapters in this book shed some light on these issues, but these problems are very deep and complex.

Regarding an architecture supporting the integration of behaviors, it is clear that Brooks' [7] layered architecture is not satisfactory because low- and high-level processes should cooperate directly and because the order of visual systems is not complete, but partial. This simply means that flexible and sophisticated vision systems may not have capabilities that simpler (apparently) systems possess. In addition, flexible and sophisticated systems need to be able to represent knowledge, and Brooks' viewpoint that the world can be used as a repository of information can give rise, at best, to some simple reactive behaviors. On the other hand, formalisms such as discrete event dynamic systems, I/O automata, Petri nets, Bayesian networks, and the like [18, 28, 20, 22, 12, 26], appropriately modified, are good candidates for formalizing behavior[3], i.e., for serving as mechanisms for knowledge representation inside a behavioral process. For lack of a better word and slightly modifying Sloman's [29] word, this architecture has been called labyrinthic [1], in order to stress

---

[3] There is a large amount of literature in theoretical computer science that basically models behaviors.

the interaction among the different cognitive modalities and action. The brain is thus a set of behaviors, and it makes a lot of sense to study it as such.

7. BUILDING VISUAL SYSTEMS

The main reason why the approach to vision suggested by Marr has not led to the development of successful artificial systems is that vision was studied in a vacuum, i.e., the utilization of vision was completely ignored. However, the vision of no system is purposeless and thus it necessarily needs to be studied in conjuction with the task the system is involved in. From this viewpoint, understanding vision means understanding a system possessing visual capabilities.

In general, if our goal is to study (or more precisely formulated, analyze in order to design) a system, we are advised by engineering considerations to follow some common principles in system design and address a set of basic questions: What is the functionality of the system? What are the autonomous subsystems (modules) the system is divided in? What is the relationship of the modules to each other? What is the representation of information within the subsystems, and how are the modules communicating with each other? Finally, we have to ask: What is the most efficient and effective way for designing the single modules?

Having these questions in mind, C. Fermüller [11] proposed a new approach for studying vision and developing artificial vision systems. This approach takes it for granted that the observer (the system) possesses an active visual apparatus. Since, furthermore, it is inspired by evolutionary, neuroethological considerations, it is called synthetic (evolutionary) approach. This approach constitutes a philosophy for how to systematically study visual systems which live in environments as complex and multifarious as those of human beings. It is substantiated by basically two principles. The first principle is related to the overall structure of the system and how it is modularized, what are the problems to be solved and in which order they ought to be addressed. The second principle is concerned with the way the single modules should be realized.

As basis for its necessary computations a system has to utilize mathematical models, which serve as abstractions of the representations employed. The first principle of the synthetic approach states that the study of visual systems should be performed in an hierarchical order according to the complexity of the mathematical models involved. Naturally, the computations and models are related to the class of tasks the system is supposed to perform. A system possesses a set of capabilities which allow it to solve certain tasks. The synthetic approach calls for first studying capabilities whose development relies on only simple models and then go on and study capabilities requiring more complex models. Simple models do not refer to environment or situation specific models which are of use in only a limited amount of situations. On the contrary, each of the capabilities requiring a specified set of models can be used for solving a well defined class of tasks in every environment and situation the system is exposed to. In other words, the employed assumptions have to be general with regard to the environment. The motivation for this approach is to gain increasingly insight in the process of vision, which is of such high complexity. Therefore the capabilities that require more complex models should be based on "simpler" already developed capabilities. The complexity of a capability is thus given by the complexity of its assumption; what has been considered a simple capability, might require complex models and vice versa. For example, the celebrated capability of egomotion estimation does not require as has been believed complex models about the geometry of the scene in view or the time evolution of the motion, but only a simple rigid motion model, while the detection of independent motion, which has been considered as primitive, requires more elaborate non-rigid motion models.

The second principle, motivated by the need for robustness, is the quest for algorithms which are qualitative in nature [1]. The synthetic approach does not have as its goal the reconstruction of the scene in view, but the development of a class of capabilities that recognize aspects of objective reality which are necessary to perform a set of tasks. The function of every module in the system constitutes an act of recognizing specific situations by means of primitives which are applicable in general environments. For example, a system, in order to avoid obstacles, does not have to reconstruct the depth of the scene in view. It merely has to recognize that the distance to a close-by object is decreasing at a rate beyond some threshold given by the system's reaction time. Recognition, of course, is much easier than general reconstruction of the scene, simply because the information necessary to perform a specific task can be represented in a space having only a few degrees of freedom. Moreover, in order to speak of an algorithm as qualitative, the primitives to be computed don't have to rely on explicit quantitative models. Qualitativeness can be achieved due to a number of reasons: The primitives might be expressible in qualitative terms or their computation might be derived from inexact measurements and pattern-recognition techniques or the computational model itself can be proved stable and robust in all possible cases.

8. SCANNING THE BOOK

The seven chapters of this book are devoted to various aspects of active perception, ranging from general principles and methodological matters to technical issues related to navigation, manipulation, recognition, learning, planning, reasoning and topics related to the neurophysiology of intelligent systems. In the first chapter, Pahlavan et al. address active vision as a methodology and elucidate its methodological superiority over passive vision; they also discuss issues of system design, purpose dependency and problems related to control. The second chapter treats the problem of navigation from the perspective of active, purposive vision and advances a methodology borrowed from the field of programming languages for formalizing the behaviors of an agent in such a way that we can reason about them (i.e., prove their properties). In Chapter 3, Fermüller discusses the problem of 3-D motion for an active observer and shows that the problems of estimating egomotion and the motion of an object, although mathematically equivalent, are perceptually different and should be addressed through the development of different behaviors. She develops novel geometric constraints that serve as the basis of a set of algorithms for 3-D motion estimation that do not rely on correspondence or optic flow computation as a preprocessing step. The fourth chapter demonstrates that the simultaneous and coordinated operation of vision and action can be used not only to simplify some traditional visual tasks, but also to extend the overall scope of vision to important new areas. The concepts of purposiveness, closed-loop control and concurrency of motion and sensing are dominant throughout the chapter and they synergistically contribute to novel solutions in problems of navigation, manipulation and gaze control. In Chapter 5, Raviv and Herman treat the problem of visual servoing for an active and purposive vision system in a novel manner. They present a solution to the problem of visually controlling a vehicle which is very different from the traditional approaches to navigation. In Chapter 6, A. Blake presents the beginnings of a theory for the computational modelling of hand–eye coordination, a topic of increasing scientific interest. Finally, Ballard and Brown present a set of ideas around cooperative gaze-control behaviors that reduces the need for explicit representation postulated in the perceiver. These ideas take the form of principles governing active vision systems and they represent a framework for sequential decision making and visual learning. There exists a good reason why most of the chapters are devoted to problems related to navigation and manipulation. This is because the most basic visual capabilities found in living systems are based on motion [17]. In addition, it is not very hard to classify categories in the visual environment in a way which is related in a purposive manner to visuomotor coordination tasks of an agent. Later, a high-level analysis of purposive recognition is given.

9. FINAL THOUGHTS

Marr was influenced by Warrington [31]. She described the capacities and limitations of patients who had suffered left or right parietal lesions. She noticed the existence of two classes of patients: The members of the first class could recognize an object provided that its view was conventional; the members of the second class could not name the object or its purpose but could still perceive its shape. To Marr these results suggested that vision alone could deliver a description of the shape of an object even when the object was not recognized in a conventional sense; Marr took this to be the main (central) purpose of vision. After many years of research and after looking at many patients, Martha Farah does not seem to be finding the same results. Her findings agree much more with a labyrinthic picture of the brain than with a Marrian modular point of view (see Appendix 1 for a very short summary of Farah's work).

It is very hard to understand a purposive approach to recognition because this problem is equivalent to the embodiment of categories. To shed some light on this complex issue, a few more appendices have been added: on intentionality and behavior (Appendix 2); on the recognition process (Appendix 3); and on functional categories (Appendix 4).

What does the future hold? Researchers will realize that general vision is a chimera. Although general vision will continue to be studied, it will become clear that it does not make much sense to insist on developing systems possessing general vision. They will develop basic visual capabilities that, in the framework of purposive, qualitative and active vision, will contribute in a synthetic manner to the development of flexible vision systems. We will see, not general, but specific invariance techniques appearing; we will find out how to achieve the most while spending the least effort. We will discover the computational capabilities of uncalibrated (or partially calibrated) vision systems. Most important, flexible vision systems will be constructed in several laboratories (see [3] for some existing ones); we will observe them and experiment with them. In the past, many discoveries have resulted from unexplained engineering observations rather than from the development of a successful theory.

Vision has a purpose, and that purpose is action. Action can be practical (motor control), theoretical (creation of a purposive representation, a decision or an internal change of state) or aesthetic [29]. Flexible and sophisticated vision without action is meaningless. Purposive vision bridges the gap between theory (general recovery) and vision systems. In this framework, we can advance the field to a post-paradigmatic stage, in the sense of Kuhn. In simple terms, we can integrate the different cognitive modalities - perception, planning, reasoning, learning - into intelligent beings. We should also note that learning can be done much more successfully in the purposive paradigm, because we learn well defined things—behaviors, instead of general-purpose representations whose beauty is only of theoretical importance. Working on general vision has discouraged the integration of learning and visual processes, something that has just started [4, 25]. In addition, the problem of photointerpretation—analysis of static images—a problem receiving increasing attention lately under the name "Image Databases" and which humans are very good at–is trivial when the researcher is allowed to collect the perceptual images and to ask the appropriate questions, and is currently impossible when general questions are asked.

REFERENCES

1. Y. Aloimonos, "Purposive and qualitative active vision," In *Proc. Image Understanding Workshop*, 1990, 816–828.

2. Y. Aloimonos, I. Weiss and A. Bandopadhay, "Active vision," *Int'l. J. Comp. Vision* **7**, 1988, 333–356.

3. Y. Aloimonos (Ed.), Special Issue on Purposive and Qualitative Active Vision, *CVGIP B: Image Understanding* **56**, 1992.

4. Y. Aloimonos, R. Michalski, P. Pachowitz and A. Rosenfeld, "Report on the NSF/DARPA Workshop on Vision and Learning," October 1992, Harpers Ferry, VA.

5. R. Bajcsy, "Active perception," *Proc. IEEE 76* **8**, 1988, 996–1005.

6. D. Ballard, "Animate vision," *Artificial Intelligence* **48**, 1991, 57–86.

7. R.A. Brooks, "Achieving Artificial Intelligence Through Building Robots," A.I. Memo 899, MIT, Cambridge, MA.

8. B. Chandrasekaran, "Design problem solving: A task analysis," *Artificial Intelligence* **11**, 1990, 59–72.

9. M. Dennis, "Dissociated naming and locating of body parts after left anterior temporal lobe resection: An experimental case study," *Brain and Language* **3**, 1976, 147–163.

10. M. Farah, *Visual Agnosia: Disorders of Object Recognition and What They Tell Us about Normal Vision*, MIT Press, Cambridge, MA, 1990.

11. C. Fermüller, *Basic Visual Capabilities*, Ph.D. Thesis, Technical University of Vienna, 1993. (also, Technical Report, Computer Vision Laboratory, University of Maryland, 1993).

12. S. Owicki and D. Gries, "An axiomatic proof technique for parallel programs," *Acta Informatica* **6**, 319-440.

13. T. Hamada, "Active vision," In *Proc. Int'l. Neuroethology Congress*, 1992.

14. J. Hart, R.S. Berndt and A. Caramazza, "Category-specific naming deficit following cerebral infraction," *Nature* **316**, 1985, 439–440.

15. J. Hopcroft, J. Schwartz and M. Sharir, "On the complexity of motion planning for multiple independent objects: PSPACE hardness of the warehouseman's problem," *Int'l. J. Robotics Research* **3**, 1984, 76–88.

16. B.K.P. Horn, *Robot Vision*, McGraw Hill, New York, 1986.

17. G.A. Horridge, "The evolution of visual processing and the construction of seeing systems," *Proc. Royal Soc. London B* **230**, 1987, 279–292.

18. Y. Ho, "Dynamics of discrete event systems," *Proc. IEEE* **77**, 1989, 3–6.

19. J. De Kleer and S. Brown, "A qualitative physics based on confluences," in D.G. Bobrow (Ed.), *Qualitative Reasoning about Physical Systems*, MIT Press, Cambridge, MA, 1985.

20. F. Lin and W.M. Wonham, "Decentralized control and coordination of discrete event systems," In *Proc. IEEE Conf. on Decision and Control*, 1988, 1125–1130.

21. H.C. Longuet-Higgins, "A computer algorithm for reconstructing a scene from two projections," *Nature* **293**, 1981, 133–135.

22. N. Lynch and M. Tuttle, "Hierarchical correctness proofs for distributed algorithms," In *Proc. ACM Symposium on Principles of Distributed Computing*, 1987.

23. D. Marr, *Vision: A Computational Investigation into the Human Representation and Processing of Visual Information*, Freeman, San Francisco, 1982.

24. A. Pentland (Ed.), *From Pixels to Predicates: Recent Advances in Computational and Robot Vision*, Norwood, NJ; Ablex, 1986.

25. T. Poggio and S. Edelman, "A network that learns to recognize 3-D objects,", *Nature*, **343**, 1990, 263–266.

26. P.J. Ramadge and W.M. Wonham, "The control of discrete event systems," *Proc. IEEE* **77**, 81–98.

27. J.R. Searle, *Intentionality*, Cambridge University Press, New York, 1983.

28. S.S. Lam and A.U. Shankar, "A relational notation for state transition systems," *IEEE Trans. Software Engineering*, 1991, 12–25.

29. A. Sloman, "On designing a visual system," *J. Experimental Theoretical Artificial Intelligence* **1**, 1989, 289–337.

30. E. Schwartz, Personal Communication, *Workshop on Active Vision*, University of Chicago, 1991.

31. E.K. Warrington and T. Shallice, "Category specific semantic impairments," *Brain* **107**, 1984, 829–854.

32. R. Wehner, "Matched filters: Neural models of the external world," *J. Comparative Physiology A* **161**, 1987, 511–531.

33. G. Wilfong, "Motion planning in the presence of movable obstacles," In *Proc. ACM Symposium on Computational Geometry*, 1988, 279–288.

34. A. Yamadori and M.L. Albert, "Word category aphasia," *Cortex* **9**, 1973, 112–115.

APPENDIX 1: HUMAN VISUAL AGNOSIA AND OBJECT RECOGNITION

The condition of visual agnosia provides interesting evidence as to how object recognition might be done by humans. Visual agnosia refers to a condition in which the patient fails to recognize objects (by sight) due to some brain damage, despite relatively well preserved sensory capacities. A common distinction is between apperceptive agnosia, in which recognition fails because of an impairment in visual perception (patients do not see objects normally, and hence cannot recognize them), and associative agnosia, in which perception seems adequate to allow recognition, and yet recognition cannot take place.

Farah [10] summarizes associative agnosia cases. Especially revealing is the categorization of objects agnostic patients fail to recognize. Farah describes patients studied by Warrington [31] in which knowledge of stimuli roughly corresponding to living things is relatively impaired compared to knowledge of most nonliving things, or vice versa. Under the definition of living things she included animals, plants and foods. Nonliving things were exemplified by small, man-made objects. Farah adds cases like Dennis' [9], in which deficits were confined to body parts; Yamadori's [34], objects typically found indoors; Hart's [14], fruits and vegetables; and prosopagnosia, which is the inability to recognize faces.

Under apperceptive agnosia, Farah describes a case of a patient who had adequate elementary visual functions and general cognitive ability, yet was dramatically impaired in the simplest forms of shape discrimination. This patient could detect differences in luminance, color, size, as well as respond to small movements of presented objects, but could not distinguish between two objects of the same size, color, etc. when the only difference between them was shape. It is important, in our opinion, to emphasize that this patient could identify and name objects from tactile, olfactory, or auditory cues without any problem. This situation is reported for other patients as well. It is interesting to note the role played in the recognition process, as well as the help given by motion. Tracing was used for contour following, orientation judgement, or search for the best view.

Another interesting disorder is dorsal simultanagnosia. Accepting Luria's definition [10], it is a specific type of perceptual deficit in which only one object, or part of an object, can be seen at one time. Luria suggests that "objecthood" is not simply a matter of size or of visual complexity. For example, a face can be viewed as an object, a collection of other objects such as eyes, nose, etc., or as a part of a larger object, the human body. Luria's patient could perceive a face, but when a detail was perceived, its relation to the whole was lost. It seems that whatever cognitive process is disrupted in dorsal simultanagnosia is sensitive to shifts in what the visual system takes to be an object.

APPENDIX 2: INTENTIONALITY AND BEHAVIOR

Vision systems that operate in different environments and perform different visual tasks do not necessarily recognize objects using similar algorithms. A vision system that recognizes ten types of objects does not necessarily work in the same way as a system that needs to recognize one type or a hundred types. A system that serves a rapidly moving agent is not necessarily built in the same way as a system for a stationary agent. Object recognition should be studied by taking into account not only the objects that have to be recognized but also the agent that has to perform the recognition. Since different agents, working with different purposes in different environments, do not recognize visually in the same manner, we should not seek a general, universal theory of object recognition. Instead, we should concentrate on developing a methodology that, given an agent will suggest how to perform particular recognition tasks.

An agent is a system (robot) that has visual (and other) sensing capabilities and is able to carry out a set of behaviors. These behaviors are direct results of a set of purposes or intentions that the agent has. A behavior is identified as anything that changes the internal state of the agent and its relationship to the environment. Carrying out a behavior calls for the performance of various recognition tasks. By performing partial recovery of attributes of an object, we can find out if the object is suitable for the desired purpose. In general, an object can be used for many purposes. The agent must recognize the one needed to carry out its behavior.

Perception is a causal and intentional transaction between the mind and the world. The intentional content of our visual perception is termed [27] "the visual experience." When we see a table there are two elements in the perceptual situation: the visual experience and the table. The two are not independent. The visual experience has the presence and features of the table as conditions of satisfaction. The content of the visual experience is self-referential in the sense that it requires that the state of affairs in the world must cause the visual experience which is the realization of the intentional content.

When we visually perceive an object we have a visual experience. This visual experience is an experience of the object. It may be that the conditions of satisfaction are not fulfilled. This is the case for illusions, hallucinations, etc. The visual experience, and not the world, is at fault. The visual experience that we have, in this case, is indistinguishable from the visual experience we would have if we actually saw the real object. The intentional content of the visual experience determines its conditions of satisfaction. A visual experience in that sense is a mental phenomenon which is intrinsically intentional.

An agent is defined as a set of intentions, $I_1, I_2, \ldots, I_n$. Each intention I_k is translated into a set of behaviors, $B_{k1}, B_{k2}, \ldots, B_{km}$. Each behavior B_{ki} calls for the completion of recognition tasks $T_{ki1}, T_{ki2}, \ldots, T_{kij}$. The agent acts in behavior B_{ki} under intention I_k. The behavior calls for the completion of recognition tasks $T_{ki1}, \ldots, T_{kin}$. The behavior sets parameters for the recognition tasks. Note that the same object can answer positively to several recognition tasks. Under one behavior a chair will answer yes to some recognition task that is asking for obstacles, under another behavior it will answer yes to a recognition task that is asking for a sitting place, and under another it will answer yes to a task that is asking for an assault weapon.

We can view the recognition process along the axis intention, behavior, recognition task. For a theory of purposive object recognition we should be able to make two basic transformations: first from the desired intention to the set of behaviors that achieve it, second from a specific behavior to some needed recognition task(s). In the following paragraphs we will show that the intention-to-behaviors (or task decomposition) problem with a finite number of behaviors is undecidable by reducing it the halting problem. We believe that the transformation from behaviors to recognition tasks is also hard.

Let the state of the world S_n be defined by the two tuples $\langle O_n, R_n \rangle$, where O_n is a set of objects $(O_{n1}, O_{n2}, \ldots, O_{nk})$ and R_n is a set of relations $(R_{n1}, R_{n2}, \ldots, R_{nl})$ between the different objects. A behavior is a transition between two states. An intention is a desired state of the world. The intention-to-behaviors problem is: Given the triplet $\langle S_0, S_n, (B_1, \ldots, B_k) \rangle$ (i.e., a start state, an intention, a set of behaviors), find a sequence of behaviors that leads from the start state to the desired intention.

Assume we are given a Turing machine M and an input sequence of symbols X. We describe the transformation from $\langle M, X \rangle$ to $\langle S_0, S_n, (B_1, \ldots, B_k) \rangle$ informally. To encode a completely blank tape containing the input X, with the indication that M's head is pointing to the leftmost symbol of X and that the state is M's start state, we write the start state as $\langle (\#, X, \#), (R_1, R_2) \rangle$ where R_1 indicates M's state and R_2 the head position. The state-transition diagram is represented by the set of behaviors. The halting state is represented by S_n (the intention). Activating a sequence of behaviors from the start state corresponds directly to a computation of M on X. Consequently, if the intention-to-behaviors problem were decidable the halting problem would be decidable too.

If we add constraints to our definition of the problem we can move from undecidability to intractability. For example, by constraining ourselves to a constant set of objects we can show a PSPACE-hard lower bound. This can be shown by reducing our problem, for example, to that of motion planning for an object in the presence of movable obstacles, where the final positions of the obstacles are specified as part of the goal of the motion. The complexity of this problem is discussed in [33, 15]. The reduction is straightforward. The set of objects contains the moving objects and the obstacles (the polygonality can be given in the relation set or as part of the objects' definition). The positions of the objects are part of the relation set. The intention encodes the final state. Grasping, pushing and moving are the behaviors. Solving the intention-to-behaviors problem gives a solution to this problem.

APPENDIX 3: THE RECOGNITION PROCESS

Object utilization is not the same problem as that of naming an object. Under this framework an agent acts in behavior B_{ki} under intention I_k. The behavior calls for the completion of recognition tasks $T_{ki1}, \ldots, T_{kin}$. The behavior sets parameters for the recognition tasks. Each recognition task activates a different collection of basic perceptual modules. Each module qualitatively finds a generic object property which is a result of one or a combination of direct low-level computations on some sensory data (possibly done by other modules). The result of a module's operation is given as a qualitative value. Each module has its own neighboring open intervals which are parameter-specific. The ith module can take one of $q_{i1}, \ldots, q_{in}$ qualitative values.

The state of our recognition system, denoted by Q_i, is a tuple of all the qualitative values of our modules $(q_1, \ldots, q_m)$ under recognition task T_{kij}. Each recognition task T_{kij} defines a system state that will constitute a positive answer to that recognition task. Recognition is done when we complete our task, which means a stable answer from our modules. At this point we want to remark that a common recognition task can be defined as a new module and unexpected object recognition could be developed along these lines. The conditions for this kind of decision are not considered here and probably should take into account some utility measures (frequency of appearance, network complexity, etc.).

Under this framework learning can be defined as the process of matching the "correct" system state with the recognition task needed by a certain behavior. This process is actually the reverse of recognition. A behavior creates a need for an object. An object is segmented by some low-level modules, and a system state is achieved. The object is tested and a satisfied result for a needed behavior starts the creation or definition of a recognition task.

When we need to perform a given recognition task T_{kij} under behavior B_{ki} and intention I_k, we may assume that some parameter setting is done by the intention and the behavior. These parameters fix the setting for the task, which includes the required system state (some of the modules might be in the don't care position) and possibly some additional "common knowledge" parameters, such as environmental parameters (outdoor, indoor), predator, size, etc. From this point of view the recognition process is using high-level information.

APPENDIX 4: FUNCTIONAL CATEGORIES

The relationships of an organism or robot to objects in its environment are functional relations: Objects can be obstacles, predators, prey, etc. Such relations are intention-dependent. Objects are related to actions from the utilitarian point of view. When we want to get a coconut from a tree, we must search for an object that provides the necessary functions—e.g., graspable, movable, rigid, elongated, long. We thus need to define transformations from these functions into the needed sensory data. Objects have observable characteristics from which we can infer which functional category an object belongs to. For example, does the object appear to be immobile or mobile? (It can be momentarily stationary.) Is the object graspable? Does the object appear to be organic or inorganic (animal, vegetable, mineral)?

This transformation is close, in some senses, to a design process. Design involves mapping from behavior to structure. A designer tries to specify an artifact that delivers some functions and satisfies some constraints [8]. It is interesting to note that general algorithms for design are computationally intractable [8], and that common methods for design use compiled knowledge, solved design cases, and the like. We believe that the general solution to this problem of finding the transformation from function to structure is hard.[4] In order to build working systems, we can use a set of common, useful, specialized functional translations.

We can define object categories like animate, inanimate, prey, predator, obstacle, etc., that belong to hierarchical structures. The hierarchies are functional and have sensory relevance, i.e., they must have perceivable characteristics that make them discriminable.

For example, consider a class of functional categories that relate to how your motion is constrained by the things in the category. Obviously the definitions of these classes depend on your motion ability: Are you a tortoise or a vehicle with wheels? Depending on the nature of your mobility and on your size, the world subdivides into different functional classes of objects in terms of their possible roles as obstacles. We can have movable obstacles, obstacles that can be climbed over, different surface classes that can be described in terms of how they impede motion (depending on their orientation), etc. We can have different taxonomies for agents that move on the ground (or the surfaces) and for agents that fly. This is only one taxonomy with which a large number of objects in the environment can be labeled with respect to how they can affect the agent's mobility. Other functional taxonomies can be built based on concepts such as prey, food, etc.

---

[4] We can see another aspect of the complexity by looking at the inverse problem of deriving function from structure. The general translation is not one to one (the same is true for our direction). In order to solve the problem there is need for many limiting assumptions [19]. With these assumptions the present solution relies on a library of generic components with their allowable paths of interaction and a set of boundary conditions which constrain the device's behavior. Even under these constraints the system (ENVISION [19]) may produce a set of behaviors, one of which corresponds to the actual behavior of the real device.

1 ACTIVE VISION AS A METHODOLOGY

Kourosh Pahlavan, Tomas Uhlin and Jan-Olof Eklundh
The Royal Institute of Technology

ABSTRACT

If vision is a way of interaction with the environment, then it must be active. That is, either the observer or the environment have to undergo certain changes in order for vision to be a meaningful process. One could say that vision is trivially active. Still, this does not legitimate active vision as a methodology.

Traditionally, active vision is considered from two points of view. One approach regards active vision as a set of techniques that can be used to simplify the computational aspects of vision in certain situations; the other points to the specific computational advantages of having *anthropomorphic* features. This chapter attempts to address active vision as a methodology, and elucidate its methodological superiority to passive vision. The idea is to formalize active vision by defining it, classifying its different components and expanding its generality rather than by isolating it as an endless list of merits. We also address implementational issues like system design, purpose dependency and control problems; these issues are discussed in accordance with the formal definition. At the end, some experiments with an active vision system, the KTH-head, are briefly discussed.

1. INTRODUCTION

Active vision is attracting an increasing interest among researchers in computational vision. A look at the outcome of more than three decades of research in machine vision points to the sources of this trend. Although the achievements in the field are by no means negligible, fundamental difficulties in developing computational theories have made progress relatively slow. Since the 70s, these complications have resulted in the use of more sophisticated physical models and in engaging high-level mathematics. Such efforts, in spite of complexity and abstraction, have not solved many of the primary problems which seem so easy for a biological observer to deal with, like motion tracking and figure-ground segmentation.

As the field of computer vision matured in the 1970s and 1980s there was an emphasis on its informational processing nature and therefore the problem was formalized as such. Computational theories were formed and substantial work was and is being done on the development of algorithms embodying these theories and taking advantage of the rich information contained in an image. Since this information in turn is contained in an enormous set of potentially available data about the scene, it was very clear at an early stage that a main issue is to have the right kind of data for the right kind of processing; this could be seen as the major explanation for why there has been such a focus on representational issues.

The attempts to find appropriate representations of the relevant information point to the need for attentional mechanisms. This insight, in conjunction with the discovery of the difficulties in finding the proper constraints for processing images in the traditional paradigm, has largely motivated the interest in active vision. Other motivations come from interdisciplinary influences from the fields of psychophysics and neurophysiology on one hand, and progress in robotics on the other.

In particular, an active vision platform could not be built without the presence of the compact CCD arrays, motors and control systems of today, as well as current microprocessor technology. Hence, the emergence of active vision is tied to general developments in hardware. Also, it could certainly not have happened without an increasing familiarity with the great achievements in physiology. In summary, with the interest in active vision, computer vision has, more than ever, developed a strong relationship with other disciplines such as robotics, psychology and physiology.

All this background cannot, however, motivate the use of active vision as a methodology until the methodological advantage of this paradigm vs. passive vision[1] is shown. Many researchers, among them the very first pioneers of active vision, like Bajcsy [6], Ballard [8] and Aloimonos [3], have in different portions and from different viewpoints elaborated the advantages of active vision in both the computational and the qualitative sense in specific applications. Hence, such arguments are available elsewhere [35]. Despite this, we will discuss what lies in the notion of active vision and why we feel it adds something to existing approaches for two reasons. First, we feel it is important to explain the methodological supremacy of active vision before working out its computational advantages in each instance, and secondly, we think that an analysis of active vision as a methodology—which *is* the objective of this chapter—provides such an explanation.

It should be noted that vision is trivially active, both because it must necessarily be tied to some action (the information is used for something) and in the sense that the world surrounding the visual agent in general is a dynamic, steadily changing environment. However, it is often not the observer that causes these changes. The observer cannot help being affected by the environmental changes and should therefore react accordingly. Nevertheless one could argue that this does not necessarily justify the active vision approach.

In active vision the observer selectively acquires visual data in space and time,

---

[1] This implies, of course, that we must specify what we mean by passive vision (see Section 2).

while in passive vision the observer relies on given (usually prerecorded) data. The question is what this actually entails.

The emphasis in much work has largely been on active vision as body movements and, more recently, as eye movements. This is clear from an early published definition like:

> An observer is called active when engaged in some kind of activity whose purpose is to control the geometric parameters of the sensory apparatus. [3] p. 35

indicating that it is particularly the manipulation of the *"geometric"* parameters which dominantly form the notion of active vision.[2]

In this chapter we will try to show that not only the observer's geometric parameters are relevant, but a whole set of other visual parameters as well. The *ability* to manipulate them in a controlled manner, both as an action and a reaction, builds the concept of active vision. However, the *way* the manipulation is done, to what extent and what kind of manipulation is done, is task dependent.

We will also discuss the components of an active vision system, i.e., the building blocks that form the system. These building blocks should enable us to construct a system that can simplify visual sensing according to the paradigm and allow not only cue integration, but also process integration. Our own work and the results from other research groups are examples that we will use to illustrate our arguments. There are indeed considerable advances in the field which substantiate our claim that methodological advantages of the paradigm exist and can be exploited in practice [1, 13, 16, 17, 24, 29].

Next we consider the implications of this discussion of active vision as a methodology on our strategy for actually studying it. We argue that a close look at biological vision is necessary and also stress the differences between reactive and active behaviors. Thereafter the control issue is discussed, which in our view is an inherent problem that cannot be separated from the other aspects of active vision. Our presentation ends with a final brief account of some of our experiments which illustrate our general discussion and findings.

2. WHAT IS ACTIVE VISION?

Active vision should not be seen as a total contradiction to passive vision. The two approaches agree, at least, upon addressing the problem of developing seeing systems. The difference is methodological, and as such it does not deal with optimality and efficiency; rather it deals with the question of whether the major tasks can be carried out by one methodology or not. Not surprisingly, there are situations where the passive approach is as good as the active approach. One example can be found in recognition, where Biederman [10] has shown that humans can perform object classification without eye movements and so rapidly that active feedback seems excluded. Note, however, that in order to recognize an object in a real situation, it should be found in the image, at the right scale and with proper visual parameters.

---

[2] In later work Aloimonos modified his view [4] p. 143.

In this context, let us point out that in our ensuing discussion of active vision we refer to seeing systems that are highly flexible and that can perform a large number of tasks. Our arguments are less relevant in more limited situations.

2.1. ACTIVE AND PASSIVE VISION

The typical property of passive vision is that the observer is not capable of choosing how to view the scene, but is instead limited to what is offered, determined by the preset visual parameters and environmental conditions, including the time sampling. The active observer, on the other hand, utilizes its capability to change its visual parameters to acquire favorable data from the scene in solving the specific task it has at the time. A passive system has to extract all information needed from the given images, possibly engaging in complicated reasoning and computations, but cannot acquire more data which could facilitate the computations.

We will now give our definition of active vision:

An active visual system is a system which is able to manipulate its visual parameters in a controlled manner in order to extract useful data about the scene in time and space.

The proponents of active vision have traditionally stressed the issue of optimality and the benefits of anthropomorphic vision techniques in specific applications, instead of pointing out the methodological superiority of active vision applied to visual tasks in general. We want to emphasize the latter aspect.

Once accepted that active vision is the methodologically superior approach to computer vision, one can begin to discuss how to do it optimally and in practice.

2.2. THE GIBSONIAN OPTIC ARRAY AND ACTIVE VISION

We defined an active system functioning in time and space. Gibson [20] introduced the notion of the spatial *optic array* as being the set of visual data that, in principle, can be acquired from the surrounding world from a given viewing point (see Figure 1). *Seeing* in particular requires sampling the optic array, and it is worthwhile to discuss concretely how both the active and passive approaches to vision could perform this function.

An observer utilizing active vision, by definition, is able to sample all visual data, limited only by its degrees of freedom. The process of data acquisition occurs in time, but the observer is of course only capable of capturing the data at the rate it can sample them. Hence, accepting the discrete steps in time and space, the active methodology, based on the given definition, is capable of acquiring all the information given by the abstract Gibsonian optic array.

As far as static vision is concerned, there are two major cases to study here. The first case is when the observer can access prerecorded data about the world and process those data. Unless the system is capable of prerecording *all* possible samplings in time and space and storing them, the system cannot process in real time, that is at the rate of the relevant events in the world. It is obvious that such

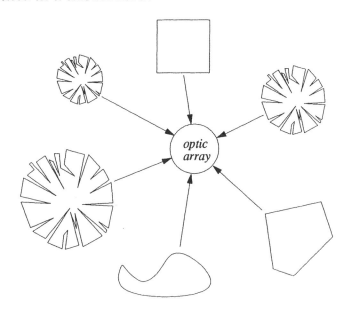

Figure 1. An illustration of the optic array. All visual data is supposed
to be gathered in the optic array from the viewing point. The question
is, what methodology makes it feasible to sample the array?

an approach either would cause delayed responses, making it insensitive to what is
happening in the world, or require an enormously large capacity to store and process
data. For instance, it has been pointed out by Schwartz that if the human eye had
the spatial resolution of the fovea all over the retinal field, then the visual system
would weigh ten thousand tons [33]. Adding other parameters, including temporal
sampling, demonstrates the awkwardness of such a solution.

Since vision is also an interaction with the physical world, it is *perceptually*
meaningless not to run it in real time.[3] Prerecorded data is certainly meaningful in
an analysis of what has happened—such as we do by referring to our memory—but
it is simply not the proper set of data we need for interaction.

In the previous paragraphs we were implicitly assuming a visual sensor like a
camera or an eye looking in certain directions in space. One could imagine another
static scheme which is capable of sampling visual data in real time. Imagine that we
have a spherical sensor with high resolution and transparent sensing elements with
different sensitivities, with many such spherical layers arranged in a concentric order
to form an onion-shaped 3-D sensor in space. Such a sensor will certainly be capable
of sampling data in real time and will have several degrees of freedom. Except for
motion blur, which can only be used as a beneficial cue together with eye movements
(see Section 3.2), the sphere could do anything we might expect from a head–eye
system. Since all needed data is available at each time interval, the system should
utilize a very high degree of parallelism in its computations. In return it could be

---

[3] Of course, this is not to say that a system can be without delays.

very fast. The only problem is that such a system is infeasible for several practical reasons.

2.3. THE ACTIVE OBSERVER

The expression "active observer" is today sometimes used to denote an observer that uses active vision. We feel that this expression could be somewhat misleading and really does not capture the essence of active vision. This is due to the original definition of the active observer first brought up by Gibson in 1950. He writes in his chapter "Stimulus variables—The active observer":

> The normal human being, however, is active. His head never remains in a fixed position for any length of time except in artificial situations. If he is not walking or driving a car or looking from a train or airplane, his ordinary posture will produce some changes of his eyes in space. Such changes will modify the retinal image in a quite specific way. [19] p. 117

The cited chapter is mainly devoted to an investigation of the ways in which the retinal image changes for different types of motion, and focuses on the resulting perception of depth by the observer. This depth perception experienced by the active observer is of course a very strong and important cue to depth, but our notion of an observer utilizing active vision incorporates much more. The active observer, as originally described by Gibson, is basically a passively perceiving moving observer. This is a very different concept from an observer that actively chooses its motion in order to perceive something. Also this is only a part of all the possibilities active vision gives to the observer that has, in general, many parameters besides motion to exploit in striving to perform its tasks.

3. COMPONENTS OF AN ACTIVE VISION SYSTEM

In the previous section we defined an active system as a system that was able to control its visual parameters. We discussed the difference between such an approach and passive vision from a general perspective. Here we will specify the most important of these visual parameters and discuss why they are useful. Notably, we do not claim that these parameters are the only existing ones.

We would like to divide the components of an active vision system into four categories:

- Optical parameters
- Sensory parameters
- Mechanical parameters
- Algorithmic integration

As far as the *optical parameters* are concerned, the parameters are well known. The optical parameters together with the position and shape of the image sensor determine the mapping of the 3-D world onto the 2-D image surface. This decrease in dimensionality, which causes many problems in passive vision, is due to projection onto the 2-D image surface and not to mapping through the optics of the system. That is, the mapping of the world through the optical system is in fact a 3-D to 3-D mapping[4] (see Figure 2), and it is obvious that there is much more information present than what is obtainable from just one 2-D projection. From this point of view it is clear that having access to and control over the optical parameters means that we can exploit this 3-D mapping and obtain more information about the 3-D world by acquiring a whole range of 2-D projections onto the image surface.

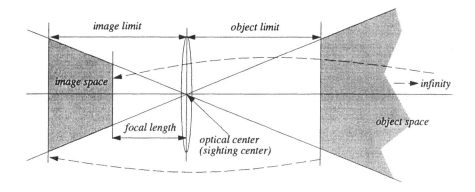

Figure 2. The 3-D to 3-D mapping from object space into image space. The infinite space spanned from the object limit (the nearest distance for sharpness) to infinity is mapped onto the limited image space spanned from the focal plane back to the image limit (the projection of the object limit plane).

We have already mentioned the image surface (retina in the eye) as a means of producing a 2-D projection of the world. The *sensory parameters* determine how this projection is sampled so as to produce an image, and this can of course be done in many ways. Contributing factors include the shape of the retina and the distribution, density and sensitivity of imaging elements, among others. The optics, together with the retina, are referred to as the imaging system or the eye.

When talking about the *mechanical parameters* in an active system, we mean the motion and positioning of the eye in the 3-D world. These parameters become important for many reasons; some are implied by the structure of the image sensor, as are eye movements in vertebrates with foveal vision, others are implied by the fact that we cannot see everything in the world from one spot, thus necessitating the need for changing the position of the eye. A third reason is that a moving object or scene (arising from observer motion) often cannot be imaged clearly unless it is stabilized on the sensor.

Once the mobility and flexibility of the system is accepted, the question that is raised is how to control these sets of visual parameters so that the system as a whole can benefit when solving a certain task. This is the stage at which control

---

[4] The mapping is not one-to-one, but geometrical optics states that to each point in space, there is a unique point of best focus in this projected image space.

algorithms and vision algorithms need to be integrated.

After this brief overview of the different components that may be useful in an active vision system, we will look at each set in more detail.

3.1. OPTICAL PARAMETERS

Optical parameters of a visual system include the focal length, the accommodation distance and the iris size. We would like to see these parameters as a means to fully exploit the rich 3-D mapping of the world produced by the optical system. Perhaps the easiest way to realize the possibilities is to note that changing *any* of these parameters results in changes in the image which systematically depend on the distance to the imaged points in the world. Having a model of how the image changes with these parameters enables the observer to acquire information about depth and hence helps in solving the figure-ground problem.

In primate vision, accommodation is a very significant parameter; this is the case in active machine vision as well. Accommodative cues to depth are of a qualitative nature due to the fact that the infinite depth range (spanning from close to the camera to infinity) of the world is projected through the lens system into a finite range (see Figure 2). This means that there will always be differences in depth, far away, that cannot be distinguished, since there will always be only a finite number of settings in any practical focusing system. Nevertheless, the cue is very stable and the problem of depth recovery from accommodation data is a well-posed one. There is biological evidence showing that in the human case the crystalline lens does not have a stable state, but is changing its accommodation distance continuously, albeit by a small amount [36]. Work in our laboratory has shown how relatively small changes in the focusing distance can give a qualitative judgement of the depth in the scene [21] (see Figure 3). Other researchers have chosen iris changes and achieved similar results [31]. Some researchers have used static approaches (with no change of optical parameters) and on the basis of a model of the optical system they have calculated depth from defocus, and from that calculated coarse depth mappings of the scene [37].

A simple way to achieve accommodation in an optical system is to move the lens back and forth relative to the image surface, and this is in fact what is done in some biological systems, such as fish, as well as in our conventional cameras. However, this simple method of accommodation causes some side effects that could be undesirable.

There are in particular two such side effects. The first one is the change of apparent size of an object as accommodation is performed. This may not be desirable, since the localization of an object in the image becomes focus dependent. The second side effect has more to do with the control aspects of a visual system which in turn have to do with the mechanical parameters of the system. As we will discuss in Section 3.2, rotating the cameras about the lens center enables us to avoid geometric distortions of the image during the rotation. This means that it is easier to predict the motion of an object projection on the retina as the eyes rotate. However, accommodation will in general change the position of the lens center unless the accommodation is performed very carefully.

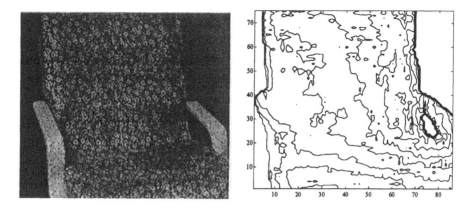

Figure 3. The image of a chair and the level curve representation of the
result obtained by active approach to depth from defocus. The chair is
at a distance of about 2 meters from the camera. Two frames are used
here, and the difference between the two images is a small change in the
accommodation distance. Each level curve stands for a relative distance
of 100 mm. For detailed information see [21].

In many vertebrate eyes there are sophisticated accommodation mechanisms that
avoid such effects. For instance, the shape rather than the position of the lens can be
manipulated. In machine vision one can have a camera that is able to accommodate
while keeping the position of the lens center fixed relative to the retina. This can be
achieved with conventional zoom lenses, by coordinating the change of focus with
an appropriate change in zoom.

Another important feature of a vision system is of course its field of view, since
this determines how much of the world the system can overlook at the same time.
The field of view is determined by the focal length, so an active vision system that
is able to change its focal length can choose with which resolution, with respect to
field of view, it wants to examine a scene or object.

Let us finally remark that although iris changes also cause depth-dependent
effects on the image, and thus can be explored as a depth cue, a more important
property of the iris parameter is to let the right amount of light through to the
retina.

3.2. MECHANICAL AND SENSORY PARAMETERS

Mechanical movements of the eye can be divided into two categories; movements
that cause motion parallax or kinetic depth (observer movements), and movements
that do not (eye movements).

The benefits of observer motion have been known since the early years of computational vision and have been addressed by many researchers within the field.
The importance of observer motion does not only lie in that it provides motion
parallax and hence information about depth. Obviously, it also provides additional
information, since different views of the objects in the scene can be acquired.

On the other hand, eye movements, in the above sense, have only recently begun to be explored in computational vision [29]. Since eye movements do not cause motion parallax, these movements cannot be motivated in the same way as observer motion. The significance of eye movements becomes apparent in conjunction with the structure of the sensor [2]. Carpenter explains it in a nice way:

> Different species vary considerably in how much they can see at any given moment. The horse, for example, can see almost all round its head, and, given an adequate system for stabilization of the retinal image, it is not obvious that it would ever need to make any other kinds of eye movements at all. The reason that it does is that it cannot see equally well in all parts of its field [15] p. 6.

This brings us to another reason for eye movements, which becomes apparent when the observer and objects begin to move in the environment, namely the effects of motion blur. Any observer that wants to examine an object that is moving relative to the observer needs to look at the object for some period of time. It may be for the reason of acquiring a snapshot of the object, and then a finite exposure time is needed. It may also be the case that the observer requires a flow of images. Then an even longer time is needed. Whatever time is needed, it is essential to keep the object projected to the same place on the sensor in order to acquire sharp images of it. Eye movements become necessary to stabilize a target on the sensor. This means that even if we have an imaging system that covers a target of interest, eye movements are needed to stabilize the target to get the best possible image. Now one may argue that by decreasing the exposure time for each image, one avoids the effect of motion blur. This is correct, and may well be applicable when the object is easily distinguished from the background. On the other hand, when the object is not easily distinguished, motion blur in the background, but not on the object of interest, allows for simpler segmentation. This can only be achieved by stabilizing the object on the retina while increasing the exposure time.

The typical parameters of a *sensing element* are its sensitivity/bandwidth and size, and these properties are usually unchanged for a single cell. Thus, it is hard to imagine situations where the sensory parameters alone could affect the responses in such a way that the same sensor elements would yield two proper sets of data, with different information about the scene, due to a manipulation.[5] It may however be desirable to be able to produce different sets of data. In many biological systems this is attained by putting together many cells with different properties to form a sensory area with a specific shape, distribution and internal connections, like the foveal-peripheral structure and receptive fields of the human eye. This will in turn make eye movements necessary (see the earlier quote from Carpenter).

---

[5] Moran and Desimone empirically discovered that:
> ...the very structure of the receptive field, recently considered to be a fixed property of the neuron, can change from moment to moment in the behaving monkey depending on the immediate task and state of attention. [26].

With sensing elements, however, we do not mean receptive fields, but rather the individual cones and rods and their counterparts in machine vision.

It should be noted here that one could imagine more complex sensory elements in which one could actively change the parameters, and this may well be attractive. Such elements might, however, be hard to realize in practice.

3.3. ALGORITHM INTEGRATION AND ACTIVITY

The algorithms involved in an active visual system have a distinguishing ability compared to the ones in a passive system, namely their ability to manipulate certain parameters. Hence, they actively change the parameters to obtain data needed at a particular time. One can therefore say that an integration of these algorithms forms the observer itself.

An elaborate active system, with the capability to change its parameters in parallel, should have many algorithms running in parallel—we will call them processes. The activity of these processes has to be coordinated in time so that they can affect the outcome of the integration. All this points to a demand for competition and cooperation between the parallel processes in such an active system, because the processes involved in the system could yield contradictory outputs and each process should therefore somehow inhibit or amplify the output of the others. An active system can feed its algorithms with different cues within the same time interval and therefore it is natural and efficient to have parallelism embedded in the system; this is however not a condition for a system to be active. The sequential component is evidently prominent.

In general, even the simplest observer at times has to choose between at least two competing alternatives in order to be active, otherwise it would not be meaningful for it to control its parameters. The activity of the system, in other words, is defined by its algorithms and their outcome. The algorithms and their integration guarantee the use of the degrees of freedom of the system. One could say that a single algorithm does nothing other than pure information processing; integration implies everything from the ability of the system to control itself, its behavior toward the changes in the environment, its tendency to change its parameters, and perhaps even its intelligence.

3.4. SUMMARY

In this section we have discussed the different parameters that could be present in an active vision system. We have also motivated the need for parallelism and activity on the algorithmic level in an active system. Before we go on with how to actually do active vision, we would like to emphasize that any visual parameter that results in a change of image data, i.e., that generates new data or reveals latent data, beneficial to the task at the time, is a parameter of an active vision system.

4. HOW TO DO ACTIVE VISION

An acceptance of the active paradigm faces one with implementational problems such as what degrees of freedom to choose (what parameters do we have to manipulate?), how to control the system actuators, what kind of feedback information is relevant, and how to integrate the flow of information to obtain useful data.

Currently there exist a number of head–eye systems designed by different research groups [1, 12, 16, 23, 30] and a steadily increasing stream of reports on experiments with these rigs are recorded. Here, we try to look at the implications from biological vision systems and try to underline the problem that forces us to look at them—the design strategy.

4.1. DESIGN STRATEGY AND BIOLOGICAL VISION

We have considered active vision as a methodology and our argument leads us to consider the issue of implementation as a task-dependent problem. From another point of view, we are still researchers who try to understand the visual phenomenon not only theoretically but also empirically. The pragmatic approach, like ours, forces one to see visual systems as combinations of flexibility and performance; in this respect human vision seems to be the most successful biological system we can find. Human vision has many shortages in terms of both bandwidth and resolution (e.g., compared to some birds whose environment constrains their vision to have a more elaborate acuity). Still, the enormous ability of human vision to integrate a well suited degree of flexibility with a high degree of performance is a very successful example of a visual system. Consequently, it is quite natural that one becomes attracted to the well designed, perfectly adapted, and at the same time high-performing vision of primates if one wants to design a flexible active machine vision system.

It is, however, important to take into consideration that the set of interests of animals, their purpose of vision, is developed tightly in conjunction with their level of intelligence and survival conditions. It could therefore be very pedagogical to study even more primitive visual systems.

There is a flora of tailored visual systems in nature, almost as many as the number of species. Some of these systems are relatively primitive and some very complex, probably due to the environment and survival conditions in which the animals exist. Some of them have no eye movements (e.g., compound eyes), some have very little, and some much more. All of them have eyes grouped into a pair, but not all of them have stereopsis and binocular vergence. Some have many visual parameters to change and some very few, if any at all, except for body motion. Our concept of machine vision should therefore cover vision in a much broader sense than what we are used to and what we experience through our own eyes.

Vision in general is preconditioned by having some goals. Active vision, however, is preconditioned also by knowing what degree of performance and flexibility is desirable. Having this knowledge, it is well established what kind of experimental facilities we need. A static camera, for example, which is only capable of focusing, has a very limited flexibility and performance, while control becomes simpler. Adding more and more parameters to the system, when properly done, enhances its capabilities and consequently its performance. At the same time the control problem becomes more and more difficult.

Knowing how to put components together is still a problem, due to the fact that we do not have any idea about the strategy of our seeing machines, and we do not have a clear understanding about what amount of complexity, flexibility and performance they should have. Developing a flexible head–eye system is not something that can be done over and over again as new demands appear. There is, however, a great affinity between the visual systems of higher species and they resemble each other quite a lot physically. This resemblance could be a good guideline to understanding these systems and it somehow urges one to follow their design.

Most vertebrates have a pair of eyes that have a rather similar construction. They are capable of accommodation in different ways, and have at least small eye movements. They usually also have neck movements, often coordinated with their eye movements. Often there is a fixation mechanism, but this is not always the case. However, all of them use the two eyes to expand their field of view, while some of them have foveal vision and others do not.

By looking at the common characteristics of biological systems and simply finding a good compromise for imitation, we could hope for a design strategy that is suitable for performing flexible and sophisticated vision.

4.2. ANTHROPOMORPHIC VISION SYSTEMS

A good compromise, following an imitation strategy, is to build an anthropomorphic system, not because we are actually capable of building a seeing agent of such complexity, but because such a system seems to be a good combination of flexibility and performance. For experimenting with fewer degrees of freedom, we can let some of the parameters be constant, or change their internal dependency by software, but of course the set of possible configurations will still be limited.

One could even argue for the benefits of the natural architecture of biological systems in general and anthropomorphic vision in particular, as Ballard has done[6] [9]. Anthropomorphic systems, however, require elaborate mechanical constructions: control electronics together with proper optics and sensors. In the end we are limited by the state of the art, technologically and scientifically. We can only come as close to our goal as we can afford, both economically and scientifically, given the mechanical, electromechanical and electronics hardware at hand. The KTH-head is such a machine (see Figure 4). It is designed to be flexible at three levels: mechanical, optical and computational.

In accordance with primate vision, the KTH-head differentiates between eye movements and neck movements. It has seven mechanical and six optical degrees of freedom and there are no hard connections between its visual components, so that the control system can make a decision on the dependency between them in a flexible manner. The two eyes are totally independent at all three levels mentioned above. The camera actuators of the system are not as fast as eyeballs in primates (about half the speed of primate eyes) but are still at an order of magnitude that affordable computational power has difficulty matching.

Currently we do not have the technology to build eyes with the quality found in biological systems and there are some virtues of primate vision that are very

---

[6] With reservation for the definition of what is an active system and what is not, some of the points mentioned in this work are essential for understanding the sophisticated solutions in biological vision.

Figure 4. The KTH-head.

difficult for us to imitate. One of these virtues is foveal vision. It is often ignored that foveal vision is not simply high-resolution in fovea centralis and low-resolution accompanied by wide field of view in the periphery. In fact, the structure of the primate retina is much more complicated than this. There are two kinds of light-sensitive cells in the human retina: cones and rods. Where the cones are densest (fovea centralis), rods are hardly present, and the opposite is true on the outskirts of the retina. In between, the cone distribution decreases monotonically from the fovea down to the retinal borders; the rod distribution, consequently, follows the opposite order. Figure 5 depicts the distribution of cones and rods in the human retina.

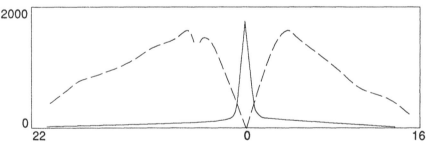

Figure 5. Distribution of rods and cones in the human retina. The figures on the horizontal axis stand for the distance (in mm) from the foveola (the center of fovea centralis) along the horizontal section of the right eye. The figures on the vertical axis represent the number of hundreds of rods and cones per mm^2. The dashed curve represents rods and the solid curve cones. Redrawn after [28].

As a partial solution, one could generate the log-polar structure of the retina electronically, optically or by obtaining the new flat foveal sensors [34]. In any case, it remains to be shown what the practical advantages are and how far they could be stretched. One problem with the electronic approach (filtering in software) is that one inserts a delay in the system without obtaining any new data. Nevertheless, our experiments, like those of others on stabilization/tracking and vergence, show that even simple foveal approaches are still of both computational and algorithmical value.

Another problem in trying to imitate nature is caused by the use of conventional optics and sensors. Traditionally the most common and popular products use flat sensors, which have drawbacks in this context. Even though spherical aberrations and similar shortages are cured in the construction of mass-produced lenses, we are left with bulky and mal-designed lenses, mal-designed in the sense that the combination of refractive surfaces is optimized for a flat image that keeps good sharpness all over the image and with a large depth of field. The latter is particularly inconvenient for algorithms estimating depth from focus and defocus.

Consequently, we are stuck with flat sensors which are also of the wrong kind. Still we can do a lot of work on active vision and even develop "seeing" systems with present technology, partly by simulating some features of the vertebrates and partly by remembering that vision is not only human vision. We have to realize that we have to build systems that work, because computer vision is an empirical and not an absolute or descriptive science. Many times, integrating processes implemented as independent algorithms is as important as the quality of the algorithms themselves, and given limited resources, it is the correct combination that makes a functioning machine. At the same time, computer vision is a basic research area with many unsolved problems. Therefore we have to be very open-minded in implementing systems and simultaneously push the research frontiers forward.

4.3. REACTIVE VISION

The major difficulty facing vision, and all computational sensing in general, is the problem of system behavior, i.e., the knowledge about and formalization of what the set of goals of the system is, and what its purposes are. There exists no species in nature that is only capable of sensing. The sensing capability is used for survival, manipulation, or similar behaviors. Machines, however, have traditionally been defined as tools. The issue of intelligent machines is, in this sense, a radically new approach to using machines and could hardly be raised if we did not have computers as tools.

Note that there is a difference between intelligent machines that act as animals which have their own purpose for existence and intelligent machines acting as tools for human beings. A horse, for example, has many more capabilities than those we expect from it as a tool. Here we are talking about synthetically building the latter type of systems, as suggested in [5].

What, then, should the behavior of such a system be? This still depends on the systems's tasks, but in building it, hopefully we know what the tasks of our tool are. The designer of the system must know exactly what the system should be sensitive to and what kinds of actions it should be engaged in, following the perception. The system might actively seek perception or passively wait for perception, depending on its design complexity and programmed behavioral scheme. The system simply becomes like a chess-playing machine programmed to be aggressive or defensive, and remains at that level of machine intelligence.

Visual processing, however, is a somewhat special situation, and indeed is much more interesting. The visual sense is broadly much more complex than the more primitive senses such as touching, temperature sensing and the like, because vision (like hearing) provides information about events far from us. This is actually what makes visual sensing intricate. Otherwise, one could always find a simpler way of solving a specific sensing problem using simple approaches. If we are only interested in task-specific solutions, vision is of hardly any interest.

There is, however, a very fundamental condition in life that makes the visual sense indispensable for truly autonomous machines—light. Light is a phenomenon in our environment that is external to us.[7] From the point of view of the human observer, light is a unidirectional phenomenon for communication that generally exists beyond our will, and it puts us in contact with the environment without any mechanical link to it.

All the background description above is aimed at explaining why even simple visual sensing is relevant and interesting. We should consequently be very interested in changes in illumination patterns, because they tell us that something is happening out there and they reveal some new information to us. We call these changes and the visual actions following these changes *reactive vision*. Reactive vision is the set of visual actions due to changes in the environment and not the will of the observer.

What we achieve by this kind of thinking is beneficial to machine vision in several ways. We can build systems capable of simple visual sensing, that perform meaningful tasks; we can isolate each aspect of a visual task as a set of reactive processes with simple implementable behavior; and finally, we might be able to integrate these simple reactive processes into a much more complicated observer in Brooks' sense [11].

With this approach in mind, we have done work on the control of the primary ocular processes, the lowest level processes engaged in the control of the KTH-head. The details of this work can be found in [29]; later, in Section 6, we will briefly describe the structure of the work as an approach for solving some of the control issues.

4.4. ACTIVITY AND VOLUNTARISM

We described behavior due to changes in the environment as reactive. The other kind of behavior, which is much more complicated, is behavior due to voluntarism; we will call this the *will* of the observer. What these voluntary behaviors depend on is hardly well understood today; the important thing is to notice the complications caused by lack of such a will. The problem can be rephrased as: What does the system do when there are no events in the environment? We can always explore the world completely by looking at all locations in the scene, but this could hardly be called a purposive behavior.

So far, the approaches to the problem of "where to look next" (e.g., [7, 32]) have only in a limited sense addressed the essence of the problem, which in fact relates to the whole issue of what intelligence is. One thing we could do is to see the will of a system as a table of interests and not expect this to work in more elaborate cases. It is, however, obvious that a foveal structure in the retina or a limited field of view requires attentional mechanisms that are tied to the structural complexities of

---

[7] Of course, this is also the case with signals carried by a wavefront in general, not excluding sound.

the scene as well. This behavior of scanning the scene structure could, however, be considered as a pure reactive behavior that is overridden by the will of the observer when needed.

Yarbus [36] has a famous series of recordings of eye movements, most of which are evidence of the influence of the interests of the observer on his choice of fixation points. Human beings are often interested in the trio eye-mouth-nose when they study another human being's face. However, when looking at a frieze, for example, with very detailed structure, the observer becomes more interested in the pure complexity of the object he is looking at. This simple example is intended to elucidate the distinction between the fixations based on embedded interests like concentrating on the eyes and the purely visual attractions toward the structure of the object. It points to the enormous complexity of the task of modeling a seeing agent that can actively pursue its goals.

5. THE CONTROL ISSUE

The control problem is inherent in active vision. An active system should address the problem of controlling its parameters based on the design strategy. Here we are not talking about the motor servo aspects, but about the visual feedback from the cameras and the control loop around that feedback. We will discuss control of both optics and mechanical axes and choose primate vision as the inspiration for our strategy.

Since our system utilizes mechanical movements, the knowledge of geometrical and optical parameters of the system, their relations in terms of position and speed control of the joints is crucial to the control system.[8] Therefore, the kinematics and inverse kinematics of the system, along with its geometrical design, are also discussed here.

5.1. GAZE CONTROL

We will discuss gaze control in view of the design of our existing head–eye system. To simplify things, we forget about the physiologically less established behaviors like cyclotorsion and micromovements. Currently our head–eye system has no inertial sensors and therefore there is no vestibulo-ocular component present in our control system. Finally, we do not explicitly address the issue of body movements, which we consider as an extension of neck movements.

Choosing primate vision as a model for our control strategy, we face two categories of oculomotor adjustments: gaze holdings and gaze shiftings. As mentioned above, we will only discuss the visual components of these adjustments and ignore the influence of inertial data in the control system. We will then have:

- optokinesis (whole image stabilization)
- smooth pursuit (foveal stabilization)

---

[8] By this we mean that in the design of the system we know what the precision of the various components is. We do not refer to precise fixed calibration, which would be difficult to obtain.

- saccades
- vergence

The first and second items are movements due to retinal slips or shifts and can be said to be involuntary. The third and fourth are more voluntary movements.This may be the right place to emphasize that the border between voluntary and involuntary behaviors is rather fuzzy. All of these items can be integrated to build a purely reactive behavior on the condition that there is a set of events in the system that attracts the interest of the system represented in the control scheme. We have implemented such a system for the KTH-head and that is why we discuss this following our discussion of reactive vision.

It is very important to realize that optokinesis and smooth pursuit, although somewhat similar in definition, are rather contradictory in action. While the subject locks the foveal image of a mobile object, it is ignoring the negative speed of the background relative to the object. The optokinetic pattern, on the other hand, is the image of the whole scene and is used to stabilize the scene due to egomotion or the motion of a large portion of the scene.

The particular stimulus for optokinesis and smooth pursuit is retinal slip or shifts in the image, and it is very difficult for a subject to simulate them when the stimuli are not present. The case is different for vergence and saccades (version). The stimulus for these is a physical point or feature and there is no need for a change in the scene to activate them. Human saccades, however, are present in faster pursuit as partial elements, and they are also present in most vergence processes as versions. That is, smooth pursuit and vergence are linked together by the saccade element. The vergence process itself comprises two different subprocesses depending on the stimuli: accommodative vergence and disparity vergence. The control of the optics, at least partially, enters the loop here.

We have deliberately postponed the discussion of a very significant characteristic of our head–eye system up to this moment—binocularity. Vergence is tightly connected to binocularity and loses its meaning without it. This is the case with the disparity component of vergence but not with the accommodative component, because accommodation is a monocular cue. Although our system is a binocular one, it should manage partial or total occlusion of one eye and still work. This is a point that is often not discussed in the approaches that advocate an object-centered coordinated system (see e.g., [9]).

The discussion above implies that the monocular elements of control should be lined up in a loop around each ocular feedback mechanism and the binocular elements in another loop joining the two monocular loops to one another.

It is reasonable to ask what happens to the occluded eye when the other is changing its fixation parameters. Since accommodative vergence, as input, takes a monocular stimulus, the occluded eye would follow the fixation point suggested by the seeing eye.

Another question that is essential to binocular vision is how the two control loops for the left and the right eye are integrated. In other words, what happens if the two stimuli of the processes on the two sides are different; which one should be chosen and why. It is not difficult to imagine that this phenomenon occurs, both when the same kind of processes do the same job on different eyes and when different processes do the same job but in different ways on the same eye. Marr puts the necessity for this elegantly (although in another context):

> The common and almost despairing feeling of the early investigators like B.K.P. Horn and T.O. Binford was that practically anything could happen in an image and furthermore that practically everything did. [25] p. 16

An example of processes doing the same job on different eyes is the attempt to fixate on a feature that appears in one image and not in the other. An example of conflicts between different processes doing the same job in different ways on the same eye is the conflict that could arise between accommodation and disparity detection processes. It is known that the problem is solved in nature by one process overriding the other. The whole idea behind integrating processes that do the same job in different ways is that these processes let the system manage ambiguities by referring to the information coming from other processes. One process overrides another one in some situations while the opposite occurs in others. We will illustrate this by the specific example of rivalry and cooperation of accommodation with disparity in Section 6, which discusses the experiments. In that section we will also mention another interesting example: the rivalry between optokinesis and smooth pursuit. In any case, there are instances in human vision where ambiguity fools the whole system of ocular control, but these cases are very rare and often illusions rather than realities.

The former category, that of information conflict between the same processes on different eyes, is a more complex problem, which seems to be closely related to the problem of ocular dominance. In machine vision one could maneuver around this problem either by choosing one eye as the dominant eye, or by altering the dominance from time to time according to some scheme. The first approach could lose information that is present in one eye but not in the other. The second could use the information in the other image, but how to define such a scheme is still unknown to us and to our knowledge no work is being done on this issue by other researchers.

These are examples from active vision of the general problem of cue integration [4], and especially cue conflicts, on which there exist a host of results in other areas (see e.g., [14, 18]).

Following the discussions in Section 4.3, it is natural to implement the control system as an integration of primary ocular processes that are reactive, in the sense that each of them has a simple, straightforward task: just react to the visual stimulus received, and cooperate or compete on both eyes. Figure 6 demonstrates the dependency and direction of dependency between the processes discussed above.

Two different representations are used in the system: the raw images from the cameras and the cyclopean representation common to both of them.[9] In any case, since cyclopean representation and ocular dominance is yet to be solved, in our

---

[9] The expression "cyclopean vision" in the psychophysical literature is used in different ways; see e.g., [22]. Here, we mean the representation that contains data about the lines of equal mean version.

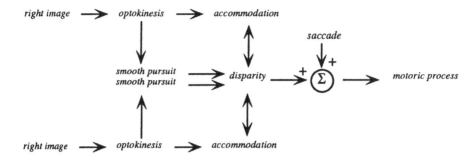

Figure 6. A scheme of some of the visuomotor processes and their dependency on each other.

experiments and the real control system of the KTH-head we have used a fixed eye as the dominant eye. More about this in Section 6, about experiments.

5.2. MECHANICAL DESIGN, KINEMATICS AND INVERSE KINEMATICS

The problem of kinematics (given the actuator data, what are the gaze direction and speed?) is basically an easy problem and is more a real-time computational burden than a mathematical one. The problem of inverse kinematics (given the gaze direction and speed, what must the actuator data be?) is, however, a bit more complicated, because in general it is not guaranteed that there is any solution to the problem at all (due to the limitation of the work space) and even if there is, it is often not unique. Even so, many times solutions can only be achieved by iterative numerical methods. This is indeed very undesirable in a real-time system.

One way of coping with the latter problem is to adapt the design so that the solutions are achievable analytically. It turns out that this is almost always possible. However, in our case it is not sufficient that an analytic solution exists, it must also be easy to compute.

When several solutions are found, the question remains which one to choose. In robotics in general, there are some standard approaches to follow; the usual one is to choose the nearest solution with respect to the present position or speed that is not constrained by the presence of probable obstacles.

In an anthropomorphic head–eye system, there is a very prominent variable to minimize, namely the asymmetry of vergence. However, this is not always suitable, since there are some other considerations involved here. The camera modules are lighter and have smaller moment of inertia compared to the whole head. This means that the acceleration time for the neck is usually longer and therefore a certain amount of asymmetry should be allowed to exist, depending on the acceleration time of both camera axes and neck axes.

All this sounds very complicated, but in fact it is not, if it is supported by a suitable design. Let us describe such a design. Actually, if the head–eye system is really anthropomorphic, then there aren't many options for the designer. One should simply copy the primate head! What we mean is that if a head–eye system is anthropomorphic, then it is not enough to have a couple of eyes and a neck module. The eye modules should mechanically function the same way they do in primates; i.e., they must rotate about the sighting center[10] and be decoupled from each other and from the neck. If so, retinal slip, during stabilization and tracking, can be compensated for by a straightforward calculation of corresponding angles without incorporating the distance to the target.

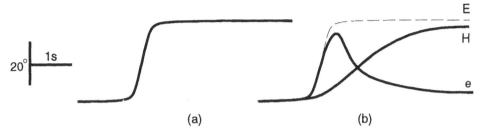

Figure 7. Head and eye movements made when looking at novel objects: (a) eye movement (saccade) made in fixating an eccentric target with the head fixed; (b) head (H) and eye (e) movements made under exactly the same conditions, but with the head free. The sum of (H) and (e) is the gaze (the dashed curve E). Redrawn after [27].

The whole problem of inverse kinematics then vanishes, because in the other case, i.e., saccades accompanied by neck movements, the procedure is even easier. Figure 7 demonstrates the whole thing pictorially. Saccades are ballistic movements and are preprogrammed. In other words once the movement has started, there is no visual feedback supporting its final position. In this way, it is a positioning movement and not an integrated velocity control. This means that the acceleration ramp is known beforehand. Knowing the acceleration ramp for both eye movements and head movements, it is very easy to find the superposition, and vice versa. It might be interesting to add here that the contribution from head movements speeds up the process of gaze shifting. The problem of inverse kinematics is converted to deciding the eye angles only.

The procedure mentioned above is possible if the the movements are ballistic and therefore the eye rotations *must* be about the optical center.

6. EXPERIMENTS ON PRIMARY OCULAR PROCESSES

We have now analyzed the methodological differences between active and passive vision and from that outlined how one can realize the components of active vision. We have several times referred to our own head–eye system. We will now describe some experiments with this system, which further illustrate the obtained functionalities.

In Section 5.1 we discussed examples of ocular control processes that could come into a collision course with each other. Optokinesis and smooth pursuit form a pair of such processes that have contradictory tasks. While optokinesis tries to stabilize the image over the whole scene as well as possible, smooth pursuit tries to stabilize

---

[10] For a definition of the sighting center see [15].

the foveal part of the image. That is, when pursuing a moving object, the negative speed of the background results in a conflict between the two processes. We learn from the psychophysical literature that the pursuing process overrides optokinesis in this case.

This is an example of two processes that have a one-way connection: one of the processes takes over in case of conflict. One can imagine another scenario where one process overrides the other one in some situations while in complementary situations the relation is the opposite. The relation between accommodative vergence and disparity vergence is an example of this. In this section we will give an example of our implementation of primary ocular processes and specifically show how the cooperation between these two processes works in practice. First a glance at the implemented and integrated processes is appropriate. They are:

- motion detection (a simple behavioral engine)
- stabilization (serving as optokinesis)
- tracking (serving as smooth pursuit)
- vergence (the disparity-based integrator of processes)
- focusing (the accommodation-based process)

These processes currently run in parallel on a transputer network which is formed around two transputer-based digitalization modules. Figure 8 depicts the hardware configuration of the system.

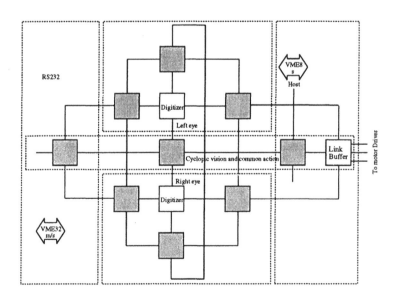

Figure 8. The processor configuration in the KTH-head. Each node is a T8 transputer.

Fixation at a point is based on a combination of vergence and version. The version component is ballistic and fed directly to the motoric processes. The vergence component, however, is formed by the set of processes illustrated in Figure 9.

The observant reader will note that in addition, the accommodation process receives feedback from the stabilization process, due to the fact that neither the object nor the head is constrained to be still. If the object and the head–eye system are not still, the focusing process will not function properly, because the evaluation function for sharpness yields only relative values for the sharpness and therefore the values for two different sharp images are not necessarily the same. Figure 10 demonstrates the result of accommodation on a sequence of stabilized images and the same sequence of unstabilized images. In the latter case there are several maxima, which certainly is unwanted.

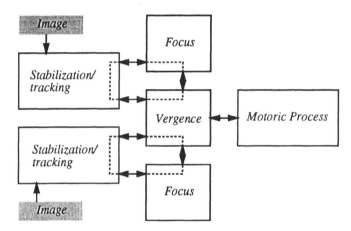

Figure 9. Process configuration in the implementation. The meeting point for the processes dedicated to the left and the right eye (the two rings) is the vergence process (disparity component).

The optokinetic process also updates the reference point of the disparity process so as to keep track of the disparities in time. A typical case when the accommodative process comes into conflict with the disparity detecting process is when the image consists mainly of a repetitive pattern. The disparity-detecting process would then find several good matches between the two images; due to noise the best match is quite often false. This is depicted in Figure 11. Figure 12 illustrates the output of the evaluation functions for the same case. Utilizing the feedback from the accommodative process would however solve the problem easily, and as long as the pattern frequency in the image in relation to depth of focus is not critical, the solution will be unique. Figures 13 and 14 illustrate the result of this cooperation.

In summary, these examples demonstrate that the design considerations above lead to an implementation that has desirable functionalities. It should be noted that these experiments have been carried out in static environments in order to achieve repeatability in the experiments. To get quantitative results during dynamic fixation we need facilities with which we can control and repeat motion patterns. Hence our current experiments on dynamic fixation are only of qualitative nature.

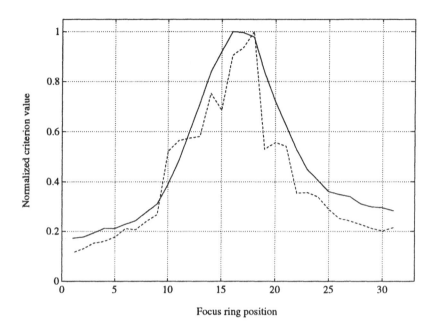

Figure 10. The evaluation function for focusing without stabilization (dashed curve), and with stabilization (solid curve). Stabilization results in a smooth curve free from local minima.

Figure 11. The repetitive pattern without the band limits of accommodation. The band (top). The pattern square is superimposed on the best match (bottom). The match, represented by the smallest value, is false.

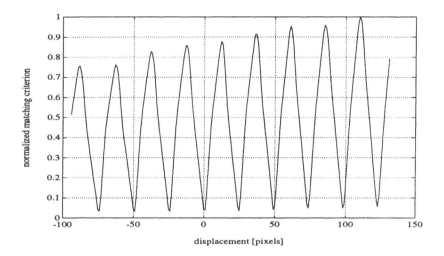

Figure 12. The evaluation function for matching. A good match here is represented by points of minima. As shown in the figure, without the dynamic constraints from the focusing process there are multiple solutions to the problem. Here the obtained match is false.

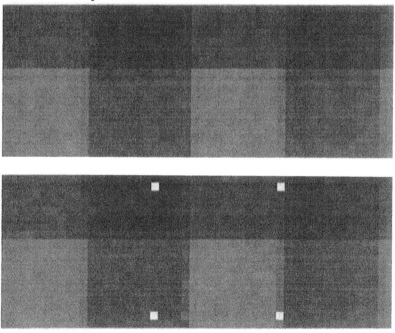

Figure 13. The repetitive pattern with the band limits suggested by accommodation. The band is shown at top. The pattern square is superimposed on the best match (bottom); in this case it is the correct match.

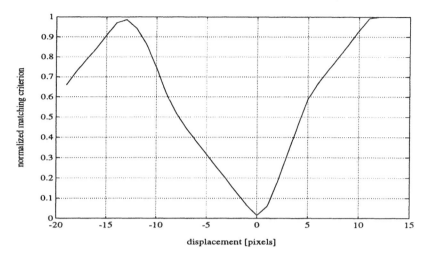

Figure 14. The evaluation function for matching. A good match is represented by the minimum point. To be compared with the curve not using the limits suggested by accommodation.

7. CONCLUSIONS

If vision is a way of interacting with the environment then it must be active. Either the observer or the environment must change over time for vision to be meaningful. Claims that active vision simplifies certain computations are substantiated in many cases, but that does not exclude that new difficulties may arise in other tasks, which must be solved to obtain a high-performing and flexible "seeing system."

Starting out from the active aspects of vision in general we considered active vision as a methodology. From this standpoint we discussed what the components of active vision are and how the approach is consistent with the notion of seeing systems. The next natural step to take is to study the design, actual development and integration of active behaviors.

REFERENCES

1. A.L. Abbott and N. Ahuja, "Surface reconstruction by dynamic integration of focus, camera vergence, and stereo," *Proc. Second Int'l. Conf. on Computer Vision*, 1988, 532–543.

2. M.A. Ali and M.A. Klyne, *Vision in Vertebrates*, Plenum Press, New York, 1985.

3. Y. Aloimonos, I. Weiss and A. Bandyopadhyay, "Active vision," *Int'l. J. Computer Vision* **2**, 1988, 333–356.

4. Y. Aloimonos and D. Shulman, *Integration of Visual Modules*, Academic Press, Boston, 1989.

5. J.Y. Aloimonos, "Purposive and qualitative active vision," In *Proc. Image Understanding Workshop*, 1990, 816–828.

6. R. Bajcsy, "Active perception vs. passive perception," *Proc. Third IEEE Workshop on Computer Vision*, 1985, 55–59.

7. R. Bajcsy, "An active observer," *Proc. Image Understanding Workshop*, 1992, 137–147.

8. D.H. Ballard, "Animate vision," *Proc. Int'l. Joint Conf. on Artificial Intelligence*, 1989, 1635–1641.

9. D.H. Ballard, "Animate vision," *Artificial Intelligence* **48**, 1991, 57–86.

10. I. Biederman, "Recognition-by-components: A theory of human image understanding," *Psychological Review* **94**, 1987, 115–147.

11. R.A. Brooks, "Intelligence without representation," *Artificial Intelligence* **47**, 1991, 137–160.

12. C.M. Brown (Ed.), D.H. Ballard, T. Becker, R. Gans, N. Martin, T. Olsen, R. Potter, R. Rimey, D. Tilley and S. Whitehead, "The Rochester Robot," Technical Report 287, University of Rochester, Computer Science Department, 1988.

13. C.M. Brown, "Gaze controls coöperating through prediction," *Image and Vision Computing* **8**, 1990, 10–17.

14. H.H. Bültoff and H.A. Mallot, "Interaction of different modules in depth perception," *Proc. Int'l. Conf. on Computer Vision*, 1987, 295–305.

15. R.H.S. Carpenter, *Movements of the Eyes*, Pion Press, London, 1988.

16. J.J. Clark and N.J. Ferrier, "Modal control of an attentive vision system," *Proc. Second Int'l. Conf. on Computer Vision*, 1988, 514–523.

17. D.J. Coombs, "Real-Time Gaze Holding in Binocular Robot Vision," Technical Report 415, University of Rochester, Computer Science Department, 1992.

18. J.P. Frisby and D. Buckley, "Experiments on stereo and texture cue combination in human vision using quasi-natural viewing," In *The Insight Project*, Springer Verlag ESPRIT series, to appear.

19. J.J. Gibson, *The Perception of the Visual World*, Houghton Mifflin, Boston, MA, 1950.

20. J.J. Gibson, *The Senses Considered as Perceptual Systems*, Houghton Mifflin, Boston, MA, 1966.

21. A. Horii, "The Focusing Mechanism in the KTH Head Eye System," Technical Report 105, Royal Institute of Technology, Computational Vision and Active Perception Laboratory, Stockholm, 1992.

22. B. Julesz, *Foundations of Cyclopean Perception*, University of Chicago Press, 1971

23. E.P. Krotkov, J.F. Summers and F. Fuma, "The Pennsylvania Active Camera System," Technical Report TR-CIS-86-22, University of Pennsylvania, 1986.

24. E.P. Krotkov, *Active Computer Vision by Cooperative Focus and Stereo*, Springer Verlag, 1989.

25. D. Marr, *Vision*, W.H. Freeman, San Francisco, CA, 1982.

26. J. Moran and R. Desimone, "Selective attention gates visual processing in the extrastriate cortex," *Science* **229**, 1985, 782–784.

27. P. Morasso, E. Bizzi and J. Dichgans, "Adjustment of saccade characteristics during head movements," *Experimental Brain Research*, 1973.

28. G. Oesterberg, *Topography of Layer of Rods and Cones in the Human Retina*, Copenhagen, 1935.

29. K. Pahlavan, T. Uhlin and J.O. Eklundh, "Integrating primary ocular processes," *Proc. Second European Conf. on Computer Vision*, 1992, 526–541.

30. K. Pahlavan and J.O. Eklundh, "A head–eye system—Analysis and design," *CVGIP: Image Understanding*, **56**, Special Issue on Purposive, Qualitative, Active Vision, Y. Aloimonos (Ed.), 1992, 41–56.

31. A. Pentland, "A new sense for depth of field," *IEEE Trans. PAMI* 91987, 523–531.

32. R.D. Rimey and C.M. Brown, "Where to look next using a Bayes net: Incorporating geometric relations," *Proc. Second European Conf. on Computer Vision*, 1992, 542–550.

33. E.L. Schwartz, Presentation given at the NSF Active Vision Workshop, Chicago, IL, August 1991.

34. J. van der Spiegel, G. Kreider, C. Claeys, I. Debusschere, G. Sandini, P. Dario, F. Fantini, P. Bellutti and G. Soncini, "A foveated retina-like sensor using CCD technology," in *Analog VLSI Implementations of Neural Systems*, Kluwer, C. Mead and M. Ismail (Eds.), 1989.

35. M.J. Swain and M. Stricker (Eds.),"Promising directions in active vision," In *NSF Active Vision Workshop*, 1991.

36. A. Yarbus, *Eye Movements and Vision*, Plenum Press, New York, 1967.

37. W. Zhang and F. Bergholm, "An Extension of Marr's "Signature" Based Edge Classification," Technical Report 104, Royal Institute of Technology, Computational Vision and Active Perception Laboratory, Stockholm, 1992.

2 Designing Visual Systems: Purposive Navigation

Yiannis Aloimonos, Ehud Rivlin and Liuqing Huang
University of Maryland

Abstract

We propose here a new approach to addressing problems related to visual motion, namely the purposive approach [4]. Instead of considering the various visual motion tasks as applications of the general structure from motion module, we consider them as independent problems and we directly seek solutions for them. As a result we can achieve unique and robust solutions without having to compute optic flow and without requiring a full reconstruction of the visual space, because it is not needed for the tasks. In the course of the exposition, we present novel solutions to various important visual tasks related to motion, such as the problems of motion detection by a moving observer, passive navigation, relative-depth computation, 3-D motion estimation, and visual interception, using as input only the spatial and temporal derivatives of the image intensity function. It turns out that the spatiotemporal derivatives of the image (i.e., the so-called normal flow) are sufficient to provide robust algorithms for the solution of many interesting visual tasks that do not require the full solution, but only part of it. Thus, we do not have to solve the general structure from motion problem. The ability to create robust nontrivial behaviors suggests the possibility that visual perception could be studied as intelligent behavior. We point out some of the benefits and drawbacks of this paradigm that studies vision as a set of behaviors that recover the visible world partially, but well enough to carry out a task (purposive, animate or behavioral vision), we contrast it to the traditional paradigm of treating vision as a general recovery problem, and we present a formal framework formalizing behaviors and tasks. This framework can be used for designing successful vision systems, by visually achieving vari-

This work was funded in part by ARPA, NSF (under a Presidential Young Investigator Award), Alliant Techsystems, Inc., Texas Instruments, Inc., and Sony Corporation.

ous tasks without reconstruction but through the recognition of patterns, objects or situations.

What to recognize is concerned with the questions we pose. The purposive paradigm calls for formulating questions that are directly related to visual tasks, i.e., that have a purpose. Knowledge of 3-D motion is much more than we need to answer the purposive question: Is this moving object coming closer to the observer? Purposive thinking leads us to pose questions whose answers will only help to solve the particular task at hand, and will not be of general use. This level of the paradigm is parallel to Marr's computational theory and insures that the resulting algorithms will be of minimal complexity.

How to recognize (patterns, objects or situations) is related to the algorithmic level of Marr's paradigm. Qualitative vision calls for the development of algorithms that are simple, robust and based on qualitative techniques, such as comparisons of quantities or discrete classifications. Qualitative vision, which in the past has been wrongly called inexact, makes sense here because it is coupled with purposive vision, which formulates questions for which qualitative solutions are possible.

1. INTRODUCTION AND MOTIVATION

The problem of structure from motion has attracted a lot of attention in the past few years [27, 39, 42] because of the general usefulness that a potential solution to this problem would have. Important navigational problems, such as detection of independently moving objects by a moving observer, passive navigation, obstacle detection, target pursuit, and many other problems related to robotics, teleconferencing, etc., would be simple applications of a structure from motion module. The problem has been formulated as follows: Given a sequence of images taken by a monocular observer (the observer and/or parts of the scene could be moving), to recover the shapes (and relative depths) of the objects in the scene, as well as the (relative) 3-D motions of independently moving bodies.

The problem has been formulated and usually treated as an aspect of the general task of recovering 3-D information from motion [30, 21]. The majority of the proposed solutions to date are based on the following modular and hierarchical approach:

1. First, one computes the optic flow on the image plane, i.e., the velocity with which every image point appears to be moving.[1]
2. Then segmentation of the flow field is performed and different moving objects are identified on the image plane. From the segmented optic flow one then computes the 3-D motion with which each visible surface is moving relative to the observer. (Assuming that an object moves rigidly, a monocular observer can only compute its direction of translation and its rotation, but not its speed.)

---

[1] For clarity, we consider only the differential case. In the case of long range motion one computes discrete displacements, but the analysis remains essentially the same.

3. Finally, using the values of the optic flow along with the results of the previous step, one computes the surface normal at each point, or equivalently, the ratio Z_i/Z_j of the depths of any two points i and j.

The reason that most approaches have followed the preceding three-step approach is two-fold. The first is due to the formulation of the problem, which insists on recovering a complete relative depth map and accurate 3-D motion. The second is due to the fact that the constraints relating retinal motion to 3-D structure involve 3-D motion in a nonlinear manner that does not allow separability. For examples of such approaches, see [1, 43, 27, 39]. However, the past work in this paradigm, despite its mathematical elegance, is far from being useful in real-time navigational systems, and such techniques have found few or no practical applications.[2] Consequently, this approach cannot be used yet to explain the ability of biological organisms to handle visual motion.

There exist many reasons for the limitations of the optic flow approach, related to all three steps listed. To begin, the computation of optic flow is an ill-posed problem, i.e., unless we impose additional constraints, we cannot estimate it [21]. Such constraints, however, impose a relationship on the values of the flow field which is translated into an assumption about the scene in view (for example, smooth). Thus, even if we are capable of obtaining an algorithm that computes optic flow in a robust manner, the algorithm will work only for a restricted set of scenes. The only available constraint at every point (x, y) of the changing image $I(x, y, t)$ for the flow (u, v) is the constraint $I_x u + I_y v + I_t = 0$ [23], where the subscripts denote partial differentiation. This means that we can only compute the projection of the flow on the gradient direction $((I_x, I_y) \cdot (u, v) = -I_t)$, i.e., the so-called *normal flow*. More graphically, it means that if a feature (e.g., an edge segment) in the image moves to a new position, we don't know where every point of the segment moved to (see Figure 1); we only know the normal flow, i.e., the projection of the flow on the image gradient at that point.

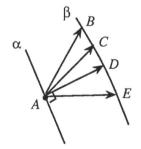

α: feature before motion

β: feature after motion

Figure 1. The aperture problem. Point A could have moved to B, C, D, E. However, whatever the value of the image motion vector is, its projection on the normal to α is always AD (known).

A second reason has to do with the very essence of optic flow. An optic flow field is the vector field of apparent velocities that are associated with the variation of

---

[2] Possible exceptions are photogrammetry and semiautonomous applications requiring a human operator.

brightness on the image plane. Clearly, the scene is not involved in this definition. One would hope that optic flow would be equivalent to the so-called motion field [21], which is the (perspective) projection on the image plane of the 3-D velocity field associated with each point of the visible surfaces in the scene. However, the optic flow field and the motion field are not equal in general. Verri and Poggio [45] reported some general results in an attempt to quantify the difference between the optic flow and motion fields. Although we don't yet have necessary and sufficient conditions for the equality of the two fields, it is clear that they are equal only under specific sets of restrictive conditions.

A third reason is related to the second step of the existing algorithms for structure from motion. These algorithms attempt to recover 3-D motion before they proceed to recover relative depth, and this problem of 3-D motion appears to be very sensitive in the presence of small amounts of noise in the input (flow or displacements) [1, 2, 40].

In [40] several experiments as well as comparisons of various algorithms were made and the finding was that an average error of 1% to 2% in the input (retinal correspondence) can create an error of about 100% in the estimated parameters. An important question to ask then is what makes this problem unstable, and to seek ways to address any inherent instabilities that might arise. There is recent work toward this direction but difficult questions still remain.

But while theoretical research on the principles of structure from motion continues in its quest for optimal recovery, we can also follow an alternative approach. We can ask the following simple question: If we had a robust structure from motion module, what would we use it for? The answer of course lies in a taxonomy of visual tasks involving motion, i.e., navigational tasks. A few such *generic* navigational tasks are, for example, the following:

- *Detection of independently moving objects in the environment, by a moving observer.* This is a nontrivial task, as everything moves on an image obtained by a moving observer, thus making it hard to distinguish independent motion. Although many general schemes have been proposed for segmentation of a flow field into areas corresponding to differently moving objects, there are still problems in practical applications involving more than one independently moving object. Other approaches of interest are those that combine measurements of flow with some 3-D interpretation which can then be used for incremental improvements to segmentation in an iterative manner. However, no practical robust system for detecting independently moving objects in general environments and based on optic flow has been demonstrated to date, with the exception of some model-based approaches.

- *Passive navigation.* Passive navigation is a term used to describe the processes by which a system can determine its motion with respect to the environment. This is important for kinetic stabilization which, in its simplest form, requires a system to maintain a fixed position and attitude in space in the presence of perturbing influences. More generally, stabilization can refer to any conditions placed on the motion parameters; for instance, the system might be required to translate without rotation. The two abilities are interrelated because stabilization is generally achieved by bringing the motion parameters to certain specified values. The capacity for passive navigation is prerequisite for any other navigational ability. In order to guide the system, some idea of the present motion and some method of setting it to known values must be available. In present robot systems the necessary information is often explicitly available as a result of a built-in coordinate system. For an autonomously moving system, however, there must be an active sensing capacity. It is possible to obtain the required information mechanically as is done by the inertial guidance systems in guided missiles. However, the task can also be performed by visual means and it is this problem that we address here.

- *Obstacle avoidance.* Obstacle avoidance refers, simply, to the ability to utilize sensory information to maneuver in an environment containing physical objects without striking them. This can be considered a second-level ability. It requires some capacity for passive navigation, but little else, and could thus be considered the lowest level of active navigation. This task can be performed nonvisually by range sensing methods, and it has been generally proposed that the problem be solved visually with a similar algorithm utilizing depth data from a scene reconstructed by the structure from motion module.

- *Avoidance of collision with a moving object.* A robust structure from motion module can detect the 3-D motion of a moving object, calculate its 3-D position with the aid of a binocular system and predict its 3-D trajectory. Thus, it can detect any possibilities for collision, by reconstructing the 3-D trajectory of the moving object.

- *Understanding of relative depth.* Visual motion provides a very rich amount of information about the relative depths of objects in the environment (which object is closer). Clearly, this is one of the outputs of the structure from motion module.

- *Visual pursuit.* A 3-D visual pursuit system consists of an eye (camera), a subject, an object and a mind. The mind uses information from the eye in order to control the movement of the subject so that it will collide with (intercept, catch) the object. Under the traditional paradigm of considering vision as a recovery problem, visual pursuit is just another application of the structure from motion module. In such a case, the camera would reconstruct the 3-D positions and motions of the camera, the subject and the object and then this information would be utilized by a planning module to generate correct control of the subject.

Given the lack of success in developing a robust structure from motion module, it would seem reasonable to consider simpler problems. There are visual problems, such as the above, which do not require the full realization of the structure from motion capability, yet which are both nontrivial and possess the sort of environmental invariance that would give them general utility. To consider a few examples from biological navigation, the housefly can maneuver visually in 3-D in a complex environment without striking obstacles; a number of bees and wasps can recognize and return to a particular location in their environment; and the frog can extend its tongue and catch flying insects. Human beings can also perform such tasks, but obviously they can be performed with far less computational equipment than humans possess. We propose here to consider, in the context of navigational tasks, some of the above problems, more specific and more restricted than the general structure from motion problem, with a view toward producing examples of visual systems that have the potential for robustness. This approach is termed *purposive* [4].

We show later that specific questions such as the preceding ones can be answered without having to go through the estimation of optic flow. The derivatives of the image intensity function are enough for the task. The approach taken in this chapter calls for the solution of specific visual tasks, such as the preceding ones, in such a way that the solution does not have more power than it is supposed to have. For example, the procedure that provides relative depth is designed only for that purpose and cannot be used to solve the passive navigation problem, or the problem of 3-D motion estimation. Of course, if information about 3-D motion is known, it can be effectively utilized in the estimation of relative depth, but this is of no concern to us here. When building a system that can deal with visual motion problems, we can visualize it as consisting of many processes working in a cooperative manner to solve various problems. For example, the theories described in this chapter could be used to design a process that computes relative depth from image measurements, independently of the process that computes 3-D motion. However, after a number of computational steps, when results about relative depth and 3-D motion become available from the two independent processes, they can be exchanged and the constraints relating them can be effectively utilized so that the results are as consistent as possible.

2. QUALITATIVE METHODS

Most visual navigation tasks, including the ones just described, have been considered to be subproblems for the reconstructive school. The connection is a natural one since most of these tasks involve shape and distance relationships between the system and the environment which can be expressed in terms of the quantitative idiom of the reconstructive school. This perception has tended to discourage explicit research on such specific problems by classifying them as special cases of an important general problem. It has also tended to obscure the fact that many of the operations necessary to implement specific visual tasks can be expressed in qualitative terms which are more aptly described in terms of the recognition idiom. Consider, for example, the problem of passive navigation. It is not necessary to know exactly how the system is moving with respect to the environment but only whether it is rotating or translating at all, and if so, in what direction forces must be applied to reduce the motion. In the case of obstacle avoidance, the most relevant information is not the exact distance in centimeters from the observer to each point in the environment, but whether the observer is on a collision course with a nearby obstacle and if so, in which direction it should move to avoid the danger of a crash. The common factor in these examples is that they do not require precise quantitative information and that in each case, the information necessary to carry out the task can be represented in a space having only a few degrees of freedom.

3. ORGANIZATION OF THE CHAPTER

We wish to develop the mathematics that will give rise to general solutions to the specific problems of detection of independent motion, passive navigation, relative depth estimation, obstacle avoidance, estimating whether an object is on a collision course with the observer, and visual pursuit using the derivatives of the image as input, as opposed to considering them as applications of the structure from motion module. Section 4 is devoted to the description of the input and Sections 5–9 describe general solutions to the specific tasks mentioned previously. Finally, Section 10 is devoted to the presentation of some experimental results. It should be pointed out that here we are mostly interested in the theoretical principles behind these perceptual processes and the geometry of the normal flow. We seek solutions that have uniqueness properties using normal flow as input, since normal flow is well defined, while optic flow is not. Thus, we only present the computational theory behind each process. For various properties of the solutions of the individual problems, a theoretical error analysis and an extensive implementation, see [6, 18, 24, 37]. It will become clear that solving the aforementioned problems using normal flow (which contains less information than optic flow) becomes possible only through the employment of an active visual agent [7]. The reason is, of course, that some of the computational burden is transferred to the activity of the agent.

Finally, the chapter ends with a formal framework describing behaviors/tasks and providing a novel methodology for designing visual systems consisting of processes that perform partial recovery of the scene in view which is adequate for accomplishing a set of behaviors.

4. THE INPUT

Our motivation is by now clear. We wish to avoid using optic flow as the input to visual motion tasks. On the other hand, we must utilize some description of the image motion. As such a description we choose the spatial and temporal derivatives $\frac{\partial I}{\partial x}, \frac{\partial I}{\partial y}, \frac{\partial I}{\partial t}$ of the image intensity function $I(x, y, t)$. These quantities define the normal flow at every point, i.e., the projection of the optic flow on the direction of the gradient (I_x, I_y). Clearly, estimating the normal flow is much easier than estimating the actual optic flow. But how is normal flow related to the 3-D motion field? Is the normal optic flow field equal to the normal motion field, and under what conditions? This question was first investigated by Verri and Poggio [45].

Let $I(x, y, t)$ denote the image intensity, and consider the optic flow field $\vec{v} = (u, v)$ and the motion field $\vec{\bar{v}} = (\bar{u}, \bar{v})$ at a point (x, y) where the local (normalized) intensity gradient is $\vec{n} = (I_x, I_y)/\sqrt{I_x^2 + I_y^2}$. The normal motion field at point (x, y) is by definition

$$\bar{u}_n = \vec{\bar{v}} \cdot \vec{n} \qquad \text{or}$$

$$\bar{u}_n = \frac{(I_x, I_y)}{\sqrt{I_x^2 + I_y^2}} \cdot \left(\frac{dx}{dt}, \frac{dy}{dt}\right) \quad \text{or}$$

$$\bar{u}_n = \frac{\nabla I}{\|\nabla I\|} \cdot \left(\frac{dx}{dt}, \frac{dy}{dt}\right) \qquad \text{or}$$

$$\bar{u}_n = \frac{1}{\|\nabla I\|} \left(I_x \frac{dx}{dt} + I_y \frac{dy}{dt}\right)$$

Similarly, the normal optic flow [23] is

$$u_n = -\frac{1}{\nabla I} I_t$$

Thus

$$\bar{u}_n - u_n = \frac{1}{\nabla I}\frac{dI}{dt}$$

From this equation it follows that if the change of intensity of an image patch during its motion $\left(\frac{dI}{dt}\right)$ is small enough (which is a reasonable assumption) and the local intensity gradient has a high magnitude, then the normal optic flow and motion fields are approximately equal. Thus, provided that we measure normal flow in regions of high local intensity gradients, the normal flow measurements can safely be used for inferring 3-D structure and motion.

We are now ready to describe our solution to the various motion related tasks. Since the input to the perceptual process is the normal flow, and the normal flow field contains less information than the motion field, in order to solve various problems we need to transfer much of the computation to the activity of the observer [7]. A geometric model of the observer is given in Figure 2. Notice that the camera is resting on a platform ("neck") with six degrees of freedom (actually only one of the degrees is used) and the camera can rotate around its x and y axes (saccades).

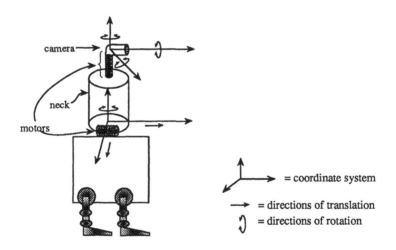

Figure 2. The active observer.

5. PASSIVE NAVIGATION

5.1. A QUALITATIVE SOLUTION

The problem of passive navigation (kinetic stabilization) has attracted a lot of attention in the past ten years [15, 27, 28, 43, 40, 42] because of the generality of a potential solution. The problem has been formulated as follows: Given a sequence of images taken by a monocular observer undergoing unrestricted rigid motion in a stationary environment, to recover the 3-D motion of the observer. In particular, if (U, V, W) and (A, B, C) are the translation and rotation, respectively, comprising the general rigid motion of the observer, the problem is to recover the following five numbers: the direction of translation $(\frac{U}{W}, \frac{V}{W})$ and the rotation (A, B, C) (see Figure 3). The problem has thus been formulated as the general 3-D motion estimation problem (kinetic depth or structure from motion) and its solution would solve several other problems.

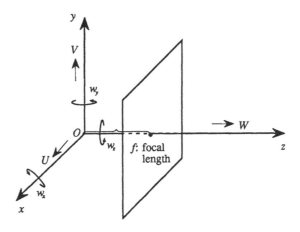

Figure 3. Geometric model of the observer.

Consider a model for a monocular observer as in Figure 3. We assume that the observer moves forward. It should be noted that the observer is equipped with inertial sensors which provide the rotation (A, B, C) of the observer at any time. As the observer moves in its environment, normal flow fields are computed in real time. Since optic flow due to rotation does not depend on depth but on image position (x, y), we know (and can compute in real time) its value (u^R, v^R) at every image point along with the normal flow.[3] That means that we know the geometrical locus of the optic flow due to translation (see Figure 4). Since the observer moves forward in a static scene, it is approaching anything in the scene and the flow is expanding. From Figure 4, it is clear that the focus of expansion (FOE) $(\frac{U}{W}, \frac{V}{W})$ (when the gradient space of directions $(\frac{U}{W}, \frac{V}{W})$ is superimposed with the image space) lies in the half plane defined by line ϵ. Clearly, at every point we obtain a constraint line which constrains the FOE to lie in a half plane. If the FOE lies on the image plane (i.e., the direction of translation is anywhere inside the sector $OABCD$, Figure 5) then the FOE is constrained to lie in an area on the image plane and thus it can be localized (see Figure 6). When the FOE does not lie inside the image, a closed area cannot be found, but the votes collected by the half planes indicate its general direction. In this case the observer, with a "saccade" (a rotation of the camera), can bring the FOE inside the image and localize it (Figure 7 explains the process).

---

[3] If computation of normal flow at some points is unreliable, we just don't compute normal flow there.

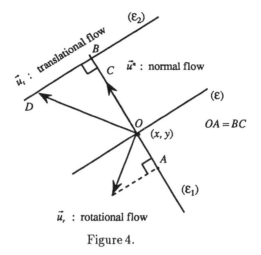

Figure 4.

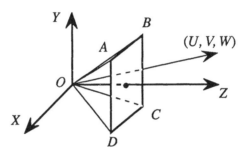

Figure 5. Consider the camera coordinate system. If the translation vector (U, V, W) is anywhere inside the solid $OABCD$ defined by the nodal point of the eye and the boundaries of the image, then the FOE is somewhere on the image.

5.2. THE ALGORITHM

We assume that the computation of the normal flow, the voting and the localization of the area containing the highest number of votes can happen in real time. In this chapter we don't get involved with real time implementation issues as we wish to analyze the theoretical aspects of the technique. However, it is quite clear that computation of normal flow can happen in real time (there already exist chips performing edge detection). According to the literature on Hough transforms and connectionist networks [11], voting can also take place in real time. Let S denote the area with the highest number of votes. Let $L(S)$ be a Boolean function that is true when the intersection of S with the image boundary is the null set, and false otherwise. Then the following algorithm finds area S. We assume that the inertial sensors provide the rotation and thus we know the normal flow due to translation.

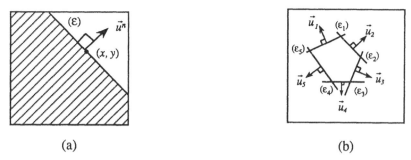

(a)   (b)

Figure 6. (a) From a measurement $\vec{u}$ of the normal flow due to translation at a point (x, y) of the image, every point of the image belonging to
the half plane defined by ϵ that does not contain $\vec{u}$ is a candidate for the
position of the focus of expansion, and collects one vote. The voting is
done in parallel for every image measurement. (b) If the FOE lies within
the image boundaries, then the area containing the highest number of
votes is the area containing the FOE. Using only a few measurements
can result in a large area. Using many measurements (all possible) results in a small area (in our experiments an area of at most three or four
pixels).

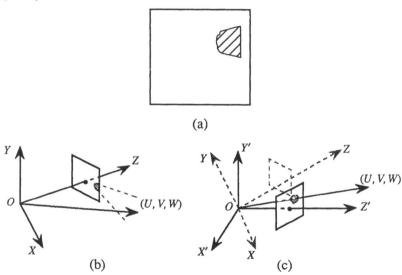

(a)

(b)   (c)

Figure 7. (a) If the area containing the highest number of votes has a
piece of the image boundary as part of its boundary, then the FOE is outside the image plane. (b) The position of the area containing the highest
number of votes indicates the general direction in which the translation
vector lies. (c) The camera ("eye") rotates so that the area containing
the highest number of votes becomes centered. With a rotation around
the x and y axes only, the optical axis can be positioned anywhere in
space. The process stops when the highest vote area is entirely inside
the image.

1.   begin {
2.   find area S
3.   repeat until $L(S)$
4.   {   rotate camera around x, y axes
                  so that the optical axis passes
                  through the center of S (saccade)
5.   find area S
                  }
            output S
            }

If the camera has a wide angle lens, then image points can represent many orientations, and only one saccade may be necessary. But if we have a small angle lens, then we may have to make more than one saccade.[4]

5.3. IMPROVEMENT OF THE SOLUTION

It is clear that the technique just described provides as an answer an area on the image containing the FOE. How large or small this area can be depends on the distribution of surface markings and thus on the measured normal flow. If the FOE lies in a featureless area, the resulting area will not be small. For some applications the knowledge of area S might be enough to accomplish the task. We can, however, narrow down a more accurate solution, with S providing one constraint.

Assuming that inertial sensors provide us with the rotation, we can derotate the normal flow field. Thus, assuming a translational normal flow field $v_n(x, y)$, we have $v_n = u \cdot n_x + v n_y$, where (u, v) is the optic flow and (n_x, n_y) the direction of the gradient at that point. Since we have derotated, the optic flow is

$$u = \frac{U - xW}{V}, v = \frac{V - yW}{Z}$$

and thus

$$v_n = -\frac{W}{Z}(x n_x + y n_y) + \frac{W}{Z}\left(n_x \frac{U}{W} + n_y \frac{V}{W}\right)$$

or

$$\frac{n_x}{v_n}\frac{U}{W} + \frac{n_y}{u_n}\frac{V}{W} - \frac{Z}{W} = \frac{n_x}{v_n} \cdot x + \frac{n_y}{u_n} \cdot y$$

This is a linear equation in the FOE $\left(\frac{U}{W}, \frac{V}{W}\right)$ and the time to collision $\left(\frac{Z}{W}\right)$ with the scene point.

If we consider a small image patch P with Z_{av} the average depth of the scene points giving rise to the patch under consideration, then the above equation, for every point $(x_i, y_i) \in P$ with depth z_i, can be written as

$$\frac{n_x}{v_n}\frac{V}{W} + \frac{n_y}{v_n}\frac{V}{W} - \frac{Z_{\text{av}}}{W} = \frac{n_x}{v_n}x + \frac{n_y}{v_n}y + \left(\frac{Z_i}{W} - \frac{Z_{\text{av}}}{W}\right)$$

---

[4] Up to this point the algorithm is similar to [22]. However, as will become clear later, it works even when rotation is present, while in [22] the solution works only for translational motion.

The expected value of the last term in the preceding equation is zero, and assuming that we can correctly compute (n_x, n_y) and v_n, equations

$$\frac{n_x}{v_n}\frac{U}{W} + \frac{n_y}{v_n}\frac{V}{W} - \frac{Z_{\text{av}}}{W} = \frac{n_x}{v_n}x + \frac{n_y}{v_n}y$$

at every point $(x, y) \in P$ constitute a linear system in the unknowns $\frac{U}{W}$, $\frac{V}{W}$ and $\frac{Z_{\text{av}}}{W}$. Solving such systems for several patches robustly provides the FOE and a hazard map (showing different time-to-collision values). The patches need at least three normal flow measurements, and so they can be quite small.

5.4. ANALYSIS OF THE METHOD

We have assumed that the inertial sensors will provide the observer with accurate information about rotation. Although expensive accelerometers can achieve very high accuracy, the same is not true for inexpensive inertial sensors and so we are bound to have some error. Thus we must assume that some unknown rotational part still exists and contributes to the value of the normal flow. As a result, the method for finding the FOE (previous section) which is based on translational normal flow information (since we have "derotated") might be affected by the presence of some rotational flow. In this section, we study the effect of rotation (the error of the inertial sensor) on the technique for finding the FOE. At the same time *we provide a technique for bounding the FOE given a normal flow field containing both rotation and translation.*

In order to avoid artificial problems introduced by perspective distortions in the case of a planar retina and to simplify the formulas without loss of generality, we employ a spherical retina. Let a sphere with radius f and center O (Figure 8) represent the spherical retina (with O the nodal point of the eye) and a coordinate system $OXYZ$ attached to it. Let

$$\vec{r}_\omega = (X, Y, Z) \text{ be a world point}$$

and

$$\vec{r} = (x, y, z) \text{ be its image on the image plane.}$$

Then

$$\frac{\vec{r}}{f} = \frac{\vec{r}_\omega}{R}, \quad R = \|\vec{r}_\omega\| = \sqrt{\vec{r}_\omega \cdot \vec{r}_\omega}$$

In the sequel we derive expressions for optic (normal) flow in the new configuration.

If the velocity of the world point $\vec{r}_\omega$ is given by

$$\dot{\vec{r}}_\omega = -\vec{t} - \vec{\omega} \times \vec{r}_\omega$$

where $\begin{array}{l}\vec{t} \text{ is translation } (\vec{t} = (U, V, W)) \\ \vec{\omega} \text{ is rotation } (\vec{\omega} = (\omega_x, \omega_y, \omega_z))\end{array}$

then

$$\frac{\dot{\vec{r}}}{f} = \frac{\dot{\vec{r}}_\omega \cdot R - \vec{r}_\omega \cdot \dot{R}}{R^2}$$

$$\dot{R} = \frac{d}{dt}\left(\sqrt{\vec{r}_\omega \cdot \vec{r}_\omega}\right) = \frac{1}{2R}(\dot{\vec{r}}_\omega \cdot \vec{r}_\omega + \vec{r}_\omega \cdot \dot{\vec{r}}_\omega) = \frac{\dot{\vec{r}}_\omega \cdot \vec{r}_\omega}{R}$$

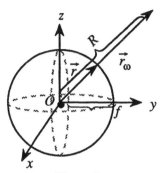

Figure 8.

We have

$$\frac{\dot{\vec{r}}}{f} = \frac{\dot{\vec{r}}_\omega}{R} - \frac{\vec{r}_\omega}{R^3}(\dot{\vec{r}}_\omega \cdot \vec{r}_\omega)$$

$$= -\frac{\vec{t}}{R} - \frac{\vec{\omega} \times \vec{r}_\omega}{R} - \frac{\vec{r}_\omega}{R} \cdot \frac{1}{R^2}\left((-\vec{t} - \vec{\omega} \times \vec{r}_\omega) \cdot \vec{r}_\omega\right)$$

$$= -\frac{\vec{t}}{R} - \frac{\vec{\omega} \times \vec{r}}{f} + \frac{\vec{r}}{f} \cdot \frac{1}{R}(\vec{t} \cdot \frac{\vec{r}}{f})$$

or

$$\dot{\vec{r}} = -\frac{\vec{t}f}{R} - \vec{\omega} \times \vec{r} + \frac{\vec{r}}{Rf}(\vec{t} \cdot \vec{r}) \qquad (1)$$

$$= \frac{1}{R}\left[-\vec{t}f + \frac{\vec{r}}{f}(\vec{t} \cdot \vec{r})\right] - \vec{\omega} \times \vec{r}$$

Thus, the translational flow is

$$\vec{u}_t = \frac{1}{R}\left[-\vec{t}f + \frac{\vec{r}(\vec{t} \cdot \vec{r})}{f}\right]$$

while the rotational flow is given by

$$\vec{u}_R = -\vec{\omega} \times \vec{r}$$

Without loss of generality we can set $f = 1$.

At this point we define two quantities that will be of use later. They are $\tau = \frac{R}{\|\vec{t}\|}$, which we term time to collision, and $k = \frac{\|\vec{\omega}\|}{\|\vec{t}\|}R = \|\vec{\omega}\|\tau$, which represents the effective ratio of rotation and translation.

The geometry of the spherical projection is then given in Figure 9. It has been shown [33] that a full (360°) visual field simplifies motion analysis. However, what we usually have is just a piece of the surface of the sphere (due to a limited field of view). Assume then that the image (the part that we see) is projected on the surface patch S. Obviously, voting for the estimation of the FOE can be performed for all points on S.

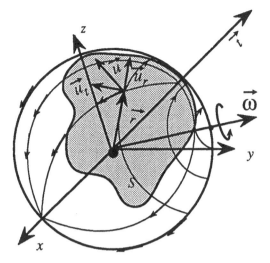

Figure 9.

Principles of voting

Consider

$\vec{r}_i = (x, y, z)$, a point in S,
$\vec{n}_i = (n_x, n_y, n_z)$, the image gradient direction
         at point $\vec{r}_i$,
$\dot{\vec{r}}_i = \vec{u}_i = (u_x, u_y, u_z)$, the flow at point $\vec{r}_i$, and
$\vec{u}_i^n = (\vec{n}_i \cdot \vec{u}_i) \cdot \vec{n}_i$, the normal flow at $\vec{r}_i$.

Then (see Figure 10) if $\vec{r} = (x, y, z)$ is a point in S, a feature point $\vec{r}_i$ will vote for $\vec{r}$ being the FOE (direction of translation) iff $\vec{u}_i^n (\vec{r} - \vec{r}_i) < 0$ (see Figure 10).

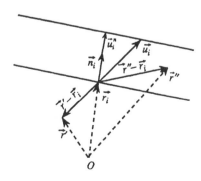

Figure 10.

If $V[\vec{r}]$ represents the number of votes collected at point $\vec{r}$, then it is easy to see that

$$V[\vec{r}] = \sum_{\vec{r}_i \in S} U\left[\vec{u}_i^n (\vec{r}_i - \vec{r})\right]$$

where

$$U(x) = \begin{cases} 1, & x > 0 \\ 0, & x \leq 0 \end{cases}$$

Let $S' = \left\{ \vec{r} | \forall \vec{r'} \in S, \ V[\vec{r}] \geq V[\vec{r'}] \right\}$ be the set of points that have acquired the maximum number of votes. There are two cases:

Case 1: S' does not intersect the border of S, in which case the FOE is in S'.
Case 2: S' touches the border of S, in which case the FOE could be outside S.

It should be clear that if there is no rotation, then S' will always contain the FOE or give the direction of the FOE—i.e., the direction toward which we need to rotate. The size of S' depends on the distribution of features.

We can investigate the performance of the voting scheme in the presence of rotation. In particular we can ask how large area S is when rotation is present. It has been shown that this depends on the angle θ_ω between the direction of translation and the axis of rotation as well as on the rotation-to-translation ratio k. In particular, θ_ω distorts area S' and k enlarges it as it grows. The interested reader can consult [6].

Correctness of voting

The normal flow (as well as the actual flow) is very small in the region close to the FOE, and in the directions close to orthogonal to the directions of the flow. Consequently, even when only translation is present, in order to avoid inaccuracies that might arise in the estimated direction of the normal flow—numerical manipulation of very small quantities is unstable—we are going to discard any normal flow whose magnitude is less than some threshold T_t. Later, it will turn out that choosing this threshold greatly facilitates the geometrical analysis of the technique. Considering an actual flow $\vec{u}$ at a point A (see Figure 11) we can compute the locus of gradient directions $\vec{n}$ along which the normal flow (i.e., the projection of $\vec{u}$ on $\vec{n}$) is bigger than the threshold T_t. In Figure 11 they are all directions inside angle BAC defined by $\beta_0 = \arccos \frac{T_t}{\|\vec{u}\|}$ for $\frac{T_t}{\|\vec{u}\|} \leq 1$, or there are no such directions for $\frac{T_t}{\|\vec{u}\|} > 1$.

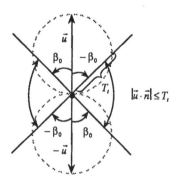

Figure 11.

We now develop a condition that needs to be satisfied in order for voting at a point to be correct in the presence of rotation.

Voting will clearly be correct only if the direction of the translational normal flow is the same as the direction of the actual normal flow, that is when

$$(\vec{n} \cdot \vec{u}_t)(\vec{n} \cdot \vec{u}) > 0 \qquad (2)$$

In addition, since we consider only normal flows greater than threshold, we need

$$|\vec{n} \cdot \vec{u}| > T_t \qquad (3)$$

Inequality (2) becomes

$$\begin{aligned}(\vec{n} \cdot \vec{u}_t)(\vec{n} \cdot \vec{u}) &= (\vec{n} \cdot \vec{u}_t)(\vec{n} \cdot \vec{u}_t + \vec{n} \cdot \vec{u}_R) = \\ &= (\vec{n} \cdot \vec{u}_t)^2 + (\vec{n} \cdot \vec{u}_t)(\vec{n} \cdot \vec{u}_R) > 0\end{aligned} \qquad (4)$$

So, if we set $|\vec{n} \cdot \vec{u}_R| = T_t$, then there are two possibilities: Either $|\vec{n} \cdot \vec{u}|$ is below the threshold, in which case it is of no interest to voting, or the sign of $\vec{n} \cdot \vec{u}$ is the same as the sign of $\vec{n} \cdot \vec{u}_t$. In other words, if we can set the threshold equal to the maximum value of the normal rotational flow, *then our voting will always be correct.* But at point $\vec{r}$ of the sphere the rotational flow is

$$\begin{aligned}|\vec{n} \cdot \vec{u}_R| &\leq \|\vec{n}\| \cdot \|\vec{u}_R\| = \|\vec{u}_R\| = \|\vec{\omega} \times \vec{r}\| = \\ &= \|\vec{\omega}\| \cdot \|\vec{r}\| \cdot |\sin(\angle \vec{\omega}, \vec{r})| \leq \|\vec{\omega}\|\end{aligned}$$

Thus if we choose $T_t = \|\vec{\omega}\|$, then the sign of $\vec{n} \cdot \vec{u}$ (actual normal flow) is equal to the sign of $\vec{u}_t \cdot \vec{n}$ (translational normal flow) for any normal flow of magnitude greater than T_t.

6. ACTIVE DETECTION OF INDEPENDENT MOTION

Among the more significant papers devoted exclusively to detecting moving objects is [41] by Thompson and Pong. It recognizes the difficulty of motion detection using only visual information in the form of optic flow, and considers additional constraints that may have to be applied for motion detection, e.g., knowledge about camera motion, moving object tracking, and information about scene depth. Though it presents a good discussion of the various trade-offs involved, all techniques proposed still depend on the computation of the optic flow.

The two approaches that are closest to the technique described here (emphasizing qualitative techniques for particular situations) are [10] and [32]. Bhanu et al. [10] identify a fuzzy FOE (see also [16]) and propose a rule-based qualitative analysis of the motion of scene points. However, this requires point correspondences that are difficult to obtain in general and involves considerable "high-level" (and hence expensive) reasoning, which would seem to be inappropriate for the relatively "low-level" task of motion detection. Nelson [32] gives motion detection techniques based on normal flow and pattern recognition that can be used in situations when the observer motion is specific, and when the object motion changes rapidly in comparison with the changes in camera motion (termed *animate vision*; see also [12]).

The basis of the technique described here lies in deviations from expectations. If the observer moves in a stationary environment then he/she expects to observe a normal flow field that obeys some properties (see Figure 12). If there exist independently moving visible objects in the scene then some of these properties will not hold in parts of the normal flow image; these unexpected "anomalies" signify the existence of independent motion.[5] However, it is possible that the normal flow field appears as expected while there still exists independent motion. In the sequel we will examine the problem in more detail.

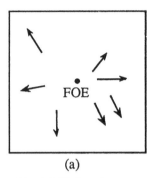 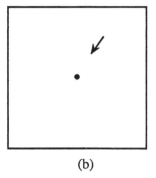

(a)   (b)

Figure 12. (a) If the observer translates along its optical axis, then the normal flow field has the property that it points away from the origin (FOE) at every point. This normal flow field is as expected and it does not signify independent motion (although it might exist). (b) There exist values of the normal flow that do not point away from the FOE. They are not as expected and thus signify independent motion.

The motion field and hence the optic flow is due to the motion of the observer (inducing a flow $\vec{u}^{eg}$) and the motion of independent objects in view, inducing a flow $\vec{u}^{ind}$. Then the normal flow at every point is: $v_n = u_n^{eg} + u_n^{ind}$, where u_n^{eg}, u_n^{ind} are the normal components of $\vec{u}^{eg}$ and $\vec{u}^{ind}$, respectively.

We consider the case where the motion of the observer is translation (if there is rotation, the observer's inertial sensors can provide it; then we can derotate the normal flow field and thus consider only translation). Also, the previous algorithm (Section 5) provides the FOE (or an area containing it). To simplify the exposition we first assume that the FOE is a known point but we can easily generalize to the case where the FOE lies in an area S.

6.1. THE COMPUTATIONAL THEORY

Consider Figure 13, which represents the normal flow at two points A, B with O being the FOE. Clearly, if the normal flow points toward the FOE (i.e., the FOE lies in the half plane defined by the line normal to the flow), then this particular point (B) is moving independently of the sensor. If, however, the normal flow points away from the FOE (as in A), this could be due to egomotion or to a combination of egomotion and independent motion. Thus further constraints need to be applied to always be able to detect independent motion. At this juncture additional information from the

---

[5] This principle of deviations from expectations and anomalies is very powerful and can be used in many other situations.

image sequence could be used, for example, the value of u_n, but in accordance with our goal of devising a strategy that uses only the "sign" of u_n, we have to define some additional activity that may make motion detection possible. It is easy to see that the following conditions are necessary and sufficient for detecting independent motion at a point for a particular position of the FOE.

(a) $\vec{u}_n^{\text{ind}}$ points toward the FOE.
(b) The length of $\vec{u}_n^{\text{eg}}$ is less than the length of $\vec{u}_n^{\text{ind}}$.

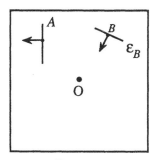

Figure 13.

In general, the conditions above will not be satisfied at every point in the image. The only "tool" that we allow ourselves at this point is shifting of the FOE by some process. The question we ask then is, what *exploratory action* (a sequence of shifts of the FOE) will guarantee motion detection at all points of the image? One condition that any exploratory activity guaranteeing "completeness" will have to satisfy is established by the following observation: If $O_1, O_2, \ldots, O_k$ is a sequence of new FOE locations (formed by an exploratory action), and the convex hull of the set of points $\{O_1 \ldots O_k\}$ encloses the entire region of interest, then complete detection of independent motion is guaranteed. This constitutes a necessary condition for the completeness of detection.

We can also observe that if the region of interest is the entire rectangular image, and the FOE is shifted at least to the four corners of the image, then the necessary condition for guaranteeing detection is satisfied. Up to now, we were mostly concerned with condition (a). Before we establish conditions under which both conditions (a) and (b) are satisfied, let us consider condition (b). If it is violated, then the length of $\vec{u}_n^{\text{eg}}$ is larger than the length of $\vec{u}_n^{\text{ind}}$, or $\|\vec{u}_n^{\text{eg}}\| > \|\vec{u}_n^{\text{ind}}\|$. Any exploratory action (since we have no control over $\vec{u}_n^{\text{ind}}$) would attempt to decrease $\vec{u}_n^{\text{eg}}$. The following two exploratory activities attempt to satisfy condition (b).

If the point of interest is point $A(x_A, y_A)$ then we can either move the FOE close to A, or decrease the angle between the line connecting the FOE to point A and the gradient of the image at point A. The first action decreases the flow due to egomotion (egomotion flow at the FOE is zero) and the second action decreases the normal flow due to egomotion.

6.2. Shifting the FOE

The shifting of the FOE is a process that can be achieved by an active observer. In [37], Sharma implemented FOE shifting through the employment of a jittering process. The engineering basis for using the "jitter" is that the shift in the FOE helps in motion detection, while the fact that it causes only momentary and controlled displacement about an equilibrium position eliminates the need for point correspondence. It was assumed that the motors responsible for moving the camera have the dynamic control capability needed for producing the jitter. With a suitably designed camera system this should be possible.[6] Sharma and Aloimonos [37] were not concerned with the details of the motor control involved but considered instead only the effect of the resulting shifts of the FOE. Note that the "jitter" does not affect the dominant motion of the observer (i.e., that of the mobile platform). Thus its effect on the image flow is only "additive." That is, the image flow pattern due to the egomotion is modified by the addition of the flow due to the jitter at a point. This constrains the nature of the changes to the flow that can be brought about.

A more feasible activity for the achievement of FOE shifting is the so-called "neck rotation" (see Figure 2). Rotation around the y-axis of the neck is equivalent to the sum of a rotation of the camera around an axis passing through the nodal point plus a translation of the camera along its x-axis. Given that ω is known (since the relative position of the neck and camera center are assumed to be known in the system) its effects can be subtracted from the image normal flow thus having as a result the effect of parallel translation along the x-axis, which can shift the FOE out of the image (to the left or to the right). Similarly, rotation of the neck around its x-axis amounts to translation of camera along its y-axis (and thus shifting of the FOE up and down).

6.3. The algorithm

For a typical robot task, detecting the motions of objects that are small, distant, or slow is not very important. On the other hand, detecting the motions of objects that are large, close, or fast may be critical for the robot, and any useful motion detection strategy should guarantee the detection of such motions.[7]

There is obviously a trade-off involved between the activity required and the parameters that describe the sensitivity of motion detection under different conditions. Computation of normal flow proceeds in real time. Normal flows pointing toward

---

[6] After all, human eyes are perpetually active and can be moved very efficiently with the help of extensive groups of muscles. Any artificial system that purports to emulate human performance— at least in achieving navigational goals (for example)—should have similar "active" capabilities [12].

[7] For example, for safe navigation a mobile robot needs to detect any sharp changes in nearby objects that are large enough to be important (e.g., another robot or a human that may move across its path), while other moving objects may not be of immediate interest if they are distant (e.g., they will not affect the robot's planned path) or if they are too small (e.g., a fly). Of course this may represent only a typical scenario; under other circumstances or for other missions all motion may be critically important, and it would be justified to pay the cost, which consists of increased exploratory activity (careful scanning of the scene) or a decrease in the overall speed of the robot. An analogy from the biological world can easily be made. When a deer or other animal senses danger it slows down or even stops completely and looks around carefully, alert to the slightest movement (and may "jump" even for a falling leaf), whereas normally it is less sensitive to the motions around it. It would be desirable to equip a robot with a similar mechanism for motion detection that would have a variable level of sensitivity.

the FOE are classified as moving independently. Additional activity by the observer (moving the FOE at least to the four image boundaries) may uncover additional independently moving points.

If we consider a point $A(x, y)$ on the image plane, then the length of the flow $\vec{u}^{eg}$ is $\|\vec{u}^{eg}\| = \frac{W}{Z} \cdot r$, where r is the distance of A from the FOE. Assume further that the detection paradigm is such that for the point of interest A at least one position of the FOE lies within distance d from A. That is $r < d$ for point A. The length of the corresponding egomotion flow is thus $\|\vec{u}^{eg}\| < \frac{W}{Z} \cdot d$ and consequently the normal egomotion component obeys

$$\|u_n^{eg}\| < \frac{W}{Z} \cdot d$$

For independent motion to be detected, we need both conditions (a) and (b) to be satisfied. One way to guarantee that (a) will be satisfied is to move the FOE to a new position so that A will be inside the segment defined by the two FOE positions. For condition (b) to be satisfied we need (worst case) that

$$\|\vec{u}_n^{ind}\| > \|\vec{u}_n^{eg}$$

so that $\qquad \|\vec{u}_n^{ind}\| > \frac{W}{Z} d$

or $\qquad d < \|\vec{u}_n^{ind}\| \frac{Z}{W}$

If the above inequality is satisfied, then we are guaranteed to detect independent motion at point A.

In the above inequality, d basically represents the cost involved in detecting motion using an exploratory strategy that guarantees detection. Obviously the cost of the exploration decreases (i.e., d increases) when the time to collision with the environment is small (large depth, small W). On the other hand, if $\|\vec{u}\|$ is the smallest retinal motion (due to independent 3-D motion) that can be detected, then

$$d = \|\vec{u}\| \cdot \frac{Z}{W}$$

If $\|\vec{u}^{ind}\| < \|\vec{u}\|$, then there is no guarantee of detection.

This formalizes the earlier intuitive discussion and also indicates a way to control the performance of the motion detection strategy. At any stage a higher precision (lower $\|\vec{u}\|$) can be achieved without changing the exploratory action (parameterized by d), by decreasing the dominant speed of the robot.

When the purpose of motion detection is to serve as an early warning system to detect independently moving objects in the scene it is not necessary to guarantee the detection of all moving (feature) points. The detection of a few moving points (that satisfy some criteria, to eliminate "false alarms") should suffice since it can trigger a more detailed analysis (perhaps over a narrower region), again depending on the task at hand. We show how the cost of motion detection may be dramatically reduced when the requirement is to guarantee detection of a compact moving object of at least a minimum projected size. In particular, the cost of the exploratory activity can be linked to the minimum (image) diameter of the objects of interest.

As discussed earlier, it may be reasonable to assume that the boundary of the image of a compact object in the scene forms a closed contour. In particular, this implies that all the points on the boundary of the object are features, and would be successful candidates for our motion detection paradigm provided the projected motion $\vec{u}^{\text{ind}}$ is sufficiently large ($\|\vec{u}^{\text{ind}}\| > \|\vec{u}\|$). We define the diameter ϵ of an arbitrary object as the diameter of the largest circle that can be inscribed in the closed contour that forms the boundary of the projected image of the object. Now it becomes clear that any exploratory paradigm that "covers" the image so that it guarantees the detection of all points distance ϵ apart will guarantee the detection of at least a few points on an object having features. The points are guaranteed to be detected by an appropriate sequence of FOE shifts as discussed earlier. Moreover, because the boundaries of objects are locally smooth, the points thus detected will be clustered together, so that it may be possible to eliminate false alarms arising due to various noise sources that result in isolated points appearing to have independent motions. In practice, the presence of larger features on the objects, e.g., lines separating regions, would make the detection even easier. Thus the effort in the exploratory activity can be reduced when the objects of interest have image diameters greater than some threshold and when there need be no guarantee of detecting objects having projected diameters below that threshold. This is most appropriate when the purpose of the robot is such that larger and nearer objects are more interesting than smaller and farther objects, as may be true for many typical robot tasks such as safe navigation in a dynamic environment. However, at any stage the precision of the detection can be increased by decreasing the diameter and threshold using closer FOE shifts in the exploratory action.

7. ESTIMATING 3-D MOTION

Assume an observer imaging an object moving in an unrestricted rigid manner. The motion of the object can be described as the sum of a rotation plus a translation. We can choose a point through which the rotation axis passes; this gives a unique rotation and translation describing the rigid motion (in general there are infinitely many combinations of rotations and translations describing the same rigid motion). In many visual tasks we are only interested in the translation of the moving object and we need no information about how it rotates around itself. This section describes how we can estimate the direction of the object's translation without being able to recover the rotation using a technique based on normal flow. Assume that the object is translating with velocity $\mathbf{V} = (U, V, W)$ and rotating with angular velocity $\Omega = (A, B, C)$ around a point $P = (X_0, Y_0, Z_0)$ on the object. Point P is on the object and its exact choice will be made clear later.

Point P is visible in the image ($p = (x_0, y_0)$) and we attach a coordinate system onto the object at point P with axes parallel to the observer's coordinate system. We express the motion of the object in this "object-based" coordinate system. The velocity of a point Q on the object is

$$\mathbf{V} = \begin{bmatrix} U \\ V \\ W \end{bmatrix} + \Omega X \begin{bmatrix} X - X_0 \\ Y - Y_0 \\ Z - Z_0 \end{bmatrix}$$

Then the normal flow v_n along direction (n_x, n_y) at point (x, y) is

$$v_n = un_x + vn_y$$

where (u, v) is the motion field. Expressing (u, v) in terms of 3-D motion we get

$$v_n = \frac{W}{Z}\left(n_x\frac{U}{W} + n_y\frac{V}{W}\right) - \frac{W}{Z}(n_x x + n_y y)$$

$$
\begin{aligned}
&-A(y - y_0)(xn_x + yn_y) + \\
&+B(x - x_0)(xn_x + yn_y) + \\
&+C[(x - x_0)n_y - (y - y_0)n_x] + \\
&+\frac{Z - Z_0}{Z}(Bn_x - An_y),
\end{aligned}
$$

or

$$\frac{n_x}{v_n}\frac{U}{W} + \frac{n_y}{v_n}\frac{V}{W} - K\frac{Z}{W} = \frac{n_x}{v_n}x + \frac{n_y}{v_n}\cdot y$$

where

$$
\begin{aligned}
k = {}&1 + A(y - y_0)\left(x\frac{n_x}{v_n} + y\frac{n_y}{v_n}\right) \\
&- B(x - x_0)\left(x\frac{n_x}{v_n} + y\frac{n_y}{v_n}\right) \\
&- C(x - x_0)\frac{n_y}{v_n} \\
&+ C(y - y_0)\frac{n_x}{v_n} \\
&- \frac{Z - Z_0}{Z}\left(B\frac{n_x}{v_n} - A\frac{n_y}{v_n}\right)
\end{aligned}
$$

Consider a small patch of the image around point $p = (x_0, y_0)$ and let us assume that the average depth there is Z_{av}. If we add the quantity $k\left(\frac{Z}{W}\right) - \frac{Z_{\text{av}}}{W}$ to both sides of the above equation, we get

$$\frac{n_x}{v_n}\frac{U}{W} + \frac{n_y}{v_n}\frac{V}{W} - \frac{Z_{\text{av}}}{W} = \frac{n_x}{v_n}x + \frac{n_y}{v_n}y + \left(k\frac{Z}{W} - \frac{Z_{\text{av}}}{W}\right)$$

One can verify that the mean of the last term in the equation above is zero (assuming that the mean of x is x_0 and of y, y_0).

We can thus consider several linear equations:

$$\frac{n_x}{v_n}\frac{U}{W} + \frac{n_y}{v_n}\frac{V}{W} - \frac{Z_{\text{av}}}{W} = \frac{n_x}{v_n}x + \frac{n_y}{v_n}y$$

in the neighborhood around P. Solution of the system provides the FOE.

The reader must have realized that it was the choice of the coordinate system in which we expressed the motion that allowed us to isolate the translational part of the problem. Since P is the center of rotation, the rotational flow at point $p = (x_0, y_0)$ is zero. In other words the preceding equation is exact at point (x_0, y_0) and approximate in its neighborhood. The error terms, however, have zero mean. This provides the potential for robust estimation. The time to collision is also estimated.

It is, however, clear that the technique for addressing the passive navigation problem (Section 5) cannot be used for the 3-D motion of an object estimation problem (while they are both the same problem if considered as general recovery problems). For example, voting for the values of normal flow produced by the motion of an object can provide a very large solution area (Figure 14).

Figure 14.

8. Obstacle Avoidance—Relative Depth

One of the most elementary forms of navigation is obstacle avoidance by a moving, compact sensor. It is a prerequisite, however, for many more complex abilities since any system performing a more complicated task must avoid obstacles in the process. Obstacle avoidance is thus one specific problem for which a general solution is highly desirable. In this context, a general solution refers to a system that works effectively in a wide range of real environments. This implies, among other things, that the system performance does not depend upon artificial constraints on the nature of objects in the environment such as assuming planar or smoothly curved surfaces, rigid or unmoving objects, mathematically uniform textures, and so forth.

The concept of "obstacleness" is a relative one. When we move about in our environment, every object might represent a potential obstacle, depending on its position and our direction of motion, and depending on its size. In addition, time plays an important role. When we move toward a building, the building itself represents a potential obstacle if our intent was to go beyond it. In other words, an object represents an obstacle if the observer is on a collision course with it, its size is comparable to the observer's size and the time to collision is smaller than some value which depends on the particular aspects of the problem under consideration.

Thus, we consider the problem of obstacle avoidance as synonymous with the problem of computing the times to collision to different parts of the scene, or finding relative depths at places of interest. This section is devoted to computing time to collision and relative depth from normal flow. The technique of the previous section will be used. We consider the most general case, where an object in view is moving rigidly (rotation plus translation).

8.1. COMPUTING TIME TO COLLISION FOR A MOVING OBJECT

Recalling the last equation of the previous section, which is exact at the position $p = (x_0, y_0)$, we have

$$v_n = \frac{W}{Z}\left(n_x \frac{U}{W} + n_y \frac{V}{W}\right) - \frac{W}{Z}(x_0 n_x + y_0 n_y)$$

with all terms defined as previously. If $\frac{U}{W}, \frac{V}{W}$ is already computed, the quantity $\frac{Z}{W}$ is directly available.

8.2. COMPUTING RELATIVE DEPTH

Assume two objects A and B moving in a rigid manner, while an active observer has the task of finding which one is closer. The camera is active and can undergo a short abrupt motion along its optical axis. Let us assume that at time t_1 the camera is stationary and then it moves with velocity W_c at time t_2. Assuming that the velocities of the two objects remain unchanged during the time interval $[t_1, t_2]$, we obtain (as in Section 7) for times t_1 and t_2

$$\frac{Z_{av}^A}{W_A} = A_1 \qquad \frac{Z_{av}^B}{W_B} = B_1$$
$$\frac{Z_{av}^A + W_A dt}{W_A + W_C} = A_2 \qquad \frac{Z_{av}^B + W_B dt}{W_B + W_C} = B_2$$

where A_1, B_1, A_2, B_2 are known.

From these equations, assuming that dt is very small, we obtain

$$\frac{Z_{av}^A}{Z_{av}^B} = \frac{A_1 A_2 (B_2 - B_1)}{B_1 B_2 (A_2 - A_1)},$$

and hence relative depth.

9. VISUAL PURSUIT[8]

In a general 3-D visual pursuit system, we have an agent, whose motion is under the control of our system; a camera, which is used to generate useful visual information to control the agent; and an object, which may be moving. If we could find the 3-D positions and motion parameters [21, 30] of the camera, the object, and the agent, it would be a simple arithmetic problem to predict and guide the collision of the agent with the object. However, we shall show here that it is not necessary to recover these parameters.

When we try to solve the visual pursuit problem through 3-D recovery, we estimate much more than we actually need in order to perform this generic visual

---

[8] This section demonstrates that depth recovery is not necessary for motion coordination problems.

task. Taking a purposive viewpoint we develop a robust, qualitative solution to the problem that does not require correspondence or full 3-D recovery.

There are two general cases of the pursuit problem. The camera can be mounted separately from the agent and the object, or the camera can be mounted on the agent or the object. In a situation where a human agent pursues a flying ball, both of these problems are involved. The "camera" is mounted on the agent (the human's body) which is intended to collide with the object. When the human is sufficiently close to the ball, the "camera," which is mounted on the head, is independent of the agent (the hand, possibly carrying a tool such as a bat), and the hand or tool is to collide with the ball. Thus the solution of both problems would provide a theoretical basis for an integrated mobile "hunting" system, or for a baseball player!

From a mathematical viewpoint it is equivalent whether the camera is mounted on the agent or the camera is mounted on the object. In such systems the collision is solely determined by the relative motion of the object and the agent, and it is equivalent whether we are controlling the motion of the entity that the camera is mounted on, or the entity that is moving separately from the camera. However, these cases may have different applications. An example of the case when the camera is mounted on the agent is an airplane that is attacking a target. An example of the case when the camera is mounted on the object is a camera that is guiding a plane to land near the camera.

Let us assume a Cartesian coordinate system with its origin at the focus of the camera, with the z-axis pointing toward the general direction of the agent and the object, such that both the object and the agent are in the full view of the camera.

Assume that the agent is located at $(X_s, Y_s, Z_s)^T$ with a velocity of $(V_{xs}, V_{ys}, V_{zs})^T$, and the object is located at $(X_o, Y_o, Z_o)^T$ with a velocity of $(V_{xo}, V_{yo}, V_{zo})^T$. If the agent or the object is also rotating at the time, we can choose the rotation axis to go through visible points on the surface of the agent or the object, chosen such that the rotation parameters are irrelevant in the prediction and guidance of a collision. However, for simplicity we assume that the motion is instantaneously translational. In the general case the analysis remains essentially the same, but the formulae become more complicated.

The agent and the object will collide after time t provided that

$$t = \frac{X_s - X_o}{V_{xo} - V_{xs}} = \frac{Y_s - Y_o}{V_{yo} - V_{ys}} = \frac{Z_s - Z_o}{V_{zo} - V_{zs}} > 0 \tag{5}$$

If the projection of the agent (i.e., a point of it) on the image plane is (x_s, y_s), and the projection of the object is (x_o, y_o), assuming unit focal length and perspective projection, we have

$$x_s = \frac{X_s}{Z_s} \tag{6}$$

$$y_s = \frac{Y_s}{Z_s} \tag{7}$$

$$x_o = \frac{X_o}{Z_o} \tag{8}$$

$$y_o = \frac{Y_o}{Z_o} \tag{9}$$

$$v_{xs} = \frac{V_{xs}}{Z_s} - x_s \frac{V_{zs}}{Z_s} \tag{10}$$

$$v_{ys} = \frac{V_{ys}}{Z_s} - y_s \frac{V_{zs}}{Z_s} \tag{11}$$

$$v_{xo} = \frac{V_{xo}}{Z_o} - x_o \frac{V_{zo}}{Z_o} \tag{12}$$

$$v_{yo} = \frac{V_{yo}}{Z_o} - y_o \frac{V_{zo}}{Z_o} \tag{13}$$

where (v_{xs}, v_{ys}), (v_{xo}, v_{yo}) is the flow produced by the agent and the object at points (x_s, y_s) and (x_o, y_o), respectively. Combining (6–9) with (5), we obtain the following relation for the prediction of collision:

$$t = \frac{x_s Z_s - x_o Z_o}{V_{xo} - V_{xs}} \tag{14}$$

$$= \frac{y_s Z_s - y_o Z_o}{V_{yo} - V_{ys}} \tag{15}$$

$$= \frac{Z_s - Z_o}{V_{zo} - V_{zs}} \tag{16}$$

$$> 0 \tag{17}$$

We call (14–17) the *Visual Constraints of Collision*. The visual pursuit problem is solved if we can guide the system to satisfy these constraints. Using the processes of Sections 7 and 8 we can estimate the locomotive intrinsics (i.e., the direction of translation and the time to collision). In what follows, we solve the visual pursuit problem in the case when the camera is mounted on the object, using only the signs of the three locomotive intrinsics, and then we present a solution in the case when the camera is mounted separately to supervise the agent, using the locomotive intrinsics, relative depth, and direction of motion.

9.1. CAMERA MOUNTED ON THE OBJECT

The problem is equivalent whether the camera is mounted on the agent or on the object. For simplicity here we assume that the camera is mounted on the object and that we can control the velocity of the agent. We choose a Cartesian coordinate system with its origin at the focus of the camera, and with its z-axis pointing towards the general direction of the agent, such that the agent is in the full view of the camera.

As the camera is mounted on the object, the coordinates of the object on the image plane are zero, as is its velocity. We have $(X_o, Y_o, Z_o)^T = 0$ and $(V_{xo}, V_{yo}, V_{zo})^T = 0$, as well as $(x_o, y_o) = 0$ and $(v_{xo}, v_{yo}) = 0$. In the following, when we write Z_o and Z_s, we always mean $E(Z_o)$ and $E(Z_s)$ (i.e., the average depth around the neighborhood), unless otherwise specified. Thus (14–17) can be simplified to

$$t = -\frac{x_s Z_s}{V_{xs}} \tag{18}$$

$$= -\frac{y_s Z_s}{V_{ys}} \tag{19}$$

$$= -\frac{Z_s}{V_{zs}} \tag{20}$$

$$> 0 \tag{21}$$

From (18) and (20) we have $x_s = V_{xs}/V_{zs}$. From (19) and (20) we have $y_s = V_{ys}/V_{zs}$. Thus if we draw a line from the origin through the focus of expansion $(V_{xs}/V_{zs}, V_{ys}/V_{zs})$, or the first two locomotive intrinsics, on the image plane, we have a set of all the points that will collide with the origin. In order to collide the agent with the object, we should control the motion of the agent so that the focus of expansion lies inside the image of the agent. The third locomotive intrinsic Z_s/V_{zs} is the negative of the time to collision (21). Note that since $t > 0$, the third locomotive intrinsic should be negative for the collision to occur. In this case, $V_{zs} < 0$, that is, the agent should be coming closer to the camera.

Since we have an active camera, for simplicity we can rotate the camera such that the image of the agent will be in the center. The agent will collide with the object if we can keep the focus of expansion at the origin and keep an expanding pattern of normal flow.

If the focus of expansion is not at the origin, we can devise a control strategy to guide the focus of expansion toward the origin of the image plane according to the signs of the three locomotive intrinsics, indicating whether the velocity of the agent needs to be increased or decreased at any time instant.

- If $Z/V_z < 0$ and $V_{xs}/V_{zs} = V_{ys}/V_{zs} = 0$, a collision will occur.
- If $Z/V_z = 0$, a collision has occurred;
- If $Z/V_{zs} > 0$, the agent is going away. Decrease V_{zs} and
    - If $V_{xs}/V_{zs} = 0$, do not change V_{xs};
    - If $V_{xs}/V_{zs} > 0$, decrease V_{xs};
    - If $V_{xs}/V_{zs} < 0$, increase V_{xs};
    - If $V_{ys}/V_{zs} = 0$, do not change V_{ys};
    - If $V_{ys}/V_{zs} > 0$, decrease V_{ys};
    - If $V_{ys}/V_{zs} < 0$, increase V_{ys};
- If $Z/V_{zs} < 0$, the agent is coming closer. Do not change V_{zs} and
    - If $V_{xs}/V_{zs} = 0$, do not change V_{xs};
    - If $V_{xs}/V_{zs} > 0$, increase V_{xs};
    - If $V_{xs}/V_{zs} < 0$, decrease V_{xs};
    - If $V_{ys}/V_{zs} = 0$, do not change V_{ys};
    - If $V_{ys}/V_{zs} > 0$, increase V_{ys};
    - If $V_{ys}/V_{zs} < 0$, decrease V_{ys}.

This constitutes a qualitative paradigm for colliding the agent with the object when the camera is mounted on the object. We only use the signs of the three locomotive intrinsics. We can predict the collision, and if a collision will not occur we qualitatively control the velocity of the agent toward a state such that the agent will collide with the object.

9.2. CAMERA MOUNTED SEPARATELY

When the camera is mounted separately, the camera may be stationary or in motion relative to the world coordinate system. But for simplicity, we choose a coordinate system with its origin at the focus of the camera and its z-axis pointing towards the general direction of the agent and the object such that both the agent and the object are in full view of the camera. In this coordinate system, the camera is stationary, and velocity is measured relative to the camera.

Object coming toward the camera

The special case when the object is coming toward the camera may need to be handled differently. If we can correctly identify cases when the object is coming toward the camera, we may want to move the camera away from the pathway of the object and then proceed as usual, or when the object is small and is not destructive, we may just put the agent in front of the camera to receive the object.

We can detect whether the object is coming toward the camera using the analysis in the previous section. When the object is coming toward the camera, the focus of expansion of the object lies inside the image of the object and the third locomotive intrinsic is negative.

If we send the agent to the front of the camera, we have the case studied in the last section. It can be determined from the time to collision of the agent and the object whether the agent is moving fast enough to intercept the object.

In the following general analysis, we assume that the object is not coming toward the camera, but moving in any other direction.

General case of camera mounted separately

From (14–15), we obtain

$$
\begin{aligned}
((x_s V_{yo} - y_s V_{xo}) - (x_s V_{ys} - y_s V_{xs}))Z_s - \\
((x_o V_{yo} - y_o V_{xo}) - (x_o V_{ys} - y_o V_{xs}))Z_o = 0
\end{aligned}
\tag{22}
$$

Note that if (x_s, y_s), $(V_{xs}/V_{zs}, V_{ys}/V_{zs})$, (x_o, y_o), and $(V_{xo}/V_{zo}, V_{yo}/V_{zo})$ are a group of parallel vectors, (22) will be satisfied. Thus in the general case of a separately mounted camera, we first obtain the direction of motion of the object; then we rotate the z-axis of the camera such that it will be in the direction of the object. Then we can move the agent in the direction parallel to the direction of motion of the object. This is a group of sufficient conditions for the collision of the agent and the object when we have good control of the original position of the agent.

To satisfy (16–17), we need to find the time to collision t and make it equal to (16). Combining (10–13) with (14–17), we obtain

$$
t = \frac{x_s - x_o \frac{Z_o}{Z_s}}{\left(v_{xo} + x_o \frac{V_{zo}}{Z_o}\right)\frac{Z_o}{Z_s} - \left(v_{xs} + x_s \frac{V_{zs}}{Z_s}\right)}
\tag{23}
$$

$$= \frac{y_s - y_o \frac{Z_o}{Z_s}}{(v_{yo} + y_o \frac{V_{zo}}{Z_o}) \frac{Z_o}{Z_s} - (v_{ys} + y_s \frac{V_{zs}}{Z_s})} \tag{24}$$

$$= \frac{1 - \frac{Z_o}{Z_s}}{\frac{V_{zo}}{Z_o} \cdot \frac{Z_o}{Z_s} - \frac{V_{zs}}{Z_s}} \tag{25}$$

$$> 0 \tag{26}$$

If we can find a point on the agent and a point on the object which have the same normal direction (n_x, n_y), from (23–24) we find the time to collision as follows:

$$t = \frac{n_x x_s + n_y y_s - (n_x x_o + n_y y_o) \frac{Z_o}{Z_s}}{(v_{no} + (n_x x_o + n_y y_o) \frac{V_{zo}}{Z_o}) \frac{Z_o}{Z_s} - (v_{ns} + (n_x x_s + n_y y_s) \frac{V_{zs}}{Z_s})} \tag{27}$$

Similar equations can be obtained if we can find two normal directions from the agent and the object which are perpendicular. Combining with (25), we have

$$\frac{V_{zs}}{Z_s} = \frac{V_{zo}}{Z_o} - \frac{(\frac{Z_s}{Z_o} - 1)(v_{no} \frac{Z_o}{Z_s} - v_{ns})}{n_x (x_s - x_o) + n_y (y_s - y_o)} \tag{28}$$

Thus, control of the agent is achieved by varying V_{xs}/V_{ys} in order to satisfy (22) and V_{zs} in order to satisfy (26) and (28). According to these equations, we can devise a system for qualitative control of the motion of the agent, so that the agent will collide with the object. This scheme can be accomplished through six sequential phases as follows. The first three phases are devised to satisfy (22). The next two phases are devised to satisfy (26) and (28). The last phase tests to see if the agent will collide with the object without further control of the agent.

1. Rotating the camera. Through the point (x_o, y_s) draw a line in the image plane with direction $(V_{xo}/V_{zo}, V_{yo}/V_{zo})$.
   - If the line goes through the origin, proceed to the next phase;
   - If the origin is on the lower left portion of the image plane, rotate the camera upward and to the right;
   - If the origin is on the upper right portion of the image plane, rotate the camera downward and to the left;
2. Position the agent.
   - If the line drawn above goes through the agent, proceed to the next phase;
   - If the agent is on the lower left portion of the image plane, move the agent upward and to the right;
   - If the agent is on the upper right portion of the image plane, move the agent downward and to the left;
3. Move the agent parallel to the image plane. Change the velocity of the agent, so that $V_{xs}/V_{ys} = x_s/y_s$.
   - If the agent is on the left of the object, V_{xs} and V_{ys} should be increased;
   - If the agent is on the right of the object, V_{xs} and V_{ys} should be decreased;
   - If the agent and the object collide on the image plane, do not change V_{xs} and V_{ys};
4. Positive time to collision. Proceed to the next phase after:

- If $Z_o/Z_s = 1$, do not change V_{zs} at present;
- If $Z_o/Z_s > 1$, adjust V_{zs} so that

$$\frac{V_{zs}}{Z_s} > \frac{Z_o}{Z_s} \cdot \frac{V_{zo}}{Z_o};$$

- If $Z_o/Z_s < 1$, adjust V_{zs} so that

$$\frac{V_{zs}}{Z_s} < \frac{Z_o}{Z_s} \cdot \frac{V_{zo}}{Z_o};$$

5. Move the agent perpendicular to the image plane.
   - If (28) is satisfied, proceed to the next phase.
   - If V_{zs}/Z_s is larger in (28), decrease V_{zs};
   - If V_{zs}/Z_s is smaller in (28), increase V_{zs};
6. Predicting collision. The agent will collide with the object if the following conditions are met, or otherwise repeat from phase 1:

$$\frac{x_o}{y_o} = \frac{\frac{V_{xo}}{V_{zo}}}{\frac{V_{yo}}{V_{zo}}} = \frac{x_s}{y_s} = \frac{\frac{V_{xs}}{V_{zs}}}{\frac{V_{ys}}{V_{zs}}}$$

$$\left(\frac{Z_o}{Z_s} - 1\right)\left(\frac{V_{zs}}{Z_s} - \frac{Z_o}{Z_s} \cdot \frac{V_{zo}}{Z_o}\right) > 0$$

and

$$\frac{V_{zs}}{Z_s} = \frac{V_{zo}}{Z_o} - \frac{\left(\frac{Z_s}{Z_o} - 1\right)\left(v_{no}\frac{Z_o}{Z_s} - v_{ns}\right)}{n_x(x_s - x_o) + n_y(y_s - y_o)}$$

In summary, in the case when the camera is mounted on the the object or the agent, we have devised a qualitative strategy to predict and guide the collision of the agent and the object. We only used the signs of the three locomotive intrinsics (FOE and time to contact) to qualitatively control the velocity of the agent such that the visual constraints of collision will be satisfied.

In the case when the camera is mounted separately to supervise the agent to collide with the object, we have devised a set of sufficient conditions to satisfy the visual constraints of collision. This set of sufficient conditions can be reached by a qualitative scheme of control without any exact 3-D depth or velocity information of the agent and the object.

Our method can also be used to control the collision even when the object is rotating in addition to having instantaneous translational motion.

10. RECAPITULATION AND EXPERIMENTS

We have presented solutions to several problems related to visual motion using normal flow as the input. Although we have not solved the general structure from motion (sfm) problem using normal flow, we have presented solutions to various important problems that are simple applications of the sfm module. The robustness of the proposed algorithms relies heavily on the robustness of the computation of normal flow, i.e., spatiotemporal derivatives of the image intensity function. But even without using any elaborate schemes for computing the normal flow (after all, some of the techniques presented only require its sign) we have performed several experiments. We report here a few of them:

(a) **Egomotion estimation**

We have performed several experiments with both synthetic and real image sequences in order to demonstrate the stability of our method. From experiments on real images it was found that in the case of pure translation or pure rotation the method computes the focus of expansion or the axis of rotation very robustly. In the case of general motion it was found from experiments on synthetic and real data that the behavior of the method is as predicted by our theoretical analysis (see [6]).

(b) **Detection of independent motion**

Figure 15 shows one of a sequence of images taken by a moving camera and containing independently moving objects. The camera, a Sony CCD miniature camera, was attached to the end effector of an Merlin American Robot arm that was moving forward (Figure 16). Figure 17 shows the detection of independent motion; no shifts of the FOE were necessary in order to achieve the result.

Figure 15.

(c) **Relative Depth**

We have performed several experiments on both synthetic and real data in order to test the feasibility and stability of our approach. We report here some experiments on real data. The setup for our experimental work with real images consists of a CCD camera mounted on a slide so that it can (purely) translate along its optical axis (Figure 18). The camera is viewing a scene consisting of a toy ("Mrs.

Figure 16.

Figure 17.

Potatohead") and a toy robot arm (Radio Shack). The arm (carrying the "vision" of Mrs. Potatohead) is initially placed closer to the camera. Figures 19 and 20 are taken with the camera stationary and the arm moving toward Mrs. Potatohead. Figure 21 shows the normal flow produced from the motion of the arm, using the straightforward gradient technique [21]. Figure 22 is taken after the camera has

Figure 18.

Figure 19.

moved forward and Figure 23 shows the normal flow produced.

Using the algorithms in Sections 5 and 7, we estimated the relative depth of the toy and the arm. We computed the quantity Z/V_c, where Z is the depth of a point and V_c is the speed of the camera, and considered the median value for the arm and the toy. It was found that this value was 7.553544 for the arm and 9.118339 for the toy, which agrees with the ground truth.

We performed the same experiment with the arm at the same distance as the toy. We found that the value of the median relative depth (Z/V_c) was 10.230856 for the arm and 10.145772 for the toy, which again agrees with the ground truth.

Figure 20.

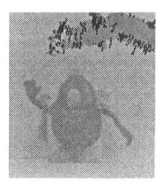

Figure 21.

Figure 22.

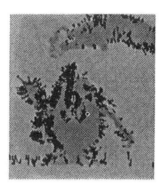

Figure 23.

11. PURPOSIVE, BEHAVIORAL, ACTIVE VISION

Vision has been studied, for the most part, as a general recovery problem, i.e., its goal has been to reconstruct an accurate representation of the visible world and its properties—for example, to recover boundaries, shape from texture, shading, motion, etc. Following this point of view, we consider the "brain"—or any intelligent system possessing vision—as consisting of vision and everything else (planning, reasoning, memory, etc.). In other words, we view the role of vision as that of creating a central database which stores accurate 3-D information about the scene. Then other cognitive processes (such as planning, for example) can access this database, extract whatever information they need and modify it to suit their needs. This central database is created by visual modules—such as the sfm module—that have been integrated in some way [3].

But if the analysis in this chapter is valid, it demonstrates that we can solve many interesting problems without creating a very accurate or full representation of the scene and its properties. Clearly, when a problem is simpler and more restricted, it is easier to solve. However, these simpler problems (in our case, simpler than the general sfm problem)—namely, passive navigation, motion detection, 3-D translation estimation, obstacle avoidance, relative depth, visual interception—are quite important and not very specific. They are generic in the sense that they have environmental invariance. In other words, developing such visual motion capabilities constitutes theoretical research. The fact that we may be able to robustly solve many less general problems—which, of course, cannot replace the reconstructive modules—demonstrates that we are capable of building machines that robustly achieve various behaviors. By putting such behaviors together, can we achieve "intelligent systems"? If this is possible, it provides an alternative way to study perception. A few publications over the past few years [8, 13, 14, 17, 31, 44] have supported such an approach, which has acquired various names such as purposive, task-based, behavioral, active, animate, utilitarian, etc. In this section we attempt to describe the paradigm in more detail and present a formal framework.

It would be convenient for our formalism to consider vision as a recognition problem. Then, the visual system consists of various processes, some of which perform visual recognition tasks while others implement different cognitive abilities. On the other hand, it is easy to demonstrate that any vision problem can be formulated as a recognition problem.

Given that behavioral vision has as its goal the development of robust behaviors displayed by a robotic agent, we should be able to formalize the concept of behavior and the concept of an agent. At the same time we need to be able to provide a formal way of generating new behaviors and a calculus of behaviors or purposes.

If there is a similarity of this approach to old ideas of goal-based vision—where systems using knowledge at all levels, including domain-specific knowledge, were built and it turned out that many corners had to be cut and many oversimplified assumptions had to be made—it exists only in spirit. *An intelligent agent (observer) is a system that has a set of goals or purposes, at all times. To pursue these goals, it has to exhibit a set of behaviors.* Not all agents have the same purposes; some are more sophisticated than others and they display different behaviors.

It would be hard to give a general definition of an agent (or such a definition would be so general that it wouldn't be useful at an engineering level). We are surrounded by agents. They are basically entities that *interact* with the world around them and *act* appropriately in each situation. As they act and sense, they display behaviors and fulfill purposes.

Coming back to the basic question of formalizing behaviors, we realize that there is a very rich set of them. Some are primitive, others more sophisticated and others quite complex. In such situations, it is nice to be able to start from primitives, that is a set of behaviors from which all others can be constructed. But it is not at all clear which behaviors are the primitive ones.

To avoid a potential philosophical snare, we sidestep the question and we ask: How can we formalize behaviors, and then generate new and more complex ones from old ones and from learning?

A behavior is a sequence of perceptual events and actions whose task is to accomplish a goal. Visual input is received in a continuous manner and various processes (such as those described here and others) work together in order to recognize perceptual events and take appropriate action (an action could be a motion—navigation, manipulation, or a change of an internal state of the agent displaying the behavior). The problem is then to control such a system. It must be emphasized that the processes performing the visual analysis in order to recognize the perceptual events perform only partial recovery of the world, i.e., to accomplish some behaviors we do not need an accurate and full scene representation.

In abstract terms, a behavior of an agent is a system broadly known as discrete event process [9]. However, despite numerous results in the literature, there is at the present time apparently no unifying theory for the control of discrete event processes. Nor is it very clear what such a theory should accomplish. Numerous approaches to the modeling of discrete processes have appeared in the literature (Boolean models, Petri nets, formal languages, temporal logic, port automata, and flow networks [19, 20, 26, 29, 34, 36]).

11.1. BEHAVIOR MODELING

When we consider recognition under the purposive framework of the agent's behaviors, we are faced with problems of behavior control. An agent can carry out a set of behaviors in parallel, and change the set of behaviors upon obtaining outputs from various recognition tasks. Controlling the agent under these conditions is not a trivial task. In what follows we suggest models for formalizing both the description of the agent as a system and the specification of the control policies that regulate it.

We consider an agent that changes its state or behavior only at discrete instants of time, not continuously. It thus belongs to the category of Discrete Event Dynamic Systems (DEDS, as opposed to continuous variable dynamic systems—CVDS). A DEDS is a dynamic system with a discrete state space and piecewise constant state trajectories [34, 35]; the state transitions are called events. The time instants at which state transitions occur, as well as the actual transitions, are in general unpredictable. A brief classification of DEDS models can be found in [19]. A short discussion of the different models can be found in [35].

Several classes of models have been proposed for describing the behavior of controlled DEDS. There is no consensus as to which of these models has the potential to serve as the analog of the differential equations for the CVDS. It seems that no single approach to modeling and analysis of DEDS will suffice for all problems of interest. For our purpose we use models that are untimed in the sense that the state sequence is emphasized without considering the holding time. We might consider Lynch's I/O automata [29], or Ramadge and Wonham's DEDS formalism that is based on Finite State Machines (FSM) [34]. These are logical models in the sense that they are used to study the qualitative properties of DEDS. A different type of model, algebraic in nature, might be based on Hoare's CSP (Communicating Sequential Processes, [20]). Both types of models allow checking for properties such as correct event ordering, stability, coordination, desirable dynamic behavior, etc.

We will use the state transition system [36, 26, 25] as a DEDS formalism that suits our purpose. The model uses nondeterministic state transition systems and fairness requirements as a mechanism that generates a set of sequences of events (assuming interleaving semantics).[9] The model gives the ability to capture the connection between the agent and the environment (this is actually the link between perception and action). The model gives the option of combining behaviors in a meaningful way and proving properties of the resulting combination. This ability to reason in a comfortable level of abstraction is important for the design of complex systems.

Following [25] we could use the aforementioned formalism to define agents and compositions between them (hierarchically). This option gives the ability to prove properties of the composition. We should note that the composition rule supports only layered compositions. Each layer contains a finite number of modules. The

---

[9] Interleaving semantics reduces concurrent execution of atomic events to nondeterministic sequential execution of atomic events. As far as safety and progress properties are concerned, interleaving semantics is equivalent to partial-ordering semantics. Of course our model will have to consider some events to be atomic.

theory allows the modules in a hierarchy to interact as follows: A module can offer a set of interfaces. Each module can use multiple (disjoint) interfaces each offered by a different module at some lower level of the hierarchy. Thus the hierarchy is in general a directed acyclic graph where each node is a module; each node offers its upper interface to its parents while using lower interfaces offered by its sons. There is the special case of a leaf node that does not use any lower interface, and an option for a root whose upper interface is offered to the user(s) of the entire hierarchy.

11.2. STATE TRANSITION SYSTEM FORMALISM AND ASSERTIONAL REASONING

Following [36, 26] we define an agent A by the quadruple: (S, I, E, F) where:

- $S = States_A$, the set of the possible different states the agent can maintain. As the level of granularity changes, the different states will capture different aspects of the agent. When we describe low level modules a state might represent some stage in the computational process. When we analyze the agent on a higher level of abstraction, for example on the high behavioral level, a state might represent some behavior like visual interception.
- $I = Initial_A$, a subset of $States_A$, specifying the possible initial states for the agent.
- $E = Events_A$, a set of events. This set is the union of three disjoint sets: $Inputs(A)$, a set of the input events for the agent; $Outputs(A)$, a set of output events of the agent; and $Internals(A)$, a set of internal events. The input events are under the control of the environment, or the user of the agent. The agent has no control over the input events, but has full control over the internal and output events. The output events are those that influence the environment, or those that are offered to other different agents. Every event is composed of two parts: enabling conditions and actions. We specify the enabling conditions of an event e by using a state formula,[10] denoted $enabled_A(e)$, and a sequential program, denoted $action_A(e)$; $enabled_A(e)$ specifies the enabling condition of e, and $action_A(e)$ must always terminate when executed in any state satisfying $enabled_A(e)$. We assume, without loss of generality, that $action_A(e)$ is deterministic.

  It is common to have recognition tasks as enabling conditions within complex agents. Recognition is a trigger between behaviors. When we deal with an agent on the behavioral level it is possible to enter an intention as part of the enabling conditions.
- $F = Fairness$ $requirements$ of A, specifying a finite set of fairness requirements. A fair behavior of the system gives an event infinitely many chances to happen. Fairness requirements are a way of imposing nonzero execution speed. The fairness requirements of A are defined with respect to a set of events. Usually they will be of the form: E has weak fairness, where $E \subseteq Events_A$. Informally, this

---

[10] A state formula is a formula in $Variables_A$ that evaluates to *true* or *false* at each state $s \in States_A$. When we say that a state satisfies a state formula we mean that the state formula evaluates to *true* at that state. A state formula can have parameters, that is, variables which are not state variables.

means that if E is continuously enabled, then one of the enabled events in E eventually occurs.

An agent starts its behavior from some initial state. From that state any event that is enabled can be executed. A possible result of an event is a change in the state of the agent. A change in the state of the agent as a result of an event e is referred to as a transition of e. We can formally define:

$Transitions_A(e) = \{(s,t) : s$ and t are states of A, s satisfies $enabled_A(e)$, and executing $action_A(e)$ in s results in $t\}$

For an agent A, a **behavior** is a sequence $< s_0, e_0, s_1, e_1, \cdots >$ such that every s_i is a state, every e_i is an event, and every (s_i, s_{i+1}) is a transition of e_i. Note that a behavior can be infinite or finite. Note that for any behavior σ, every finite prefix of σ ending in a state is also a behavior. For an agent A a behavior σ is allowed behavior iff for every fairness requirement F of A σ is finite and F is not enabled in its last state, or σ is infinite and satisfies F.

An example: A motion detector

Using the preceding formalism we describe an agent whose purpose is to detect motion in the environment by identifying changes in the normal flow field. The agent has one state variable S that can be in one of the states $\{nf\text{-}constant, nf\text{-}changes\}$; initially it is set to $nf\text{-}constant$. Another state variable env indicates the state of the environment; it can be in one of the states $\{nobody, moving\}$. We have six events:

Input events: $gen\text{-}flow, no\text{-}flow$
Internal events: $nf_a, nf_{b1}, nf_{b2}, nf_e$
Output events: $, nf_c, nf_d$

gen-flow:
$enabled \equiv true$
$action \equiv env \leftarrow moving$
no-flow:
$enabled \equiv true$
$action \equiv env \leftarrow nobody$
nf$_a$:
$enabled \equiv env = moving$
$action \equiv NF$
nf$_b$:
$enabled \equiv env = nobody$
$action \equiv NF$
nf$_c$:
$enabled \equiv NF < threshold$
$action \equiv S \leftarrow nf\text{-}constant$
nf$_d$:
$enabled \equiv NF >= threshold$
$action \equiv S \leftarrow nf\text{-}changes$

The motion detector starts with the initial state $S = nf\text{-}constant$. When something is moving in the environment, env is set to $moving$, and nf_a is enabled. As a result a computation of the normal flow field will take place (we assumed fairness). This can be considered as an internal event. The result of the computation will enable nf_c or nf_d, and S will get some value. Consider S as a variable that records the state of the agent. S might be a shared variable, that is, it is also used by other agents. From this point of view these are output events. Another option is to couple these events with events of some other agents.

The first two events, $gen\text{-}flow, no\text{-}flow$, are controlled by the environment. They are input events. We model the normal flow detector in such a way that permits motion ($env = moving$) in the environment, but still NF will not detect it ($NF < threshold$). We could include the environment as part of our system. The environment controls the flow generation. We could describe the environment using the following output events:

gen-flow:

$enabled \equiv actor = stop$

$action \equiv actor \leftarrow move$

no-flow:

$enabled \equiv actor = move$

$action \equiv actor \leftarrow stop$

The output event $gen\text{-}flow$ is coupled with the motion detector input event $gen\text{-}flow$. The same holds for the $no\text{-}flow$ event. The events happen together and this is an example of simultaneous modelling of perception and action (observation).

End of example

In assertional reasoning, we consider two types of properties, namely, safety properties and progress properties. Safety assertions are of the form $Invariant(P)$, where P is a state formula. For a sequence $\sigma = < s_0, e_0, s_1, e_1, \cdots >$ over alternating states and events, σ satisfies $Invariant(P)$ iff every state in σ satisfies P.[11]

Progress assertions are constructed from leads-to assertions of the form P leads-to Q, where P and Q are state formulas, like the ones described in the preceding paragraphs. For a sequence $\sigma = < s_0, e_0, s_1, e_1, \cdots >$ over alternating states and events, σ satisfies P leads-to Q iff the following holds: If, for some i, state s_i in σ satisfies P then there is a state s_j in σ, $j \geq i$, that satisfies Q. A progress assertion is satisfied by an agent A iff it is satisfied by every *allowed* behavior of system A.[12]

Proving safety and progress assertions

The first step in reasoning about behaviors is to reason about single transitions, that is, actions and individual events. To reason about actions, we use a terminology derived from weakest preconditions.[13] Let P and Q denote state formulas, and S denote an action. P is a sufficient precondition of Q wrt S iff for every state s

---

[11] Similarly for an agent A, A satisfies $Invariant(P)$ iff every finite behavior of A satisfies $Invariant(P)$.

[12] A behavior σ of A is *allowed* iff σ satisfies every fairness requirement of A.

[13] Throughout we shall use "wrt" as an abbreviation for "with respect to."

satisfying P, the execution of S starting from s terminates in a state that satisfies Q. Using this definition we follow [36] and define weakest precondition: P is the weakest precondition of Q wrt S iff P is a sufficient precondition of Q wrt S, and for any state formula R, if R is a sufficient precondition of Q wrt S, then $R \Rightarrow P$ holds. Note that the qualifier "weakest" means that P specifies the largest set of states where the execution of S terminates with Q holding. $wp(Q, S)$ is used to denote any state formula that is a weakest precondition of Q wrt S. Thus, $P \Longleftrightarrow wp(Q, S)$ denotes "P is a weakest precondition of Q wrt S", and $P \Longrightarrow wp(Q, S)$ denotes "P is a sufficient precondition of Q wrt S."

The weakest precondition can be extended to events. The following are proof rules for establishing invariant assertions [26]:

1. $inv(P)$ is satisfied by system A if the following hold:
   (a) $Initial_A \Longrightarrow P$
   (b) For every event e of A: $P \Longrightarrow wp(P, e)$
2. Given that system A satisfies $inv(Q)$, it satisfies $inv(P)$ if $Q \Longrightarrow P$ holds.

For leads-to assertions we have the following options. Trivially it will be established by event set rule. That is, given a system A with weak fairness for event set E that is a subset of $Events_A$, P leads-to Q is satisfied by A if every event $e \in E$ establishes $P \Longrightarrow wp(Q, e)$. For the rest of the events of $Events_A$ we demand that $P \Longrightarrow wp(P \vee Q, e)$. So, if $Invariant(P \Longrightarrow enabled_A(E))$ is satisfied by A eventually we will get Q. Another option to establish leads-to is by using closure rules (like transitivity, disjunction, etc.).[14]

An example: An interceptor

We describe an agent that gets as an input event a call for target acquisition and triggers a locking process, an intercepting process, and an acquiring process for a complete target acquisition. The agent can be stopped at any time by the input event *Stop-It*.

M state variables, initial conditions, and events:
$S = \{stop\text{-}all, get\text{-}target, lock, intercept, acquired\}$, initially *stop-all*.
$i, j, k \in \{go, done, stop\}$, initially all are *go*.

Get-Target:
$enabled \equiv true$
$action \equiv S \leftarrow get\text{-}target$

---

[14] As an option [26]:
   P leads-to Q is satisfied if *one* of the following is satisfied:

- $Invariant(P \Longrightarrow Q)$ [Implication]

- For some R, P leads-to R and R leads-to Q [Transitivity]

- $P = P_1 \vee P_2$, P_1 leads-to Q, and P_2 leads-to Q [Disjunction]

- $Invariant(R)$ and $P \wedge R$ leads-to $R \Longrightarrow Q$ [Substitution]

Stop-It:
$enabled \equiv true$
$action \equiv S \leftarrow stop\text{-}all$
Start-Lock:
$enabled \equiv i = go \wedge S \neq stop\text{-}all$
$action \equiv S \leftarrow lock; i \leftarrow done$
End-Lock:
$enabled \equiv i = done \wedge S \neq stop\text{-}all$
$action \equiv if\ S = acquired\ then\ i \leftarrow stop\ else\ i \leftarrow go$
Start-Intercept:
$enabled \equiv j = go \wedge S \neq stop\text{-}all$
$action \equiv if\ S = lock\ then\ S \leftarrow intercept\ else\ S \leftarrow get\text{-}target;\ j \leftarrow done$
End-Intercept:
$enabled \equiv j = done \wedge S \neq stop\text{-}all$
$action \equiv if\ S = acquired\ then\ j \leftarrow stop\ else\ j \leftarrow go$
Start-Acquire:
$enabled \equiv k = go \wedge S \neq stop\text{-}all$
$action \equiv if\ S = intercept\ then\ S \leftarrow acquired\ else\ S \leftarrow get\text{-}target;\ k \leftarrow done$
End-Acquire:
$enabled \equiv k = done \wedge S \neq stop\text{-}all$
$action \equiv if\ S = acquired\ then\ k \leftarrow stop\ else\ k \leftarrow go$

Assuming that every event has weak fairness, we can prove the following safety property: If the agent terminates, then its state equals *acquired*; that is $Invariant(A)$ holds, where
$A \equiv i = stop \wedge j = stop \wedge k = stop \Rightarrow S = acquired.$
Using the first invariance rule we can prove this property. The property holds initially and for every event of the agent $A \Rightarrow wp(A, e)$ holds.

We can check for the following progress property: Does the agent eventually terminate? That is, does B hold, where $B \equiv i = go \wedge j = go \wedge k = go$ leads-to $i = stop \wedge j = stop \wedge k = stop$
It is clear that the system has terminating behaviors, for example:
$\sigma_0 =<$ *get-target, start-lock, start-intercept, start-acquire, end-lock, end-intercept, end-acquire* $>$
We can disprove B by presenting allowed behavior that is nonterminating.[15]
$\sigma_1 =<$ *get-target, start-lock, end-lock, start-intercept, start-acquire, end-intercept, end-acquire, start-lock, end-lock, start-lock,* $\cdots >$
After a certain point in the behavior only *start-lock* and *end-lock* are active. The *start-acquire* and *end-acquire* behaviors are permanently disabled. Because only *start-acquire* can set S to *acquired*, the agent has no possibility of terminating after that point. This is a state from where termination is impossible. Of course that B does not hold.

---

[15] The infinite behavior $<$ *get-target, start-lock, end-lock, start-lock, end-lock,* $\cdots >$ is nonterminating. We cannot conclude from this behavior that the system does not satisfy B because it is not an allowed behavior (*start-intercept*, for example, is continuously enabled but never occurs).

11.3. COMPOSITION

We want to be able to model a complex agent by composing the descriptions for
simpler agents which constitute its components. To model the composition we follow
[25] and concentrate on the notion of interface. Interactions between the using agent
and its components (or the environment) take place at an interface. An interface is
specified by a set of allowed sequences of interface events. Each allowed sequence
defines one possible sequence of interactions between the agent and a component.

The motivation is as follows: Suppose an interface I has been specified through
which an agent interacts with its environment. Instead of designing and implementing a monolithic agent A that offers I, we would like to implement the agent as a
collection of simpler agents A_i that interact through interfaces such that the composition of A_i offers I. To achieve this objective, the following approach may be used:
First derive a set of interfaces I_i from I, one for each agent in the collection. Then
design agents individually, and prove that A_i offers I_i assuming that the environment of A_i satisfies I_i in some manner. (Some interface events of I_i are controlled
by the environment of A_i. To design an agent that guarantees properties of I_i, we
generally need to assume that the agent's environment satisfies I_i in some manner.)
In designing the different agents we can use the state transition formalism described
earlier and check for existence of the desired properties. After the completion of this
stage we can apply an inference rule (the composition theorem) to infer from the
results of the former stage that the composition of A_i offers I.

The approach has the following highly desirable feature: Given interfaces I_i,
agents can be designed and implemented individually. By so doing the process of
deriving the interfaces I_i from I becomes the core of the design process. This is a
typical top-down approach, and it is a natural characteristic of a purposive process.

The composition itself is based on the identification of an output event of one
agent with an input event of another agent. When an agent performs some output event e, another agent that has e as input event performs e simultaneously.
For example, in our normal flow detector example, when the environment performs
gen-$flow$, we identify this output event of the environment with the input event
gen-$flow$ of the normal flow detector. This synchronization models a form of communication from the environment to the detector, or the using agent. This is the first
characterization of the interaction, namely simultaneous participation. The second
notion is that each interface event is under the control of either the using agent
or its environment (unilateral control), i.e., the occurrence of an interface event is
initiated by either the agent or its environment (but not both). From this point of
view the set of interface events is partitioned into a set of input events controlled
by the environment and a set of output events controlled by the agent. The entity
(agent or environment) with control of an interface event is the only one that can
initiate the occurrence of the event.

An interface I is defined by:

- Events(I), a set of events that is the union of two disjoint sets, $Inputs(I)$, a set
  of input events, and $Outputs(I)$, a set of output events.

- $AllowedEventSeqs(I)$, a set of sequences over $Events(I)$, each of which is referred to as an allowed event sequence of I.

For a given interface I, we define $SafeEventSeqs(I)$ to be: $\{w : w$ is a finite prefix of an allowed event sequence of $I\}$. We now define an allowed behavior wrt an interface, and a safe behavior wrt to an interface: σ is allowed wrt I iff $image(\sigma, Events(I)) \in AllowedEventSeqs(I)$, where $image(\sigma, E)$ denotes the sequence of events in E obtained from σ by deleting states and deleting events that are not in E. Similarly, σ is safe wrt I iff one of the following holds: σ is finite and $image(\sigma, Events(I)) \in SafeEventSeqs(I)$, or σ is infinite and every finite prefix of σ is safe wrt I.

Denoting $last(\sigma)$ to be the last state in finite behavior σ, and @ to be concatenation, we can define "A offers I" for an agent A and an interface I.

Definition [25]: Given an agent A and an interface I, A offers I iff the following conditions hold:

- Naming constraints:
  - $Inputs(A) = Inputs(I)$ and $Outputs(A) = Outputs(I)$.
- Safety constraints:
  For all $\sigma \in FiniteBehaviors(A)$, if σ is safe wrt I, then
  - $\forall e \in Outputs(A): last(\sigma) \in enabled_A(e) \Rightarrow \sigma@e$ is safe wrt I, and
  - $\forall e \in Inputs(A): \sigma@e$ is safe wrt $I \Rightarrow last(\sigma) \in enabled_A(e)$.
- Progress constraints:
  For all $\sigma \in AllowedBehaviors(A)$,
  - σ is safe wrt $I \Rightarrow \sigma$ is allowed wrt I.

Informally, the safety constraints state that whenever an output event of A is enabled to occur, the event's occurrence would be safe, i.e., if the event occurs next, the resulting sequence of interface event occurrences is a prefix of an allowed event sequence of I. The second constraint states that whenever an input event of A (controlled by its environment) can occur safely, A must not block the event's occurrence. However, the agent A may block the occurrence of an input event whenever the event's occurrence would be unsafe.[16]

Given an agent A and an interface I, the preceding definition provides the conditions under which they satisfy A offers I. Similarly we can define an agent that, using interface L provided by another agent, offers U as an interface. The agent is required to satisfy its interfaces U and L only if its environment satisfies the safety requirements of these interfaces. The agent satisfies the safety requirements of both U and L, and whenever an environment-controlled event can occur safely, the agent must not block the event's occurrence. Formally we define A using L offers U iff the following conditions hold:

- Naming constraints:

---

[16] In this respect, this model differs from that of I/O automata [29], which require modules to be always input-enabled. Since we require modules to be input-enabled only for input event occurrences that are safe, our model is more general.

  $- Events(U) \cap Events(L) = \emptyset,$
  $- Inputs(A) = Inputs(U) \cup Outputs(L),$ and
  $- Outputs(A) = Outputs(U) \cup Inputs(L).$

- Safety constraints:
  For all $\sigma \in FiniteBehaviors(A)$, if σ is safe wrt U and L, then
  $- \forall e \in Outputs(A): last(\sigma) \in enabled_A(e) \Rightarrow \sigma@e$ is safe wrt U and L, and
  $- \forall e \in Inputs(A): \sigma@e$ is safe wrt U and $L \Rightarrow last(\sigma) \in enabled_A(e).$

- Progress constraints:
  For all $\sigma \in AllowedBehaviors(A)$,
  $- \sigma$ is safe wrt U and L and σ is allowed wrt $L \Rightarrow \sigma$ is allowed wrt U.

The main difference between the definitions of A offers I and A using L offers U is in the progress constraint. There is no requirement that A satisfies any progress requirement of interface L and A is required to satisfy the progress requirements of interface U only if the agent that offers L satisfies the progress requirements of L.

To compose agents we need them to be compatible. Since internal events of an agent A_i are intended to be unobservable by any other agent A_j, a composition is allowed only if the internal events of A_i are disjoint from the events of A_j. If this is not the case there is an option that one of A_i's internal events will cause A_j to act. The principle of unilateral control prevents A_i and A_j from being composed unless the output events of A_i and A_j form disjoint sets.

Definition: A finite set of agents $\{A_j : j \in S\}$ are compatible iff $\forall j, k \in S, j \neq k$:

- $Internals(A_j) \cap Events(A_k) = \emptyset$, and
- $Outputs(A_j) \cap Outputs(A_k) = \emptyset$.

Given a compatible set of agents $\{A_j : j \in S\}$, their composition is an agent $A = (S, I, E, F)$ defined as follows:

- $S = States_A = \prod_{j \in S} States(A_j)$
- $I = Initial_A = \prod_{j \in S} Initial_{A_j}$
- $E = Events_A =$
  $- Internals(A) = [\bigcup_{j \in S} Internals(A_j)] \cup [(\bigcup_{j \in S} Outputs(Aj)) \cap (\bigcup_{j \in S} Inputs(A_j))]$
  $- Outputs(A) = [\bigcup_{j \in S} Outputs(A_j)] - [(\bigcup_{j \in S} Inputs(A_j)]$
  $- Inputs(A) = [\bigcup_{j \in S} Inputs(A_j)] - [\bigcup_{j \in S} Outputs(A_j)]$
- $F =$Fairness requirements of $A = [\bigcup_{j \in S}$ Fairness requirements of $A_j]$.

The following basic results from [25] give the approach to the agents' composition: Let agents A and B, and interfaces U and L, satisfy the following:

- $Internals(A) \cap Internals(B) = \emptyset$
- A using L offers U
- B offers L

Then A and B are compatible and their composition offers U.

Let $A_1, I_1, A_2, I_2, ..., A_n, I_n$ be a finite sequence over alternating agents and interfaces, such that the following hold:

- For all j, k, if $j \neq k$ then $Events(I_j) \cap Events(I_k) = \emptyset$ and $Internals(A_j) \cap Internals(A_k) = \emptyset$.
- A_1 offers I_1.
- For $j = 2, ..., n$, A_j using I_{j-1} offers I_j.

Then agents $A_1, ..., A_n$ are compatible and their composition offers I_n. This second result gives the basis for hierarchical composition.

Composition of modules: An example

To illustrate the use of the state transition system to describe agents and to compose them, we give a description of a main module and a service-providing module. We prove some safety properties of the main module, and then combine it with the lower module to create a new machine. The main module is a floor cleaning agent (using the visual abilities described in the first part of the chapter). The lower module is an interceptor. Our intention is to combine this interceptor module into the basic agent configuration. By so doing we will get a new machine with added capabilities. Safety and progress assertions about the combined machine can be proven. For historical reasons [4] and to ease the exposition, in the sequel we refer to an agent capable of performing the visual tasks described in Sections 5–10 as "Medusa."

We start by giving a general description of the main module. For every behavior we indicate the appropriate recognition tasks that are needed. These recognition tasks will be executed in parallel.

We assume here that the agent has three basic behaviors:

- $M\&C$ ("move and clean")
- $S\&W$ ("stop and wait," when an independently moving object is within some distance)
- $PASS$ ("bypass an obstacle")

These behaviors are based on the following recognition tasks:

MCA	- detect the main cleaning area
DE	- detect a dead end
OBJD	- detect potential obstacles and their dimensions
IMO	- detect independently moving objects

We also need to specify the recognition tasks involved in each behavior and those that trigger switches from behavior to behavior. A behavior transition diagram is depicted in Figure 24. Each node in the diagram represents a distinct behavior. To accomplish a behavior we need to carry out recognition tasks which are not shown in the diagram. The arcs represent those recognition tasks that trigger a change in behavior. These tasks are running in parallel with whatever tasks are taking place during any behavior. Since two or more events may happen simultaneously a priority scheme is needed to arbitrate; larger numbers indicate higher priorities.

The default behavior of the system is $M\&C$. Under $M\&C$ recognition of the main cleaning area (MCA) is carried out. The following recognition tasks are carried out in

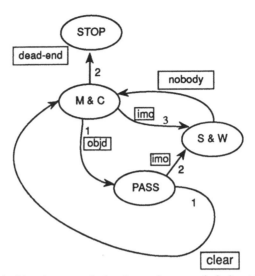

Figure 24. Switching between behaviors: the agent's behavior-transition diagram. Each node represents a distinct behavior; the arcs are recognition tasks.

parallel with the *M&C* behavior: independently moving object detection (IMO), object detection (*OBJD*), and dead-end detection(DE). The highest priority is given to IMO, which runs in parallel with all other activities and triggers the *S&W* behavior. Similarly *OBJD* triggers the *PASS* behavior, and *DE* triggers the *S&W* behavior.[17] We model our agent using the state transition formalism. We assume three visual modules are running. The first one detects independently moving objects. The second and the third detect obstacles, the main cleaning area and independently moving objects, using different algorithms.[18] The agent is moving in the M&C (move and clean) behavior; when it detects an independently moving object it switches to S&W (stop and wait). When an obstacle is detected the agent goes to the PASS behavior (bypassing the obstacle). The agent and the three visual modules are modeled as different processes. Processes VM1...VM3 are environment dependent. Their states are changed "internally." Process S model the state of the agent. S changes states by VM1...3, and this is why it will be constantly enabled.

VM1 state variables, initial conditions, and events:

$S_1 = \{moving, nobody\}$ Initially nobody.

vm1$_a$:

$enabled \equiv S_1 = moving$

$action \equiv S_1 \leftarrow nobody; S_b$

vm1$_b$:

---

[17] In CSP notation, the transition diagram of Figure 24 can be expressed as follows: $M\&C = [mca :: MCA \| imo :: IMO \| objd :: OBJD \| dead\text{-}end :: DE]$
$PICK = [imo :: IMO \| clear :: CLEAR]$
$OBS = [imo :: IMO \| clear :: CLEAR]$
$S\&W = [nobody :: NOBODY]$

[18] The first can use a threshold on velocities, the second can use time to collision, and the third can detect anomalies.

$enabled \equiv S_1 = nobody$
$action \equiv S_1 \leftarrow moving; S_a; S_e$

VMi, i=2,3 state variables, initial conditions, and events:
$S_i = \{moving, nobody, obst, clear\}$ Initially nobody.
vmi$_a$:
$enabled \equiv S_i = moving$
$action \equiv S_i \leftarrow nobody; S_b$
vmi$_b$:
$enabled \equiv S_i = nobody \lor S_i = obst \lor S_i = clear$
$action \equiv S_i \leftarrow moving; S_a; S_e$
vmi$_c$:
$enabled \equiv S_i = nobody$
$action \equiv S_i \leftarrow obst; S_c$
vmi$_d$:
$enabled \equiv S_i = obst$
$action \equiv S_i \leftarrow clear; S_d$

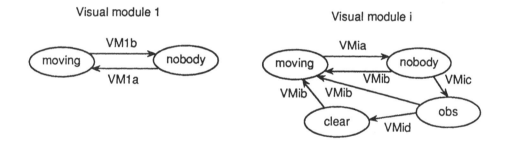

Figure 25. A state transition s for the visual modules S_1, S_i. Each node represents a state; the arcs are recognition tasks.

S state variables, initial conditions, and events:
$S = \{m\&c, s\&w, pass\}$ Initially m&c, an integer count initially 0;
S$_a$:
$enabled \equiv true$
$action \equiv$ if $S = m\&c$ then $S \leftarrow s\&w; count + +$
S$_b$:
$enabled \equiv true$
$action \equiv count -$; if $S = s\&w$ and count=0 then $S \leftarrow m\&c$
S$_c$:
$enabled \equiv true$
$action \equiv$ if $S = m\&c$ then $S \leftarrow pass$
S$_d$:

$enabled \equiv true$

$action \equiv$ if $S = pass$ then $S \leftarrow m\&c$

S_e:

$enabled \equiv true$

$action \equiv$ if $S = pass$ then $S \leftarrow s\&w$; count++;

We will use the above notation to prove a safety property of our cleaning agent. We will prove that when VM2 identifies an independently moving object the agent will enter to a S&W state. The agent will stay there as long as VM2 detects IMO. Marking the VM2 state by S_2 and the agent state by S we want to prove $Invariant(A_0)$ where $A_0 \equiv Invariant(S_2 = moving \implies S = S\&W)$. We will use invariance rule 2, and show that $Invariant(A_1)$, $Invariant(A_2)$, and because $A_1, A_2 \implies A_0$, $Invariant(A_0)$ holds.

We define A_1 to be $A_1 \equiv (count <> 0 \implies S = S\&W)$. We define A_2 to be $A_2 \equiv (S_2 = moving \implies count <> 0)$. We prove $Invariant(A_1), Invariant(A_2)$ by using invariance rule 1. We start with A_2. Initially it holds (vacuously). We need to show that for every event e of the system $A_2 \implies wp(A_2, e)$. The only event that concerns us is $vm2_b$, but there the action part changes the count. A_1 holds initially (again vacuously). The only events that can change $count$ are S_a, S_b, S_e. Both S_a and S_e set S to $S\&W$; S_b is conditioned on $count = 0$. So $inv(A_0)$ is proved. The ease of the proof is a result of the system's simplicity. Introducing counter or weighting schemas, adding states, or changing the level of atomicity will complicate the proof.

THE INTERFACE

We describe the lower interface between Medusa and the interceptor. We first define the interface events that are needed.

Input events: (These events are under the control of the consumer—that is, the main module, Medusa)

{**Intercept, Stop-Intercept**}

A possible definition can be:

Intercept:

$enabled \equiv Interceptor = stop \wedge target = locked$

$action \equiv Interceptor \leftarrow run$

Stop-Intercept:

$enabled \equiv Interceptor = run \wedge Clock > bound$

$action \equiv Interceptor \leftarrow stop$

Output events: (These events are under the control of the providing module—that is, the interceptor)

{**Lost-Target, Intercepted**}

A possible definition can be:

Lost-Target:

$enabled \equiv Interceptor = run \wedge target = locked$

$action \equiv target = lost \wedge Interceptor \leftarrow stop$

Intercepted:

$enabled \equiv Interceptor = run \wedge target = in\text{-}range$

$action \equiv target = intercepted \wedge Interceptor \leftarrow stop$

AllowedEventSeq: We allow for any combination of *Intercept* and *Stop-Intercept*; we do not allow an event sequence like $\{Intercepted, Lost\text{-}Target, Intercepted, \cdots\}$. After an *Intercept* event we allow only one occurrence of either *Lost-Target* or *Intercepted*. After *Stop-Intercept* we allow for any combination of *Intercepted* and *Lost-Target*, until a new *Intercept* event occurs.

Now we describe the interceptor. The interceptor offers the above interface using some lower interface with different perceptual modules. We then describe the events that are added to the basic agent configuration (Medusa) for the composition. Then we are in a position to show that the interceptor indeed offers I, and that the agent M offers a new interface U (that includes new interception capabilities) using I, the interface that is offered by the interceptor.

The interceptor

In what follows we describe the interceptor module. The control strategy of the interceptor follows the lines presented in [38]. The interceptor is getting as inputs the relative angular displacement of the optical axis of the camera with respect to the agent base, as the camera rotates to track the prey ($\Delta\Theta$), and information on whether or not the target has moved closer in the control interval Δt (this fact can be determined by a simple qualitative computation using the concept of focus of expansion—FOE). The interceptor declares a success when the target is at a prespecified distance, or failure when it has lost it. The using module can end the interception because of a change in the intention, or because a bound on the interception time was reached. The module has access to a range finder. The module can activate the range finder, but this energy-consuming operation is not done continuously. The module uses it only to check for termination.

Interceptor state variables, initial conditions, and events:

Input events: The following are three input events of the interceptor, two from the upper module, and one from the lower interface with the range finder. (The range finder is implemented here as one event; in reality it might be coupled with three events: far-out, in-range, far-in. This is a kind of abstraction.) :

Intercept:
$enabled \equiv true$
$action \equiv S \leftarrow run$

Stop-Intercept:
$enabled \equiv true$
$action \equiv S \leftarrow stop$

Get-Range:
$enabled \equiv true$
$action \equiv if\ range > upper\text{-}range\ then\ target \leftarrow lost\ else$
$if\ range < lower\text{-}range\ then\ target \leftarrow intercepted$

Input events: The following are two output events:

Lost-Target:
$enabled \equiv target = lost \vee FOE = out$

$action \equiv S \leftarrow stop$

Intercepted:

$enabled \equiv target = intercepted$

$action \equiv S \leftarrow stop$

The following are internal events:

Move:

$enabled \equiv S = run$

$action \equiv \Delta\Theta; if \Delta\Theta < 0\ move\text{-}left\ else\ move\text{-}right$

FOE$_1$:

$enabled \equiv foe\text{-}state = further$

$action \equiv foe\text{-}state = lost; target = lost$

FOE$_2$:

$enabled \equiv foe\text{-}state = further$

$action \equiv foe\text{-}state = closer$

FOE$_3$:

$enabled \equiv foe\text{-}state = closer$

$action \equiv foe\text{-}state = lost; target = lost$

FOE$_4$:

$enabled \equiv foe\text{-}state = closer$

$action \equiv foe\text{-}state = further$

The using agent—Medusa

Medusa state variables, initial conditions, and events (interface events):
The following two events are output events of the using module.

Intercept:

$enabled \equiv Target = locked \wedge Intention = intercept$

$action \equiv Clock \leftarrow run$

Stop-Intercept:

$enabled \equiv Clock > Bound \vee Intention \neq intercept$

$action \equiv Control \leftarrow main$

The following are input events of the using module.

Lost-Target:

$enabled \equiv true$

$action \equiv Target \leftarrow lost$

Intercepted:

$enabled \equiv true$

$action \equiv Target \leftarrow intercepted$

The range finder is defined as (interface events):

Get-Range:

$enabled \equiv Clock\ mod\ 5 = 0$

$action \equiv Range$

Now we combine the interceptor with the basic Medusa agent to get a composition of modules. We consider Medusa to be the upper module that using L offers U, and the interceptor offers L. The composition offers U. The interface events are designed to fulfill the needs of the user. We use the basic result for agent composition with Medusa being agent A, and the interceptor agent B. It is clear that $Internals(A) \cap Internals(B) = \emptyset$. We have to verify that B (the interceptor) offers L, and then that Medusa using L offers U; then according to the theorem we have a composition that offers U.

The interceptor offers L: The naming constraints hold. As for the safety constraints, we should note that once S is set to *stop*, the only event that can set it back to *run* is the output event *Intercept*. Because the result of *Lost-Target* or *Intercepted* is the assignment $S \leftarrow stop$, it is clear that $\forall e \in Outputs(B): last(\sigma) \in enabled_B(e) \Rightarrow \sigma@e$ is safe wrt L. The second safety constraint: $\forall e \in Inputs(B):$ $\sigma@e$ is safe wrt $I \Rightarrow last(\sigma) \in enabled_B(e)$, holds because the input events are always enabled (that is, they will not be blocked). The progress constraint, that for all $\sigma \in AllowedBehaviors(A)$, σ is safe wrt $I \Rightarrow \sigma$ is allowed wrt I, clearly holds.

Now we need to show that Medusa using L offers U and then the composition is complete. For that we need to go over the naming, safety and progress constraints in a similar manner. What actually should be checked is the influence of the new behaviors that were added to the behavior of Medusa. Because the addition is simple the check is not complicated. The combined agent has new set of input, output, and internal events. The new states of the agent are the products of the different states of the constituting agents.

12. CONCLUSIONS

We have presented the foundations of a set of processes that interpret visual motion in a purposive manner. We showed that an active observer can solve a series of important problems through the use of the derivatives of the image intensity function. In particular, we presented direct solutions to the problems of kinetic stabilization (passive navigation), detection of independent motion, obstacle avoidance, relative depth and 3-D motion (translation) computation and visual interception. Although the aforementioned problems are applications of the general structure from motion problem, we addressed them as independent problems in their own right and produced solutions that depend on data which can be measured.

The possibility that important behaviors can be realized by the cooperation of processes that recognize perceptual events without having to create a full representation of the outside world suggests that vision can be studied as a part of a system that has purposes which translate into behaviors. This point of view opens several interesting research areas, all related to the development of intelligent visual behaviors.

Finally, we presented a mathematical framework (borrowed from the literature on distributed processing) formalizing the concept of behaviors and showed how an agent can be composed from a set of behaviors and how it can be controlled.

Research in this paradigm will become more interdisciplinary with time, since the basic premise is that vision should not be studied in isolation but as part of an intelligent system. New questions about control arise, and the integration of vision with planning, manipulation, memory and learning will provide interesting research avenues.

REFERENCES

1. G. Adiv, "Determining three-dimensional motion and structure from optical flow generated by several moving objects," *IEEE Trans. PAMI* **7**, 1985, 384–401.

2. G. Adiv, "Inherent ambiguities in recovering 3d motion and structure from a noisy flow field," In *Proc. IEEE Conference on Computer Vision and Pattern Recognition*, 1985, 70–77.

3. J. Aloimonos and D. Shulman, *Integration of Visual Modules: An Extension of the Marr Paradigm*, Academic Press, Boston, 1989.

4. Y. Aloimonos, "Purposive and qualitative active vision," In *Proc. Image Understanding Workshop*, 1990, 816–828.

5. Y. Aloimonos (Ed.), *CVGIP: Image Understanding* **56**, Special Issue on Purposive, Qualitative, Active Vision, 1992.

6. Y. Aloimonos and Z. Duriç, "Active egomotion estimation: A qualitative approach," In G. Sandini (Ed.), *Lecture Notes in Computer Science* **588**, Springer-Verlag, 1992, 497–510.

7. Y. Aloimonos, I. Weiss, and A. Bandopadhay, "Active vision," *Int'l. J. Comp. Vision* **2**, 1988, 333–356.

8. M.A. Arbib, "Perceptual structures and distributed motor control," In V.B. Brooks (Ed.), *Handbook of Physiology: The Nervous System II. Motor Control*, 1981, 1449–1480.

9. R. Bajcsy, "Active perception," *Proc. IEEE* **76**, 1988, 996–1005.

10. B. Bhanu and W. Burger, "Qualitative target motion detection and tracking," In *Proc. Image Understanding Workshop*, 370–398, 1989.

11. D.H. Ballard, "Parameter networks," *Artificial Intelligence* **22**, 1984, 235–267.

12. D.H. Ballard, "Reference frames for animate vision," In *Proc. Int'l. Joint Conference on Artificial Intelligence*, 1989, 635–1641.

13. R.A. Brooks, "Achieving artificial intelligence through building robots," AI Memo 899, Massachusetts Institute of Technology, Cambridge, MA, 1986.

14. R.A. Brooks, "A robust layered control system for a mobile robot," *IEEE J. Robotics Automation* **2**, 1986, 14–23.

15. A. Bruss and B.K.P. Horn, "Passive navigation," *Computer Vision, Graphics, Image Processing* **21**, 1983, 3–21.

16. W. Burger and B. Bhanu, "On computing a 'fuzzy' focus of expansion for autonomous navigation," In *Proc. IEEE Conference on Computer Vision and Pattern Recognition*, 1989, 563–568.

17. C.H. Chen and A.C. Kak, "A robot vision system for recognizing 3-d objects in low-order polynomial time," *IEEE Trans. Systems, Man, Cybernetics, Special Issue on Computer Vision* **19**, 1989, 1535–1563.

18. C. Fermüller and Y. Aloimonos, "Estimating 3-d motion from image gradients," Technical Report CAR-TR-554, Center for Automation Research, University of Maryland, College Park, MD, 1991.

19. Y. Ho, "Dynamics of discrete event systems," *Proc. IEEE* **77**, 3–6.

20. C.A.R. Hoare, *Communicating Sequential Processes*, Prentice-Hall, Englewood Cliffs, NJ, 1985.

21. B.K.P. Horn, *Robot Vision*, McGraw Hill, New York, 1986.

22. B.K.P. Horn and E.J. Weldon Jr, "Computationally-efficient methods of recovering translational motion," In *Proc. Int'l. Conference on Computer Vision*, 1987, 1–11.

23. B.K.P. Horn and B.G. Schunck, "Determining optical flow," *Artificial Intelligence* **17**, 1981, 185–203.

24. L. Huang and Y. Aloimonos, "Relative depth from motion using normal flow: An active and purposive solution," In *Proc. Workshop on Visual Motion*, 1992, 196–204.

25. S.S. Lam and A.U. Shankar, "Understanding interfaces," In *Proc. Int'l. Conference on Formal Description Techniques (FORTE)*, 1991.

26. S.S. Lam and A.U. Shankar, "A relational notation for state transition systems," *IEEE Trans. Software Engineering* **16**, 1991, 12–25.

27. H.C. Longuet-Higgins, "A computer algorithm for reconstructing a scene from two projections," *Nature* **293**, 1981, 133–135.

28. H.C. Longuet-Higgins and K. Prazdny, "The interpretation of a moving retinal image," *Proc. Royal Soc. London B* **208**, 1984, 385–397.

29. N. Lynch and M. Tuttle, "Hierarchical correctness proofs for distributed algorithms," In *Proc. ACM Symposium on Principles of Distributed Computing*, 1987.

30. D. Marr, *Vision*, W.H. Freeman, San Francisco, 1982.

31. H.P. Moravec, "Towards automatic visual obstacle avoidance," In *Proc. Int'l. Joint Conference on Artificial Intelligence*, 1977, 584.

32. R.C. Nelson, "Qualitative detection of motion by a moving observer," In *Proc. Image Understanding Workshop*, 1990, 329–338.

33. R.C. Nelson and J. Aloimonos, "Finding motion parameters from spherical flow fields (or the advantages of having eyes in the back of your head)," *Biological Cybernetics* **58**, 1988, 261–273.

34. P.J. Ramadge and W.M. Wonham, "Supervisory control of a class of discrete event processes," *SIAM J. Contr. Optimization* **25**, 1987, 206–230.

35. P.J. Ramadge and W.M. Wonham, "The control of discrete event systems," *Proc. IEEE* **77**, 1989, 81–98.

36. A.U. Shankar and S.S Lam, "Construction of network protocols by stepwise refinement," In J. W. de Bakker, W.P. de Roever and G. Rozenberg (Ed.), *Stepwise Refinment of Distributed Systems*, Springer-Verlag, 1990.

37. R. Sharma and Y. Aloimonos, "Robust detection of independent motion: An active and purposive solution," Technical Report CAR-TR-534, Center for Automation Research, University of Maryland, College Park, MD, 1991.

38. R. Sharma and Y. Aloimonos, "Visual motion analysis under interceptive behavior," In *Proc. IEEE Conf. on Computer Vision and Pattern Recognition*, 1992.

39. M.E. Spetsakis and J. Aloimonos, "Structure from motion using line correspondences," *Int'l. J. Computer Vision* **4**, 1990, 171–183.

40. M.E. Spetsakis and Y. Aloimonos, "Optimal computing of structure from motion using point correspondences in two frames," *IEEE Trans. PAMI* **14**, 1992, 959–964.

41. W.B. Thompson and T-C. Pong, "Detecting moving objects," *Int'l. J. Computer Vision* **4**, 1990, 39–57.

42. R.Y. Tsai and T.S. Huang, "Uniqueness and estimation of three dimensional motion parameters of rigid objects with curved surfaces," *IEEE Trans. PAMI* **6**, 1984, 13–27.

43. S. Ullman, *The Interpretation of Visual Motion*, MIT Press, Cambridge, MA, 1979.

44. S. Ullman, "Visual routines," *Cognition* **18**, 1984, 97–157.

45. A. Verri and T. Poggio, "Against quantitative optic flow," In *Proc. Int'l. Conference on Computer Vision*, 1987, 171–180.

3 | NAVIGATIONAL PRELIMINARIES

Cornelia Fermüller
University of Maryland
and Technical University of Vienna

ABSTRACT

It has been proposed by neuroethologists that the most basic visual capabilities found in animals are based on motion [25, 39]. Machine vision, of course, does not have to copy animal vision, but the existence of vision in biological organisms gives us at least some reason to believe that it is possible for a system to work in the same or a similar way. Robots equipped with visual sensors which move autonomously in their environments must possess basic visual motion capabilities. The importance of visual motion understanding has been recognized for many years and as a consequence a lot of research has been done, most of it formulated in the framework of reconstructive vision as the general structure from motion module. Although research along these lines has been accompanied by many experiments, none of the existing techniques can be used in an unrestricted (general) environment. The reasons for this lack of applicability to general situations are that the problem was formulated in such a way that specific assumptions had to be employed, and furthermore it was studied for the case of a passive observer.

The recently emerging paradigm of *active and qualitative vision* advocates studying visual problems in form of modules that are directly related to visual tasks for observers that are active. Along these lines, we argue that the problems of egomotion estimation and 3-D object motion estimation are conceptually different. In this chapter a computational framework for robust motion estimation for an active observer is presented. It is shown how different activities (fixation and tracking) facilitate motion perception. Furthermore, new constraints of a global nature relating 2-D image measurements to 3-D motion parameters are presented. Local image measurements form global patterns in the image

This work was funded in part by NSF, the Österreichisches Bundesministerium für Wissenschaft und Forschung and the Österreichische Bundeskammer der Gewerblichen Wirtschaft.

plane and the position of these patterns determines the 3-D motion parameters. The robustness of the approach is due to the fact that neither correspondence nor optical flow is computed and that the constraints used are global and qualitative in nature.

1. INTRODUCTION

Many researchers no longer consider computer vision as a scientific field of independent study. The scope of computer vision should not be limited to the study of mappings of a given set of visual data into representations on a more abstract level. It is becoming clear that image understanding should be extended to include the process of selective acquisition of data in space and time. This has produced a paradigm that has established itself under the term active vision [5, 7]. The main idea behind this approach is that visual capabilities only make sense for systems (biological or artificial) that interact with their environments and engage in some kind of movement. A good theory of vision is one that can create the interface between perception and other cognitive motor abilities (such as reasoning, planning, navigation, manipulation) through the employment of an observer that has the capability to change visual parameters in a controlled way.

Since computer vision is considered as one of the main subfields of Artificial Intelligence (AI),[1] it has been addressed since the earliest years of its appearance using general AI methodology. The main emphasis in AI research has been on finding general purpose methodologies and general purpose representations that preserve as much information as possible. A three-step approach to solving any problem has been taken for granted. The conversion of external data (sensor data, actuator commands, decision making, etc.) into an internal representation and vice versa has been separated from the phase of developing algorithms to perform computations on internal data. Most research has been devoted to processing the internal data, and as a consequence different subfields such as planning, machine learning, knowledge-based data bases and many more have appeared. Therefore it is not surprising that the first influential theory of computational vision (Marr [33]) mainly concentrated on the computational and representational aspects. In this theory, vision is described as a reconstruction process, that is, a problem of creating representations of increasingly high levels of abstraction leading from 2-D images over the primal sketch through the $2\frac{1}{2}$D sketch to object-centered descriptions ("from pixels to predicates" [38]).

Important results have been achieved at the level of computational theories and algorithms dealing with internal representations. Nevertheless, it has to be admitted that vision, and AI in general, are far from the ultimate goal of building machines possessing capabilities of living organisms. Critics of the general AI philosophy argue that the study of intelligence cannot be separated from the study of the system's interaction with its environment. Applied to machine vision, this has led to the paradigm of active vision, sometimes also referred to as purposive, animate or behavioral vision [5, 2, 8, 9, 10]. This paradigm states that by engaging the system in interaction with the world, additional information can be supplied and problems

---

[1] About 40% of the human brain is devoted to visual processing.

that were originally considered to be ill posed, ill conditioned and nonlinear may be solved. It further states that the approach of complete scene recovery should be avoided if possible, and vision should be studied in connection with the behavior of the organism. Finding a general purpose representation is not necessary for performing many tasks. The classical problems that have been addressed have to be reconsidered as well. The question, of course, still remains: What are these easier problems to be solved?

Most ideas in machine vision are inspired by the abilities of humans or animals. There has always been much cross-fertilization between AI and psychology, therefore the study of the human visual system has received a lot of attention. Interaction with other fields, like psychophysics and neurology, has increased, and hopefully this interaction will lead to the understanding of visual capabilities and the knowledge needed to create artificial ones. Horridge, working on insect vision, attempts to present a hierarchical classification of visual systems ordered by their degree of evolution [26]. He argues that the most basic visual capabilities found in animals are based on motion[25]. Machine vision, of course, does not have to copy animal vision, but the existence of vision in biological organisms gives us at least some reason to believe that it is possible for a system to work in the same or a similar way.

We believe that a synthetic approach should be taken to building a vision system, where nature should serve as a source of inspiration. After understanding basic capabilities of the visual system, we want to supply the system with components of increasing complexity and study more complex capabilities. If a system can robustly measure its motion relative to a static scene or relative to some object then it possesses a basic capability that can serve as a basis for more elaborate tasks. A system will operate successfully in the real world only if it uses algorithms which are insensitive to noise in the sensor measurements. This leads us to believe that studying active vision also means focusing on robustness issues. We present here a computational framework for motion estimation by an active observer that leads to a series of algorithms which are robust and qualitative in nature.

2. VISUAL MOTION ANALYSIS

For years visual motion interpretation has been approached through studying the "structure from motion" problem. The idea is to find methods of recovering the 3-D motion parameters and the structure of the objects in view from the dynamic imagery ([28, 27, 33, 46]). The way the problem has been addressed was first to compute the exact position to which each point in the image has moved. In cases of small motion the vector field that represents the change of every point in the image, the so-called optical flow field, is computed from the spatio-temporal derivatives of the image intensity function [6, 13, 20, 24, 34, 47]. This requires the employment of additional constraints, such as smoothness. In cases where the motion is large, features such as points, lines or contours in images taken at different time instants are corresponded [18, 46]. From the derived optical flow field or the correspondences between features the 3-D motion is then determined [1, 15, 22, 31, 32, 43, 45, 48, 49].

One can distinguish three phases in the evolution of research on the structure from motion problem. Early work dealt with the question of the existence of a solution, i.e., can we extract any information from a sequence of images about the structure and 3-D motion of the scene that cannot be found from a single image? Intensive research has been conducted in this field and several theoretical results have appeared that deal with questions such as: What can be recovered from a certain number of feature points in a given number of frames ([4, 46])? Then the uniqueness aspects of the problem were studied. Nonlinear algorithms for the recovery of structure and motion from point [31] or line correspondences [30] or optical flow [48] increasingly appeared in the literature. Such algorithms were based on iterative approximation techniques, so they lacked guarantees of convergence as well as clear analytical formulations that would make proofs of uniqueness possible and allow other researchers to build on them. Later, "linear" algorithms and uniqueness proofs came out for points [45] and lines [42], as well as flow [1]; all were based on the same linearization technique. Although research along these lines has been accompanied by many experiments, none of the existing techniques can be used as a basis for an integrated system, working robustly in a general environment.

The reasons for the lack of applicability to real world problems are due to the difficulty of estimating retinal correspondence, which is an ill-posed problem, the assumptions that have to be made to derive optical flow; and the sensitivity of 3-D motion estimation to small changes in the data. Even optimal algorithms [43]—optimal under the assumption of Gaussian noise—perform quite poorly in the presence of moderate noise. Since the existence and most uniqueness aspects [14, 21, 35, 42, 45] of the problem are now well understood and initial attempts to construct algorithms that perform well in realistic domains have failed, motion research has shifted its focus to the robustness issue. With the advent of active vision a new door leading to the development of robust visual motion techniques has opened. An observer is active if it has the capability of controlling the geometric parameters of its sensory apparatus. Through interaction with the environment it can gain additional information and classical ill conditioned problems can become well conditioned. The fact that active vision has mathematical advantages over passive vision was first shown by Aloimonos et al. [5] in connection with several recovery problems.

Like many other visual problems, motion estimation has usually been addressed as a reconstruction problem: the so called "structure from motion" problem. In this approach the most general strategy is being used. Clearly, if we can recover from a sequence of images the involved structure of the imaged scene and the relative 3-D motion, then various subsets of the computed parameters provide sufficient information to solve many practical problems, such as detection of independent motion, passive navigation, obstacle avoidance, prey catching, etc., as well as many other problems related to robotics and automation—hand-eye coordination, automatic docking, teleconferencing, etc. However, the intermediate computation of structure and 3-D motion is not a prerequisite for solving many navigational tasks. Since the structure from motion problem turned out to be extremely difficult we may choose to seek direct solutions to the aforementioned problems that do not presume complete recovery. In this chapter we solve the problem of 3-D motion estimation independently from the recovery of depth. We describe various aspects of the motion estimation problem and investigate properties of the motion field. As a result we obtain constraints that can be used for finding the motion parameters. By exploiting the advantages of different kinds of activities we develop algorithms based on these geometrical findings to solve various navigational tasks very efficiently.

3. OVERVIEW

We address the problem of 3-D motion estimation on the basis of a sequence of images acquired by a monocular observer. From measurements on the image we can only compute the relative motion between the observer and any point in the 3-D scene. The model that has been employed most in previous research to relate 2-D image measurements to 3-D motion and structure is that of rigid motion. Consequently, egomotion recovery for an observer moving in a static world has been treated in the same way as the estimation of an object's 3-D motion relative to an observer. We argue here that the rigid motion model is appropriate if only the observer is moving, but it holds only for a restricted subset of moving objects—mainly man-made ones. Indeed, all objects in the natural world move non-rigidly. However, considering only a small patch in the image of a moving object, a rigid motion approximation is legitimate. For the case of egomotion, data from all parts of the image plane can be used, whereas for object motion only local information can be employed. Hence, we develop conceptually different techniques for explaining the mechanisms underlying the perceptual processes of *egomotion recovery* and *3-D object motion recovery*.

In this chapter we analyze the following two problems:

(a) Given an active observer viewing an object moving in a rigid manner (translation + rotation), recover the direction of the 3-D translation and the time to collision by using only the spatio-temporal derivatives of the image intensity function. Although this problem is not equivalent to "structure from motion," because it does not fully recover the 3-D motion, it is of importance in a variety of situations. If an object is rotating around itself and also translating in some direction, we are usually interested in its translation—for example in problems related to tracking, prey catching, interception, obstacle avoidance, etc.

(b) Given an active observer moving rigidly in a static environment, recover the direction of its translation and its rotation. This is the process of passive navigation, a term used to describe the set of processes by which a system can estimate its motion with respect to the environment. Passive navigation is a prerequisite for any other navigational ability. A system can be guided only if there is a way for it to acquire information about its motion and to control its parameters.

Our approach to egomotion estimation is based on an analysis of the properties of the motion field. The fact that motion is rigid defines geometric relations between certain values of the spatio-temporal derivatives of the image intensity function. By considering only the sign of the selected values we find patterns in the image plane which are dependent on only some of the motion parameters. For the most general case (an observer moving with three translational and three rotational parameters) we show how these patterns can be searched for in order to find the parameters describing this motion. Then we discuss how these general results can be used in a number of motion estimation algorithms for an observer with restricted motion capabilities. Finally, we show that if the observer is active and supplies additional information, these general constraints can be exploited to solve various navigational tasks with only a small computational effort.

4. INPUT

If our goal is to develop robust algorithms that can perform successfully in general environments, we should abandon all computational steps which are provably unstable. Any 3-D motion estimation technique must make use of a representation for the image motion. Most existing algorithms rely at this stage on the computation of optic flow or correspondence, but the estimation of retinal correspondence is an ill posed problem.[2] The only image motion that can be uniquely defined from a sequence of images is the normal flow—the projection of the optical flow on the gradient direction (see Figure 1). This is the well known "aperture problem." Normal flow can be computed in different ways, either from the image motion of edges (the edge flow) or from the image gradients (the spatio-temporal derivatives of the image intensity function) by employing the motion constraint equation. The difficulty in its computation is due only to the discrete aspect of digital images. Computing normal flow in images is as difficult as computing edges. Since normal flow constitutes a uniquely definable image motion representation, we choose to use it as input to the estimation of 3-D motion, although the normal flow field appears to contain less information than the optical flow field.

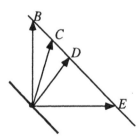

Figure 1. The aperture problem: Only the projection of the flow on the image gradient can be computed.

Methods for estimating 3-D motion from only the normal flow field without going through the intermediate stage of computing optical flow have appeared in [3, 23, 36]. In [3] the case of purely rotational motion was studied, and linear equations relating the rotation parameters to the normal flow were derived. A similar result was

---

[2] The estimation of optical flow is an underconstrained problem and in order to solve it additional assumptions have to be made. For special applications valid assumptions can be found; this is the case with certain model-based systems [16, 29]. In the general case, however, any algorithm will produce imperfect output (erroneous, if the assumptions do not hold).

reported by Horn and Weldon [23], who presented several methods for the problem of motion and structure computation in addition to the purely rotational case, for translation only, for known rotation, and for known structure. The constraint of positive depth was used by Negadharipour [36] to estimate the focus of expansion for purely translational motion. In [50] translation and rotation were estimated for an observer rotating around the direction of translation, and recently a hybrid technique has appeared, using both optical flow and image gradients for addressing 3-D motion in the general case (rotation and translation). Our contribution here lies in the introduction of several novel geometric properties of a normal flow field due to rigid motion that give rise to simple pattern matching techniques for recovering 3-D motion, Furthermore, it is shown how activities such as tracking and fixation facilitate motion estimation.

5. IMAGE FORMATION AND THE CHOICE OF THE COORDINATE SYSTEM

Consider the monocular imaging situation, where the observer and the scene are in relative motion to each other. In order to obtain the equations relating the 3-D scene to the image measurements in a general form, two coordinate systems are employed. The reference coordinate system (X, Y, Z) is fixed to the observer with the center O being the nodal point of the camera. Another coordinate frame, which we will call the "scene frame," is fixed at a point $S = (X_s, Y_s, Z_s)$ on an object in the scene. At the time of observation the reference frame and scene frame axes are parallel. The rigid motion of any point $P = (X, Y, Z)$ in the scene can then be described through a translation $T_s = (U_s, V_s, W_s)$ of the scene frame with respect to the reference frame and a rotation $\omega = (\alpha, \beta, \gamma)$ with respect to the scene frame, which leads to the following equations [12]:

$$\dot{X} = -U_s - \beta(Z - Z_s) + \gamma(Y - Y_s)$$
$$\dot{Y} = -V_s - \gamma(X - X_s) + \alpha(Z - Z_s)$$
$$\dot{Z} = -W_s - \alpha(Y - Y_s) + \beta(X - X_s) \tag{1}$$

As image formation model we use perspective projection on the plane. The image plane is parallel to the XY plane and the viewing direction is along the positive Z axis (see Figure 2). Under this projection the image position $p(x, y)$ of a 3-D point $P(X, Y, Z)$ is defined by the relation

$$(x, y) = (\frac{fX}{Z}, \frac{fY}{Z}) \tag{2}$$

The constant f denotes the focal length of the imaging system. The equations relating the velocity (u, v) of an image point p to the 3-D velocity can be derived by differentiating (1) and substituting from (2):

$$u = \frac{(-U_s f + x W_s)}{Z} + \alpha(\frac{xy}{f} - \frac{xX_s}{Z}) - \beta(\frac{x^2}{f} + f - \frac{xX_s}{Z} - \frac{Z_s f}{Z}) + \gamma(y - \frac{Y_s f}{Z})$$
$$v = \frac{(-V_s f + y W_s)}{Z} + \alpha(\frac{y^2}{f} + f - \frac{yY_s}{Z} - \frac{Z_s f}{Z}) - \beta(\frac{xy}{f} - \frac{yX_s}{Z}) - \gamma(x - \frac{X_s f}{Z}) \tag{3}$$

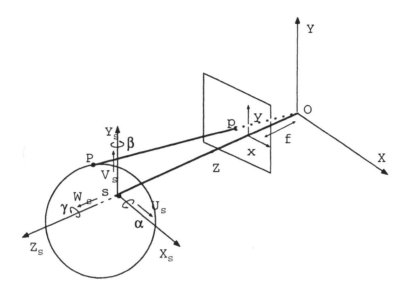

Figure 2. Imaging geometry and motion representation.

The above equation is a more general form of the optical-flow based constraint equation first derived by Longuet-Higgins and Prazdny [32]. In fact, if the origin of the scene frame coincides with the origin of the reference frame, then $X_s = Y_s = Z_s = 0$ and $T = T_0 = (U, V, W)$ and (3) becomes

$$u = \frac{(-Uf + xW)}{Z} + \alpha\frac{xy}{f} - \beta(\frac{x^2}{f} + f) + \gamma y$$
$$v = \frac{(-Vf + yW)}{Z} + \alpha(\frac{y^2}{f} + f) - \beta\frac{xy}{f} - \gamma x \tag{4}$$

Since the motion parameters are expressed relative to the scene coordinate system, prediction of the position of the moving entity (object or observer) at the next time instant is dependent on the choice of this coordinate system's position. In the case of egomotion it makes sense to attach the scene coordinate system to the observer, simply because the quantities recovered are directly related to the way the observer moves. On the other hand, when the observer needs to make inferences regarding another object's motion, the ideal place to put the origin of the scene coordinate system would be the mass center of the object (the natural system).

Since the mass center is not known, different choices have to be made. Most commonly the camera's nodal point is chosen as the center of the scene coordinate system (a "camera-centered" coordinate system). Rotation is described around the nodal point. In the case of object motion this leads to different values for the motion parameters for each new frame, which is an unwelcome effect in the task of finding translational motion.

We therefore decided to attach the center of rotation to the object's point of intersection with the optical axis (an "object-centered" coordinate system). The active observer is free in its choice of the center and will therefore decide on a point belonging to a neighborhood of nonuniform brightness with distinguishable features.

This approach can be justified by the following argument: When choosing as fixation point the mass center of the object's image or a point in its neighborhood, the resulting motion parameters are in many cases close to those of the natural system. In the natural coordinate system with center O_{natural} the velocity v at point P is due to the translational and the rotational component:

$$v = t_{\text{natural}} + \omega \times \overrightarrow{O_{\text{natural}}P}$$

and in the object-centered coordinate system with center O_{object} the same velocity is expressed as

$$v = t_{\text{object}} + \omega \times \overrightarrow{O_{\text{object}}P}$$

Therefore the difference in translation between t_{natural} and t_{object} (see Figure 3) is given by

$$t_{\text{natural}} - t_{\text{object}} = \omega \times (\overrightarrow{O_{\text{object}}P} - \overrightarrow{O_{\text{natural}}P})$$
$$= \omega \times \overrightarrow{O_{\text{object}}O_{\text{natural}}}$$

This value becomes smaller as $\overrightarrow{O_{\text{object}}O_{\text{natural}}}$ decreases. In order to stress the different analyses for different coordinate systems throughout the chapter we denote rotation in an object-centered coordinate system by $(\omega_1, \omega_2, \omega_3)$ and a camera-centered coordinate system by (α, β, γ).

6. ACTIVE 3-D MOTION ESTIMATION

We present a method for estimating the direction of translation and the time to collision for a monocular observer that has the capability of tracking. The observer derives its required tracking movement from the image sequence and uses these tracking parameters as input to the computation of the object's 3-D motion.

To begin with, the observer detects independent motion [41] and fixates on the object, thus causing the optical axis to pass through the object. The translational direction of an object moving with translational parameters (U, V, W) and rotating with velocity $(\omega_1, \omega_2, \omega_3)$ is represented in the image plane by the point $(\frac{U}{W}, \frac{V}{W})$, the Focus of Expansion (FOE). To give a graphical explanation: If we put the object at a distance equal to the focal length f in front of the nodal point of the camera, the FOE represents the intersection point of the image plane and the motion trajectory which passes through the nodal point (see Figure 4).

It has been argued that tracking is used in biological vision for the sake of simplifying the estimation of motion. Since we are studying computer vision for an active observer, our first question concerns the nature of the activities themselves. Therefore we should ask why one should proceed in a roundabout way and derive the tracking movement as an intermediate step. What do we gain from tracking?

Through tracking we can accumulate information over time and therefore add the parameter of time as additional component to the input information. Another

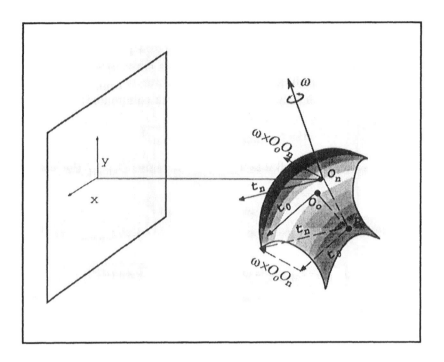

Figure 3. The difference in translation between t_n in the natural system with center O_n and t_o in the object centered system with center O_o is $\omega \times O_o\vec{O}_n$.

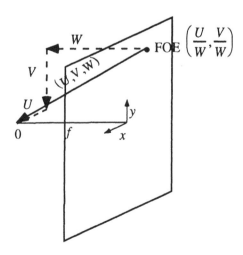

Figure 4. FOE in the image plane.

advantage of tracking is that since it is accomplished over a number of steps, the tracking parameters can be corrected sequentially (smoothed) and we need not rely on just one measurement.

The idea of using the tracking parameters for motion estimation was used previously by Bandopadhay and Ballard [12]. They provide closed form solutions for the computation of the egomotion parameters for a binocular observer by employing the rotation angle and its first and second derivatives (angular velocity and acceleration). In their paper they did not show how tracking was actually done, whereas we propose a complete solution: We first show how to compute the tracking parameters using normal flow and then how to use them for 3-D motion estimation.

We accomplish the computation of the FOE and the time to collision through three modules that involve the activities of fixation and tracking.

1. By fixating on an object point, which we consider to be the origin of the coordinate system, we obtain the image velocity at the center that represents the projection of parallel translation. We show how tracking can be used to derive the projection of parallel translation from just the spatio-temporal derivatives.

2. In the next step, the output of the first module is used to acquire information about translation parallel to the optical axis. Again tracking is used, here as a tool for accumulating depth information over time.

3. In the third module we show that time to collision is related to the FOE and how to estimate it from the spatio-temporal information at the fixated point.

6.1. TRACKING GIVES PARALLEL TRANSLATION

The first activity used in this approach is fixation. This action provides us with linear relations between the 3-D and the 2-D velocity parameters. An object at distance Z in front of the camera moves in the 3-D environment with translational velocity (U, V, W) and rotational velocity $(\omega_1, \omega_2, \omega_3)$. In an object-centered coordinate system with center $P(X_0, Y_0, Z_0)$ under perspective projection the optical flow (u, v) is related to these parameters through the following equations:

$$\frac{dx}{dt} = u = \frac{Uf}{Z} - \frac{Wx}{Z} - \frac{xy\omega_1}{f} + \omega_2\left(\frac{x^2}{f} + \frac{f(Z-Z_0)}{Z}\right) - \omega_3 y$$
$$\frac{dy}{dt} = v = \frac{Vf}{Z} - \frac{Wy}{Z} - \omega_1\left(\frac{y^2}{f} + \frac{f(Z-Z_0)}{Z}\right) + \frac{\omega_2 xy}{f} + \omega_3 x$$

In a small area around the center x, y and $\frac{(Z-Z_0)}{Z}$ are close to zero. The optical flow components due to rotation and due to translation parallel to the optical axis converge to zero; u becomes $\frac{Uf}{Z}$ and v becomes $\frac{Vf}{Z}$.

The flow at the center of the image gives the projection of parallel translation, but only normal flow is available. We show that tracking can be used for the evaluation of optical flow by an iterative technique and prove the convergence of the method to the exact solution.

The problem of current optical flow algorithms is that additional constraints are employed. Constraints that impose a relationship on the values of the flow field are usually used, and this amounts to assumptions, such as smoothness, about the scene in view. This basic problem is overcome by providing the observer with activity.

The computation is thus transferred to the active observer, which has the ability to iteratively adjust its motion to the given situation through its control mechanism.

In cases where the dominant motion of the object is translation toward the observer, the resulting optical flow vectors emanate from a point which lies inside the object's image. The coordinates of this point, the FOE, are consequently close to zero. Otherwise the optical flow pattern is due to vectors that are approximately parallel and have about the same magnitude. Typical normal flow patterns for both cases are shown in Figure 5.

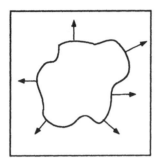 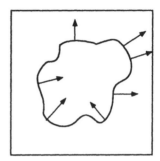

Figure 5. (a) Normal flow vectors emanating from a point inside the object. (b) Normal flow vectors, when the translational component parallel to the image plane is not much larger than the component perpendicular to the plane.

For these cases, where the FOE lies inside the object, the normal flow vectors are mainly due to translation, because the rotational components near the object center are very small. Therefore a simple technique using only the direction of the normal flow measurements can be applied. Given the normal flow vector at a point, we know that the FOE lies in the half-plane which is on the opposite side of the graylevel edge from the normal flow vector. Considering every available normal flow measurement will narrow the possible location of the FOE to a small area (see Figure 6) (see also [2, 23]). When dealing with such normal flow patterns, it would make no sense to use the method introduced in this chapter; we are concerned here with the more complicated case as displayed in Figure 5b.

Let us compute the normal flow in a set of directions in a small area around the origin (fixation point). The normal flow is the projection of the optical flow on the gradient direction. The largest of the normal flow values in the different directions is therefore the one closest to the optical flow. Let us call this normal flow vector the "maximum normal flow" and denote it by (u^n, v^n) (see Figure 7a). We take it as an approximation to the correct optical flow and use it to track the fixated point. The purpose of tracking is to correct for the error in the approximation. In order to keep a point with optical flow (u, v) in the center of the image the observer has to perform a movement that produces the same value of optical flow in the opposite direction. The way our observer accomplishes this task is by rotating the camera around the nodal point about the X- and Y-axes. While the observer is moving it takes the next image and again computes the normal flow vectors. If the maximum

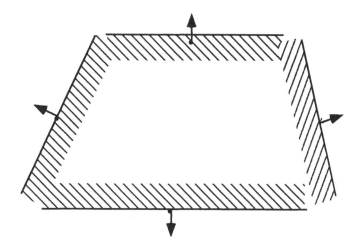

Figure 6. Each available normal flow measurement constrains the possible location of the FOE.

normal flow was equal to the optical flow, a new optical flow (due to object motion and egomotion) of zero will be achieved.

Usually, however, the maximum normal flow and the optical flow are not equal; they differ in magnitude or in direction, or both. An error in magnitude results in a flow vector in the direction of maximum normal flow, and an error in direction creates a flow vector perpendicular to it (see Figure 7b). The actual error is usually in both magnitude and direction. Thus the new flow vector is a vector sum of the two components. Again it can be approximated by the largest normal flow vector measurement. The new measured normal flow is used as a feedback value to correct the optical flow and the tracking parameters; the new normal flow vector is added to the maximum normal flow vector computed in the first step. Proceeding by applying the same technique to the successive estimated errors will result in an accurate estimate of the actual flow after a few iterations. The proof of convergence to the exact solution follows.

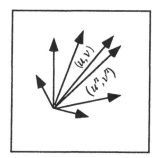

Figure 7. (a) Normal flow vectors measured in different directions. (b) The new flow vector (resulting from object motion and tracking) is due to 1) the error in magnitude, and due to 2) the error in direction.

We use here a simplified model to explain tracking. The change of the local coordinate system during tracking and the fact that the object is coming closer are not considered. Since for the purpose of optical flow estimation the number of tracking steps is small, the error originating from this model is not serious. In a specific application, the algorithm will stop when the computed error is smaller than a given threshold, which will cover model errors.

At each iteration step we are computing an approximation to the difference between the observer's egomotion and the object motion. Considering the possible sources of error we have to show that the approximation error will become zero.

Deviations of the chosen maximum normal flow from the optical flow value are due to the following causes:

- *Deviations covered through the model:*
  The fact that normal flow measurements are computed in a finite number of directions causes an error in direction of up to half the size of the angular separation between normal flow measurements. If measurements in n directions are performed, the maximum error y is bounded by $y < \frac{\pi}{n}$.
- *Deviations coming from simplifications and discrete computations:*
  In the evaluation of flow measurements the parts that are linear and quadratic in x, y, and $Z - Z_0$ are ignored. Furthermore, each measurement in one direction is computed as the average of the normal flow values in a range y of directions. These factors may cause errors in magnitude as well as direction, and a vector different from the closest normal flow vector may be chosen.
- *General errors occuring in normal flow computation:*
  Sensor noise in normal flow measurements and the numerical computation of the derivatives of the image intensity function can influence the magnitude and the direction of the estimated value.

Let v be the magnitude of the actual optical flow. The error sources lead to specifying the error in magnitude, x, as a percentage of the actual value. x_i is the magnitude error in the maximum normal flow measurement at step i and y_i is the the angle between the maximum normal flow vector and the optical flow vector, where $x_i < x$ and $y_i < y$. Therefore the difference between the optical flow and the first measurement of maximum normal flow is given by $diff_1 = \begin{pmatrix} v x_1 \cos y_1 \\ v \sin y_1 \end{pmatrix}$, where the x-axis is aligned with the maximum normal flow vector (see Figure 8). The square of its magnitude is computed as

$$||diff_1||^2 = v^2 x_1^2 \cos^2 y_1 + v^2 \sin^2 y_1$$

The second normal flow vector, if measured from the direction of the maximum normal flow vector derived at the second step, is given by $diff_2 = \begin{pmatrix} ||diff_1|| x_2 \cos y_2 \\ ||diff_1|| \sin y_2 \end{pmatrix}$, and the square of its magnitude is therefore

$$||diff_2||^2 = x_1^2 x_2^2 v^2 \cos^2 y_1 \cos^2 y_2 + x_1^2 v^2 \cos^2 y_1 \sin^2 y_2 + v^2 \sin^2 y_1 \sin^2 y_2 + x_2^2 v^2 \sin^2 y_1 \cos^2 y_2$$

In general, if we denote by $\{a, b\}$ the fact that either a or b has to be chosen, then $||\mathit{diff}_n||^2$ can be expressed as

$$||\mathit{diff}_n||^2 = v^2 \sum_{\text{all permutations}} \prod_{i=1}^{n} \{x_i^2 \cos y_i^2, \sin y_i^2\}$$

Since $x_i < 1$ and $\sin y_i < 1$ it follows that $\prod_i \{x_i^2 \cos y_i^2, \sin y_i^2\}$, and thus the whole term converges to zero. Therefore, we have shown the convergence of the approximation value to the actual optical flow value for the "simplified tracking model."

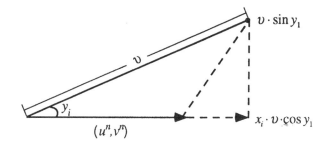

Figure 8. Difference between optical flow vector and maximum normal flow vector.

6.2. ESTIMATING THE FOE USING TRACKING

When tracking continues over time, as an object comes closer and the value of Z becomes smaller, the optical flow value increases. In order to track correctly and adjust to the increasing magnitude of the optical flow value, the tracking parameters have to be changed. From the change of the tracking parameters the change in Z can be derived. If tracking is accomplished by rotation with a certain angular velocity, this means that the change in depth is derived from the angular acceleration. In the sequel we show the relation between image motion and tracking movement. The exact process of tracking is explained for a geometric setting consisting of a camera that is allowed to rotate around two fixed axes: X- and Y-. These axes coincide with the local coordinate system in the image plane at the beginning of the tracking process.

We describe rotation by an angle ϕ around an axis which is given by its directional cosines n_1, n_2, n_3, where $n_1^2 + n_2^2 + n_3^2 = 1$. The transformation of a point P with coordinates (X, Y, Z) before motion and (X', Y', Z') after motion is described through the linear relation

$$\begin{pmatrix} X' \\ Y' \\ Z' \end{pmatrix} = R \begin{pmatrix} X \\ Y \\ Z \end{pmatrix}$$

where the transformation matrix R is of the following form:

$$\begin{pmatrix} n_1^2 + (1 - n_1^2)\cos\phi & n_1 n_2 (1 - \cos\phi) - n_3 \sin\phi & n_1 n_3 (1 - \cos\phi) + n_2 \sin\phi \\ n_1 n_2 (1 - \cos\phi) + n_3 \sin\phi & n_2^2 + (1 - n_2^2)\cos\phi & n_2 n_3 (1 - \cos\phi) - n_1 \sin\phi \\ n_1 n_3 (1 - \cos\phi) - n_2 \sin\phi & n_2 n_3 (1 - \cos\phi) + n_1 \sin\phi & n_3^2 + (1 - n_3^2)\cos\phi \end{pmatrix}$$

$$\equiv \begin{pmatrix} r_1 & r_2 & r_3 \\ r_4 & r_5 & r_6 \\ r_7 & r_8 & r_9 \end{pmatrix}$$

Since the image coordinates (x, y) are related to the 3-D coordinates through $x = Xf/Z$ and $y = Yf/Z$, we get the following equations:

$$x' = \frac{(r_1 x + r_2 y + r_3 f)f}{(r_7 x + r_8 y + r_9 f)}$$

$$y' = \frac{(r_4 x + r_5 y + r_6 f)f}{(r_7 x + r_8 y + r_9 f)}$$

In order to compensate for the image motion (u, v) of the point P_o, which moves from $(0, 0)$ to (u, v) in one time unit, the camera has to be rotated by ϕ, n_1, and n_2, where

$$u = n_2 f \tan\phi$$
$$v = -n_1 f \tan\phi$$

Taking the flow measurements (u, v) at the center of the image at the beginning of the tracking process (time t_1), and assuming that the object doesn't change its distance Z_1 to the camera, we can conclude that during time interval Δt an image flow $(u\Delta t, v\Delta t)$ should be measured. The tracking motion necessary for compensation is given by

$$\frac{Uf}{Z_1} = n_2 \tan\phi.$$

But at time t_2 the object has moved to distance Z_2 and we measure a rotation

$$\frac{Uf}{Z_2} = n_2' \tan\phi'$$

Figure 9 shows the relationship between the 3-D motion and the tracking parameters. Since $Z_2 - Z_1 = W\Delta t$, the change in the reciprocal of the rotation angle is proportional to $\frac{W}{U}$, because

$$\frac{1}{n_2 \tan\phi} - \frac{1}{n_2' \tan\phi'} = \frac{Z_2 - Z_1}{U\Delta t} = \frac{W\Delta t}{U\Delta t}$$

and the FOE $(\frac{U}{W}, \frac{V}{W})$ can be computed as

$$\frac{U}{W} = 1/(\frac{1}{n_2' \tan\phi'} - \frac{1}{n_2 \tan\phi}) = 1/(\frac{1}{n_2' \tan\phi'} - \frac{f}{u\Delta t})$$

and

$$\frac{V}{W} = \qquad\qquad 1/(\frac{1}{-n_1' \tan\phi'} - \frac{f}{v\Delta t}).$$

It remains to be explained how tracking is actually pursued, since we are facing the problem of a constantly changing local coordinate system. The interested reader may consult [19], in which the tracking parameter computation is given.

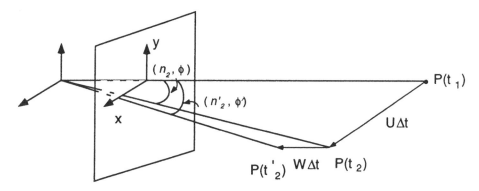

Figure 9. From the optical flow value, which is due only to translation parallel to the image plane, a translation of P from $P(t_1)$ to $P(t_2)$ is inferred, and therefore the tracking parameters (n_2, ϕ) are expected. But actually the point has moved to $P(t_{2'})$ and a rotation described by $(n_{2'}, \phi')$ is measured.

6.3. ESTIMATING THE TIME TO COLLISION

If the values of the motion parameters don't change over the tracking time, the value $\frac{Z}{W}$, the time to collision, expresses the time remaining until the object will hit the infinitely large image plane. A relationship between FOE and time to collision is inherent in the scalar product of the optical flow vector $\overrightarrow{(u, v)}$ with the unit vector in the gradient direction $\overrightarrow{(n_x, n_y)}$:

$$\begin{pmatrix} u \\ v \end{pmatrix} \begin{pmatrix} n_x \\ n_y \end{pmatrix} = ||v^n||$$

For the pixels near the center, for which we ignore the linear and quadratic parts in x, y and $\frac{Z-Z_0}{Z}$ in the relation between optical flow and the 3-D parameters, we get the relationship

$$\frac{Uf}{Z}n_x + \frac{Vf}{Z}n_y = ||v^n||$$

$$\frac{Uf}{W}n_x + \frac{Vf}{W}n_y = ||v^n||\frac{Z}{W}$$

Since we know the FOE, we can compute the time to collision from this relationship by measuring the normal flow value in each of a set of directions and by solving an overdetermined system of linear equations by minimizing the squared error.

7. EGOMOTION ESTIMATION

For a monocular observer undergoing unrestricted rigid motion in the 3-D world we compute the parameters describing this motion. Using a camera-centered coordinate system, the equations relating the velocity (u, v) of an image point to the 3-D velocity and the depth Z of the corresponding scene point are

$$u = \frac{(-Uf + xW)}{Z} + \alpha\frac{xy}{f} - \beta(\frac{x^2}{f} + f) + \gamma y$$

$$v = \frac{(-Vf + yW)}{Z} + \alpha(\frac{y^2}{f} + f) - \beta\frac{xy}{f} - \gamma x$$

The number of motion parameters a monocular observer is able to compute under perspective projection is limited to five: the three rotational parameters and the direction of translation. We therefore introduce coordinates for the direction of translation, $(x_0, y_0) = (Uf/W, Vf/W)$, and rewrite the righthand sides of the above equations as sums of translational and rotational components:

$$u = u_{\text{trans}} + u_{\text{rot}} = (-x_0 + x)\frac{W}{Z} + \alpha\frac{xy}{f} - \beta(\frac{x^2}{f} + f) + \gamma y$$

$$v = v_{\text{trans}} + v_{\text{rot}} = (-y_0 + y)\frac{W}{Z} + \alpha(\frac{y^2}{f} + f) - \beta\frac{xy}{f} - \gamma x$$

Since we can only compute normal flow, the projection of flow on the unit gradient direction (n_x, n_y), only one constraint can be derived at every point. The value u_n of the normal flow vector along the gradient direction is given by

$$u_n = u n_x + v n_y$$

$$u_n = ((-x_0 + x)\frac{W}{Z} + \alpha\frac{xy}{f} - \beta(\frac{x^2}{f} + f) + \gamma y)n_x$$

$$+ ((-y_0 + y)\frac{W}{Z} + \alpha(\frac{y^2}{f} + f) - \beta\frac{xy}{f} - \gamma x)n_y \qquad (5)$$

This above equation should demonstrate the difficulties of motion computation using normal flow. A monocular observer not being able to measure depth is confronted with a motion field of five unknown motion parameters and one scaled depth component (W/Z) at every point. Since there is only one constraint for a single point and since we do not want to make assumptions about depth, there is no straightforward way to compute the motion parameters analytically.

7.1. MOTION FIELD INTERPRETATION

A motion field is composed of a translational and a rotational component. Only the first of these is dependent on distance from the observer. Therefore it seems reasonable to look for a way of determining the motion components by disregarding the depth components. The motion under consideration is rigid. Every point in 3-D moves relative to the observer along a constrained trajectory. The rigidity constraint also imposes restrictions on the motion field in the image plane and these restrictions are reflected in the normal field as well. This is the motivation for investigating geometrical properties inherent in the normal flow field. The motion estimation problem then amounts to resolving the normal flow field into its rotational and translational component.

If the observer undergoes only translational motion, all points in the 3-D scene move along parallel lines. Translational motion viewed under perspective results in a motion field in the image plane, in which every point moves along a line that passes through a vanishing point. This point is the intersection of the image plane with the translational trajectory passing through the nodal point. Its image coordinates are $x = Uf/W$ and $y = Vf/W$; the flow there has value zero. If the sensor is approaching the scene, all the flow vectors emanate from the vanishing point, which is then called the *focus of expansion* (FOE) (Figure 10). Otherwise the vectors point toward it, in which case we speak of the *focus of contraction* (FOC). The direction of every vector is determined by the location of the vanishing point; the lengths of the vectors depend on the 3-D positions of the points in the scene. The vanishing point also constrains the direction of the normal flow vector at every point; it can only be in the half-plane containing the optical flow vector.

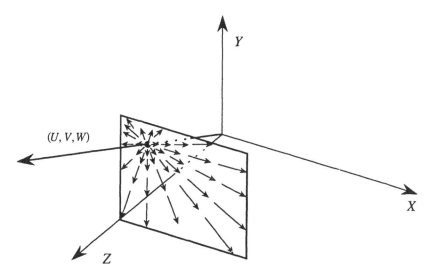

Figure 10. Translational motion viewed under perspective projection: The observer is approaching the scene.

In the case of purely rotational motion, every point in 3-D moves along a circle in a plane perpendicular to the axis of rotation. The perspective image of this circular path is the intersection of the image plane with the cone defined by the circle and the rotation axis (see Figure 11). Depending on the relation between the aperture angle of the cone for a given image point and the angle that the image plane forms with the rotation axis, different second order curves are obtained for the intersection: ellipses, hyperbolas, parabolas, and even circles when the rotation axis and the optical axis coincide. The specific conic sections due to rotational motion are defined by the axis of rotation. The rotation axis given by the two parameters $\left(\frac{\alpha}{\gamma}\right)$ and $\left(\frac{\beta}{\gamma}\right)$ defines a

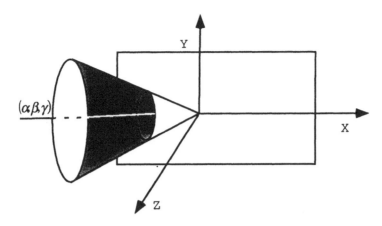

Figure 11. The intersection of the image plane with the cone (determined by the circular path in 3-D and the rotation axis) defines the projection of rotational motion on the image plane.

family $M(\frac{\alpha}{\gamma}, \frac{\beta}{\gamma}; x, y)$ of conic sections:

$$M(\frac{\alpha}{\gamma}, \frac{\beta}{\gamma}; x, y) = (\frac{\alpha^2}{\gamma^2}x^2 + 2xy\frac{\alpha}{\gamma}\frac{\beta}{\gamma} + y^2\frac{\beta^2}{\gamma^2} + 2xf\frac{\alpha}{\gamma} + 2yf\frac{\beta}{\gamma} + f^2)/(x^2 + y^2 + f^2) = C$$

$$\text{with } C \text{ in } [0, \ldots, (1 + \frac{\alpha^2}{\gamma^2} + \frac{\beta^2}{\gamma^2})] \tag{6}$$

8. PROPERTIES OF SELECTED VECTORS

A motion vector consists of a rotational component which can be parameterized by three unknowns and a translational vector which is everywhere directed away from (or toward) a point. However, the estimates we can compute at every point are only projections of the motion vector on the gradient direction. In this section geometrical relations of normal flow vectors in selected directions are investigated. To be more precise, we study the sign of the normal flow in certain directions and the locations of normal flow vectors of the same sign. Vectors which are perpendicular to rotational vector field lines and vectors perpendicular to lines emanating from a point are considered. For these vectors we find that the FOE and the axis of rotation separate the normal flow values in the image according to their sign by a second order curve and a straight line.

The normal flow vector $\vec{u_n}$ is the projection of the optical flow vector $\vec{u}$ on the gradient direction and the value of the normal flow is therefore defined by the scalar product of the optical flow vector and the unit vector in the gradient direction. The flow vector can be decomposed into its translational and rotational components and the right hand side of Equation (5) can be written as a sum of scalar products:

$$u_n = \frac{W}{Z}((-x_0 + x), (-y_0 + y))(n_x, n_y) +$$

$$((\alpha\frac{xy}{f} - \beta(\frac{x^2}{f} + f) + \gamma y), (\alpha(\frac{y^2}{f} + f) - \beta\frac{xy}{f} - \gamma x)(n_x, n_y) \qquad (7)$$

Our goal is to achieve some kind of separation between translation and rotation. Therefore we classify the normal flow vectors according to their direction by defining two kinds of classes which are motivated by the concepts of rotation axis and FOE.

Any possible axis given by an orientation vector (A, B, C), where $A^2 + B^2 + C^2 = 1$, defines an infinite class of cones with axis (A, B, C) and apex at the origin. The image plane gives rise to a set of conic sections, hereafter called vector field lines, or field lines of the axis (A, B, C), or just (A, B, C) field lines. It is worth noting that the (A, B, C) field lines are the lines along which the image points would move if the observer rotated around axis (A, B, C). Normal flow vectors are combined into a single class if they are perpendicular to the vector field lines of the same axis (A, B, C). At a point (x, y) the orientation perpendicular to the vector field lines (A, B, C) is given by a vector $\vec{M} = (M_x, M_y)$:

$$(M_x, M_y) = ((-A(y^2 + f^2) + Bxy + Cxf),$$
$$(Axy - B(x^2 + f^2) + Cyf))$$

and its unit vector $\vec{m} = (m_x, m_y)$ is thus $\vec{m} = \frac{\vec{M}}{\|\vec{M}\|}$. We call the vectors of the class corresponding to the axis (A, B, C) the coaxis vectors (A, B, C). These are the normal flow vectors where the gradient (n_x, n_y) is equal to (m_x, m_y). In order to establish conventions about the vector's orientation, a vector will be said to be of positive orientation if it is pointing in direction (m_x, m_y). Otherwise, if it is pointing in direction $(-m_x, -m_y)$, its orientation will be said to be negative[3] (see Figure 12).

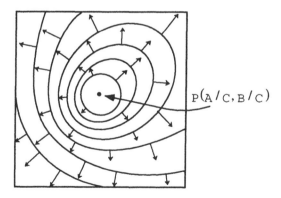

$P(A/C, B/C)$

Figure 12. Field lines corresponding to an axis (A, B, C) and positive coaxis vectors (A, B, C).

Next we evaluate the translational components of the normal flow vectors in the chosen direction. The value t_n of any translational vector component at point (x, y)

---

[3] Obviously, the proposed classification is not based on an equivalence relation, since the intersection between normal flow vectors belonging to different axes is not zero. However, for our purpose this is not of importance.

in direction (n_x, n_y) is given by

$$t_n = ((x - x_0, y - y_0)\frac{W}{Z})\vec{n}$$

Since $\frac{W}{Z}$ is positive in case the observer is approaching the scene, a classification into positive and negative values independent of the distance from the image plane is possible. The translational components of the coaxis vectors (A, B, C) are separated by a second order curve $h(A, B, C, x_0, y_0; x, y)$ given by

$$h(A, B, C, x_0, y_0, ; x, y) = x^2(Cf + By_0) + y^2(Cf + Ax_0) - xy(Ay_0 + Bx_0)$$
$$-xf(Af + Cx_0) - yf(Bf + Cy_0) + f^2(Ax_0 + By_0) \quad (8)$$
$$= 0 \quad (9)$$

Where $h(x, y) > 0$, the normal flow values are positive; where $h(x, y) < 0$, they are negative; and where $h(x, y) = 0$, the normal flow values have value zero. For any selected class of coaxis vectors there exists a curve h which is uniquely defined by the two coordinates x_0, y_0 of the FOE; furthermore it is linear in x_0 and y_0 (see Figure 13a).

The rotational components of the flow vectors are defined only by the three rotational parameters α, β and γ. Along the positive direction of the coaxis vectors the value r_n of the rotational component is

$$r_n = ((\alpha\frac{xy}{f} - \beta(\frac{x^2}{f} + f) + \gamma y), (\alpha(\frac{y^2}{f} + f) - \beta\frac{xy}{f} - \gamma x)(n_x, n_y)$$

The coaxis vectors (A, B, C) and the rotational flow vectors form a right angle for all points on a straight line. Thus considering only the sign of the rotational component along the coaxis vectors (A, B, C) the image plane is separated by a straight line $g(A, B, C, \alpha, \beta, \gamma)$ into two halves containing values of opposite sign, where

$$g(A, B, C, \alpha, \beta, \gamma; x, y) = y(\alpha C - \gamma A) - x(\beta C - \gamma B) + \beta Af - \alpha Bf = 0 \quad (10)$$

Again the sign of $g(x, y)$ at a point (x, y) determines the sign of the coaxis vectors (A, B, C). The straight line is defined by only two parameters which characterize the axis of rotation, namely $\frac{\alpha}{\gamma}$ and $\frac{\beta}{\gamma}$ (see Figure 13b).

In order to investigate constraints for general motion the geometrical relations due to rotation and due to translation have to be combined. A second order curve separating the plane into positive and negative values and a line separating the plane into two half-planes of opposite sign intersect. This splits the plane into areas of only positive coaxis vectors, areas of only negative vectors, and areas in which the rotational and translational flow have opposite signs. In these last areas, no information is derivable without making depth assumptions (Figure 13c).

We thus obtain the following geometrical result for the case of general motion. Any class of coaxis vectors (A,B,C) is separated by a rigid motion into two groups. The FOE (x_0, y_0) and the rotation axis $(\frac{\alpha}{\gamma}, \frac{\beta}{\gamma})$ geometrically define two areas in

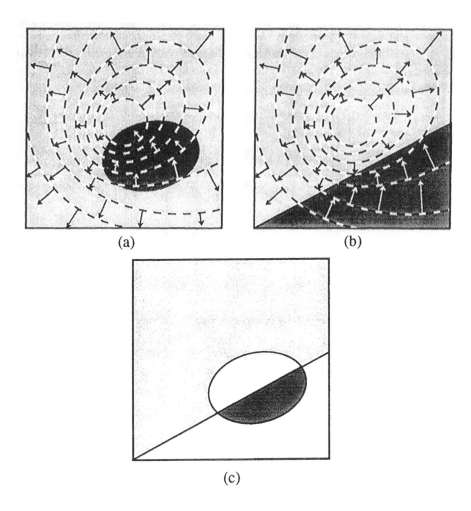

(a)   (b)

(c)

Figure 13. (a) The coaxis vectors (A, B, C) due to translation are negative if they lie within a second-order curve defined by the FOE, and are
positive at all other locations. (b) The coaxis vectors due to rotation
separate the image plane into a half-plane of positive values and a half-
plane of negative values. (c) A general rigid motion defines an area of
positive coaxis vectors and an area of negative coaxis vectors. The rest
of the image plane is not considered.

the plane, one containing positive and one containing negative values. We call this structure on the coaxis vectors the coaxis pattern. It depends on the four parameters x_0, y_0, $\frac{\alpha}{\gamma}$ and $\frac{\beta}{\gamma}$.

For the second kind of classification of the normal flow vectors, namely the one defined as "perpendicular to the lines emanating from a defined point" (see Figure 14), similar patterns are obtained. In this case, the rotational components are separated by a second order curve into positive and negative values and the translational components are separated by a straight line. We call the vectors perpendicular to straight lines passing through a point (r,s) the copoint vectors (r,s).[4]

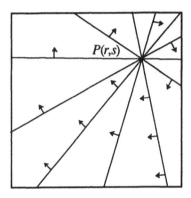

Figure 14. Positive copoint vectors (r,s).

At point (x,y) a copoint vector of unit length in the positive direction is defined as

$$\frac{(-y+s, x-r)}{\sqrt{(x-r)^2 + (y-s)^2}}.$$

The functions which define the curves are given as follows: The straight line $k(r,s,x_0,y_0,x,y)$ separating the translational components is

$$k(r,s,x_0,y_0;x,y) = y(x_0 - r) - x(y_0 - s) - x_0 s + y_0 r = 0 \qquad (11)$$

and the second-order curve $l(r,s,\alpha,\beta,\gamma;x,y)$ separating the rotational components is (similar to $h(A,B,C,x_0,y_0;x,y)$) defined as

$$l(r,s,\alpha,\beta,\gamma;x,y) = -x^2(\beta s + \gamma f) - y^2(\alpha r + \gamma f) + xy(\alpha s + \beta r)$$
$$+ xf(\alpha f + \gamma r) + yf(\beta f + \gamma s) - f^2(\alpha r - \beta s) = 0 \qquad (12)$$

The superposition of translational and rotational values again defines patterns in the plane which consist of a negative and a positive area. These patterns, called copoint patterns, are defined by the same four parameters which characterize the coaxis patterns.

---

[4] The copoint and coaxis vectors are dual to each other.

9. SEARCH FOR MOTION PATTERNS

Utilizing the geometrical constraints developed in the last section, motion estimation for a rigid moving observer will now be addressed through a search technique. The strategy involves checking constraints that a certain solution would impose on the normal flow field and in this way discarding impossible solutions. The search is performed in three steps, where from the first to the third step the constraints become more restrictive, hence the number of possible solutions computed at each step decreases. First a set S_1 of possible solutions for the FOE and axis of rotation is estimated by fitting a small number of patterns to the normal flow field. Two techniques, which use different patterns defined on certain coaxis vectors, are proposed for solving this task. Both fitting processes use the input in a qualitative way, since only the sign of the normal flow is employed. In the second step the third rotational parameter is computed, and the space of solutions is further narrowed to a set S_2. This can be performed by using normal flow vectors that do not contain translation (certain copoint vectors) and approximating the remaining rotational parameter from the given rotational vectors. An alternative approach is to have the active observer change its rotation and compute the third rotational component from the change in the perceived motion patterns. In the second approach loyalty to the exclusively qualitative use of normal flow is maintained. Finally, in the last step all impossible solutions are discarded by checking the validity of the motion parameters at every point.

9.1. FIRST STEP: PATTERN FITTING

The direction of translation and the axis of rotation define patterns on subsets of the normal flow vectors. In the general case these patterns are described by four independent variables and searching for the solution would mean searching in a 4-D parameter space. By concentrating, in an initial search, only on a small number of normal flow vectors, we show how to tackle the problem. Clearly, such a restricted use of data will generally not result in a unique solution, but it allows us to either reduce the dimensionality of the problem ($\alpha\beta\gamma$-algorithm), or to employ motion vectors from all parts of the image plane (ARS-algorithm).

$\alpha\beta\gamma$-algorithm

One way to look at the optical flow vector is to imagine it as a sum of five vectors, each being due to only one of the motion parameters (either one of the two translational or one of the three rotational components). Consequently the value of the normal flow vector at a point is computed as the sum of the five scalar products of these vectors and the unit vector in the gradient direction. The scalar product of two vectors is zero if the vectors are perpendicular to each other. Thus, by selecting normal flow vectors in particular directions, one or more of the motion components vanish.

The coaxis vectors which are dependent on only two of the three rotational parameters correspond to one of the three coordinate axes. These normal vectors and their patterns have special properties.

The coaxis vectors (A, B, C) when the orientation vector (A, B, C) is the Z-axis are perpendicular to circles whose center is the origin of the image plane, and we call them γ-vectors. Similarly, when (A, B, C) is the X- or Y-axis, the (A, B, C) coaxis vectors are called α-vectors and β-vectors and the corresponding field lines are hyperbolas whose major axes are the image plane's x- and y-axes, respectively. Figure 15 depicts these sets of vector field lines and the corresponding γ-, α- and β-vectors in positive orientation.

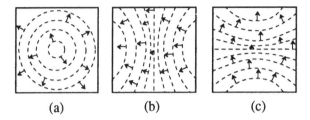

(a)   (b)   (c)

Figure 15. If the (A, B, C) axis is the Z-, X-, or Y-axis, the corresponding vector field lines are circles with center O (a), or hyperbolas whose axes coincide with the coordinate axes of the image plane (b and c). Normal flow vectors perpendicular to these field lines are called γ-, α-, and β-vectors.

The value of the α-, β- and γ- vectors due to rotation only can be described by a one-parameter function. Thus the dimensionality of the corresponding patterns is also reduced by one and the search for these patterns can be limited to a 3-D parameter space. This becomes clear by substituting into Equation (10) for the triple (A,B,C) the orientation vectors of the coordinate axes $((1, 0, 0), (0, 1, 0)$ and $(0, 0, 1))$. The rotational components of the γ-vectors are separated by a line passing through the center, which has equation $y = \frac{\beta}{\alpha}x$. For the rotational components of the α-vectors the line is parallel to the x-axis and is defined by the equation $y = \frac{\beta}{\gamma}f$. The β-vectors are separated by a line parallel to the y-axis having equation $x = \frac{\alpha}{\gamma}f$.

The second-order curves separating the translational components of the α-, β- and γ-vectors are obtained from Equation (9). For the γ-vectors the curve reduces to a circle, which has the FOE and the image center as two diametrically opposite points. Equation (9) reduces to

$$h(0, 0, 1, x_0, y_0, ; x, y) = f(x - \frac{x_0}{2})^2 + f(y - \frac{y_0}{2})^2 - (\frac{x_0 f}{2})^2 + (\frac{y_0 f}{2})^2 = 0$$

The curves separating the α- and β-vectors become hyperbolas of the form

$$h(1, 0, 0, x_0, y_0, ; x, y) = y^2 x_0 - xy y_0 - xf^2 + f^2 x_0 = 0$$

and

$$h(0, 1, 0, x_0, y_0, ; x, y) = x^2 y_0 - xy x_0 - yf^2 + f^2 y_0 = 0$$

Figure 16 shows the α-, β- and γ-vectors for a general rigid motion.

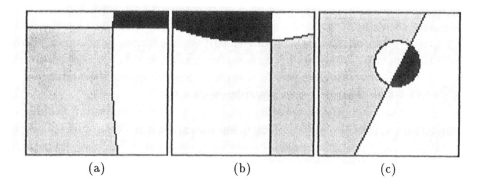

Figure 16. α-, β- and γ-patterns for a general rigid motion.

The algorithm which computes the FOE and the axis of rotation from a given normal flow field by using only the α-, β- and γ-vectors works as follows. With each subset of normal flow vectors is associated a 3-D parameter space that spans the possible locations of the FOE and of a line defined by the quotient of two of the three rotational parameters. A search in the 3-D subspaces is accomplished by checking the patterns that the subspaces' parameter triples define on selected values of the normal flow field. The α-patterns are fitted to the α-vectors, that provides possible solutions for the coordinates of the FOE: x_0, y_0, and the quotient $\frac{\beta}{\alpha}$. Similarly, the fitting of the β- or γ-patterns results in solutions for x_0, y_0 and $\frac{\beta}{\gamma}$ or $\frac{\alpha}{\gamma}$. The objective is to find the four parameters defining the directions of the translational and rotational axes that give rise to three successfully fitted patterns. Therefore the three subspaces' patterns are combined and the parameter quadruples that define possible solution are determined. Since only subsets of the normal flow values are considered in the fitting process, the fitting alone does not uniquely define the motion, but just constitutes a necessary condition. Usually there will be a number of parameter quadruples $\{x_0, y_0, \alpha/\gamma, \beta/\gamma\}$ that are selected as candidate solutions through pattern fitting.

The range of values for the coordinates of the FOE and for $\frac{\beta}{\gamma}$ and $\frac{\alpha}{\gamma}$ is $[-\infty, +\infty]$. If a wide-angle lens or a logarithmic retina [44] is employed, most of the directions representing the FOE lie in a bounded area of the image plane. Alternatively, in order to cover all possible cases, a coordinate transformation on the sphere can be performed, in which case the coordinates are expressed by two angles.

ARS-algorithm (Axis of rotation search algrithm)

For any rigid motion there exists one class of coaxis vectors that does not contain any rotational components. This set is defined by the actual rotation axis $\frac{A}{C} = \frac{\alpha}{\gamma}$ and $\frac{B}{C} = \frac{\beta}{\gamma}$. Coaxis vectors of this kind are due only to translation and the pattern of these vectors is solely defined by the two-parameter second-order curve $h(\alpha, \beta, \gamma, x_0, y_0; x, y)$. There is only one curve separating the positive from the negative values and thus the pattern is defined on the whole image plane. Since $h(\alpha, \beta, \gamma, x_0, y_0; x, y)$ is linear in x_0 and y_0, the problem of finding the FOE from the normal vectors due only to rotation reduces to estimating the linear discriminant function separating two classes of values (labeled positive and negative).

The pattern is due to only two parameters. In order to find the axis of rotation a search in the 2-D parameter space of $\frac{\alpha}{\gamma}$ and $\frac{\beta}{\gamma}$ is performed. For every possible rotation axis the data is checked for linear discrimination. If a second-order curve can be found that separates the positive from the negative values the quadruple $(x_0, y_0, \frac{\alpha}{\gamma}, \frac{\beta}{\gamma})$ will be added to the set of possible solutions.

Concerning the computational aspect of solving the discrimination problem, different algorithms from the pattern recognition literature can be applied. For example, the Ho-Kashyap algorithm decides whether a data set is linearly discriminable and will also find the best discrimination.

9.2. SECOND STEP: COMPUTATION OF COMPLETE ROTATIONAL MOTION

Detranslation

Proper selection of normal flow vectors also enables the elimination of the normal flow's translational components. By choosing as normal flow vectors the copoint vectors defined by the locus of the FOE, this can be achieved. With the location of the FOE the directions of the translational motion components are defined. The optical flow vectors lie on lines passing through the FOE. The normal flow vectors perpendicular to these lines (the copoint vectors (r, s) where $r = x_0$ and $s = y_0$) do not contain translational, but only rotational components. This can be seen from equation (5). If the selected gradient direction at a point (x, y) is $((y_0 - y), (-x_0 + x))$ the scalar product of the translational motion component and a vector in the gradient direction is zero. This technique of eliminating the translational component, in the future referred to as "detranslation," is applied to compute the third rotational component and to further reduce the possible number of solutions.

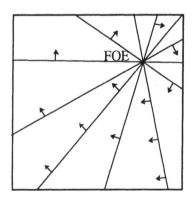

Figure 17. Normal flow vectors perpendicular to lines passing through the FOE are due only to rotation.

For each of the possible solutions computed in the second module the normal flow vectors perpendicular to the lines passing through the FOE have to be tested to see if they are due only to rotation (see Figure 17). This results in solving an overdetermined system of linear equations. Since two of the rotational parameters are already computed, there is only one unknown, the value γ. Every point supplies an equation of the form

$$\gamma = u_n \ /(\frac{\alpha}{\gamma}(\frac{xy}{f}n_x + (\frac{y^2}{f} + f)n_y) - \frac{\beta}{\gamma}((\frac{x^2}{f} + f)n_x + \frac{xy}{f}n_y) + (yn_x - xn_y)) \ (13)$$

Provided the chosen normal flow vectors are due only to rotation, the solution to the overdetermined system gives the γ value. In a practical application a threshold has to be chosen to discriminate between possible and impossible solutions. The value of the residual is used to confirm the presumption that the selected normal flow values are purely rotational. Usually "detranslation" will not result in only one solution, but will provide a set S_2 of possible parameter quintuples.

Alternatively to detranslation a different approach to computing the third rotational component may be taken. It requires the observer to be active in order to acquire, through a controlled motion, additional information about its rotation.

Pattern change through rotation

From one pattern search alone, we can only derive the ratio of the three rotational components. However, if the observer is active it has the capability of changing its rotational velocity. In the image plane such a change will result in the superposition of an additional flow field on the existing one. A pattern search on the new image measurements will provide the new rotation axis. From the change of the rotation axes the complete rotation can then be derived.

The first pattern fitting supplies the two parameters k_1 and l_1, where

$$k_1 = \frac{\alpha_1}{\gamma_1} \text{ and} \tag{14}$$

$$l_1 = \frac{\beta_1}{\gamma_1}. \tag{15}$$

A change of the rotational velocity by $(\alpha^*, \beta^*, \gamma^*)$ will alter the parameters of the rotation axis to k_2 and l_2:

$$k_2 = \frac{\alpha_2}{\gamma_2} = \frac{\alpha_1 + \alpha^*}{\gamma_1 + \gamma^*} \tag{16}$$

$$l_2 = \frac{\beta_2}{\gamma_2} = \frac{\beta_1 + \beta^*}{\gamma_1 + \gamma^*} \tag{17}$$

From (14) and (15) we obtain

$$\gamma_1 = \frac{k_2\gamma^* - \alpha^*}{k_2 - k_1}.$$

Similarly from (16) and (17) we obtain

$$\gamma_1 = \frac{l_2\gamma^* - \beta^*}{l_2 - l_1}$$

In this analysis the change of the local coordinate system between the two measurements is not considered. If the measurements are performed within a small interval of time, such a simplification is legitimate. Concerning the amount of search to be performed, knowledge about the first pattern allows us to restrict the search in the new normal flow field to a small fraction of the complete parameter space. If the additional rotation is performed for a small amount of time only, this will result in a very small change in the location of the FOE. Thus only a tiny spatial neighborhood of the original FOE has to be considered. Furthermore, the parameters of the additional rotation supply information about the direction in which $g(A, B, C, \alpha, \beta, \gamma)$ (the straight line separating the positive from the negative rotational components) will change its slope and intercept. Additional reduction of the search space can be achieved by restricting the change of velocity to only one of the rotational motion parameters.

9.3. THIRD STEP: DEROTATION

The modules described so far considered only subsets of the normal flow vectors. Clearly, after having found possible solutions for the FOE and the axis of rotation, we can test every candidate solution for its correctness by employing any class of coaxis vectors. Since the quadruple $(x_0, y_0, \frac{\alpha}{\gamma}, \frac{\beta}{\gamma})$ defines a pattern on every class of coaxis vectors, we just have to test for the existence of this pattern. However, a pattern in the general case is defined only on parts of the image plane. Thus even by testing every possible class of coaxis vectors not every normal flow vector will be tested.

In order to eliminate all motion parameters which are in contradiction to the given normal flow field, every normal flow vector has to be checked. This check is performed in the "derotation" technique. With every parameter quintuple computed in the second step a possible FOE and a rotation are defined. The three rotational parameters are used to derotate the normal flow vectors by subtracting the rotational component $(u_{\text{rot}}, v_{\text{rot}})$. At every point the flow vector $(u_{\text{der}}, v_{\text{der}})$ is computed:

$$u_{\text{der}} = u_n n_x - u_{\text{rot}} n_x$$
$$v_{\text{der}} = v_n n_y - v_{\text{rot}} n_y \tag{18}$$

If the parameter quintuple defines the correct solution, the remaining normal flow is purely translational. Thus it has to have the property of an emanating motion field. Since the direction of optical flow for a given FOE is known, the possible directions of the normal flow vectors can be determined. The normal flow vector at every point is confined to lie in a half-plane (see Figure 18). The technique checks all points for this property and eliminates solutions that cannot give rise to the given normal flow field.

9.4. THE COMPLETE CAPABILITY

In this section we give a summary of the complete technique in the form of a block diagram. The computation of an observer's egomotion is performed in three steps,

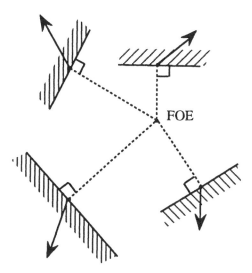

Figure 18. Normal flow vectors due to translation are constrained to lie in half-planes.

where for each of the first two steps two alternative modules can be chosen. The sets of candidate solutions which are determined in the five modules are called S_1, S_2, S_3. To denote single solutions or single parameters, subscripts are used: $S_{1,i}$, $S_{2,i}$, $x_{0,i}$, $y_{0,i}$, and so on. Input to the algorithm is a normal flow field and outputs are all possible solutions for the direction of translation and the rotation which can give rise to this normal flow field.

It can easily be shown that from normal flow fields, in general, 3-D motion cannot be uniquely computed. From two flow fields a common normal flow field can be constructed: Take two different normal flow fields that originate from different scenes and different rigid motions. At every point in the image plane there exist two motion vectors. A normal flow vector, which is defined as the projection of a flow vector, is constrained to lie on a circle. Thus the intersection of the two circles defines the normal flow vector which is due to both motions (Figure 19).

The algorithm determines the complete set of solutions. If for a given normal flow field the algorithm finds more than one solution, then from the normal flow field alone the 3-D motion cannot be determined uniquely. In this case one is obliged to use matching of prominent features to eliminate the incorrect motion parameters.

The computed 3-D motion parameters and the normal flow values supply two linear equations in u and v at every point from which the optical flow field can be determined:

$$\frac{u - u_{\text{rot}}}{v - v_{\text{rot}}} = \frac{u_{\text{trans}}}{v_{\text{trans}}}$$
$$u_n = u n_x + v n_y \tag{19}$$

The unique solution is then derived by checking prominent feature points of the first frame for their existence in the second frame at the locations computed by the optical flow values.

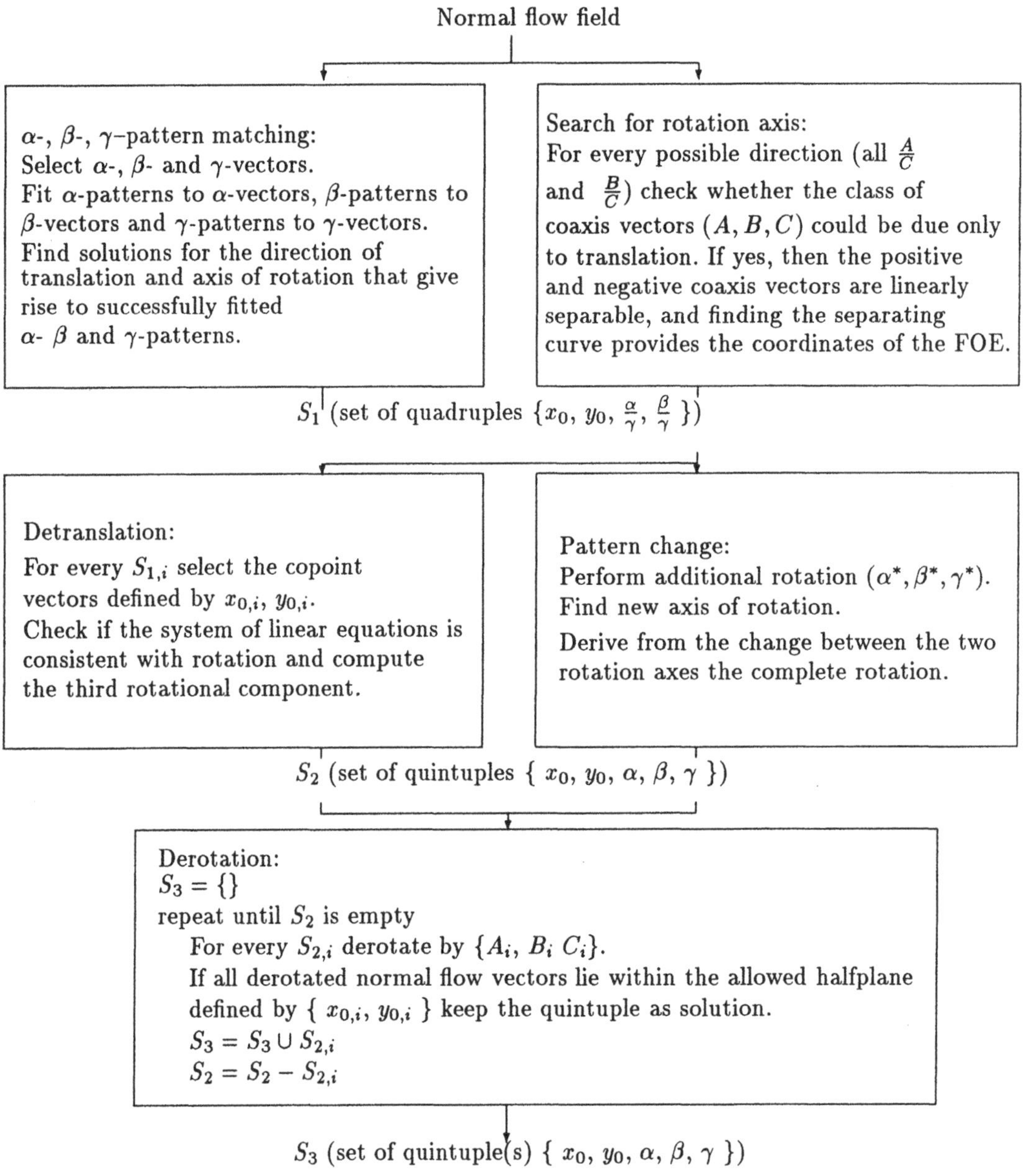

Normal flow field

α-, β-, γ–pattern matching:
Select α-, β- and γ-vectors.
Fit α-patterns to α-vectors, β-patterns to
β-vectors and γ-patterns to γ-vectors.
Find solutions for the direction of
translation and axis of rotation that give
rise to successfully fitted
α- β and γ-patterns.

Search for rotation axis:
For every possible direction (all $\frac{A}{C}$
and $\frac{B}{C}$) check whether the class of
coaxis vectors (A, B, C) could be due only
to translation. If yes, then the positive
and negative coaxis vectors are linearly
separable, and finding the separating
curve provides the coordinates of the FOE.

S_1 (set of quadruples $\{x_0, y_0, \frac{\alpha}{\gamma}, \frac{\beta}{\gamma}\}$)

Detranslation:
For every $S_{1,i}$ select the copoint
vectors defined by $x_{0,i}, y_{0,i}$.
Check if the system of linear equations is
consistent with rotation and compute
the third rotational component.

Pattern change:
Perform additional rotation $(\alpha^*, \beta^*, \gamma^*)$.
Find new axis of rotation.
Derive from the change between the two
rotation axes the complete rotation.

S_2 (set of quintuples $\{x_0, y_0, \alpha, \beta, \gamma\}$)

Derotation:
$S_3 = \{\}$
repeat until S_2 is empty
    For every $S_{2,i}$ derotate by $\{A_i, B_i C_i\}$.
    If all derotated normal flow vectors lie within the allowed halfplane
    defined by $\{x_{0,i}, y_{0,i}\}$ keep the quintuple as solution.
    $S_3 = S_3 \cup S_{2,i}$
    $S_2 = S_2 - S_{2,i}$

S_3 (set of quintuple(s) $\{x_0, y_0, \alpha, \beta, \gamma\}$)

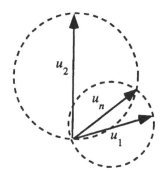

Figure 19. The intersection of two circles defines the possible location of the normal flow vector which corresponds to two different optical flow vectors.

9.5. RESTRICTED MOTION CAPABILITIES

In the previous sections we showed how to compute an observer's 3-D motion in the most general case, i.e., if the motion conists of three translational and three rotational components. In many practical applications, however, the observer has only restricted motion capabilities. For our motion decoding strategy a limited degree of freedom in the 3-D motion will result in a reduction of the parameter space in which the search is performed. Here we will discuss algorithms for two of the most common limitations: the case of an observer moving with only translational parameters and the case of an observer that cannot rotate around the Z-axis.

For the case of purely translational motion, techniques that only employ normal flow measurements have previously been proposed by Horn and Weldon [23] and Negahdaripour [36]. These authors make use of the the the fact that the scaled depth $\frac{W}{Z}$ is positive for all points in the image plane if the observer is approaching the scene. Therefore, every normal flow measurement constrains the location of the FOE; it has to be in the half-plane (or hemisphere in case of spherical projection) which is on the opposite side of the graylevel edge from the normal flow vector. Algebraically speaking, every normal flow measurement supplies an inequality; thus methods like linear programming or perceptron learning were suggested as algorithmic strategies. Here, however, we discuss an algorithm which is based on constraints different from those used by the above authors.

If the observer is moving only translationally, there won't be any constraints due to rotation on the patterns. For both the coaxis and the copoint vectors, this means that only one curve separates the positive from the negative values. The coaxis vectors are separated by the second-order curve $g(A, B, C, \alpha, \beta, \gamma)$ and the copoint vectors by the straight line $l(r, s, \alpha, \beta, \gamma)$. Both curves are linear in the two unknowns x_0 and y_0. Thus finding the FOE is a problem of determining the linear discriminant function which separates the positive from the negative values. Linear discrimination can be solved using iterative methods, such as the perceptron algorithm [40, 17], for which convergence to a correct solution is guaranteed.

For a purely translational flow field any class of coaxis vectors (A,B,C) and copoint vectors (r,s) is linearly separable. The larger the number of normal flow

vectors in the class, the more accurately the discrimination function and thus the
FOE can be determined. If, in a normal flow field, there does not exist any direction
with a large enough number of vectors, we can compute the discriminant functions
for several classes of coaxis vectors and take the average of the computed parameters
as the final FOE.

The most common motion restriction we are dealing with in practical applications
is the case of an observer with only two rotational degrees of freedom. One can
consider the eyes of mammals to obtain an example.[5]

In such a case motion estimation through pattern fitting becomes much easier.
The fact that the axis of rotation is defined by only one parameter $(\frac{\alpha}{\beta})$ affects our
motion estimation technique in the two modules of the first step.

If the $\alpha\beta\gamma$-algorithm in employed there does not exist a line g due to rotation
for the α- and β-patterns because γ is zero. Depending on the sign of α or β all
normal flow vectors have either positive or negative rotational components. The
pattern that has to be located for these cases is an area covered by a hyperbola.
This means that the search problem is 3-D for the γ-patterns, but only 2-D for the
α- and β-patterns.

On the other hand, if pattern fitting is performed through a search for the rotation axis, only the 1-D space spanning the possible values for $\frac{\alpha}{\beta}$ needs to be considered. After having found candidate solutions for the axis of rotation and the FOE,
the algorithm proceeds as described in the general case.

10. Active Pattern Techniques

In this section we give two examples of the applicability of the global geometrical constraints to navigational tasks for an active observer. We first show how the
egomotion estimation problem becomes easier if additional information is obtained
through tracking. Then we discuss a strategy for bringing the FOE to the center of
the image plane. This is achieved by having the observer associate a pattern in the
image plane with the motion it wants to obtain. The observer iteratively changes
its motion parameters, where the change is derived from measurements of the current pattern. In this way the observer attains its goal without going through the
intermediate computation of the parameters describing its motion.

10.1. The tracking constraint

Assume that an active observer in rigid motion is tracking, as before (Section 6.2.),
an environmental point whose image (x, y) lies at the center of the visual field
$((x, y) = (0, 0))$. Assume also that during a small time interval $[t_1, t_2]$ the motion
of the observer remains constant and that during this time the camera, in order to
correctly track, rotates around its x- and y-axes with rotational velocities $\omega_x(t), \omega_y(t)$
respectively, with $t \in [t_1, t_2]$. The tracking rotation adds to the existing flow field

---

[5] Actually the human eye can be rotated around the Z-axis by a small amount (a motion referred
to as cyclotorsion [37]).

(u, v) a rotational flow field (u_{tr}, v_{tr}), where

$$u = \frac{-Uf + xW}{Z} + \frac{\alpha xy}{f} - \beta\left(\frac{x^2}{f} + f\right) + \gamma y$$

$$v = \frac{-Vf + yW}{Z} + \alpha\left(\frac{y^2}{f} + f\right) - \beta\frac{xy}{f} - \gamma x$$

$$u_{tr} = \omega_x\frac{xy}{f} - \omega_y\left(\frac{x^2}{f} + f\right)$$
$$v_{tr} = \omega_x\left(\frac{y^2}{f} + f\right) - \omega_y\frac{xy}{f}.$$

Here ω_x, ω_y are the tracking velocities at the time of the observation, and Z is the depth of the tracked point.

As before, if tracking rotation is represented by an angle ϕ around a rotation axis $(n_1, n_2, 0)$ with directional cosines n_1, n_2, then the introduced flow (u_{tr}, v_{tr}) is given by

$$u_{tr} = n_2 f \tan\phi$$
$$v_{tr} = -n_1 f \tan\phi$$

Since the camera is continuously tracking the point at the origin, at any time $t \in [t_1, t_2]$ the introduced tracking motion compensates for the existing flow there, i.e.

$$n_{2_t} f \tan\phi_t = \frac{Uf}{Z_t} + \beta f$$
$$n_{1_t} f \tan\phi_t = -\frac{Vf}{Z_t} + \alpha f$$

with the subscript t denoting the time of observation. Writing the above two constraints at times t_1 and t_2 we have

$$n_{2_{t_1}} f \tan\phi_{t_1} = \frac{Uf}{Z_{t_1}} + \beta f \tag{20}$$

$$n_{1_{t_1}} f \tan\phi_{t_1} = -\frac{Vf}{Z_{t_1}} + \alpha f \tag{21}$$

$$n_{2_{t_2}} f \tan\phi_{t_2} = \frac{Uf}{Z_{t_2}} + \beta f \tag{22}$$

$$n_{1_{t_2}} f \tan\phi_{t_2} = -\frac{Vf}{Z_{t_2}} + \alpha f \tag{23}$$

Subtracting (22) from (20) and (23) from (21), we obtain:

$$f(n_{2_{t_1}} \tan\phi_{t_1} - n_{2_{t_2}} \tan\phi_{t_2}) = Uf\left[\frac{1}{Z_{t_1}} - \frac{1}{Z_{t_2}}\right]$$
$$f(n_{1_{t_1}} \tan\phi_{t_1} - n_{1_{t_2}} \tan\phi_{t_2}) = -Vf\left[\frac{1}{Z_{t_1}} - \frac{1}{Z_{t_2}}\right]$$

or by dividing,

$$\frac{V}{U} = \frac{n_{1_{t_2}} \tan\phi_{t_2} - n_{1_{t_1}} \tan\phi_{t_1}}{n_{2_{t_1}} \tan\phi_{t_1} - n_{2_{t_2}} \tan\phi_{t_2}}$$

In the sequel we denote the known quantity $\frac{n_{1_{t_2}} \tan\phi_{t_2} - n_{1_{t_1}} \tan\phi_{t_1}}{n_{2_{t_1}} \tan\phi_{t_1} - n_{2_{t_2}} \tan\phi_{t_2}}$, which is defined by the ratio of the tracking accelerations in the vertical and horizontal directions, by T. If $(x_0, y_0) = \left(\frac{Uf}{W}, \frac{Vf}{W}\right)$ is the FOE, the above Equation becomes $\frac{y_0}{x_0} = \frac{V}{U} = T$, which is a linear constraint on the FOE. It restricts the location of the FOE to a straight line passing through the origin of the image coordinate system with slope T.

Furthermore, we obtain a constraint on the rotational motion. Tracking adds a rotational flow field to the existing one. Let us call the composited rotational parameters A and B, where $A = \alpha + \omega_x$ and $B = \beta + \omega_y$. From Equations (20) and (21) at the origin we have

$$\frac{n_{1t_1} f \tan \phi_{t_1} - \alpha f}{n_{2t_1} f \tan \phi_{t_1} - \beta f} = -\frac{V}{U}$$

Since at the center $n_{1t_1} f \tan \phi_{t_1}$ is equal to $-\omega_x f$ and $n_{2t_1} f \tan \phi_{t_1}$ is equal to $-\omega_y f$, we obtain

$$\frac{\omega_x + \alpha}{\omega_y + \beta} = \frac{A}{B} = -\frac{V}{U} = -\frac{y_0}{x_0} = -T$$

or $\frac{B}{A} = -T^{-1}$ and $\frac{y_0}{x_0} = T$.

In other words, tracking provides not only the line $\frac{y_0}{x_0} = T$ on which the FOE lies, but also defines the ratio of the two rotational parameters $\left(\frac{B}{A}\right)$ (see Figure 20).

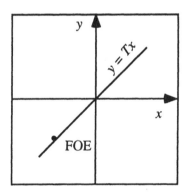

Figure 20. Fixation constrains the FOE to lie on the line $y = Tx$ and provides the value for the ratio $\frac{\beta + \omega_y}{\alpha + \omega_x} = -T^{-1}$.

When analyzing the motion field composed of the original motion and the tracking motion, these two constraints can be directly employed to reduce the dimensionality of the search for the γ-pattern. From the original three unknowns two are supplied by the tracking constraint. The line due to rotation ($y = \frac{B}{A}$) and the line through the center on which the FOE lies are known. Thus only the diameter of the circle which defines the FOE has to be found. Locating the pattern becomes a 1-D search problem.

After having found candidate solutions for the FOE and $\frac{A}{B}$, the two remaining rotational parameters can be found from the copoint vectors defined by the possible FOE's. As in the detranslation-algorithm, for every (x_{0_i}, y_{0_i}) the copoint vectors (x_{0_i}, y_{0_i}) have to be tested to see if they are due only to rotation. This results in solving an overdetermined system of linear equations, now in two unknowns. By considering all normal flow vectors $\vec{u}_{n_i} = u_{n_i}(n_{x_i}, n_{y_i})$, $i = 1, \ldots, k$, perpendicular to the lines passing through (x_{0_i}, y_{0_i}), we obtain

$$u_{n_i} = \left(A\frac{xy}{f} - B\left(\frac{x^2}{f} + f\right) + Cy \right) n_{x_i} + \left(A\left(\frac{y^2}{f} + f\right) - B\frac{xy}{f} - Cx \right) n_{y_i}$$

and since $\frac{A}{B} = -T$, we have

$$u_{n_i} = \left(-B\left(\frac{Txy}{f} + \frac{x^2}{f} + f\right) + Cy \right) n_{x_i} - \left(BT\left(\frac{y^2}{f} + f + \frac{xy}{f}\right) + Cx \right) n_{y_i} \quad i = 1, \ldots, k.$$

DSo, if the above k linear equations in the two unknowns B, C are consistent, we have found a possible FOE $((x_{0_i}, y_{0_i}))$ and we have computed its corresponding rotation. As a last step, in order to eliminate impossible solutions, derotation, as described in the general case, is performed.

10.2. SERVOING THE HEADING DIRECTION

The observer wants to translate in the direction toward which it looks. Stated in terms of motion parameters, this means that translation is along the Z-axis, and the FOE is thus to be found at the center of the image coordinate system. One possibility for solving this problem is by computing the motion parameters and changing them in such a way that $\frac{U}{W}$ and $\frac{V}{W}$ become zero. Another way to accomplish this task is to iteratively change the motion parameters through rotation, where the change in rotation is obtained by checking necessary requirements on the pattern of the current image. We will explain here the idea behind this approach.

The task can be solved by employing only the α- and β-patterns. As can be seen from Section 9.1., the hyperbola separating the positive from the negative translational components of the α-vectors is given by $h(1, 0, 0, x_0, y_0, ; x, y) = y^2 x_0 - xy y_0 - xf^2 + f^2 x_0 = 0$

This curve passes through the point (x_0, y_0) and the point $(x_0, 0)$. The part of the curve for which the absolute value of the x-coordinate is is smaller than $|x_0|$ has a y-coordinate between zero and y_0 ($0 < y < y_0$); elsewhere the absolute value of x is larger than $|x_0|$. Figure 21 depicts two different α-hyperbolas and the corresponding FOE's.

If the observer is approaching the scene, i.e., if there exists an FOE, then the area on the left side of a large enough image plane will contain positive values and the area on the right side will contain negative values. If the FOE coincides with the center of the coordinate system, the hyperbola degenerates to the y-axis.

Symmetrically, the β-vectors are separated by the hyperbola $h(0, 1, 0, x_0, y_0, ; x, y) = x^2 y_0 - xy x_0 - yf^2 + f^2 y_0 = 0$, which passes through the two points (x_0, y_0) and $(0, y_0)$. The absolute value of the y-coordinate is smaller than $|y_0|$ for all points with x between 0 and x_0 and larger otherwise. The hyperbola coincides with the x-axis if the FOE is the image center.

The lines separating the rotational components in the α- and β-patterns are defined by the equations $y = \frac{\beta \cdot f}{\gamma}$ and $x = \frac{\alpha \cdot f}{\gamma}$. If γ is small in relation to α and

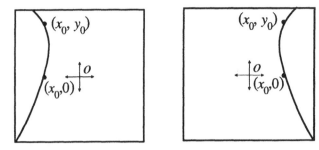

Figure 21. Possible α-hyperbolas.

β or even zero, the line will be found outside the image plane and the rotational contributions to the α- and β-vectors will be either all positive or all negative.

For the α-pattern this means that if we add a large enough positive rotation around the Y-axis, all α-vectors will have positive rotational values. On the other hand, since during the rotation the local coordinate system changes, the x-coordinate of the FOE will become larger (move to right in the image plane). The translational component of the pattern, which corresponds to the motion along the Z-axis, consists of a positive left half-plane and a negative right half-plane (see Figure 22a,b).

The translational components of the β-vectors, when the FOE is at the center, are positive in the lower half-plane and negative in the upper half-plane. A rotation with a large enough negative α-component causes all rotational components of the β-vectors to be positive and a positive β causes a negative rotational contribution (see Figure 22c,d). In order to bring the FOE to the center, the observer pursues the following strategy. It starts by changing its motion by a high positive rotation around the Y-axis and a negative rotation around the X-axis. In this way it adds a purely positive rotational field and at the same time changes the location of the FOE. This change occurs not because the actual direction of translation changes, but due to the fact that the FOE takes on a new value in a new local coordinate system. The observer continues rotating and continuously makes measurements. When the right half-plane of the α-pattern and the lower half-plane of the β-pattern become completely positive, it reverses its rotational components. It changes to a negative rotation around the Y-axis and a positive rotation around the X-axis, and thus makes the rotational contributions to all the investigated coaxis vectors negative. The rotation is performed until the left half-plane of the α-vectors and the upper half-plane of the β-vectors become negative. The final goal is to have the right and the lower half-plane positive at one step, and the left and the upper half-plane negative at the next step, where the camera should be looking at both measurements in the same direction. This means that compensation for the additional rotation has to be considered. If this is achieved, we have brought the FOE to the center of the coordinate system. Clearly the changes cannot be performed abruptly, but a smart control strategy has to developed to cope with the inertia of the system.

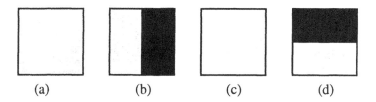

Figure 22. Rotational (a, c) and translational (b, d) patterns to be obtained if positive rotation around the Y-axis and negative rotation around the X-axis is added.

11. EXPERIMENTS

The technique for computing object motion was tested on synthetic imagery by using the graphics package Swivel. In this way object motion as well as camera rotation were simulated. In order to analyze the robustness of the method, the accuracy of the normal flow values at the centers of the images was evaluated. At every point v_{act}, the projection of the known optical flow value on the gradient direction computed there, was determined. The error (err) in the normal flow values was defined as the standardized difference between v_{act} and the normal flow value, v_{meas} ($err = (v_{act} - v_{meas})/v_{act}\%$). In this way an average error of 76.14% and a standard deviation of 179.64% was computed for the motion sequence at the beginning of the tracking process. This constitutes a large error and is comparable to the errors appearing in noisy real imagery.

The object displayed in Figure 23 moves in the direction $U/W = 4$ and $V/W = 2$, with an image motion at its center of $u = 0.004$ and $v = 0.002$ focal units; It was tracked over a sequence of 100 images. As regards the implementational details, normal flow measurements were computed in ten directions in a 9×9 pixel area at the center of the image. When testing the first module, in which parallel translation is estimated, a threshold of 0.0002 focal units was used. The method converged very quickly, usually after two to three iterations. Rotation of increasing magnitude was added to the object motion, and it turned out that the algorithm converged for this set-up even for relatively large rotations. (The object was 25 units away from the camera and moved with a translational velocity of $U = 0.1$, $V = 0.05$, $W = 0.025$ units per unit time and the method converged for rotations of up to 0.3° per time unit around the x-, y- and z-axes.) Some graphical representations are given in the following figures. Figure 24 shows, for the case of no rotation, the three normal flow fields that were computed in the the 9×9 pixel area, before convergence was achieved. In Figure 25 two maximum normal flow vector sequences are displayed ((a) for no rotation, (b) for rotation $\omega_x = 0.1°$, $\omega_z = 0.1°$). Using the estimates of parallel translation from this module and continuing the tracking over 100 steps resulted in FOE values having less than 15% error (e.g., for the case of no rotation an FOE of $U/W = 4.21$ and $V/W = 1.79$ was computed). These experiments demonstrate that the technique for computing object motion can tolerate a large amount of noise in the input (normal flow). In particular, they show that tracking can be successfully accomplished using only normal flow under noisy conditions and that tracking acceleration can be employed for robust parameter estimation.

Figure 23. First image in the sequence used for tracking.

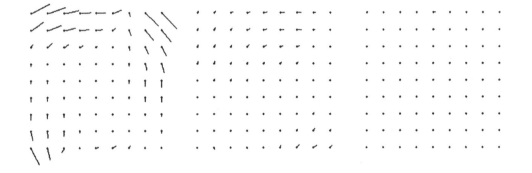

Figure 24. Normal flow fields for a tracking sequence.

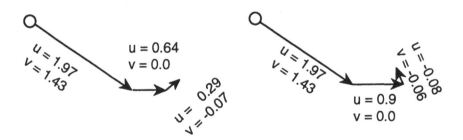

Figure 25. Maximum normal flow vectors for (a) no rotation and (b) rotation $\omega_x = 0.1°/\Delta t$, $\omega_z = 0.1°/\Delta t$.

In a second series of experiments four modules of the general egomotion recovery strategy were tested: α-, β-, γ- pattern matching, search for rotation axis, detranslation and derotation. In the implementation of these modules the following approach was taken. The elimination of impossible parameters from the space of solutions involves discrimination on the basis of quantitative values. This was implemented in the following way. Normal flow values in certain directions are selected if they are within a tolerance interval of 10°. This relatively large degree of freedom will of course introduce some error, but there is a trade-off between accuracy and the amount of data used by the technique. In the pattern fitting and the derotation modules counting is applied to discriminate between possible and impossible solutions. The quality of the fit, the "success rate," is measured by the number of values with correct signs normalized by the total number of selected values. The amount of rotation in the derotation module is computed through simple linear least squares minimization and the discrimination between accepted and rejected motion parameters is based on the value of the residual.

In the pattern fitting and derotation modules no quantitative use of values is made, since only the sign of the normal flow is considered. The limited use of data makes the modules very robust, and the correct solutions are usually found even in the presence of high amounts of noise. To give some quantitative justification of this we define the error in the normal flow at a point as a percentage of the correct vector's length. Since the sign of the vector is not affected as long as the error does not exceed the correct vector in value, "pattern fitting" will find the correct solution in cases of up to 100% error.

Several experiments have been performed on synthetic data. For different 3-D motion parameters normal flow fields were generated; the depth value (in an interval) and the gradient direction were chosen randomly. In all experiments on noiseless data the correct solution was found as the best one. Figure 26 shows the optical flow field and the normal flow field for one of the generated data sets. The image size was 100 × 100, the FOE was at $(-5, +30)$ and the ratio of the rotational components was $\alpha : \beta : \gamma = 10 : 11 : 150$. In Figure 27 the fitting of the circle and the hyperbolas to the α- β- and γ-vectors and the coaxis pattern (α, β, γ) is displayed. Points with positive normal flow values are rendered in a light color and points with negative values are dark. Perturbation of the normal flow vectors' lengths by up to 50% did not prevent the method from finding the correct solution.

As an example of a real scene, the NASA–Ames sequence[6] was chosen. The camera undergoes only translational motion, and different amounts of rotation were added. For all points at which translational motion can be found the rotational normal flow is computed, and the new position of each pixel is evaluated. The "rotated" image is then generated by computing the new grey levels through bilinear interpolation. The images were convolved with a Gaussian of kernel size 5 × 5 and standard deviation $\sigma = 1.4$. The normal flow was computed by using 3 × 3 Sobel operators to estimate the spatial derivatives in the x- and y-directions and by subtracting the 3 × 3 box-filtered values of consecutive images to estimate the temporal derivatives. When adding rotational normal flow on the order of a third to three times the amount of translational flow, the exact solution was always found among the best fitted parameter sets. In Figure 28 the computed normal flow vectors and the fitting of the α- β- and γ-patterns for one of the "rotated" images are shown.

---

[6] This is a calibrated motion sequence made public for the Workshop on Visual Motion, 1991.

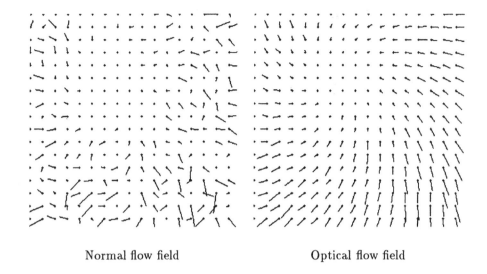

Normal flow field   Optical flow field

Figure 26. Flow fields of synthetic data.

Areas of negative normal flow vectors are marked by horizontal lines and areas of positive values by vertical lines. The ground truth for the FOE is $(-5, -8)$, the focal length is 599 pixels, and the rotation between the two image frames is $\alpha = 0.0006$, $\beta = 0.0006$, and $\gamma = 0.004$. The algorithm computed the solution exactly.

12. CONCLUSIONS

The realization that vision is not a cognitive modality which exists in isolation, but is part of a larger system in interaction with its environment, opens new avenues for the study of problems involving visual processing.

To begin with, from a mathematical point of view, as has been shown throughout this chapter, activities of the observer introduce additional constraints which reduce the dimensionality of the problem space.

More important, the problems that are relevant to an observer/actor are different in nature [2] from the problems defined in passive, reconstructive vision [33]. We elaborated this viewpoint for the problem of motion perception, which in the past was studied under the framework of the general structure-from-motion module. Consequently, egomotion perception and 3-D-object motion perception were considered to be the same problem, whereas in this chapter these two problems are studied as perceptually different processes.

These ideas translate into a philosophy for building vision systems, which calls for a synthetic approach [25]. This means that we should first develop basic capabilities and then equip the system with more and more memory and study capabilities of increasing complexity. The viewpoint taken in this chapter is that active vision also means robust vision. Two basic capabilities (egomotion estimation and the estimation of translational object motion) have been developed in a robust way. These two capabilities can form a basis of a system on which other capabilities can

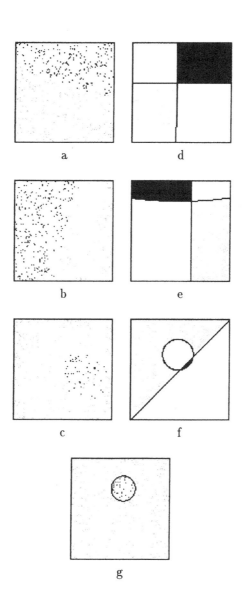

Figure 27. (a), (b), (c): Positive and negative α-, β- and γ-vectors. (d), (e), (f) Fitting of α-, β and γ-patterns. (g): Separation of coaxis pattern (α, β, γ).

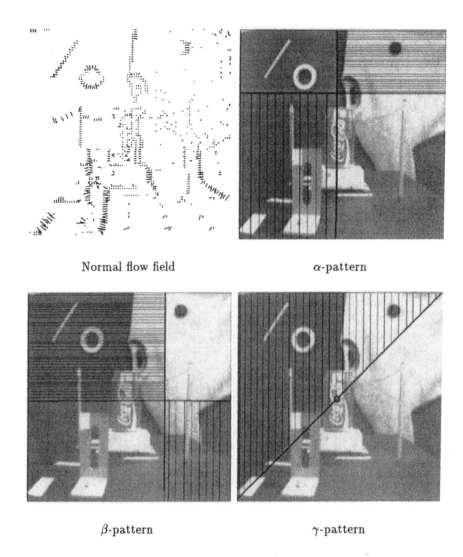

Figure 28. Real scene: Normal flow field and fitting of α-, β- and γ-patterns.

be developed. These capabilities include independent motion detection by a moving observer, landing or docking, target pursuit, and various manipulation tasks.

To summarize the technical results of this chapter, the problem of motion recovery has usually been treated by using as input local image motion, with the published algorithms utilizing the geometric constraint relating 2-D local image motion (optical flow, correspondence, derivatives of the image flow) to 3-D motion and structure. Since it has proved very difficult to achieve accurate input (local image motion), a lot of effort has been devoted to the development of robust techniques. In this chapter a new approach to the problem of egomotion estimation is taken, which is based on constraints of global nature. It has been shown that normal flow measurements form global patterns in the image plane. The positions of these patterns are related to the three dimensional motion parameters. By locating some of these patterns, which depend on only subsets of the motion parameters, using a simple search technique, the 3-D motion parameters are found. The proposed algorithmic procedure is very robust, since it is not affected by small perturbations in the local image measurements (normal flow). As a matter of fact, since only the signs of the image measurements are employed, the direction of translation and the axis of rotation can be estimated in the presence of up to 100% error in the image measurements. If the observer is active and supplies additional information, the general constraints can be exploited to reduce the dimensionality of the parameter space, in which the search is performed. Thus various navigational problems can be solved with only a small computational effort. If, for example, the observer possesses tracking and fixation capabilities, the egomotion estimation problem is reduced in dimension from five to one.

In contrast to egomotion estimation where a camera-centered coordinate system is used, for object motion estimation an object-centered coordinate system is more appropriate. The main difference between the two techniques described in the chapter lies in the fact that egomotion estimation is based on global data while object motion is computed from local data. It has been argued by psychologists that biological organisms use tracking in the motion estimation process. In this chapter the advantages of tracking have been exploited to solve, for a monocular observer, the problems of computing a moving object's translational direction and time to collision. A complete solution to this problem was presented by showing how tracking can be performed when only normal flow measurements are used and how these parameters are of use in the 3-D motion parameter decoding strategy.

The theoretical analysis and the experiments described in this chapter demonstrate that the algorithms introduced here have the potential of being implemented in real hardware active vision systems, such as the ones described in [11, 37].

REFERENCES

1. G. Adiv, "Determining 3-D motion and structure from optical flow generated by several moving objects," *IEEE Trans. PAMI* **7**, 1985, 384–401.

2. J.Y. Aloimonos, "Purposive and qualitative active vision," In *Proc. Image Understanding Workshop*, 1990, 816–828.

3. J. Aloimonos and C. Brown, "Direct processing of curvilinear sensor motion from a sequence of perspective images," In *Proc. Workshop on Computer Vision: Representation and Control*, 1984, 72–77.

4. J. Aloimonos and C.M.Brown, "On the kinetic depth effect," *Biological Cybernetics* **60**, 1989, 445–455.

5. J. Aloimonos, I. Weiss, and A. Bandopadhay, "Active vision," *Int'l. J. Computer Vision* **2**, 1988, 333–356.

6. P. Anandan and R. Weiss, "Introducing a smoothness constraint in a matching approach for the computation of optical flow fields," In *Proc. Workshop on Computer Vision: Representation and Control*, 1985, 186–194.

7. R. Bajcsy, "Active perception vs. passive perception," In *Proc. IEEE Workshop on Computer Vision*, 1985, 55–59.

8. R. Bajcsy, "Active perception," *Proc. IEEE* **76**, 1988, 996–1005.

9. R. Bajcsy and M. Campos, "Active and exploratory perception," *CVGIP: Image Understanding* **56**, Special Issue on Purposive, Qualitative, Active Vision, Y. Aloimonos (Ed.), 1992, 31–40.

10. D. Ballard, "Animate vision," *Artificial Intelligence* **48**, 1991, 57–86.

11. D. Ballard and C. Brown, "Principles of animate vision," *CVGIP: Image Understanding* **56**, Special Issue on Purposive, Qualitative, Active Vision, Y. Aloimonos (Ed.), 1992, 3–21.

12. A. Bandopadhay and D.H. Ballard, "Egomotion perception using visual tracking," *Computational Intelligence* **7**, 1991, 39–47.

13. S. Barnard and W. Thompson, "Disparity analysis of images," *IEEE Trans. PAMI* **2**, 1980, 333–340.

14. F. Bergholm, "Motion from flow along contours: A note on robustness and ambiguous cases," *Int'l. J. Computer Vision* **3**, 1988, 395–415.

15. A. Bruss and B.K.P. Horn, "Passive navigation," *CVGIP* **21**, 1983, 3–20.

16. P. Burt, J. Bergen, R. Kolczynski, W. Lee, A. Leung, J. Lubin, and H. Shvaytser, "Object tracking with a moving camera," In *Proc. IEEE Image Understanding Workshop*, 1989, 2–12.

17. R. Duda and P. Hart, *Pattern Classification and Scene Analysis*, Wiley, New York, 1962.

18. O. Faugeras, *Three Dimensional Computer Vision*, MIT Press, Cambridge, MA, 1992.

19. C. Fermüller and Y. Aloimonos, "Tracking facilitates 3-D motion estimation," *Biological Cybernetics* **67**, 1992, 259–268.

20. E. Hildreth, *The Measurement of Visual Motion*, MIT Press, Cambridge, MA, 1983.

21. B.K.P. Horn, "Motion fields are hardly ever ambiguous," *Int'l. J. Computer Vision* **1**, 1987, 259–274.

22. B.K.P. Horn, "Relative Orientation," MIT AI Memo 94, 1988.

23. B.K.P. Horn and J. Weldon, "Computationally efficient methods for recovering translational motion," In *Proc. Int'l. Conf. on Computer Vision*, 1987, 2 –11.

24. B.K.P. Horn and B. Schunck, "Determining optical flow," *Artificial Intelligence* **17**, 1981, 185–203.

25. G. Horridge, "The evolution of visual processing and the construction of seeing systems," *Proc. Royal Society London B* **230**, 1987, 279–292.

26. G. Horridge, "Evolution of visual processing," In J. Cronly-Dillon and R. Gregory (Eds.), *Vision and Visual Dysfunction*, Macmillan, New York, 1991.

27. J. Koenderink, "Optic flow," *Vision Research* **26**, 1986, 161–180.

28. J. Koenderink and A. van Doorn, "Invariant properties of the motion parallax field due to the movement of rigid bodies relative to an observer," *Optica Acta* **22**, 1975, 773–791.

29. D. Koller, K. Daniilidis, T. Thorhallson, and H. Nagel, "Model-based object tracking in traffic scenes," In *Proc. European Conf. on Computer Vision*, 1992, 437–452.

30. Y. Liu and T.S. Huang, "Estimation of rigid body motion using straight line correspondences," *CVGIP* **43**, 1988, 37–52.

31. H.C. Longuet-Higgins, "A computer algorithm for reconstruction of a scene from two projections," *Nature* **293**, 1981, 133–135.

32. H.C. Longuet-Higgins and K. Prazdny, "The interpretation of a moving retinal image," *Proc. Royal Society London B* **208**, 1980, 385–397.

33. D. Marr, *Vision*, W.H. Freeman, San Francisco, 1982.

34. H. Nagel, "Displacement vectors derived from second order intensity variations in image sequences," *CVGIP* **21**, 1983, 85–117.

35. S. Negadharipour, "Critical surface pairs and triplets," *Int'l. J. Computer Vision* **3**, 1989, 293–312.

36. S. Negahdaripour, *Direct Passive Navigation*, PhD thesis, Department of Mechanical Engineering, MIT, 1986.

37. K. Pahlavan and J.-O. Eklundh, "A head-eye system–Analysis and design," *CVGIP: Image Understanding* **56**, Special Issue on Purposive, Qualitative, Active Vision, Y. Aloimonos (Ed.), 1992, 41–56.

38. A. Pentland, *From Pixels to Predicates: Recent Advances in Computational and Robot Vision*, Ablex: Norwood, NJ, 1986.

39. W. Reichhardt and T. Poggio, "Figure-ground discrimination by relative movement in the visual system of the fly," *Biological Cybernetics* **35**, 1979, 81–100.

40. F. Rosenblatt, *Principles of Neurodynamics: Perceptrons and the Theory of Brain Mechanisms*, Spartan, Washington, D.C., 1962.

41. R. Sharma and J. Aloimonos, "Robust Detection of Independent Motion: An Active and Purposive Solution," Technical Report CAR-TR-534, Center for Automation Research, University of Maryland, 1991.

42. M. Spetsakis and J. Aloimonos, "Structure from motion using line correspondences," *Int'l. J. Computer Vision* **1**, 1990, 171–183.

43. M.E. Spetsakis and J. Aloimonos, "Optimal computing of structure from motion using point correspondences," In *Proc. Int'l. Conf. on Computer Vision*, 1988, 449–453.

44. M. Tistarelli and G. Sandini, "Dynamic aspects in active vision," *CVGIP: Image Understanding* **56**, Special Issue on Purposive, Qualitative, Active Vision, Y. Aloimnonos (Ed.), 1992, 108–129.

45. R.Y. Tsai and T.S. Huang, "Uniqueness and estimation of 3-D motion parameters of rigid objects with curved surfaces," *IEEE Trans. PAMI* **6**, 1984, 13–27.

46. S. Ullman, "The interpretation of structure from motion," *Proc. Royal Society London B* **203**, 1979, 405–426.

47. S. Uras, F. Girosi, and V. Torre, "A computational approach to motion perception," *Biological Cybernetics* **60**, 1988, 79–87.

48. A. Waxman, "Image flow theory: A framework for 3-D inference from time-varying imagery," In C. Brown (Ed.) *Advances in Computer Vision*, Lawrence Erlbaum Assoc., Hillsdale, NJ, 1987.

49. A.M. Waxman, B. Kamgar-Parsi, and M. Subbarao, "Closed-form solutions to image flow equations for 3D structure and motion," *Int'l. J. Computer Vision* **1**, 1987, 239–258.

50. G. White and E. Weldon, "Utilizing gradient vector distributions to recover motion parameters," In *Proc. IEEE Workshop on Computer Vision*, 1987, 132–137.

4 | Vision during Action

G. Sandini, F. Gandolfo, E. Grosso and M. Tistarelli
University of Genoa

Abstract

The research topics presented in this chapter have been selected from among those carried out at our institution in the field of *active vision*, in order to explain the importance and the intimate relationship between visual processing and motion for the solution of difficult visual tasks. Although the results presented are taken from different application areas (such as navigation, manipulation and gaze control), three common and important aspects represent the *fil rouge* and the motivation of the work presented: purposiveness, closed-loop control, and concurrency of motion and sensing. This last aspect, in particular, will be stressed in order to demonstrate that the *simultaneous and coordinated* operation of vision and action can be used not only to simplify some "traditional" visual tasks but also to extend the overall scope of vision to new important areas.

1. Introduction

The visual system of a behaving actor, either natural or artificial, has to cope with motion in at least two ways: It should be able to detect, measure and interpret the motion of "external" objects, and it must be able to use dynamic visual information to control, plan and coordinate its own motion. These two aspects have been more or less extensively studied in the past by neuroscientists and computer vision researchers with the aim of understanding the functionalities of the human brain and developing algorithms that can be adopted in the real world to solve general motion problems.

The research described in this chapter has been supported by the ESPRIT Projects FIRST and VOILA and by the Special Projects on Robotics of the Italian National Council of Research. The authors wish to thank many students of the LIRA-Lab for their work and enthusiasm. Among them: M. Accordino, C. Capurro, F. Curotto, F. Ferrari, M. Fossa, S. Garibaldi, M. Magrassi, E. Martinuzzi, G. Metta, A. Oddera, F. Panerai, A. Portunato and P. Questa.

From the neurophysiological side, however, the emphasis has been directed mainly toward the study of ballistic motions and/or the analysis of visually guided motor behaviors where vision provides the information to initiate and program the motor act more than the closed-loop information necessary to monitor and control motion.

Conversely, from the computer vision side the emphasis has been directed toward the extraction of *metric information* in different forms: depth, speed, trajectory, shape and so on, either with single measures or by integrating in time or across modalities (e.g., stereo and motion). The identification and extraction of those visual measures necessary to control and monitor motor acts have received comparatively less attention (apart from the research recently carried out on gaze control [8, 18, 19, 20, 53].

Apparently most of the work carried out in the field of robot navigation has focused on the analysis of motion. On the other hand looking more deeply at *how* it has been done, most of the work was aimed more at the reconstruction of the external environment than at the closed-loop control of robot motion. Apart from a few exceptions [35, 82], the motion of the robot has been used as a means to change the vantage point and, consequently, to acquire different views of the environment, disregarding the computation of what is really necessary to keep the robot "on track," to terminate the motion, or to execute more complex motor actions (such as turning to enter a door, slowing down in front of an obstacle, avoiding the obstacle, etc.).

Starting from the (more or less implicit) assumption that geometry has a predominant role (in some sense it is the goal) generates a somehow limited, and perhaps distorted, view of the role of vision and, consequently, of what to compute and how to compute it. It is not rare to see experiments performed with robots moving along linear (or piecewise linear) trajectories, or presenting as a final result the reconstructed map of the environment in terms of *surfaces*. This approach, although important for many reasons (and for some industrial applications), fails, in our opinion, to highlight the role of vision *during* the execution of motor actions and, to some extent, makes the overall process more complex, requiring a degree of accuracy much higher than what is really necessary, and certainly outside current (and possibly even future) technology.

This *geometrical approach* is even more evident in the field of manipulation. In this case a "typical" experiment involves the use of vision *prior* to the initiation of the arm motion as a way to reconstruct the 3-D structure of the environment and to plan a collision-free trajectory. The motion of the arm is executed in open loop (at least from the visual view point). As a consequence, the execution of motor actions is based only on the kinesthetic information coming from the sensors mounted on the joints and, being entirely preprogrammed, cannot cope with changes in environmental conditions; moreover, it requires a precision in the computation of 3-D parameters which may be much higher than what is really necessary. The task of grasping an object can be achieved either by providing the spatial coordinates of the object to be grasped or by constantly controlling the relative position of the end effector with respect to the object itself. How this second solution can be implemented without explicitly computing depth information will be presented in Section 3, which illustrates the use of *vision during action* to extend the relevance of visual information for the execution of manipulative tasks.

Schematically we can identify at least three situations in which the use of visual information is not only important but essential for the completion of a complex motor task.

The first one is related to the task of *learning motor actions.* In this case vision provides the only independent way to measure motor performance and, consequently, to tune motor programs. Considering humans (although examples from robotics could be presented as well), besides the process of learning basic motor actions like walking or grasping typical of infants and children, we are faced, during our entire life, with the task of learning to use "tools" such as forks, pens, computer keyboards or cars, or with the more or less slow process of aging which changes the parameters of our own body and muscles. Whether this process is defined as a learning activity or is attributed to the plasticity of the human brain is not relevant in this context. What matters is the role of vision. A similar example is the use humans often make of visual examples in learning complex, coordinated actions. Professional tennis players, skiers or dancers often try to improve their motor performance by looking at movies of their own motor acts or practicing in front of a mirror. In this sense it can be said that the fine-tuning of these complex motor behaviors requires a precision that is much higher than the proprioceptive information available and must be based on an "independent" measure (something like an independent referee) in order to evaluate and correct the execution of motor strategies. The process of mapping the visually acquired error into changes in the motor programs is a fascinating problem in itself. After the learning phase is terminated (if such a time exists), even complex motor actions can be executed more or less in open loop (at least visually), and the role of vision may be "limited" to the premotor phase.

The second situation in which vision plays a fundamental role is in *monitoring motor acts and detecting self-generated events.* In this case vision is used to monitor the execution of motor actions in order to detect unexpected events (such as collisions) or to perform more accurately. The detection of these anomalies in the expected visual input is another topic that will be extensively discussed in subsequent parts of this chapter. It is worth stressing here, moreover, that the purposive selection of specific motor tasks along with the computation of visual parameters during motion can also be used to acquire information about an object's intrinsic properties, such as hardness, stability, or shape. This aspect will also be discussed later in the chapter (Section 3).

The third situation where visual information is essential is during *interaction with "unconstrained" (e.g., moving) objects*, or whenever the accuracy of proprioceptive information is not sufficient to carry out a specific task. Examples of this kind can be found in most manipulative tasks requiring two-arms manipulations or fine, dextrous manipulation [1, 60] (e.g., capping a fountain pen, inserting a thread in a needle's head or, more simply, during writing). If one thinks, for example, of the task of hammering a nail, it is evident that in spite of the fact that all the necessary information should be available through proprioception (the nail is held with one hand and the hammer with the other), very few hammerers, even though skilled, would perform with eyes closed.

It is worth noting here that other sensory modalities like force and tactile feedback are useful **after** the contact; kinesthetic (postural) signals are not precise enough in many cases (e.g., in two-arm, fine manipulation). A very interesting problem in this context is to identify and extract the simplest (in terms of computational requirements) visual cues that allow the system to accomplish the task. A geometrical approach would require the computation of trajectory information in a 4-D space and a predictive mechanism acting on the motor controller. This approach would be based on indirect measures obtained from image data (typically the spatiotemporal coordinates of the end effector) by means of calibration parameters. Our opinion is that iconic (i.e., direct) measures can be used as well without any loss in generality. This aspect will be discussed in Sections 2 and 3.

The main points presented so far can be summarized as follows:

- A motor system of finite accuracy needs an independent (i.e., not coming from the motor system or from proprioception) estimate of its own motor performance.
- The sensory system of a robot (or of a living system) should not be designed (or studied) as a metric system but within the context of the task it is performing (its purpose). In this context, in fact, the detection of expected or unexpected events can be simplified, particularly if the system is acting in an unpredictable environment.
- A great extension of visual processing capabilities is possible if vision is used during the execution of motor acts. One of the major extensions, in this respect, is the possibility of increasing the accuracy of motor control beyond the limits imposed by proprioceptive and kinesthetic sensors.

These concepts will be presented on the basis of selected research results obtained at DIST, Lira-Lab within the framework of active and purposive vision and considering two different behavioral situations: navigation (Section 2), and manipulation (Section 3). In Section 4, some of these aspects will be discussed in relation to the use of a space-variant visual sensor. A final discussion will be presented in Section 5.

2. CONTINUOUS VISION AND NAVIGATION

Robot navigation, conceived as the ability to move safely in unstructured environments coping with other moving objects, is a very attractive field and seems to be an ideal test-bed for vision-based control techniques. Navigation is usually a bidimensional problem; therefore, compared with redundant manipulators, for instance, motor control can be very simple, and all the attention can be devoted to visuomotor coordination.

The central question in this discussion is what can be gained in terms of navigation control when vision is continuously operating during motion, and how this can be accomplished. The first important observation is how vision relates to other sensors during the execution of navigation tasks. As an example we would like to consider briefly the sources of information available to humans for the perception of self-motion.

In humans, perception of self-motion is based upon three sensorial inputs:

- visual information (mainly optical flow);
- vestibular information;
- kinesthetic information (the knowledge of the motion of the body).

From these sources of information, behaviorally important perceptions can be obtained, but possibly the most important is the evaluation of the direction and (qualitative) speed of motion with respect to points in the environment or to the heading direction.

Interesting experiments have been reported recently, to establish which are the most reliable source of information in this case [72]. The key feature of these experiments was to create conflicting visual, vestibular and kinesthetic stimuli in different combinations and to evaluate the perceived motion. In these experiments subjects walked at subthreshold accelerations (motor-kinesthetic stimulation), or were passively conveyed at suprathreshold accelerations (vestibular stimulation) along a rectilinear path. Visual information was provided using a helmet-mounted optical system in which the visual heading could be dissociated from the direction of body motion by providing a stereoscopic view from a pair of cameras located above the subject's head and pointing laterally (30 to 180 degrees) to generate visual information conflicting with the vestibular information. The conclusions derived from the experiments (at least those relevant to the current work) show that subjects are aware of visuo-kinesthetic conflicting information while, in case of visuo-vestibular conflicts, the heading direction was estimated from visual information only (or the conflict become evident in case of rather large angles). This suggests that dynamic visual information is of primary importance to the perception of self-motion when vestibular information is available, but not in the presence of competing signals from the motor-kinesthetic system.

Besides the evaluation of heading direction, however, navigation requires full visual processing capabilities. Typically it relies both on reflexive behaviors, like the avoidance of sudden obstacles, and purposive behaviors, related to the task that is being executed. To deal correctly with this topic, we first need to clarify two major issues that deeply affect the practical implementation of a visual control system.

First, and probably most important, is the concept of *visuomotor modularity*. If we describe a visual system as a set of different visual modules, each extracting information useful for a specific task, we have to understand how those modules cooperate to the global control of the robotic system. To explain this point in more detail, let us suppose a visual system composed of two simple modules, the first one capable of detecting moving obstacles and the second one aimed at recognizing and following a visual target. Target following can be considered as the main task for the system, but in this case we have to specify in detail what kind of actions the system must undertake when an obstacle is detected in its proximity. A reasonable solution of this problem is based on the fact that the robot should know that its own safety has higher priority than other behaviors; as a consequence an obstacle-avoidance procedure must be immediately activated, leaving aside, for a while, the target following goal. Moving from these ideas, Brooks [13] pointed out the need for a *visual architecture* to coordinate different visual modules. In a visual architecture, visual modules are connected in a specific order and with different priorities; control of motor actuators obviously depends on the output of the single modules, but this dependency can be quite complex and can rely on either logical or algebraic relations. A simple example of visual architecture, derived from [25], is

Table 1. The multilevel architecture

	MODULE 1 (COGNITIVE LEVEL)	MODULE 2 (EXPLORATORY LEVEL)	MODULE 3 (SAFETY LEVEL)
OUTPUT MOTOR PROCESSES	`move-to(object)`	`move-along-dir(x)`	`avoid-obstacles()`
VISUAL PROCESSES	`recognize(object)`	`look-for-corridor(x)`	`detect-obstacles()`
COMPUTATIONAL PROCESSES	object feature extraction, invariant shape recognition, others	relative depth computation, time to impact computation, dynamic stereo	rough disparity processing, optical flow anomalies

outlined in Table 1. In this case the architecture includes a third module aimed at detecting corridors of free space. Each visual module implements a specific behavior, processing the available visual information for this purpose. The motor action `move-to(object)`, for instance, requires the recognition of the target on the basis of its characteristic features; in principle those features can present different degrees of complexity: They can be points, segments, colors or complex 3-D representations. Module 2 implements a more exploratory behavior; its motor action depends on the presence of corridors of free space, which are detected using early visual processing. Finally, the motor action `avoid-obstacles()` provides self-safety to the system, detecting moving obstacles by rough disparity processing or optical flow analysis. It is worth noting that modules presented in Table 1 are simply examples of what can be done using visual processing; we could use vision to follow a wall, to find a door, to travel in the middle of a corridor (exploiting vanishing points), or to continuously reorient the robot system in a partially known environment.

A global motor control for the system can be obtained considering at least two different criteria. The first one is based on an obvious order of priority among different modules, using inhibition to solve possible conflicts (obstacle avoidance can inhibit corridor detection which, in turn, can inhibit target following); the second one, suggested in [27], is based on a set of control histograms (one for each module) covering the interval of the possible directions around the robot (from 0 to 360 degrees). Each histogram stores a continuous function, with values in the range [0,1], representing how much the requirements of the navigation module would be satisfied by a motion of the robot along this direction. A null value represents an absolute incompatibility between an eventual motion of the robot along the corresponding direction and the navigational requirements of the module. Let us consider the situation depicted in Figure 1: Using a couple of different modules the robot starts from a given point and has to reach a goal point following a planned straight trajectory. In the first part of the trajectory (Figure 1, point A), no obstacles are detected; therefore the short-range navigation module produces a flat histogram allowing all possible directions. The long-range navigation module, on the other hand, produces a histogram with a peak in the direction pointing toward the goal point (perhaps a landmark) and a minimum in the opposite direction. The combination of the two histograms drives the robot toward the goal point along a rectilinear trajectory.

When an obstacle is detected (Figure 1, point B), the obstacle avoidance module produces a histogram containing a cone of forbidden directions. Consequently, this time the result of the cooperation module is a selected direction different from the planned one, and the robot will curve to its left to try to reduce the difference between its current heading and the desired one.

It is worth noting that a system built on modules can easily be extended by addition of other navigational capabilities based on the existing or on further sensors. In fact, the combination of different histograms usually requires simple processing and never constitutes a computational bottleneck for the system, even when new navigation modules are added.

A second relevant, and sometimes misunderstood, issue in visual control concerns the *perceptual delay*. If each module is responsible for a specific task or behavior, reasonably it will have a different computational delay. Typically, the delay will be minimal for reflexive behaviors and will increase in relation to the amount of knowledge and information involved in the task. The presence of delay in closed and continuous control loops is a major cause of instabilities; a perfectly stable controller can become unstable if the feedback is delayed, or can generate undesired ringing around a stable trajectory. Delay problems must be carefully evaluated when designing vision-based control systems; in particular two requirements should be satisfied:

- different visual modules must run in parallel, avoiding interaction among different delays and processing information at their maximum speed;
- each visual module, in relation to its characteristic delays and its major functionalities, must be provided with a specific motor controller. Obviously, reflexive or simple cognitive behaviors will admit fast visual processing and simple motor control; in this sense they can be considered as best candidates for continuous time implementations.

The following sections describe in detail some visual modules that have been implemented and tested, singularly or as a part of a visual architecture. Generally speaking, they share two common features that make them very interesting from the

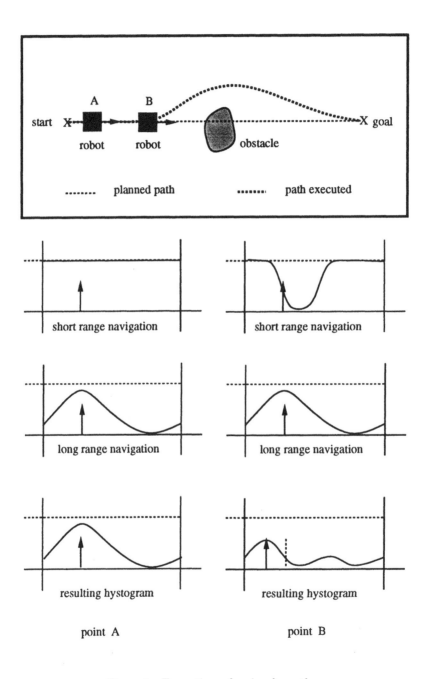

Figure 1. Execution of a simple path.

perspective of continuous vision and navigation: They are based on simple visual processing, for which an almost real-time implementation has been possible, and they don't make use of explicit metrics. This last point, in particular, will be clearly explained with the help of practical examples.

2.1. CONTINUOUS ORIENTATION USING VISUAL LANDMARKS

Navigation in a known environment cannot be based only on odometric information because of the cumulative effects of unavoidable wheel slippage (or, more generally, the difficulties in measuring absolute positioning information with on-board sensors). Solutions to this problem have been proposed in the past based on the use of beacons [15] or visual landmarks enabling the system to self-locate with respect to known positions in the environment and, consequently, to correct positional errors. Limiting the discussion to vision, landmarks can be used in two rather different ways: to verify the current absolute position of the robot in the environment, or to measure the position of the robot relative to the landmark itself. The difference can be explained with a simple example. Suppose the current task of the robot is to follow a corridor and to turn right at the end, and that in order to accomplish the task a landmark (either natural or artificial) is available at the end of the corridor.

One possibility would be to give the robot a motor command based upon the length of the corridor: *proceed x meters and check your position with respect to the landmark* (the addition of real-time visual control information like following wall or floor features or pointing toward the vanishing point can be considered without altering the overall concept). The second possibility would be to give the robot a motor command based only on the relative position of the robot with respect to the landmark: *proceed until you are at a given position with respect to the landmark*. This second solution requires a continuous monitoring of the landmark (and in this sense is more demanding computationally); on the other hand, it reduces the relevance of odometric information and does not require a metric representation of the environment. The extension of this simple example to complex tasks and environments is not straightforward but, in our opinion, shifts the estimation of self-motion from "length" to angles (which from the behavioral viewpoint seem more reliable in humans for learning the topology of new environments and planning complex trajectories).

Other qualitative uses of visual landmarks in this context could be instructions such as: *move toward a landmark, pass at the right (left) of a landmark, pass between two landmarks*, etc. Some interesting examples of this approach can be seen in the behavior of insects, particularly in so-called homing strategies where, apart from other absolute references derived by the position of the sun, the polarization of light, or from the earth's magnetic field, visual landmarks also play a very important role in orienting toward a goal by a *piloting method* rather than by a *beacon method* [31]. The piloting approach involves orienting toward the to-be-approached (or away from the to-be-avoided) point by adopting an appropriate orientation with respect to other stimuli with a known geometric relation to the goal [31]. In this case the kind of *cognitive map* used does not rely on metric information and, nonetheless, is used by the "navigator" to return to previous positions ("home") which, by their very nature cannot have any distinctive feature (e.g., in the case of hoverflies "home" is a position in mid-air).

2.2. REFLEX BEHAVIOR USING BINOCULAR DISPARITY

At a lower level we can see the use of vision to plan the avoidance of obstacles or to perform other low-level control strategies like following a wall, remaining in the middle of a corridor, pointing toward a distant point in the visual environment and so on. Even if some of these tasks could be performed using other sensors (such as ultrasound), it is our opinion that the generality, and to some extent, the reliability of vision will be superior in the medium term. If we consider, for example, the problem of obstacle avoidance, in spite of the effort devoted so far to its solution by means of ultrasonic sensors, an acceptable robustness is achieved only in very constrained situations. On the other hand, vision has been used, in many cases, to extract volumetric information redundant to accomplishing the task. The implicit assumption, in this case, is that the world is static (in the sense that there is "a lot of time" available to compute what is relevant); consequently, it is not so important to be selective. Only recently examples of obstacle detection approaches have been presented which are not based on explicit computation of volumes or shape of obstacles, or both [26, 28, 55]. One of the major achievement is, in this respect, the demonstration that reliable, real-time vision does not always require large computational power.

In order to support the above mentioned concepts, we describe briefly an approach to obstacle detection and avoidance based on a stereo set-up (the details of the algorithm can be found in [25, 28]). The main advantage in using stereo analysis [23] is that the two images are acquired simultaneously, and instantaneous visual information is totally unaffected by the motion of the vehicle.

The algorithm is based on the assumption that, in the absence of obstacles, the spatial relation between the stereo pair and the ground floor does not change during the motion. In practice, this means that the robot system possesses only two degrees of freedom: translation in a plane parallel to the ground floor and rotation around an axis perpendicular to this plane.

The algorithm is composed of two steps:

1. an off-line, self-calibration phase
2. the on-line obstacle detection

During the first phase a disparity map of the ground floor is computed by means of a stereo algorithm based on a coarse-to-fine correlative procedure [33]. The basic idea is to observe the ground floor from different positions and to recompute, at each time, the related disparity map. As the position of the stereo system does not change with respect to the floor, it is possible to average the disparity for each point of the map, obtaining a reference disparity map and its point-by-point variance.

It is worth noting that this procedure does not require any previous calibration phase (the two cameras are pointed, by hand, so that the fixation point is approximately 1 m in front of the vehicle); depth is not computed explicitly and the only assumption is that the stereo system will maintain, during the on-line phase, the same configuration with respect to the floor.

Figure 2 shows, on the left side, a disparity map obtained from a single measure of the ground floor; on the right side the final reference map, obtained by averaging 20 maps, is shown.

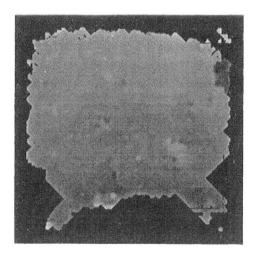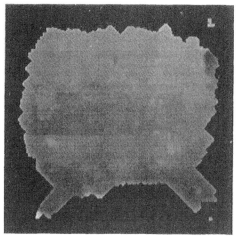

Figure 2. Disparity maps obtained from a single view and averaging multiple views.

The on-line obstacle detection is based on a fast comparison between the reference map and the disparity maps computed during navigation. Let us denote by $d(x_0, y_0)$ the value stored in the reference map at the corresponding coordinates. If we want to check the presence of an obstacle in correspondence to this image point we have to compute a similarity measure between the left image point $I_l(x_0, y_0)$ and the right image point $I_r(x_0 + d(x_0, y_0), y_0)$. In practice we use to this purpose a correlation measure computed over a square, 8-pixel-wide patch; the dimensions of the patch and the computation performed are exactly the same as those used by the off-line algorithm at the finest level. Denoting the correlation function generically with $C(x, y)$, if $C(x_0 + d(x_0, y_0), y_0)$ is far from a correlation peak, this fact indicates the presence of an obstacle.

The overall performance of the system is such that it is possible to detect even small obstacles (e.g., 5 cm height from the ground floor, and 2 cm wide) at about 12Hz.

With reference to the concepts presented previously, the main peculiarities of this approach (or of similar ones) are the following:

- No depth computation (or 3-D reconstruction) is required (this, of course, does not mean that, for other purposes, reconstruction is not important).
- Due to the simplicity of the algorithm (and consequently its speed) no single measure is considered fundamental and therefore isolated errors do not cause the system to break apart (graceful degradation).

- Performing obstacle detection during the motion of the vehicle allows a true, short-range exploration of the environment to be performed. The avoidance strategies can, therefore, be based on continuous visual measurements performed during coordinated motion: "If an obstacle is blocking the left side of the path, then slow down and turn right until the path is free." This strategy is, in our implementation, based on a short-term, short-range representation of free space which does not require precise odometric measurements.

In spite of the obvious limitations of this approach (the major one being the need of texture on the obstacle's surface), the overall performance and simplicity of the control system make the visual approach even more robust than the one based on ultrasonic sensors. For example, factors like the orientation of the obstacle's surface, or its material, or its height (above few centimeters), or its speed (if compatible with processing speed), do not affect the overall results, making this system very robust.

Finally, the extension of this approach to visual systems based on more degrees of freedom (e.g., with a pan-tilt-vergence head) is possible with a limited increase in complexity; experiments in this area have already been performed by Mayhew and his coworkers [55].

2.3. REFLEX BEHAVIOR USING OPTICAL FLOW

The topic we would like to present here is that of identifying the visual measures used to control navigation that do not rely on precise geometric information, but take full advantage of the continuous (in time) nature of visual information and are based upon simple, direct estimation of "range" extracted from 2-D (or even 1-D) optical flow [81, 67].

The inspiration of these ideas derives from some recent research results on the behavior of honeybees [45, 70], and more generally, from the use some insects make of flow field information [39] to control their flying trajectory in unconstrained environments [29]. From the computational viewpoint the problems to be solved are far more complex than what we usually do in controlling a mobile robot moving on a flat surface.

A simple example would suffice to explain the kind of simplifications that can be gained by solving apparently complex navigation problems using qualitative measures of optical flow. In the experiment of Srinivasan [70] honeybees were trained to navigate along corridors in order to reach a source of food. The behavioral observation is the fact that, in spite of the fact that the corridor was wide enought to allow for "irregular" trajectories, bees were actually flying on a quasi-linear trajectory in the middle of the corridor (i.e., maintaining the same distance from the left and the right wall). This finding is even more surprising if we take into consideration that:

- the two eyes of the honeybees are ponting laterally (at about 180 degrees);
- the distance between the two eyes is so small that, even in the binocular field of view, depth-from-stereo does not provide any useful depth information;
- no accommodation mechanism is present to provide depth-from-focus information .

Apparently, then, no depth information can be derived using traditional methods. What kind of information is used to maintain the bee in the middle of the corridor and how it is computed is, therefore, a nontrivial question. The answer presented in [70] is rather simple, and it is based on the difference between the velocity information computed from the left and the right eye: If the bee is in the middle of the corridor the two velocities are the same; if the bee is closer to one wall, the velocity of the ipsilateral eye is larger. A simple control mechanism (very similar to a reflex), then, may be based on motor actions that tend to minimize this difference: Move to the left if the velocity measured by the right eye is larger than that measured by the left (or vice versa).

In the experiments reported in [67, 81] navigation is controlled on the basis of the optical flow field computed over windows of images acquired by a pair of cameras pointing (analogous to the position of the eyes in honeybees and other insects) laterally and with nonoverlapping visual field. We call this camera placement *divergent stereo*.

The important points are:

- no explicit depth information is necessary;
- the control strategy is rather simple, and the only constraint is the presence of texture on the image;
- a reflex-like control is possible (i.e., no geometric and/or a priori information about the environment is necessary);
- range is measured in terms of image velocity. Even if this solution may seem limited, it is, in our opinion very well suited to navigation. For example, the perceived range is implicitly tuned to the speed of the robot: If the robots move faster, the objects are perceived as closer. If one considers that the "reaction time" to unexpected events is constant in all physical systems, it seems very efficient to scale distance with velocity; what is important is not how far the object is but how much time one has to react to it. In other words, if the velocity of the vehicle is small, a close object is "less dangerous" than if the velocity is higher because the system will have a longer time to react (this fact is very evident in driving through a narrow path).

The set-up used in the experiments is shown in Figure 3; it is essentially based upon a mobile platform moving on a flat floor. As the robot's motion is constrained to the ground plane, it can be assumed that the flow along the vertical direction will be negligible. Hence, we can use a simpler computation procedure, which will be faster and robust (since for example it is not necessary to compute the second derivatives), by simply assuming that the vertical flow component, v, is 0 we have:

$$\frac{\partial I}{\partial x}u + \frac{\partial I}{\partial y}v + \frac{\partial I}{\partial t} = 0 \tag{1}$$

$$v = 0 \tag{2}$$

and u is given by:

$$u = -\frac{I_t}{I_x} \tag{3}$$

Figure 3. The vehicle with the divergent stereo camera setup.

where I_x and I_t stand for the x spatial derivative and the temporal derivative of the image.

The difference between the average flow on the left and right images is then used for synthesizing the control law. More details about the actual implementation can be found in [67, 81].

The robot control system gives the possibility of performing rotations at a given speed while still moving forward. The rotational velocity is used to control the direction of motion of the robot. One could also consider the possibility of controlling the forward velocity of the robot, so that it could accelerate if the lateral flow is low (meaning that the walls are farther away) and slow down whenever the flow becomes larger (meaning that it is navigating in a narrow environment).

The flow difference is used as a misplacement error signal and we implemented a PID controller that actuates on the vehicle rotational speed.

The closed-loop behavior of the visually guided robot was the aim of the experiment reported here. For this purpose, we have considered an experiment which involves obstacle avoidance and navigating in a funneled corridor. Figure 4 shows, along with a map of the environment, the trajectory followed by the robot under closed-loop control. Notice how the trajectory allows the obstacle avoidance, and tends to a proper alignment later on.

In Figure 5 we show both the error signal (i.e., the difference between the right and left average flow vectors) under the closed-loop operation, and the control action (i.e., the angular rotation imposed on the forward-moving robot) applied to the robot.

Although the error and control signals present some sharp variations, it should be noted that the error is in the order of magnitude of 1 pixel per frame, while the changes in the rotation speed (that actually determine the direction of motion), are seldom larger than 3 degrees. Finally, as it is shown in Figure 4, the trajectory of the robot is quite smooth.

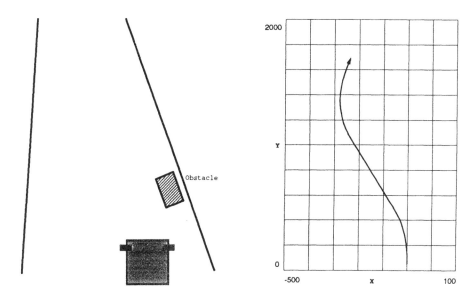

Figure 4. Closed-loop operation. The diagram on the left shows the setup for the closed-loop test, while on the right we show the trajectory followed by the robot (the two diagrams are not drawn on the same scale).

It is worth noting here that, during the rotational motions of the vehicle (e.g., while avoiding an obstacle), the values of the flow fields are not only proportional to the distance of the walls but also to the rotational velocity of the vehicle. This, of course, interferes with the simple control strategy adopted. However if, as in our case, the rotational velocity is kept small, this added error (which causes the system to perceive the wall contralateral to the direction of rotation as closer) does not degrade the performance significantly.

3. CONTINUOUS VISION AND MANIPULATION

The use of vision in robotics has been mainly devoted to localization, reconstruction, and matching problems. Tasks like 3-D reconstruction of shape (for manipulation) or free-space (in case of navigation) have attracted considerable research efforts along with the problem of recognition, either model-based or driven by a priori knowledge. We present a different perspective in relation to the use of vision for monitoring robot actions and robot control. This research activity reflects an exploratory approach to object understanding and manipulation, driven by the observation that, apart from trivial situations, the structure of the environment is never perfectly known. Therefore, the planning of motor actions cannot be based entirely on prestored models. To stress these ideas, some experiments were performed on a scene composed of unknown objects laying on a flat surface.

The adopted sensory-motor system has much in common with the "active vision" approach proposed by Bajcsy and Aloimonos [4, 6, 7, 50, 63], the "quali-

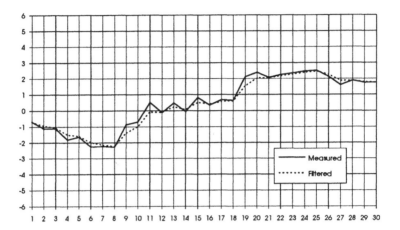

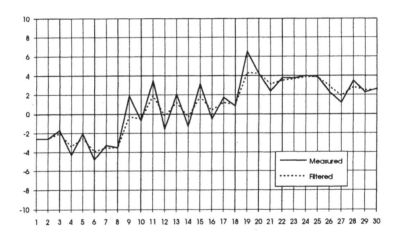

Figure 5. On top, we show the time evolution of the error during the closed-loop experiment (the difference between the right and left average flow vectors). On the bottom, we show the control action being applied to the robot (i.e., the angular rotation imposed on the forward-moving robot). Both signals are presented, together with the corresponding time-smoothed signals. The x-axis represents time expressed as the number of frames in the sequence of real-time images.

tative/purposive vision" paradigm proposed by Aloimonos [2], and also with the "animate vision" paradigm proposed by Ballard [9]. In these approaches the ability to "move" is exploited to simplify visual computations, but also to make visual information richer. Moreover, purposively planned movements of the observer, driven by visual information, facilitate the motor control of robot actions. For example, in a very simple case represented by the motion of a camera or cameras with stabilized direction of gaze, not only is it possible to simplify the computation of environmental measurements like depth or time to impact from visual data, but also the fixation point can be used as a reference point in the environment for driving the robot motion. This behavior is also coupled by saccadic motions which are used to change the focus of attention.

The major difference with the approach presented here is related to the "use" of visual information which, in the former approaches, is mainly devoted to the "exploration" of the environment, whereas, in our approach, it is devoted to monitoring the execution of motor actions as well. The commonality arises not only from the visuo-motor cooperation but also from the fact that monitoring also provides information about the environment (and, in this sense, is similar to active exploration): If some unexpected events occur, then the assumptions made on the environment are wrong or incomplete (for example if a moving object enters the camera field of view) and the system knowledge can be updated (learning from mistakes). This assertion can be formalized in terms of a "theory of expectations," and, in our case, as "anomalies" in input visual patterns [65, 75].

In order to explain our approach, some experiments have been performed in the field of object manipulation. The outcome of the experiments is that, not only does it seem possible to detect unexpected events, it is also possible to control a robot arm in such a way as to achieve a complex task like pushing an unknown object along a predetermined trajectory.

3.1. HAND–EYE SELF-CALIBRATION

In order to extract the features of interest from an object being manipulated, it is necessary to rely on an architecture able to coordinate the sensory and motor systems. The architecture that we have developed is shown in Figure 6. It is composed of an action planning module and a sensory processing module which cooperate to reach the goal, i.e., to successfully execute the desired action. Both modules act as independent cooperating agents, sending information to and requesting information from each other.

The sensory modality that has been taken into account so far is vision. Since the vision system refers to a reference frame and the robot system works in another one, it is necessary to provide a means by which to convert measurements between the two frames. This can be achieved through a calibration phase. The first step toward the implementation of the architecture is then the self-calibration procedure.

Cameras are calibrated using the method described in [33]: Only the focal length, the vergence angle, the conversion factor between mm and pixels, and the distance between the cameras are needed to be able to recover the depth of a point from the stereo images. Then a correspondence is sought between the camera's reference frame and the robot's reference frame; this latter phase is the self-calibration process. It basically consists of the estimation of the transfer matrix between the two systems. It is computed by moving the end effector into three different positions in turn and by letting the stereo system observe them. In order to simplify the visual processing, a LED is mounted onto the robot's end effector. In this way, it can be located on the images via thresholding, and the disparity computation is limited to a single point on each image. Using the geometric relationships established in the calibration phase, the 3-D position of the end effector is recovered.

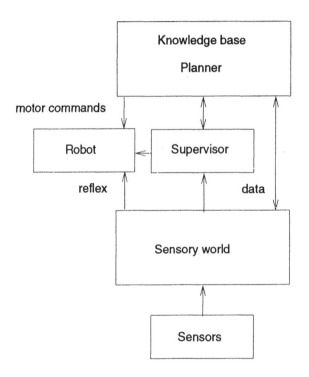

Figure 6. Schema of the architecture.

Such information can also be obtained from the joint positions of the arm (derived using proprioceptive sensing). Using the direct kinematic, it is possible to compute the position of the end effector in the robot's reference frame.

By repeated measurements of these positions in both reference frames, it is possible to compute a matrix that allows switching between the systems. Such a matrix is most accurate close to the calibration points, but its efficiency decreases away from them due to the nonlinearities of both the robotic and the vision system. To cope with this problem, the matrix can be updated periodically during the robot motion; the matrix estimate is therefore improved through repeated measurements. Moreover, if the robot changes its work area the matrix is updated during the arm motion, providing a suitable matrix for the new work space.

3.2. SENSORY-MOTOR STRATEGIES FOR OBJECT UNDERSTANDING

Given a calibrated system integrating sensory and motor actions, we investigated which kind of data can be gathered by analyzing the information that can be extracted using pushing and tapping (or impulsive pushing) as manipulative actions. The features we succeeded in retrieving include both geometrical parameters such as the object's silhouette, and "physical parameters" such as rigidity.

The methodology which has been chosen to extract these features is the computation of the optical flow, giving particular attention to the detection of anomalies with respect to the predicted velocity field [63]. An example of a moving object and the optical flow extracted from it is shown in Figure 7.

Figure 7. Silhouettes of a cat and the hand pushing it.

Object equilibrium

A property that can easily be determined by the observation of an object's reaction to manipulation is its stability with respect to external forces applied on its surface. The object's equilibrium can be determined by performing a tapping action on the object's surface and then observing its motion: If the object is in stable equilibrium it will stop very shortly after the touching. On the image plane, the number and amplitude of optical flow vectors will gradually decrease after tapping until the object stops. In this case, it is possible to characterize this behavior by computing the histogram of the mean amplitude of optical flows versus time. The standard case, which corresponds to a stable equilibrium, is determined by an approximately bell-shaped histogram, where the maximum is very close to the time instant of the contact.

Two possible anomalies can be detected (corresponding to two different events):

- if the object falls (from unstable equilibrium) after the touching, the histogram will have a steep slope (corresponding to the progressive acceleration of the object) with the maximum far from the touching instant, and then will suddenly fall, (corresponding to the quick stop of the object on the ground);

- if the object oscillates (from unstable equilibrium, but with the impulsive force applied on a particular point of the object's body), then the histogram will be double-bell shaped, the two peaks corresponding to the two opposite motions in two different time instants.

An experiment has been carried out in which a tapping action is performed on two different points of an object lying, in unstable equilibrium, on a flat table. The same experiment was then performed with the same object in stable equilibrium.

The histograms relative to these experiments are shown in Figures 8, 9 and 10.

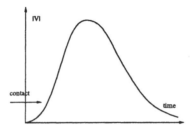

Figure 8. Histogram of mean |V| for an object in stable equilibrium.

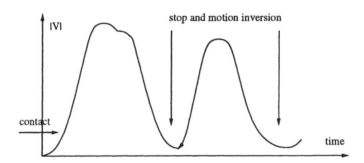

Figure 9. Histogram of mean |V| for an oscillating object.

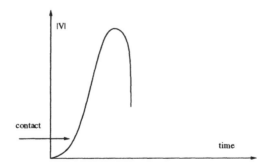

Figure 10. Histogram of mean |V| for a falling object.

Motion opposition

Another interesting feature is "motion opposition," which is qualitatively similar to friction in that it gives an idea of how an object should behave when pushed with a known force while it lies on a particular surface. Two methods can be used to exploit this measurement. The first one is to softly touch the object with a hand and to increase the pushing force until it starts moving, to find the minimal force that makes the object move; the second method consists of striking the object by an impulsive tapping action and observing how long it takes for the object to stop.

Overall dimensions of objects in the 2-D image

Having found a stable pushing point and the force to push the object, we can begin to study the behavior that will emerge during the pushing action. To obtain this it is necessary to perform a segmentation of the object, that is, to separate its points from those of the hand in the 2-D binary image obtained by optical flow in the way just described. This is obtained by initially determining the hand's shape and speed before the contact and after it, by subtracting the velocities of the hand's points from the current image. From the images of the hand and of the object used as "masks" we can compute the object's and the hand's mean velocities separately. Figure 11 shows the silhouettes computed while a human hand was pushing a toy cat.

Figure 11. Silhouettes of a cat and of the hand pushing it.

Object rigidity

Most research in manipulation has been carried out under the assumption that the world is composed of rigid objects. This has been done both because of the complexity of modelling deformations for manipulative tasks and because of the difficulty in automatically detecting deformations. We developed a procedure to discriminate among translation, rotation or object deformation during a pushing task.

The optical flow of a sequence of images is computed and the vectors composing the flow field have then been grouped into classes depending on phase and module. Each class groups the vectors whose module does not differ by more than a value δA and whose phase does not differ from a given angle θ_i by more than a $\delta\theta$ value.

In the case of pure translation along the pushing direction, there should be a limited number of neighbor classes, only one in the ideal, noiseless case. In the compression case, instead, making the hypothesis of dealing with a homogeneous object, the classes should be distributed among the allowed spectrum $(0 \div 2\pi)$. The compression causes the object points around the pusher to collapse toward the pushing center giving rise to an ideally homogeneous distribution in the phase and to an increasing module when approaching the pusher.

In the experiments performed using real objects such as balls and boxes, the resulting flow differs from the ideal one both due to the nonuniformity of the objects and noise in the images, and to possible reflections due to illumination conditions.

To cope with real-world situations, the flow vector is considered as being the sum of two vectors, one involving pure translation and one due either to the rotation or the compression. The translational flow is then subtracted from the global field; this should lead to major changes in the remaining flow in the translational case, while leaving the situation almost unchanged in a compression action.

The histogram of the modules shows the following features:

- Translation: A spike centered around the object mean velocity (which is also the pusher mean velocity) and few vectors in between zero and the spike. The rate between the number of vectors significantly different from the mean velocity and the total number of vectors on the object (see "Diff" in Table 2) is small.
- Compression: A spike centered around zero and few vectors around the pusher mean velocity.

Similarly the phase histogram can be classified as:

- Translation: A spike around the phase of the pusher mean velocity and very few noise vectors in the other phases.
- Compression: Phases are spread almost equally in the 360 degrees.
- Rototranslation: Phases are spread, but on a narrower bandwidth.

From these observations, it has been possible to discriminate among: *translation*, *rotation* or *compression*, by analyzing the histograms of the modules and the phases.

The module histogram is considered first, and the vector class grouping more vectors is selected as a reference if it is near the pusher mean velocity, otherwise this latter velocity is chosen. By comparing the number of vectors between zero velocity and the reference minus a threshold with the number of vectors around the reference, a measure of the width of the bell is obtained.

It has been found experimentally that these measures allow discrimination of a translational movement since in this case more than 70% of the vectors seem to be centered around the peak, while in the compression case and if the rotational component is relevant, the vectors are spread to a larger amount. In Table 2, Mod is the ratio between the number of vectors in the band between zero and the pusher mean velocity and the number of vectors in a band centered around the pusher mean velocity and with a width of the 10% of it.

In order to validate this result, the difference between the pusher mean velocity and each single vector is evaluated and its variance is computed, showing that it is possible to enforce the translational hypothesis by this means.

In order to discriminate between compression and rotation, the phase histogram has been considered. The reference point for the phase has been considered as the phase associated to the vector representing the movement of the geometric center of the object silhouette. In Table 2, "Phs" is the rate between the number of vectors whose phase is not in the neighborhood of the phase of the vector representing the motion of the geometric center of the object and the total number of vectors in the object.

In the rototranslational case, the translational component is composed of about 40% of the vectors, while in the compression case, they result to less than 10%, so the two cases can be discriminated.

The pure rotation case has not been considered yet, because it is unlikely to occur in a pushing experiment. Table 2 shows some results obtained from experiments.

Table 2.   An example of classification.

Seq	Mod	Phs	Diff	Result
1	0.75	0.94	0.35	compression
2	0.74	0.88	0.88	compression
3	0.49	0.52	0.42	rotation
4	0.63	0.62	0.40	rotation
5	0.22	0.58	0.14	translation
6	0.34	0.30	0.09	translation
7	0.75	0.87	0.63	compression
8	0.78	0.55	0.83	rotation
9	0.71	0.96	0.64	compression

Analysis of object's trajectory in response to a pushing action

The other features which we now consider are not intrinsic properties of the object since they are related to the motion characteristics of the object during a particular pushing experiment. They are not absolute properties, but they are a measure of the behavior of an object at a time instant during a manipulation action. A feature that is easy to detect is the relative motion between the pusher and the pushed object. It can be computed by comparing the directions of the mean velocity of the hand and the object. If the two vectors are almost aligned, then the object and the hand are translating concordingly. If this is not the case, it is necessary to discriminate between an object's translation along a direction different from that of the hand[1] and an object's rototranslation (this happens when the direction of pushing does not pass through the object's center of friction [10, 47, 54]. This information can be used to correct the pushing point so to make the object follow a predefined trajectory. If the object is rotating, this means that its center of mass does not lie along the pushing direction and the counterclockwise rotation provides a hint to the semi-space on which the center of mass lies, guiding the choice of a new pushing point. By iterating this process, a suitable pushing point is found.

Quantitative measurement of rotation

Since it is possible to detect a rotational component in the object's motion, it may be useful to compute some of its parameters (such as the angular velocity and the center of instantaneous rotation) to help the pusher to correct the pushing point. The center of instantaneous rotation can be located by exploiting two characteristics of a rotating object: The object's points lie at a distance from the center of instantaneous rotation which is directly proportional to their mean velocities, and their displacement vectors are perpendicular to the line joining them with the center of rotation. From these properties, it is possible to compute the center of rotation relative to the supporting plane (that is, the intersection between the axis of instantaneous rotation and the plane). Figure 12 shows the position of the center of rotation for a planar object. The first image shows the center of rotation and the second shows the optical flow relative to the rotating object.

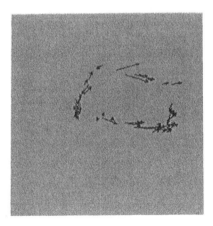

Figure 12. Optical flow for a rotating object and center of rotation.

3.3. CONCLUDING REMARKS

To manipulate objects in the real world, it is necessary to have a sensory apparatus to perceive what is going on. The sensory apparatus must be able to interact with the

---

[1] this may happen if it is sliding along an eventual obstacle or, more in generally, if the pusher is sliding along the object not causing it rotate.

motor system in order to make its information useful; a calibration phase is then necessary to tune the two systems to make them cooperate. The sensory system is in charge of the exploration of the world. The visual processing technique we employ for the dynamic evaluation of object motion is the optical flow analysis, [37, 32, 51, 36, 49, 3] performed on data extracted from images acquired during a manipulation action. The processing does not involve the recovery of exact data from optical flows, but rather the exploitation of some qualitative properties of the motion field. Using optical flow as a means of analyzing pushing sequences, it has been possible to retrieve both geometrical and physical properties of the manipulated object.

4. SPACE-VARIANT SENSING IN CONTINUOUS VISION

The scope of this paragraph is to present some ideas and experimental results in relation to the features of a visual sensor specifically designed and adapted to continuous vision: the human retina. Our intent here is not to try to transfer some knowledge of human physiology to robotics per se, but, on the contrary, to demonstrate the superiority of a space-variant sensor (such as the human retina) in motor control. In fact, even if we believe that the space-variant sampling strategy adopted by the human retina is mainly motivated by the need of compromising between high resolution and width of the visual field, other interesting features can be discussed specifically related to continuous vision. One of the consequences of the nonhomogeneous distribution of photoreceptors in the fovea of the human retina is the fact that input images are mapped into topologically distorted images in which the foveal part is "magnified" with respect to the peripheral one [40, 41]. This fact can be intuitively understood if one realizes that each photoreceptor (or receptive field) actually acquires the same amount of information regardless of its size. Moreover if the retinal image is sampled with a polar strategy (something like radar scanning) each concentric circle can be mapped into a column (or row) of a Cartesian image). The overall result, described as a log-polar mapping, has been extensively studied in the literature [30, 62, 68, 69, 79, 83]. The logarithm resulting from the fact that the size of the photoreceptors (or the nearest neighbor distance) increases in a linear manner with eccentricity (the distance from the fovea), or alternatively, the exponential increase in photoreceptor's density from the peripheral field to the fovea.

Alternative approximations of the abovementioned structure have been proposed, based upon the use of pyramids (stacks of images at different resolution and size) [14]. The similarity with the human retina stands on the fact that a small portion of the image is sampled at the highest resolution, while larger and larger areas are acquired at lower and lower resolution. This solution, although similar to the one mentioned above, has been mainly motivated by technical reasons (it is simpler to implement using currently available electronics) but does not embed the log-polar mapping. Recently two groups have been working on the realization of a space-variant visual sensor and a working prototype has been built based on CCD technology [21, 78].

Among the advantages of log-polar mapping some are related to the evaluation of shape parameters for 2-D shapes and are based on the rotation and scaling invariance of the mapping [30, 48, 83], others stress the optimality of the mapping in relation to filtering [12] and scale-space [46]. As to the dynamic features the advantages in tracking, vergence and computation of time to impact [11, 43, 84] will be discussed briefly in the following paragraphs.

4.1. EYE MOVEMENTS AND SPACE-VARIANT VISION

In the case of space-variant sensors (like the human retina) the role of eye movements is fundamental in directing the fovea toward "interesting" points of the scene, either static (to analyze shape and other local features) or dynamic (to track moving objects or to stabilize the image during self-motion).

This requirement transforms visual exploration from an entirely parallel process to a partially serial one. Although this may be seen as a limitation of this approach, one should consider the fact that the building of a perceptual image is based on the acquisition of bits of information linked to each other in a causal way: What is relevant in a given situation depends strongly on what had been perceived so far (and to the visual task being performed). The evolution of a perceptual process (particularly recognition) is intrinsically serial; even in the case of a constant resolution system (like current TV cameras), not all the image is necessary at each instant of time and the selection of relevant information adds an extra burden to visual processing (or, at least, to the required bandwidth). On the contrary, a space-variant topology of photoreceptors reduces the amount of detailed information right where the information is generated.

Moreover, we argue that the active control of fixation is not always driven by cognitive processes, but in most cases this mechanism is activated by task-related parameters. For example, a fast moving object within the field of view catches one's attention, invoking a fast saccadic movement of the eye to *foveate* and track the object. A preattentive, reflex like process must drive gaze control for fixation.

Usually, *visual attention* is related to the process of *interpretation* of the visual scene: "If I want to recognize a face I need to shift my attention to the eyes and the mouth." Our point is that "attention" also has a very strong *behavioral* basis: "If I want to walk I need to look in front of my feet." The major difference between these two different views is that while in the former case an a priori hypothesis is necessary, based on some high-level processing or expectation, in the latter everything is based on self-generated actions which are usually task driven. In the examples given above, both focusing and vergence involve the selection of a point in space *before the processing can even start*.

An interesting problem is to determine how to direct attention to a particular point in space. Although different control mechanisms are described in the literature [17], the most relevant, with respect to the contents of this chapter, is **task driven gaze control**. A very common example of this kind of control is the strategy adopted during walking. In this case the smooth reflex like movements described previously are interrupted by saccadic movements which are, in general, directed alternatively to the ground plane (to detect small obstacles and to evaluate the roughness of the floor [16, 24, 26, 66]) and to points far away (used to self-orient in space). During this period the peripheral part of the visual field plays a double role. The first, usually limited to the peri-foveal region, is to evaluate image velocity (used to maintain fixation); the second is to detect unexpected changes in the image brightness (or color) distribution. It is worth noting that in this case also, the direction of gaze does not depend on high-level reasoning processes.

This behavioral connotation is stressed even more during tracking and for the computation of time to impact. In fact, if we consider the requirements of a tracking process, the only situation in which this process is not active is when the camera is fixed and looking at a steady environment. In all other situations the need to reduce motion blurring forces the activation of the tracking system which, consequently, cannot be actively suppressed.

Tracking a point of the environment, on the contrary, gives the system a reference point which does not move in the environment and simplify the computation of time to impact [9, 34]. It is worth noting, moreover, that the tracking process is data-driven as it is the case for focusing and vergence. The role of high-level processing is "limited" to the selection of the target to track, which is often based on the behavioral task being executed (think, for instance, of the visuo-motor coordination during walking which has been discussed before). Therefore, the peculiarities of a retina like space-variant sensor in relation to visual tracking and vergence control are among the major advantages of this approach.

The relevance of a space-variant sensor for active vision is furthermore stressed by the advantages in the computation of parameters for motor control. In the remainder of the chapter we will illustrate a simple algorithm for vergence control and a new method for the estimation of time to impact[2] which take advantage of the use of a space-variant visual sensor.

Active control of fixation

The active control of fixation is a fundamental aspect of active vision systems [9, 18, 19]. Fixation control implies tracking skills, either of a moving target from a steady observer (except for rotational movements) or keeping the optical axis directed toward the same point in space while the observer is moving. The most difficult task is clearly to track a moving object while the observer is also moving. The difficulty arises not only from the complexity of the visual motion pattern, but also from the motor control part which requires the coordination of two independent motions, activated by two different goals.[3]

Generally speaking, the tracking process can be decomposed into three phases:

- detection of the target or focus of attention;
- foveation of the target;

---

[2] The time to impact represents a parameter that directly relates the observer with the environment, by taking into account the dynamic evolution of events. It is very useful for navigation and has a very distinct role from depth or range.

[3] For example, the tracking of a flying ball while walking activates a "walking" goal and a "track the ball" goal which will generally be competitive, generating movements of the body and the eye–head system with opposite directions.

• tracking.

Each phase has its own computational peculiarities related both to processing and to the constraints imposed on the system.

Considering the requirements necessary to track a textured object moving over a textured background, the detection and tracking phases are substantially different. In fact, while the detection phase must be based on a segmentation process driven "simply" by the computation of the image velocity field, the tracking itself must take into account the apparent motion due to the motion of the sensor. If the rotation axes intersect at the nodal point of the lens, this apparent motion only involves angular displacements. Therefore, the motion field does not depend on object distance and can be computed from the known rotation of the sensor. In this case the optical flow is computed to detect, isolate and foveate the target and then to track it. In order to estimate the tracking error, the expected optical flow obtained from the known rotational motion of the sensor is subtracted from the optical flow computed from the sequence of log-polar images. [4]

At this stage the control strategy is the same as that applied for the tracking of a light spot, described previously.

Binocular vergence control

In binocular systems gaze and fixation control involve keeping the optical axes directed at the point in space currently fixated. This is accomplished through active vergence control.

Olson and Coombs [52] and also Coombs and Brown [18, 19] demonstrated a simple and efficient vergence control system based on cepstral filtering of stereo images. The rationale was the computation of a gross cross-correlation score between the left and right views, the maximum correlation identifying the correct vergence of the cameras.

A similar algorithm has been devised for space-variant stereo images sampled with the retinal sensor. The basic idea is that of computing a pointwise cross-correlation between log-polar projections of the left and right views. The vergence between the cameras is varied by moving the *nondominant* camera, while the cumulative cross-correlation is computed. Even though the log-polar images do not differ for a simple translation, such as for uniformly sampled raster images, the global correlation of the images still provides a measure of the displacement between them. When the cameras are almost correctly verged, the global cross-correlation becomes very high. Therefore, if the global cross-correlation decreases, then the nondominant camera is moved in the opposite direction until the maximum is reached. It is interesting to note that the "disparity function," obtained considering the global cross-correlation values over time, has a sharper peak at the correct vergence for space-variant images than for regularly sampled images. With standard TV images (like those in Figure 13), a smoother peak is obtained. This fact implies a faster

---

[4] The optical flow is computed by solving an over-determined system of linear equations in the unknown terms $(u, v) = \vec{V}$. The equations impose the constancy of the image brightness over time [38] and the stationarity of the image motion field [77, 22].

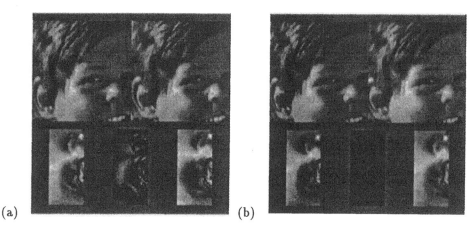

(a)   (b)

Figure 13. Results of the vergence control algorithm. On top are the original images and on the bottom are the log-polar maps, with the result of the inverse cross-correlation in the middle. (a) Starting vergence. (b) Correct vergence found by the gradient descent algorithm. Notice that the values of the correlation are almost zero.

convergence of the algorithm using space-variant images. It is worth noting that the space-variant sampling intrinsically emphasizes the relevance of the central part of the image during the cross-correlation procedure. In fact, the number of pixels near or inside the fovea is much higher than the pixels on the periphery. Therefore, the central part of the image is weighted more than the periphery. As a result the cross-correlation function is much sharper, making the vergence control much easier.

4.2. MOTION, OPTICAL FLOW AND TIME TO IMPACT

The ability to quickly detect an obstacle in order to react to avoid it is of vital importance for animates. Passive vision techniques can be beneficially adopted if active movements are performed [4, 5, 9, 34, 50, 59, 61, 64]. A dynamic spatiotemporal representation of the scene, which is the *time to impact* with the objects, can be computed from the optical flow which is extracted from monocular image sequences acquired during *tracking* movements of the sensor [9, 56, 63, 64, 71, 80]. The image velocity can be described as function of the camera parameters and split into two terms depending on the rotational and translational components of camera velocity respectively [63, 64]:

$$\vec{V}_r = \begin{bmatrix} \dfrac{x\,y\,\phi - \left[x^2 + F^2\right]\theta + F\,y\,\psi}{F} \\[2ex] \dfrac{\left[y^2 + F^2\right]\phi - x\,y\,\theta - F\,x\,\psi}{F} \end{bmatrix}^{t} \tag{1}$$

$$\vec{V}_t = \begin{bmatrix} \dfrac{x\left[D_1 - D_2\cos\phi\cos\theta\right] - F\,D_2\cos\phi\sin\theta}{Z} \\[2ex] \dfrac{y\left[D_1 - D_2\cos\phi\cos\theta\right] - F\,D_2\sin\phi}{Z} \end{bmatrix}^{t}$$

D_1 and D_2 are the distances of the camera from the fixation point in two successive instants of time; ϕ, θ and ψ are the rotations of the camera referred to its coordinate axes, shown in Figure 14; and Z is the distance of the world point from the image plane. As we are interested in computing the time to impact $\frac{W_z}{Z}$, then $\vec{V}_t$ must be derived from the total optical flow.

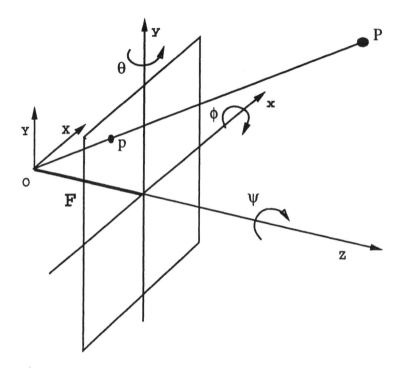

Figure 14. Diagram of the camera coordinate system, with the dynamic parameters referred to in the text.

The optical flow is computed on the (ξ, γ) plane, therefore it is necessary to define an expression to derive $\vec{V}_t$ on the Cartesian plane, given the known velocity on the log-polar plane and the motion parameters [64, 74]:

$$\vec{V}_t = \begin{bmatrix} x\,\dot{\xi}\,\log_e a & - & \frac{y\dot{\gamma}}{q} & - & \frac{xy\phi - \left[x^2 + F^2\right]\theta + Fy\psi}{F} \\ y\,\dot{\xi}\,\log_e a & + & \frac{x\dot{\gamma}}{q} & - & \frac{\left[y^2 + F^2\right]\phi - xy\theta - Fx\psi}{F} \end{bmatrix} \quad (2)$$

$(\dot{\xi}, \dot{\gamma})$ is the velocity field computed from the sequence of log-polar images. It is worth noting that expressing the Cartesian coordinates of a retinal sampling element in microns, the focal length and the retinal velocity $\vec{V}$ are also expressed in the same units.

Adopting the constrained tracking egomotion, the rotational angles are known, as they correspond to the motor control generated by the fixation/tracking system. The time to impact of all the image points on the retinal plane can be recovered using a well-known relation [44]:

$$T_{ti} \;=\; \frac{Z}{W_Z} \;=\; \frac{D_f}{\left|\vec{V_t}\right|} \tag{3}$$

D_f is the displacement of the considered point from the focus of the translational field on the image plane, and W_Z is the translational component of the sensor velocity along the optical (Z) axis. The ratio on the left-hand side represents the time to impact with respect to the considered world point. The location of the FOE is estimated by computing the least squares fitting of the pseudo intersection of the set of straight lines determined by the velocity vectors $\vec{V_t}$ [64, 74].

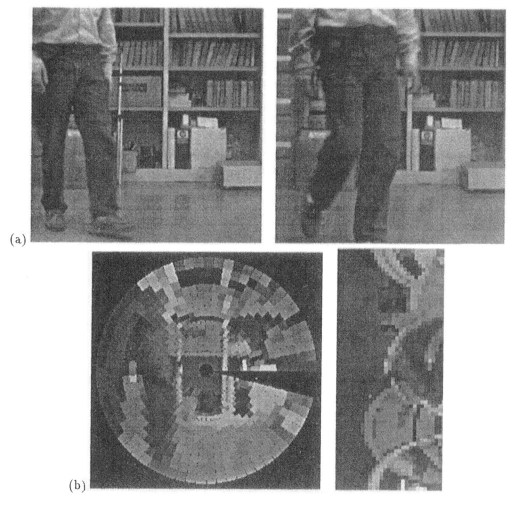

Figure 15. (a) First and last image of the sequence. (b) Retinal sampling applied to the first image, and simulated output of the retinal CCD sensor, represented in the Cartesian (x, y) and log-polar (ξ, γ) planes.

Even though this algorithm requires few constraints (including the assumption of a static environment), they still do not limit the generality of its possible applications. It can be successfully applied, for example, to locate obstacles and detect corridors of free space during robot navigation [73]. The accuracy of the measurements depends on the resolution of the input images, which, for the retinal sensor, is very low. Nevertheless, the hazard map computed with this method can still be exploited for its qualitative properties in visual navigation.

Dynamic properties of log-polar mapping

Jain [11, 42], Weiman [84] and Sandini [58] pointed out the advantages of processing the optical flow due to camera translation by using a log-polar complex mapping of the images and choosing the position of the FOE as the center for the representation.

It is possible to generalize this property to a more general and complex kind of motions. Generally, any expansion of the image of an object, due to the motion either of the camera or the object itself, will produce a radial component of velocity on the retinal plane. This intuitive observation can be stated in the following way: *The time to impact of a point on the retinal plane affects only the radial component of the optical flow.* A formal proof of this observation is given in [76].

It turns out that the most convenient way of representing and analyzing velocity is in terms of its radial and angular components with respect to the fovea [76].

Considering a general motion of the camera, both rotational and translational, the velocity on the image plane along the radial and angular coordinates is:

$$\begin{cases} \dot{\rho} = \frac{xu+yv}{\rho} = u\cos\eta + v\sin\eta \\[2ex] \dot{\eta} = \frac{xv-yu}{\rho^2} = \frac{v\cos\eta - u\sin\eta}{\rho} \end{cases} \tag{4}$$

$(u, v) = (\dot{x}, \dot{y})$ is the retinal velocity with respect to a Cartesian coordinate system centered on the fovea. Plugging in the motion equations for small angular rotations (as from Equation 1) and expressing the image velocity on the (ξ, γ) plane:

$$\begin{cases} \dot{\xi} = \frac{\dot{\rho}}{\rho}\log_a e \\[2ex] \quad = \left[\frac{1}{Z}\left[W_z - F\left(W_x\cos\frac{\gamma}{q} + W_y\sin\frac{\gamma}{q}\right)\right] + \left(\frac{\rho}{F} + \frac{F}{\rho}\right)\left(\phi\sin\frac{\gamma}{q} - \theta\cos\frac{\gamma}{q}\right)\right]\log_a e \\[2ex] \dot{\gamma} = q\dot{\eta} \\[2ex] \quad = \frac{qF}{\rho}\left[\left(\frac{W_x}{Z} + \theta\right)\sin\frac{\gamma}{q} + \left(\phi - \frac{W_y}{Z}\right)\cos\frac{\gamma}{q}\right] - q\psi \end{cases} \tag{5}$$

The above equations, although they have been derived through some simplifying assumptions, demonstrate that, while both components of the optical flow depend upon the depth Z of the objects in space, only the *radial* component $\dot{\xi}$ depends upon the time to impact $\frac{Z}{W_z}$, and this decoupling proves to be very useful. Moreover, only the *angular* component $\dot{\gamma}$ depends upon rotations around the optical axis, while the radial component is invariant with respect to ψ. Notice that up to now we have not made any hypothesis about the motion of the sensor. Therefore equation (5) certainly holds for any kind of camera motion.

Figure 16. Optical flow of the sequence in Figure 15(b), represented in the log-polar (ξ, γ) plane.

Even though the analysis has been conducted for a moving camera in a static environment the result obtained in (5) holds for any combination of object *and* camera motion. All the motion parameters are expressed in terms of translational velocities in space (W_x, W_y, W_z) and rotational velocities (ϕ, θ, ψ) referred to a camera-centered Cartesian coordinate system. These velocities do not have to be absolute velocities but can represent the relative motion of the camera with respect to the objects, which is the sum of the two velocities.

Equation (5) can be further developed in the case of tracking egomotion by imposing $\vec{V}(0,0) = \vec{0}$ in the general optical flow equations.

Many formulations of the optical flow equations and the time-to-impact computation in polar and log-polar coordinates are given in [76]. Within the scope of this chapter, the most interesting one is obtained by computing the second order partial derivative of $\dot{\xi}$:

$$\frac{Z}{W_z} = \left[\dot{\xi} \, \log_e a - \frac{\partial^2 \dot{\xi}}{\partial \xi^2} \, \log_a e \right]^{-1} \tag{6}$$

This equation is based on the assumption that the camera is actually tracking a point in space and on the assumption that the depth Z is *locally* constant. [5]

It is worth noting that Equation (6) does not depend on the position of the FOE and the motion of the fixated object; therefore it is not necessary to differentiate the optical flow with respect to the rotational component $\vec{V_r}$ to estimate the translational component $\vec{V_t}$ [57].

Moreover, time to impact can be computed from direct computations based on image features only and, more precisely, only from the the radial component of

---

[5] This concept of locality is defined by the neighbor set for the numerical computation of the derivatives of the optical flow components. In fact, any variation in depth outside this range does not affect the computation for the considered image point.

velocity with respect to the fovea.

The results of one of the experiments performed are shown in Figures 15, 16 and 17. The first and last image of a sequence of 10 are shown in Figure 15(a).

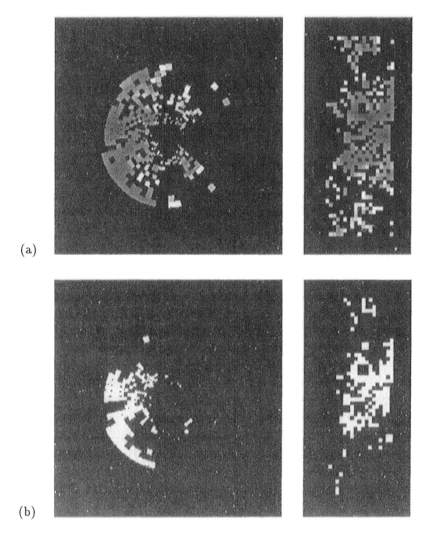

Figure 17. (a) Time to impact of the scene in Figure 15 computed by applying equation (13) to the optical flow in Figure 16. (b) Time to impact of the scene in Figure 15, computed by applying equation (6) to the optical flow in Figure 16. For clarity, data is represented on the retinal plane.

The images have been acquired at the resolution of 256×256 pixels and then resampled performing the log-polar mapping. The motion of the camera was a translation plus a rotation θ around its vertical axis Y. The direction of gaze was controlled so as to keep the fixation on the apple in the center of the basket (which is the object nearest to the observer).

In Figure 17(b) the time to impact of the scene in Figure 15, computed by applying Equation (6) to the optical flow in Figure 16, is shown. Despite the low resolution, the closest object is correctly located.

It has been shown that a space-variant velocity representation seems to be best suited to recover the time to impact from image sequences. Even though technology has been very conservative in producing only raster CCD arrays and imaging devices (therefore strongly linked to a Cartesian coordinate system), a conformal mapping can be performed in real time by using commercially available hardware, enforcing the feasibility of the proposed methodology.

5. CONCLUSIONS

Some considerations and examples of the use of "vision during action" have been presented in this chapter, with reference to manipulative and navigation tasks. Apart from the specific points described previously, the main concept presented is the fundamental, reciprocal role of vision and action in controlling "actors" behaving in unconstrained environments.[6] Within this framework vision and action cannot be decoupled, but they should be seen as concurrent, cooperating processes driven by the goal.

The advantage is that vision can be simplified by the knowledge of the intended behavior (the motor purpose) by selecting the visual measures most suited to the ongoing task and by constraining the control variables to those measurable with enough robustness and accuracy during the execution of the intended behavior.

Moreover, the exploitation of cooperative visuo-motor processes relaxes the relevance of geometric and accuracy issues by setting the requirements in terms of behavioral performance and not in terms of absolute precision and robustness of the sensory and motor components. We believe that this is the main engineering solution adopted by biological systems to overcome the intrinsic inaccuracy of the sensing and actuation components.

REFERENCES

1. M. Accordino, F. Gandolfo, A. Portunato, G. Sandini and M. Tistarelli, "Object understanding through visuo-motor cooperation," In *Proc. Int'l. Symposium on Experimental Robotics*, 1991.

2. J. Aloimonos, "Purposive and qualitative active vision," In *Proc. Image Understanding Workshop*, 1990, 816–828.

3. J. Aloimonos and D. Shulman, *Integration of Visual Modules: An Extension of the Marr Paradigm*, Academic Press, Boston, 1989.

4. J. Aloimonos, I. Weiss and A. Bandyopadhyay, "Active vision," *Int'l. J. Computer Vision* 1, 1988, 333–356.

5. R. K. Bajcsy, "Active perception vs passive perception," In *Proc. IEEE Workshop on Computer Vision: Representation and Control*, 1985, 13–16.

---

[6] In real situations the environment is never perfectly known.

6. R. Bajcsy and C. Tsikos, "Assembly via disassembly: A case in machine perceptual development," In *Proc. Int'l. Symp. Robotic Research*, 1988, 355–362.

7. R. Bajcsy and C. Tsikos, "Perception via manipulation," In *Proc. Int'l. Symp. and Exposition on Robots*, 1988, 237–244.

8. D. H. Ballard, "Eye movements and visual cognition," In *Proc. Workshop on Spatial Reasoning and Multi-Sensor Fusion*, 1987, 188–200.

9. D.H. Ballard, R.C. Nelson and B. Yamauchi, "Animate vision," *Optics News* **15**, 1989, 17–25.

10. Z. Balorda, "Reducing uncertainty of objects by robot pushing," In *Proc. IEEE Int'l. Conf. on Robotics and Automation*, 1990, 1051–1056.

11. S.L. Bartlett and R.C. Jain, "Depth determination using complex logarithmic mapping," In *Proc. SPIE Int'l. Conf. on Intelligent Robots and Computer Vision: Neural, Biological and 3-D Methods*, 1990.

12. C. Braccini, G. Gambardella, G. Sandini and V. Tagliasco, "A model of the early stages of the human visual system: Functional and topological transformation performed in the peripheral visual field," *Biological Cybernetics* **44**, 1982, 47–58.

13. R. Brooks, "A robust layered control system for a mobile robot," *IEEE J. Robotics and Automation* **2**, 1986, 237–244.

14. P. J. Burt, *Smart Sensing in Machine Vision*, Academic Press, 1988.

15. B.F. Buxton, D.A. Castelow, M. Rygol, P. McLauchan, P. Courtney and S.B. Pollard, "Developing a stereo vision system for control of an agv," In *Proc. IEEE Int'l. Seminar on the Design and Application of Parallel Digital Processors*, 1991.

16. S. Carlsson and J.O. Eklundh, "Object detection using model based prediction and motion parallax," In *Proc. European Conf. on Computer Vision*, 1990, 297–306.

17. R.H.S. Carpenter, *Movements of the Eyes*, Pion Ltd., England, 1977.

18. D.J. Coombs and C.M. Brown, "Intelligent gaze control in binocular vision," In *Proc. IEEE Int'l. Symposium on Intelligent Control*, 1990.

19. D.J. Coombs, T.J. Olson and C.M. Brown, "Gaze control and segmentation," In *Proc. AAAI Workshop on Qualitative Vision*, 1990.

20. J.L. Crowley, P. Bobet and M. Mesrabi, "Gaze control with a binocular camera head," In *Proc. European Conf. on Computer Vision*, 1992.

21. I. Debusschere, E. Bronckaers, C. Claeys, G. Kreider, J. Van der Spiegel, P. Bellutti, G. Soncini, P. Dario, F. Fantini and G. Sandini, "A 2d retinal ccd sensor for fast 2d shape recognition and tracking," In *Proc. Int'l. Conf. on Solid-State Sensor and Transducers*, 1989.

22. E. DeMicheli, G. Sandini, M. Tistarelli and V. Torre, "Estimation of visual motion and 3d motion parameters from singular points," In *Proc. IEEE Int'l. Workshop on Intelligent Robots and Systems*, 1988.

23. U.R. Dhond and J.K. Aggarwal, "Structure from stereo - a review," *IEEE Trans. SMC* **19**, 1989.

24. W. Enkelmann, "Obstacle detection by evaluation of optical flow fields from image sequences," In *Proc. European Conf. on Computer Vision*, 1990, 134–138.

25. F. Ferrari, M. Fossa, E. Grosso, M. Magrassi and G. Sandini, "A practical implementation of a multilevel architecture for vision-based navigation," In *Proc. Int'l. Conf. on Advanced Robotics*, 1991, 1092–1098.

26. F. Ferrari, E. Grosso, G. Sandini and M. Magrassi, "A stereo vision system for real time obstacle avoidance in unknown environment," In *Proc. IEEE IROS-90*, 1990, 703–708.

27. M. Fossa, E. Fuiano and G. Sandini, "A vision architecture for navigation," In *Proc. Conf. on Intelligent Autonomous Systems*, 1989, 325–335.

28. M. Fossa, E. Grosso, F. Ferrari, G. Sandini and M. Zapendouski, "A visually guided mobile robot acting in indoor environments," In *Proc. IEEE Workshop on Applications of Computer Vision*, 1992.

29. N. Franceschini, J. Pichon and C. Blanes, "Real time visuomotor control: from flies to robots," In *Proc. Int'l. Conf. on Advanced Robotics*, 1991.

30. B.V. Funt, "Problem-solving with diagrammatic representations," *Artificial Intelligence* **13**, 1980, 201–230.

31. C.R. Gallistel, *"The Organization of Learning,"* MIT Press., Cambridge, Massachusetts, 1990.

32. F. Girosi, A. Verri and V. Torre, "Constraints for the computation of optical flow," In *IEEE Int'l. Conf. on Robotics and Automation*, 1989, 116–124.

33. E. Grosso, G. Sandini and C. Frigato, "Extraction of 3d information and volumetric uncertainty from multiple images," *Proc. ECAI-88*, 1988, 683–688.

34. E. Grosso, G. Sandini and M. Tistarelli, "3d object reconstruction using stereo and motion," *IEEE Trans. SMC* **19** 1989.

35. C.G. Harris and J.M. Pike, "3d positional integration from image sequences," *Image and Vision Computing* **6**, 1988, 87–90.

36. E.C. Hildreth, *"The Measurement of Visual Motion,"* MIT Press, Cambridge, 1983.

37. B.K.P. Horn, *Robot Vision*, McGraw Hill, NY, 1986.

38. B.K.P. Horn and B.G. Schunck, "Determining optical flow," *Artificial Intelligence* **17**, 1981, 185–204.

39. G.A. Horridge, "A theory of insect vision: Velocity parallax," *Proc. Royal Soc. London B* **229**, 1986, 13–27.

40. D.H. Hubel and D.C. Freeman, "Projection into the visual field of ocular dominance columns in macaque monkey," *Brain Research* **122**, 1977, 336–343.

41. D.H. Hubel and T.N. Wiesel, "Uniformity of monkey striate cortex: A parallel relationship between field size, scatter and magnification factor," *J. Comp. Neur.* **158**, 1974, 295–306.

42. R.C. Jain, S.L. Bartlett and N. O'Brian, "Motion stereo using ego-motion complex logarithmic mapping," *IEEE Trans. PAMI* **9**, 1987, 356–369.

43. C. Jerian and R. Jain, "Determining motion parameters for scenes with translation and rotation," *IEEE Trans. PAMI*, 1984, 523–529.

44. D.T. Lawton, "Processing translational motion sequences," *CVGIP* **22**, 1983, 116–144.

45. M. Lehrer, M.V. Srinivasan, S.W. Zhang and G.A. Horridge, "Motion cues provide the bee's visual world with a third dimension," *Nature* **332**, 1988, 356–357.

46. T. Lindeberg and L. Florack, "On the Decrease of Resolution as a Function of Eccentricity for a Foveal Vision System," Technical Report TRITA-NA-P9229, CVAP111 - Stockholm, 1992.

47. M. Mason, "Mechanics and planning of manipulator pushing operations," In *Int'l. J. Robotic Research*, 1986, 53–70.

48. L. Massone, G. Sandini and V. Tagliasco, "Form-invariant topological mapping strategy for 2-d shape recognition," *CVGIP* **30**, 1985, 169–188.

49. E. De Micheli, G. Sandini M. Tistarelli and V. Torre, "Estimation of visual motion and 3d motion parameters from singular points," In *Proc. IEEE Workshop on Intelligent Robots and Systems*, 1988, 543–548.

50. P. Morasso, G. Sandini and M. Tistarelli, "Active vision: Integration of fixed and mobile cameras," In *NATO ARW on Sensors and Sensory Systems for Advanced Robots*, 1986.

51. H. Nagel, "On the estimation of optical flow: Relations between different approaches and some new results," *Artificial Intelligence* **33**, 1987, 299–323.

52. T.J. Olson and D.J. Coombs, "Real-time vergence control for binocular robots," Technical Report 348, Dep't. of Computer Science, University of Rochester, 1990.

53. K. Pahlavan, T. Uhlin and J.-O. Eklundh, "Integrating primary ocular processes," In *Proc. ECCV92 - European Conf. on Computer Vision*, 1992.

54. D.T. Pham, K.C. Cheung and S.H. Yeo, "Initial motion of a rectangular object being pushed or pulled," In *Proc. IEEE Int'l. Conf. on Robotics and Automation*, Cincinnati, Ohio, 1990, 1046–1050.

55. S.B. Pollard, J. Porrill and J.E.W. Mayhew. "Experiments in vehicle control using predictive feed-forward stereo processing," *Image and Vision Computing* **8**, 1990, 63–70.

56. D. Raviv and M. Herman, "Towards an understanding of camera fixation," In *Proc. IEEE Int'l. Conf. on Robotics and Automation*, 1990, 28–33.

57. J.H. Rieger and D.T. Lawton, "Processing differential image motion," Technical Report, COINS Dep't., University of Massachusetts, Amherst, 1984.

58. G. Sandini, F. Bosero, F. Bottino and A. Ceccherini, "The use of an anthropomorphic visual sensor for motion estimation and object tracking," In *Proc. OSA Topical Meeting on Image Understanding and Machine Vision*, 1989.

59. G. Sandini and P. Dario, "Active vision based on space-variant sensing," In *Proc. Int'l. Symposium on Robotics Research*, 1989.

60. G. Sandini, F. Gandolfo, G. Metta and A. Oddera, "The role of vision in two-arms manipulation," Technical Report, DIST University of Genoa - LIRA Lab., Genoa, Italy, 1992.

61. G. Sandini, P. Morasso and M. Tistarelli, "Motor and spatial aspects in artificial vision," In *Proc. Int'l. Symposium on Robotics Research*, 1987.

62. G. Sandini and V. Tagliasco, "An anthropomorphic retina-like structure for scene analysis," *CGIP* **14**, 1980, 365–372.

63. G. Sandini and M. Tistarelli, "Active tracking strategy for monocular depth inference over multiple frames," *IEEE Trans. PAMI* **12**, 1990, 13–27.

64. G. Sandini and M. Tistarelli, "Vision and space variant sensing," In H. Wechsler (Ed.), *Neural Networks for Perception*, Academic Press, 1992, 398–425.

65. G. Sandini and M. Tistarelli, "Understanding Optical Flow Anomalies," Technical Report, DIST University of Genoa - LIRA Lab., Genoa, Italy, 1990.

66. G. Sandini and M. Tistarelli, "Robust obstacle detection using optical flow," In *Proc. IEEE Int'l. Workshop on Robust Computer Vision*, 1990.

67. G. Sandini, J. Santos Victor, F. Curotto and S. Garibaldi, "Robotic Bees," Technical Report, DIST University of Genoa - LIRA Lab., Genoa, Italy, 1992.

68. E.L. Schwartz, "Spatial mapping in the primate sensory projection: Analytic structure and relevance to perception," *Biological Cybernetics* **25**, 1977, 181–194.

69. E.L. Schwartz, "A quantitative model of the functional architecture of human striate cortex with application to visual illusion and cortical texture analysis," *Biological Cybernetics* **37**, 1980, 63–76.

70. M.V. Srinivasan, M. Lehrer, W.H. Kirchner and S.W. Zhang, "Range perception through apparent image speed in freely flying honeybees," *Visual Neuroscience* **6**, 1991, 519–535.

71. M.A. Taalebinezhaad, "Direct recovery of motion and shape in the general case by fixation," In *Proc. IEEE Int'l. Conf. on Computer Vision*, 1990, 451–455.

72. L. Telford, I.P. Howard and M. Ohmi, "The effects od discordant visual-motor and visual-vestibular information on judgements of heading," In *Proc. European Conf. on Visual Perception*, 1992.

73. M. Tistarelli and G. Sandini, "Robot navigation using an anthropomorphic visual sensor," In *Proc. IEEE Int'l. Conf. on Robotics and Automation*, 1990, 374–383.

74. M. Tistarelli and G. Sandini, "Estimation of depth from motion using an anthropomorphic visual sensor," *Image and Vision Computing* **8**, 1991, 271–278.

75. M. Tistarelli and G. Sandini, "Dynamic aspects in active vision," *CVGIP: Image Understanding* **56**, Y. Aloimonos (Ed.), Special Issue on Purposive and Qualitative Active Vision, 1992, 108–129.

76. M. Tistarelli and G. Sandini, "On the advantages of polar and log-polar mapping for direct estimation of time-to-impact from optical flow," *IEEE Trans. PAMI*, 1993.

77. S. Uras, F. Girosi, A. Verri and V. Torre, "Computational approach to motion perception," *Biological Cybernetics* **60**, 1988, 69–87.

78. J. Van der Spiegel, G. Kreider, C. Claeys, I. Debusschere, G. Sandini, P. Dario, F. Fantini, P. Bellutti and G. Soncini, *Analog VLSI and Neural Network Implementations*, Kluwer, 1989.

79. A.J. van Dorn, J.J. Koenderink and M.A. Bouman, "The influence of the retinal inhomogeneity on the perception of spatial patterns," *Kibernetic* **4**, 1972, 223–230.

80. D. Vernon and M. Tistarelli, "Using camera motion to estimate range for robotic parts manipulation," *IEEE Trans. on Robotics and Automation* **5**, 1990, 509–521.

81. J. Santos Victor, G. Sandini, F. Curotto and S. Garibaldi, "Divergent Stereo for Robot Navigation: Learning from Bees," Technical Report, DIST University of Genoa - LIRA Lab., Genoa, Italy, 1992.

82. H. Wang, C. Bowman, M. Brady and C. Harris, "A parallel implementation of a structure from motion algorithms," In *Proc. European Conf. on Computer Vision*, 1992, 272–276.

83. C.F.R. Weiman and G. Chaikin. "Logarithmic spiral grids for image processing and display," *CGIP* **11**, 1979, 197–226.

84. C.F.R. Weiman and R. D. Juday. "Tracking algorithms using log-polar mapped image coordinates," In *Proc. SPIE Int'l. Conf. on Intelligent Robots and Computer Vision VIII: Algorithms and Techniques*, 1990, 843–853.

5   VISUAL SERVOING FROM 2-D IMAGE CUES

Daniel Raviv[1,2] and Martin Herman[2]
[1]Florida Atlantic University and
[2]National Institute of Standards and Technology

ABSTRACT

Visual servoing is a mode of navigation in which the motion of a robot vehicle is controlled through servoing on visual cues. Many visual servoing behaviors can be achieved using direct 2-D image cues, without requiring 3-D information reconstructed from the imagery. Usually, only a few *relevant* image cues need to be extracted for each behavior. Each behavior will, in general, need different relevant information, which may be a set of visible or invisible, spatial or temporal image features. The advantages of this approach are that it is potentially simpler, faster and more robust than the approach that uses 3-D reconstructed information. It results in tight perception-action control loops to directly generate action commands from image cues. We present three case studies to demonstrate these ideas: road following, landing on a surface and visual looming for obstacle avoidance and object approach. For each of these we show what kind of 2-D information can be used directly to control the robot's motion.

1. INTRODUCTION

An important mode of visual navigation is visual servoing, in which the motion of an autonomous vehicle is controlled through servoing on visual cues. There seems to be a primitive set of robot motion behaviors that can be achieved through visual servoing. Some of these are obstacle avoidance, boundary following, motion relative to environmental objects, approaching an object without collision, pursuing a moving target and landing on a surface.

This work was supported in part by a grant to Florida Atlantic University from the National Science Foundation, Division of Information, Robotics and Intelligent Systems, Grant No. IRI-9115939.

1. *Obstacle avoidance through visual servoing.*
   This involves using stereo, motion and other visual cues to identify obstacles and to servo around them. Obstacles can be either protrusions (things lying on top of the ground) or depressions (holes in the ground). They may be stationary or moving.
2. *Boundary following through visual servoing.*
   A boundary in this case is any extended curvilinear feature (in 2-D) or surface (in 3-D) that serves to (partially) bound something of interest, such as a road boundary, wall boundary, edge of forest boundary or other such features. Boundary following through visual servoing involves detecting and tracking features related to the boundary and servoing based on properties of these features.
3. *Visually servoed motion relative to objects in the environment.*
   This involves using visual cues to identify objects of interest and to servo the robot's motion relative to these objects. This is very similar to obstacle avoidance, except that the motion relative to these objects might be more structured than for obstacle avoidance. For example, motion relative to a particular object might be "bear left." Also, fine motions relative to the object can be executed here, such as executing a predetermined precise trajectory relative to the object.
4. *Approaching an object without collision.*
   This involves using visual cues to servo the robot's direction of motion and speed relative to the object of interest, such that the object is gradually approached.
5. *Pursuing a moving target.*
   This involves using visual cues to control the robot's direction of motion and speed relative to a moving target, such that the target is being followed (see also Chapter 2).
6. *Landing on a surface.*
   This involves detecting and tracking features on the surface, and servoing the robot's direction of motion and orientation in space based on these features.

In this chapter we argue that in many cases visual servoing behaviors can be achieved using direct 2-D image cues (both spatial and temporal). These cues serve as inputs to the motion control algorithms. In such cases, an explicit reconstruction of the 3-D scene may not be required. Usually, only a few *relevant* image cues need to be extracted for each behavior. For example, boundary following (as in road following) can be achieved using isolated image information contained in either the inner or outer boundaries of curved roads. As will be shown below, for inner boundaries (which are convex), a feature that may be sufficient for road following is the tangent point on the inner road edge (i.e., the point on the inner road edge lying on an imaginary line tangent to the road edge and passing through the camera) and its image velocity. Therefore, during the boundary following behavior, all image processing effort may be directed toward reliably finding and tracking the tangent point and extracting its image velocity.

In some cases important features do not exist (and are meaningless) in 3-D and can be extracted only in the 2-D image. An example is the vanishing point, which is meaningful only in the 2-D image. As will be shown below, this feature is useful for autonomous landing of an air vehicle. Another example is the focus of expansion, which indicates the instantaneous heading of the camera. Sometimes, *relevant* features do not exist in the image and need to be extracted from other visible features. The vanishing point and the focus of expansion are two examples of this. Of course, many image features are temporal and have meaning only if motion is involved.

The advantages of this 2-D approach are that it is simple, fast and robust. There is no need for 3-D reconstruction. It results in a tight perception-action loop to directly generate action commands from image cues.

The approach taken here derives from several approaches currently in the literature, including "purposive and active vision" [1, 2], "animate vision" [4] and "direct perception" [10]. The common element between these approaches and our approach is that only visual information that can be used specifically and directly for the desired task or behavior is sought.

We present three case studies to demonstrate these ideas. In each of these, there is a tight perception-action loop, i.e., 2-D information can be used *directly* to control the robot's motion. Also, in each of these cases, information dealing with the speed of the robot is not needed.

1. *Road following.*

   A visible 2-D image feature on the road boundary (theoretically a point) can be used to directly generate control signals for road following. Although the feature can be reconstructed in 3-D, we show that there are advantages to not doing so.

2. *Autonomous landing.*

   An invisible 2-D image feature (theoretically a point) can be used to generate two independent control signals for vision-based autonomous landing. This feature, a vanishing point, is extracted from other image features, has meaning only in the 2-D projection of 3-D space, and cannot be reconstructed in 3-D (since it represents a point at infinite distance).

3. *Visual looming for obstacle avoidance and object approach.*

   Looming is a temporal feature that is closely related to the time-to-contact [12, 13, 16, 14, 15, 17, 18, 20, 24, 23, 26]. Its value can be used to generate control signals for obstacle avoidance or for approaching an object without collision. It has no meaning when observing one image only. The information lies in the temporal change of a spatial feature. In many cases it is easier to extract this feature directly from a 2-D image sequence than from 3-D reconstructed information.

2. SERVOING THE HEADING VECTOR

The heading vector at any instance of time is the instantaneous translation vector of the robot. Many of the primitive navigation behaviors involving visual servoing can be thought of as servoing the heading vector.

Consider the case of road following. We define a *road* as any continuous, extended curvilinear feature. The goal of road following is to follow along this feature over an extended period of time. In what we normally think of as road following, a road is defined either by its boundaries or by an extended solid or dashed white line. Here the goal is not only to follow along these features but also to stay within a constant lateral distance from these features. In general, the feature to be followed need not define a real road. For example, it could be a boundary line of vegetation, a stripe painted on the ground, or even a wall. For a low-flying air vehicle the feature to be followed could be a river. Road following is therefore a subset of the more general behavior of boundary following.

Visual road-following requires the ability to continuously detect and track features in imagery obtained from an onboard camera and to make steering decisions based on visual properties of these features.

Figure 1 shows a vehicle and the left-hand side road edge. The unit vector $\hat{h}$ is the instantaneous heading of the vehicle, O is the instantaneous center of curvature of the vehicle path and r is the instantaneous radius of curvature of this path. Road following is an activity that involves servoing $\hat{h}$ so that it follows the road edge. It is desired that $\hat{h}$ be servoed so that it is always parallel to the tangent to the local curvature of the road edge (Figure 1b), and so that the distance s of a point on the vehicle from the road edge is maintained at a constant value. In other words, the instantaneous center of curvature of the road edge and the instantaneous center of curvature of the vehicle path should coincide, and the tangent to the edge of the road at the intersection point B should be parallel to $\hat{h}$.[1]

In the image domain, the heading vector is represented by the instantaneous *Focus of Expansion* (FOE), i.e., the 3-D vector extending from the camera focal point to the image FOE point is in the same direction as the heading vector. Therefore, servoing the heading vector is equivalent to servoing the robot's motion using as feedback the position and motion of image features relative to the FOE. We think of this as servoing the FOE in the image. For example, we will show that road following can be achieved using a feedback loop where the position and motion of the road tangent point relative to the FOE are used as feedback variables.

3. MOBILITY CONTROL USING 2-D IMAGE DOMAIN INFORMATION

Many current vision-based mobility control systems use 3-D visually derived information when making motion control decisions [8, 9, 25, 27, 28]. This 3-D information might take the form of range points or range images, 3-D line or surface descriptions, 3-D object descriptions, etc. For example, many existing road following algorithms convert the information extracted from images into a 3-D, vehicle-centered coordinate system, often aligned with the ground plane. Steering, acceleration, and braking decisions are then determined in this coordinate system. A 3-D reconstruction is therefore performed before control decisions are made. In this chapter, we show that control algorithms can be developed that *directly* use observable image information represented explicitly or implicitly in the 2-D image sequence. For example, the position and motion of features in the image can be used to determine steering decisions. A 3-D reconstruction is not required.

---

[1] Normally, these constraints will not be met if the vehicle is attempting to avoid an obstacle or if the vehicle is changing lanes on a road. If a road has two boundaries, then road following will normally involve staying within both boundary edges.

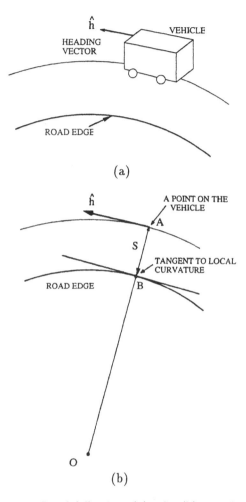

Figure 1. Road following: (a) 3-D; (b) top view.

There are several advantages to this 2-D-based approach.

1. It is more robust. Fewer hypotheses, sensor measurements, and calibrations need to be performed for control when using 2-D information rather than 3-D information. The reason is that the problem of converting 2-D image information to 3-D world information requires the making of hypotheses about the world (e.g., smoothness hypotheses, lighting hypotheses, object hypotheses), calibrations (e.g., stereo calibrations, inertial navigation system calibrations), or many sensor measurements (e.g., inertial navigation system measurements). In using visual information as part of control algorithms, the closer the visual information is to raw data form, the closer it reflects the real world, and the more robust will the control algorithms based on this information be. An example of this is converting image velocity of points to range. Such a process requires that the

velocity of the camera be known. However, the measurement of velocity will have errors which will lead to range errors. Therefore we expect that it would be more robust not to use velocity to perform navigation control. Further, a control algorithm that does not require velocity is simpler and less expensive.

2. The approach is task-dependent, therefore only relevant information has to be extracted from the images. For example, the road following behavior may only require information dealing with the road tangent point [22]. Other portions of the road edge, although important for extracting the tangent point, may not be necessary as inputs to the steering control algorithm. Each navigation behavior will, in general, need different *relevant* information. Such relevant information may be a set of visible or invisible, spatial or temporal features. Using only a small set of information from a sequence of images implies simpler and less expensive processes.

3. The closer the relevant visual information is to raw form, the less computation is required to extract this information. Such an approach is therefore simpler and much faster.

4. Using an active vision approach (in particular a multiresolution fixating camera) some vision-based control computations can be significantly simplified. An example is the measurement of visual looming. Computations become simpler (or may not be needed at all) when using a fixating foveal-peripheral logarithmic retina [20].

Figure 2a shows the 3-D based approach. The image sequence is transformed to 3-D information. Based on 3-D data and the task to be taken, a path and control signals are generated. Figure 2b shows the 2-D based approach. The information for generating control signals lies in the *relevant 2-D cues*. This information is used to *directly* control the vehicle.

Next we present the three case studies.

4. Case Study 1: Road Following

4.1. Coordinate system

The equations for this case study are defined in a coordinate system which is fixed with respect to the camera on board the vehicle. This coordinate system is shown in Figure 3. We assume that the camera is mounted on a vehicle (later we explain how) moving in a stationary environment. Assume a pinhole camera model and that the pinhole point of the camera is at the origin of the coordinate system. This coordinate system is used to measure angles to points in space and to measure optical flow at these points. We use spherical coordinates $(R - \theta - \phi)$ for this purpose. In this system, angular velocities ($\dot{\theta}$ and $\dot{\phi}$) of any point in space, say P, are identical to the optical flow values at P' in the image domain. Figure 4 illustrates this concept: θ and ϕ of a point in space are the same as θ and ϕ of the projected point P' in the image domain, and therefore there is no need to convert angular velocities of points in 3-D space to optical flow. In Figure 4 the image domain is a sphere. However, for practical purposes the surface of the image sphere can be mapped onto an image plane (or other surface).

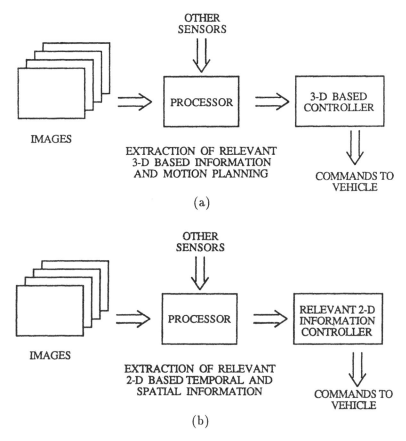

Figure 2. Block diagrams showing how commands are generated: (a) Generating 3-D based commands; (b) Generating 2-D based commands.

4.2. TWO-WHEELED VEHICLE

For our analysis we use a theoretical two-wheeled vehicle as illustrated in Figure 5. A rigid frame of length $2m$ holds both wheels. A steering wheel angle is applied to both wheels simultaneously, i.e., if one wheel is rotated by an angle β relative to the frame, the other wheel will rotate by the same angle. This apparatus assures that both wheels will always stay at the same distance from the instantaneous center of curvature of the vehicle's path. The camera is mounted so that its pinhole point is located above the front wheel center, and it rotates with the front wheel. The optical axis of the camera coincides with the instantaneous translation vector (heading) of the front wheel. Note that the heading vector of other points on the vehicle will, in general, not be the same as that of the front wheel.

The following geometrical relationship holds for the vehicle in Figure 5:

$$r = \frac{m}{\sin \beta} \tag{1}$$

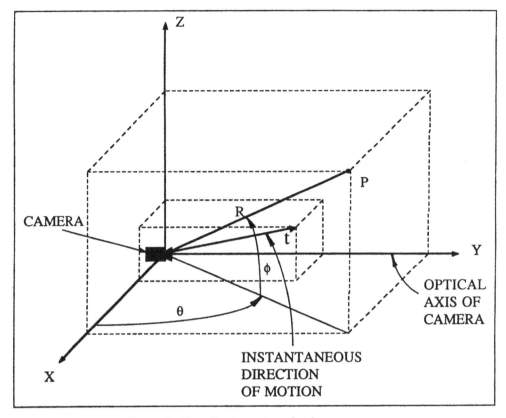

Figure 3. Coordinate system fixed to camera.

The frame length m is usually known. Thus the instantaneous radius of curvature r of the vehicle path can be determined by measuring the steering angle β.

Figure 6 is an overall description of the system including the spherical coordinate system, and Figure 7 is the related top view. For convenience we chose to have the Z- axis pointing down. However the same coordinate system as described in Figure 3 is used here. The camera is mounted at some height above the ground and rotates with the front wheel. The position of any point on the road can be expressed with the coordinates R, θ and ϕ, as shown in Figure 6.

In the following analysis, we assume a moving vehicle in a stationary environment. The road is assumed to be planar, and road edges are assumed to be extractable. Figure 8 shows examples of road images obtained from a camera mounted on a vehicle.

4.3. EQUATIONS OF MOTION AND OPTICAL FLOW

We have recently developed a new visual field theory that relates six-degree-of-freedom camera motion to optical flow for a stationary environment [19, 21]. This theory provides us with a theoretical and scientific basis for developing constraints, control schemes and optical flow-based visual cues for road following. This section reviews this theory as it relates to the road following problem.

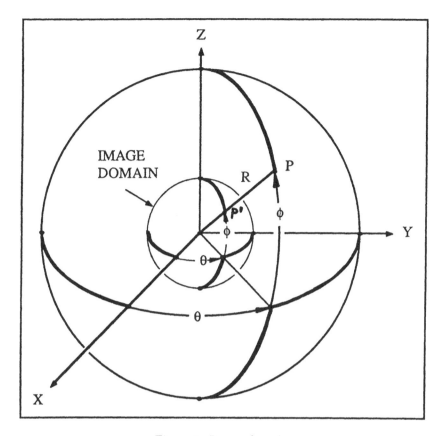

Figure 4. Image domain.

First we describe the equations that relate a point in 3-D space to the projection of that point in the image for general six-degree-of-freedom motion of the camera. Some of the equations can be found in many books, e.g., see [11].

Let the instantaneous coordinates of a 3-D point P (Figure 3) be $\mathbf{R} = (X, Y, Z)^T$ (where the superscript T denotes transpose), the instantaneous translational velocity of the camera be $\mathbf{t} = (U, V, W)^T$, and the instantaneous angular velocity of the camera be $\omega = (A, B, C)^T$. Now consider a specific motion in the instantaneous XY ($\phi = 0$) plane of the camera coordinate system defined by:

$$\mathbf{t} = (U, V, 0)^T \tag{2}$$

$$\omega = (0, 0, C)^T \tag{3}$$

This means that the translation vector may lie anywhere in the instantaneous XY plane, while the rotation is about the Z-axis. It can be shown [19] that

$$\begin{bmatrix} \dot{\theta} \\ \dot{\phi} \end{bmatrix} = \begin{bmatrix} \frac{-Y}{X^2+Y^2} & \frac{X}{X^2+Y^2} & 0 \\ \frac{-XZ}{\sqrt{X^2+Y^2}(X^2+Y^2+Z^2)} & \frac{-YZ}{\sqrt{X^2+Y^2}(X^2+Y^2+Z^2)} & \sqrt{\frac{X^2+Y^2}{X^2+Y^2+Z^2}} \end{bmatrix} \begin{bmatrix} -U + CY \\ -V - CX \\ 0 \end{bmatrix} \tag{4}$$

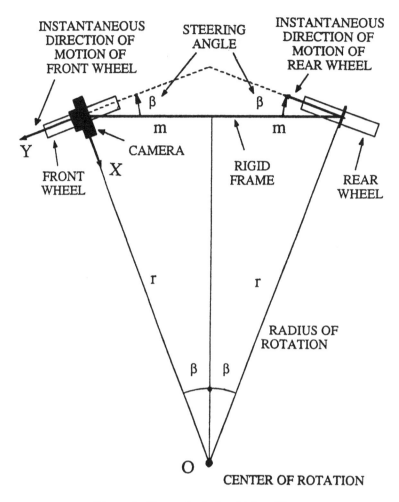

Figure 5. Two-wheeled vehicle with camera.

As mentioned earlier, $\dot{\theta}$ and $\dot{\phi}$ of a point in space (i.e., the angular velocities in the camera coordinate system) are the *same* as the optical flow components $\dot{\theta}$ and $\dot{\phi}$ (Figure 4).

Consider the case where the optical flow value of $\dot{\theta}$ is constant. From equation set (4), the points in space that result from constant $\dot{\theta}$ (regardless of the value of $\dot{\phi}$) form a cylinder of infinite height whose equation is

$$\left(X + \frac{V}{2(C + \dot{\theta})}\right)^2 + \left(Y - \frac{U}{2(C + \dot{\theta})}\right)^2 = \left(\frac{V}{2(C + \dot{\theta})}\right)^2 + \left(\frac{U}{2(C + \dot{\theta})}\right)^2 \quad (5)$$

as displayed in Figure 9.

Figure 10 shows a horizontal section of the cylinder of equation (5). The section is a circle that lies in the XY plane. This plane is perpendicular to the axis of symmetry of the cylinder. The radius of the circle is $\left[\left(\frac{V}{2(C+\dot{\theta})}\right)^2 + \left(\frac{U}{2(C+\dot{\theta})}\right)^2\right]^{\frac{1}{2}}$ and

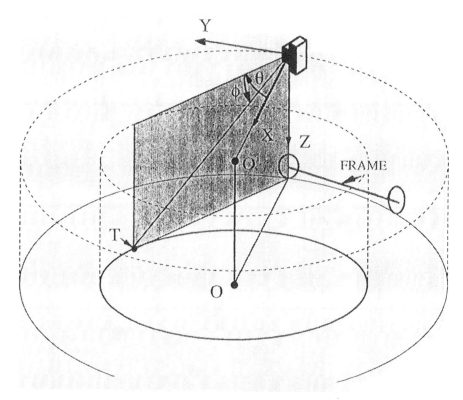

Figure 6. Overall description of system.

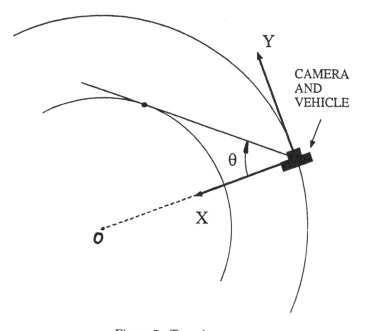

Figure 7. Top view.

Figure 8. Images obtained from camera mounted on a vehicle.

its center is at $\left(-\frac{V}{2(C+\dot{\theta})}, \frac{U}{2(C+\dot{\theta})}\right)$. The circle is tangent to the camera translation vector at the origin.

The meaning of Equation (5) is the following: All points in 3-D space that lie on the cylinder described by Equation (5) and which are visible (i.e., unoccluded and in the field of view of the camera) produce the same instantaneous horizontal optical flow $\dot{\theta}$. We call the cylinder on which equal flow points lie the *equal flow cylinder*.

4.4. ZERO FLOW CYLINDERS

One of the equal flow cylinders corresponds to points in 3-D space that produce zero horizontal flow. We call this cylinder a *zero flow cylinder*. The equation that describes the zero flow cylinder can be obtained by setting $\dot{\theta} = 0$ in Equation (5),

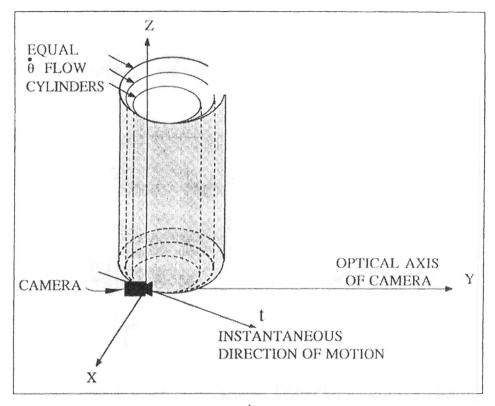

Figure 9. Equal $\dot{\theta}$ flow cylinders.

i.e.,

$$\left(X + \frac{V}{2C}\right)^2 + \left(Y - \frac{U}{2C}\right)^2 = \left(\frac{V}{2C}\right)^2 + \left(\frac{U}{2C}\right)^2 \tag{6}$$

We have shown [22] that if the Z component of the camera rotation vector ω is positive (i.e., $C > 0$), then visible points in the XY plane that are inside the zero flow cylinder produce positive horizontal optical flow ($\dot{\theta} > 0$), while visible points outside the zero flow cylinder produce negative horizontal optical flow ($\dot{\theta} < 0$) in the image (see Figure 11). If ω is negative (i.e. $C > 0$) then the opposite is true.

4.5. EQUAL FLOW CYLINDERS AS A FUNCTION OF TIME

As the camera moves through 3-D space, the equal flow cylinders move with it. Figure 12 shows sections of equal flow cylinders as a function of time. At each instant of time, the radii of the equal flow cylinders are a function of the instantaneous motion parameters $\mathbf{t}$ and ω. The locations of the equal flow cylinders are such that they always contain the origin of the camera coordinate system (the same as the camera pinhole point), they are tangent to the instantaneous translation vector $\mathbf{t}$, and their symmetry axes are parallel to the instantaneous rotation vector ω. (In Figure 12, the direction of ω varies over time.) Each zero flow cylinder lies to the left or right of the translation vector depending on whether the instantaneous rotation is positive or negative, respectively.

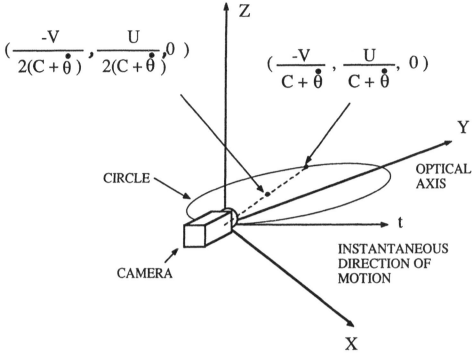

Figure 10. Section of a zero flow cylinder.

4.6. ROAD FOLLOWING BY GAZING AT INNER ROAD EDGE

In this section, we consider following along a circular road by gazing at the inner road edge. Given visual cues, a goal of the control system is to find the steering angle. If the vehicle is already on a path that follows the road, then only *changes* in steering angle are necessary. Figure 13 shows a vehicle moving around a circular road of radius l. The path traversed by the vehicle is a circle of radius r. Let the unit vector $\hat{t}$ indicate the direction of the *tangent line*, a line that contains the camera pinhole point and is tangent to the inner road edge.

We will show next that the tangent point T lies on the instantaneous zero flow cylinder if the camera orientation is fixed relative to the vehicle. The proof for this is as follows. Let us consider the planar case first, as shown in Figure 13. Given that the line AT is tangent to the road edge, then AT is perpendicular to OT. We will now show that OA is the diameter of the section of the zero flow cylinder displayed in Figure 13. From Equation (5), we can see that the center of the zero flow cylinder section is at $\left(-\frac{V}{2(C+\dot{\theta})}, \frac{U}{2(C+\dot{\theta})}\right)$ (Figure 10). Further, the location of the camera is at $(0,0)$. Now the center of rotation of the camera's circular path must lie on the zero flow cylinder section. To see why, we first note that the vector from the camera to the center of rotation O is always perpendicular to the camera heading vector. (Remember that the heading vector and camera optical axis coincide.) Therefore the center O can be considered as a fixation point for the camera during its motion, i.e., the position of point O does not change relative to the camera's coordinate system [19, 21]. This means that this point must theoretically produce zero horizontal optical

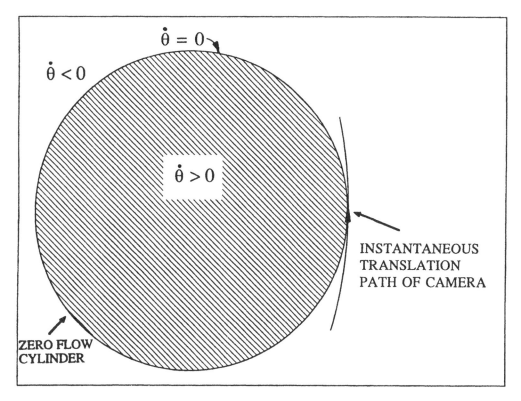

Figure 11. Section of a zero flow cylinder.

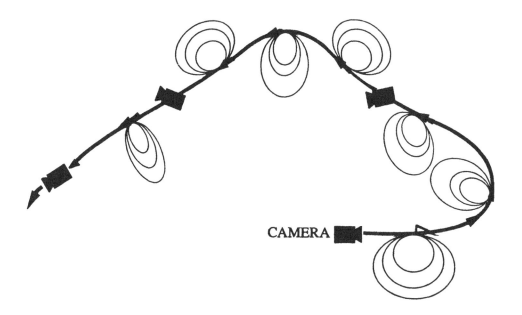

Figure 12. Sections of equal flow cylinders as a function of time.

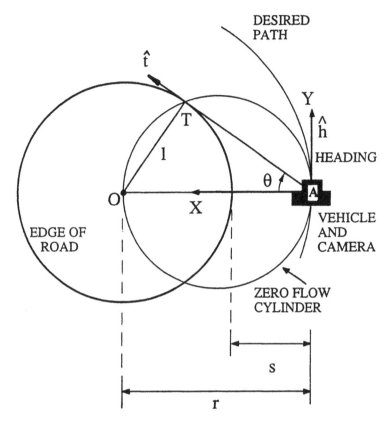

Figure 13. Circular edge: top view.

flow in the camera (assuming the camera has a wrap-around lens). Therefore, point O must lie on the zero flow cylinder section. Then the center of rotation of the camera's circular path must be at $\left(-\frac{V}{(C+\theta)}, \frac{U}{(C+\theta)}\right)$ (Figure 10). Therefore line OA is the diameter of the zero flow cylinder. Since the angle OTA is a right angle, point T must lie on the circle whose diameter is OA. Since this circle is a section of the zero flow cylinder, point T must lie on this cylinder. For the case where the inner road edge does not lie in the X-Y plane of the camera, all points above or below the point T (including the one on the edge of the road) lie on the zero flow cylinder.

Notice that this proof holds no matter what the diameter of the circular road edge is. This means that no matter how far the vehicle is from the inner road edge (Figures 14 and 15), the tangent point lies on the zero flow cylinder. Thus the horizontal component of optical flow of the tangent point is always zero.

Note that although the tangent point appears as a feature point in the image, it is not generated by a single point in space. Rather, the points in space that generate this feature constantly change. We call this point a *virtual feature point*.

In Figure 13 therefore, the optical flow $\dot{\theta}$ due to point T is zero. Let the distance from the vehicle to the inner road edge be s, and let θ be the positive angle to $\hat{t}$

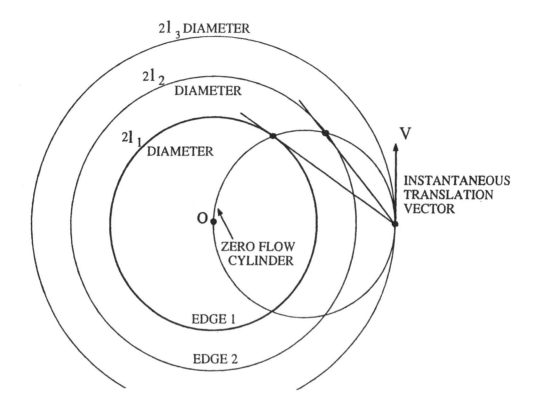

Figure 14. Road edges, zero flow cylinder and tangent points.

measured from the X-axis. From Figure 13, the following relationships hold:

$$l = r \sin \theta \tag{7}$$

$$s = r - l = r(1 - \sin \theta) \tag{8}$$

Differentiating Equation (7) with respect to time:

$$\dot{l} = \dot{r} \sin \theta + r \dot{\theta} \cos \theta \tag{9}$$

where dot denotes derivative with respect to time. For a circular road, l is constant and thus $\dot{l}$ can be set to zero in Equation (9):

$$0 = \dot{r} \sin \theta + r \dot{\theta} \cos \theta$$

$$\dot{r} = -r \dot{\theta} \cot \theta \tag{10}$$

When the vehicle is moving on a perfect circular path, both $\dot{r}$ and $\dot{\theta}$ are equal to zero. However, suppose the vehicle's path is not a perfect circle. Since r is the instantaneous radius of curvature of the vehicle motion, $\dot{r}$ is the rate at which the curvature changes. Equation (10) suggests a way of controlling the vehicle motion so

Figure 15. Road tangent points.

as to achieve a constant circular motion. Consider the two-wheeled vehicle described above. From Equation (1), we could derive the following:

$$\beta = \sin^{-1}\left(\frac{m}{r}\right) \tag{11}$$

Equation (11) gives a value of the steering angle β as a function of the instantaneous radius of curvature r and the distance $2m$ between the two wheels. Normally the value m is known. For a more realistic vehicle (such as a four-wheeled vehicle with front-wheel steering) some other relationship will hold.

In Equation (10), $\dot{r}$ is the rate at which the radius of curvature of the vehicle motion is changing. We can express $\dot{r}$ as a function of the steering angle β by differentiating Equation (1) with respect to time:

$$\dot{r} = \frac{-m\cos\beta}{\sin^2\beta}\dot{\beta} \tag{12}$$

Substituting Equations (12) and (1) into (10) and solving for $\dot{\beta}$:

$$\dot{\beta} = \dot{\theta}\tan\beta\cot\theta \tag{13}$$

Equation (13) suggests a partial control scheme whose inputs are the current steering angle β, the current angle θ of the tangent line relative to the X-axis, and the optical flow $\dot{\theta}$ of the tangent point. All of these inputs can be measured. The variable being computed is the rate of change of the steering angle, $\dot{\beta}$. Equation (13) provides the gain $\tan \beta \cot \theta$ by which $\dot{\theta}$ should be multiplied in order to get the correct change in steering wheel angle. This gain depends on the current steering wheel angle β and the angular location θ of the tangent point in the image. Note that the change in steering control command should be the negative of the value of $\dot{\beta}$ derived in Equation (13).

Figure 8 shows a sequence of images taken from a camera mounted on a vehicle. The images in the figure are numbered in the same order in which they were taken. The road is almost circular. Note that the tangent point stays (almost) at the same location in each image in the sequence. If the road were perfectly circular and the vehicle were moving on a perfect circular path, then the position of the tangent point would not change from image to image. However, if the vehicle's path is not a perfect circle, then its steering can be controlled by measuring horizontal changes in the position of the tangent point. These changes are the horizontal component of optical flow at that point, and can be used to generate changes $(\dot{\beta})$ in the steering wheel command β.

Note that Equations (1) and (11) hold only for certain types of vehicles. Vehicles with other wheel and steering configurations will result in different expressions relating steering angle to the radius of curvature of motion. In all such expressions, however, there should be a one-to-one relationship between β and r. These expressions can then be substituted into Equation (10) to derive the relevant control signals. It is important to emphasize that the derivation of $\dot{\beta}$ takes into account the kinematics of the system but *not* the dynamics. This is also the reason why we emphasize that the control scheme is not complete.

If the rate of change of the steering angle, $\dot{\beta}$, is the only variable being controlled (as indicated in Equation (13)), then in practice the vehicle may not maintain a constant distance from the edge of the road. Therefore, in addition to Equation (13), Equation (8) can also be used to control the vehicle to achieve a constant circular motion. Substituting Equation (1) into (8) and solving for β:

$$\beta = \sin^{-1}\left[\frac{m}{s}(1 - \sin\theta)\right] \qquad (14)$$

Equation (14) suggests a partial control scheme whose inputs are the measured angle θ of the tangent line relative to the X-axis, the desired distance s of the vehicle from the inner road edge, and the distance $2m$ between the front and rear wheels. The variable being computed is the steering angle β.

The control signals ($\dot{\beta}$ and $\dot{\beta}$) and partial control schemes suggested above assume that the road is circular, that the center of curvature of the desired vehicle path coincides with the center of curvature of the circular road, and that the road is planar. It is also assumed that the tangent point (in the image) can always be determined, and that the vehicle heading coincides with the camera optical axis. The main significance of this approach is that (a) it shows that the tangent point and its optical flow are important visual control signals for road following, and that potentially they are sufficient to achieve road following; (b) a tight perception-action loop is possible for road following which is simple and therefore computationally inexpensive; (c) image information can potentially be used *directly* as input into a control algorithm; (d) only a few measurements may be needed to control the vehicle; (e) the approach is independent of the speed of the vehicle; (f) it is independent of the camera height above the road; and (g) only a very small portion of the image—the portion around the tangent point—may need to be analyzed, in principle. (Of course, item (g) may not be true in practice since larger portions of the road may have to be extracted in order to reliably find the tangent point.)

Suppose we want to follow a road which is curved but not circular. Figure 16 shows two cases. In Figure 16a the radius of curvature increases as the vehicle moves. In Figure 16b, the radius of curvature decreases. In Figure 16a, the tangent point lies on some equal flow cylinder whose $\dot\theta$ optical flow is negative. In Figure 16b, the tangent point lies inside the zero flow cylinder and its $\dot\theta$ optical flow is positive. Therefore, intuitively, if the horizontal component of the optical flow, $\dot\theta$, at the tangent point is measured, then its value can be used as a control signal for steering the vehicle. If $\dot\theta$ is negative (Figure 16a) then the steering command is to increase the radius of curvature of the vehicle's current motion. If $\dot\theta$ is positive (Figure 16b), then the steering command is to decrease the radius of curvature of the vehicle's current motion by sharpening the turn.

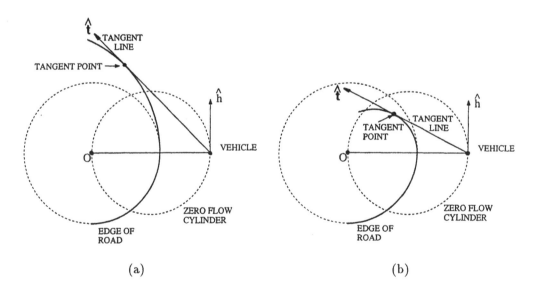

Figure 16. Road following: (a) Increasing radius of curvature; (b) Decreasing radius of curvature.

4.7. ROAD FOLLOWING BY GAZING AT OUTER ROAD EDGE

We have thus far considered road following using information about the inner edge of curved roads. In this section, we look at the problem of road following using information about the outer edge of curved roads. Figure 17 shows the outer edge of a circular road. In the figure, a vehicle is following a road whose outer edge has radius l_o. The path traversed by the vehicle is a circle of radius r. Consider the direction $\theta = \alpha$ in the camera. Refer to the definition of θ in Figure 6. This angle determines a direction defined by the plane $\theta = \alpha$. The intersection of this plane with the outer road edge is at point V. The ray from the camera to point V is (α, ϕ) for some ϕ. Figure 17 shows the top view, where a is the horizontal projection of the line connecting the camera pinhole point with point V.

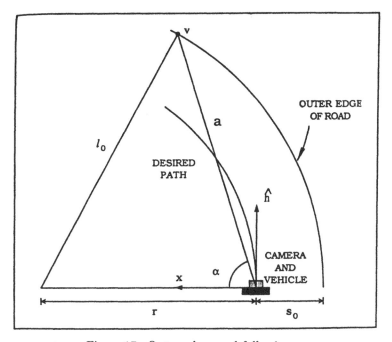

Figure 17. Outer edge road following.

Let h_c be the height of the camera above the ground as in Figure 18. During driving, this height is constant. We see that

$$a = \frac{h_c}{\tan \phi} \tag{15}$$

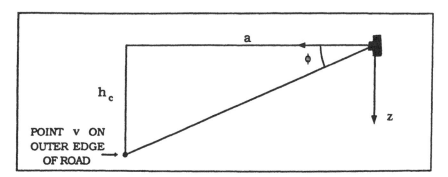

Figure 18. Outer edge road following.

In this section, we show that road following can be achieved, in principle, from information at a single point on the outer road edge, the point V. During driving, for constant azimuth direction α, the elevation angle ϕ can change as the value a changes. The point V is a virtual feature point and the value α, which defines this point for a given road, is arbitrarily chosen.

Let the distance from the vehicle to the outer road edge be s_o. From Figure 17, the following relationships hold:

$$l_o^2 = r^2 + a^2 - 2r\,a\cos\alpha \tag{16}$$

$$s_o = l_o - r \tag{17}$$

Combining Equations (15) and (16) yields:

$$l_o^2 = r^2 + \frac{h_c^2}{\tan^2\phi} - \frac{2r\,h_c\cos\alpha}{\tan\phi} \tag{18}$$

Combining Equations (17) and (18) and solving for r:

$$r = \frac{h_c^2 - s_o^2\tan^2\phi}{2\tan\phi(s_o\tan\phi + h_c\cos\alpha)} \tag{19}$$

Substituting Equation (1) into (19) and solving for β:

$$\beta = \sin^{-1}\left[\frac{2m\tan\phi(s_o\tan\phi + h_c\cos\alpha)}{h_c^2 - s_o^2\tan^2\phi}\right] \tag{20}$$

This equation suggests a partial control scheme whose inputs are the arbitrarily chosen azimuth angle α, the measured elevation angle ϕ of the virtual feature point V, the desired distance s_o of the vehicle from the outer road edge, the known distance $2m$ between the front and rear wheels of the vehicle and the known height h_c of the camera. The variable being computed is the steering angle β.

Similarly, equations of the following kind can be found for $\dot{r}$ and $\dot{\beta}$:

$$\dot{r} = f(\dot{\phi}, \phi, r, \alpha, h_c) \tag{21}$$

$$\dot{\beta} = g(\dot{\phi}, \phi, \beta, \alpha, h_c, m) \tag{22}$$

Equation (22) is for the two-wheeled vehicle described above, and may be formed by substituting Equations (1) and (12) into (21) and solving for $\dot{\beta}$.

Equations (20) and (22) can be used to achieve constant circular motion. However, suppose we want to follow a road which is curved but not circular. In this case, the radius of curvature may either increase (Figure 16a) or decrease (Figure 16b) as the vehicle moves. We can use the rate $\dot{\phi}$ at which the position of the outer road edge changes as measured in the $\theta = \alpha$ plane. For increasing radius of curvature $\dot{\phi}$ will be negative, while it will be positive for decreasing radius of curvature. This value can therefore be used as a control signal for steering the vehicle. If $\dot{\phi}$ is negative, then the steering command is to increase the radius of curvature of the vehicle's current motion. If $\dot{\phi}$ is positive, then the steering command is to decrease the radius of curvature of the vehicle's current motion by sharpening the turn.

5. CASE STUDY 2: AUTONOMOUS LANDING

5.1. THE VANISHING POINT

This section discusses how the vanishing point of a runway may be used for the autonomous landing task. The vanishing point is a visual cue which is relevant primarily for highly structured environments; the runway is an example. This cue does *not* exist (and is meaningless) in 3-D and can be extracted in 2-D only. In fact, this cue does not even exist in the 2-D image; it must be extracted from other visible 2-D features. By using an active vision approach (in particular a fixating camera) and this visual cue, some vision-based control computations can be significantly simplified (see also Chapter 3).

Figure 19 shows a simplified top view of a runway. The aircraft must land between the *threshold* and the *end* of the runway. Figure 20 shows a camera and related coordinate systems. The idea behind the active vision landing approach is based on fixating the camera at the vanishing point of the projection of the runway onto the image.

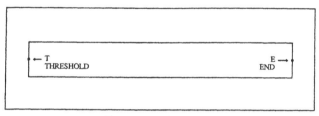

Figure 19. Runway.

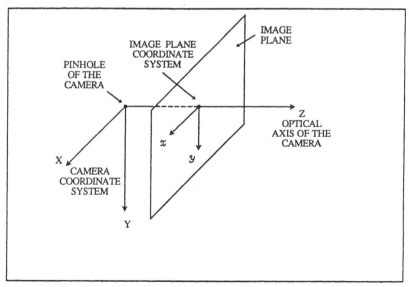

Figure 20. Camera and image plane coordinate system.

The vanishing point of the imaged runway is the point in the image plane where the projection of the two parallel side lines of the runway intersect. Obviously, this intersection point does not exist in a finite 3-D world and cannot be "reconstructed."

Since the vanishing point is a projection of a point "located" at infinity, any translational motion of the camera does *not* change the location of the vanishing point in the image plane. However, rotational motions of the camera will, in general, cause the vanishing point to shift in the image plane.[2]

5.2. VANISHING POINT AND FIXATION

The runway vanishing point provides information about aircraft orientation which can serve as a key visual feature for autonomous landing. If the camera is continuously fixated at the vanishing point through a visual feedback loop so that the optical axis of the camera (the Z- axis in Figure 20) contains the vanishing point, then there will be no pitch and yaw rotational motions of the camera (i.e., rotations about the X- and Y- axes, respectively, as shown in Figure 20). The camera may, however, rotate about its roll axis (the Z- axis). This also means that if the vanishing point does shift in the image, it is due to pitch and/or yaw rotational motions only.

When the camera undergoes translation along its optical axis, the vanishing point becomes the focus of expansion (FOE). Figures 21, 22, and 23 show the effect on the imaged runway due to camera translation along the X-, Y-, and Z- axes, respectively. Note that in all three cases the vanishing point is *stationary* in the image.

Next we shall explain how the vanishing point, as it evolves as a function of time, can be used to extract valuable information about aircraft orientation, which can be used for landing. Suppose the camera is mounted on the aircraft and it has independent pan/tilt control. Then by maintaining fixation on the vanishing point it is possible to:

1. Measure the two-degree-of-freedom orientation (pitch and yaw) of the aircraft relative to the fixating camera by measuring the camera pan/tilt angles, thus allowing the measurement of the aircraft's 2-D orientation relative to the runway. (Note that when the camera fixates at the vanishing point the optical axis becomes parallel to the longitudinal axis of the runway.)
2. Reduce the need for other rotation sensors (e.g., gyroscopes).

Practically, during the fixation process, the vanishing point which is being used to close the fixation loop may shift from the optical axis due to computation delay and loop response. In this case, it may be useful to add the velocity of the vanishing point, i.e., its optical flow, (in addition to its location) relative to the optical axis to generate control signals to maintain fixation (and the resulting camera stabilization).

Other landing-related visual cues that are based on fixating the camera on the runway vanishing point have also been developed and are discussed in [29].

5.3. CONTROL LOOP BASED ON THE VANISHING POINT

Figure 24 shows possible control loops for maintaining the vanishing point at the center of the image. The desired location of the vanishing point is the input to the

---

[2] Of course, a rotation about the line extending from the camera pinhole point to the vanishing point in the image will not cause the vanishing point to shift in the image plane.

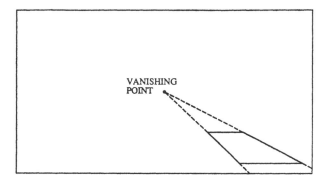

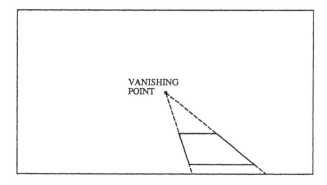

Figure 21. Translation along $+x$-axis.

closed loop system. The feedback signals are the location of the vanishing point in the image and its velocity (flow). The parameters being controlled are the pan and tilt of the camera. These control loops allow us to use the fixating camera system as a gyroscope, thus aiding in the autonomous landing task.

6. CASE STUDY 3: VISUAL LOOMING

6.1. THE VISUAL LOOMING EFFECT

The visual looming effect deals with the expansion of an object's size in the image. Usually, this expansion is a result of a decrease in the relative distance between the camera and the viewed object. This effect has been shown to be very important in biological systems when they interact with the environment [5, 6, 24, 23]. Visual looming is a quantitative temporal feature which can be very useful for generating control signals for obstacle avoidance or for approaching an object without collision. It has no meaning when considered only in the context of a single image, since the information lies in the *temporal change of a spatial feature*.

The perception of looming is critical to survival for creatures of nature, since it is an indication for possible collision. It is necessary for locomotion in a complex natural 3-D world. The reaction to this visual stimulus is the result of some kind

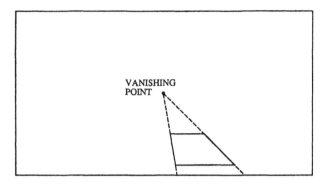

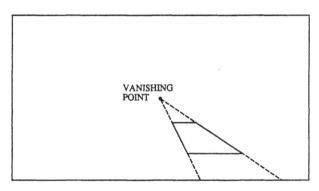

Figure 22. Translation along $+y$-axis.

of "perceived threat," i.e., the measured relative rate of expansion of objects on the retina corresponds to a visual timing parameter that causes the subject to defensively react to reduce the visual threat. The looming effect [10, 23] has been shown to cause defensive reaction in several animals as well as babies [7, 23].

Although looming and looming-related actions have been studied by many researchers (primarily psychologists), most of the work is qualitative or limited-quantitative. In order to use the existing results for robotics applications a more mathematically-oriented approach for looming is needed. The following sections present such an approach.

6.2. QUANTITATIVE LOOMING

Assume an observer is moving in a 3-D environment filled with several balls (Figure 25). During the motion of the observer relative to the balls, both the size of each ball and the location of its centroid, when projected into the image, are continuously changing (Figure 26). If the distance between a ball and the center of the camera decreases, then the projected image of the ball will increase in area. The relative rate of expansion of the area over time of the imaged ball causes the "looming" effect, and it is proportional to the time derivative of the relative distance (range) between the observer and the ball *divided* by the relative distance (range) itself. The

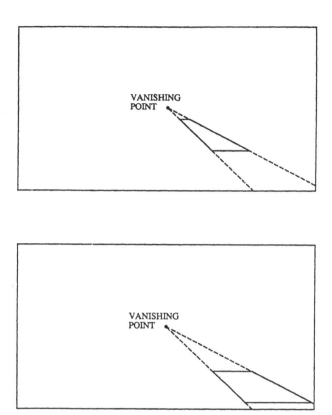

Figure 23. Translation along $+z$-axis.

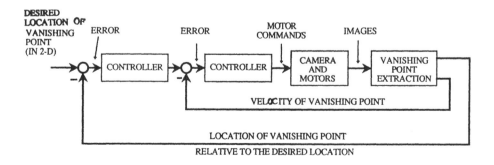

Figure 24. A control loop for fixating the camera at the vanishing point.

looming is a measurable variable and can be extracted *directly* from a sequence of 2-D images using optical flow, relative change in area, etc.

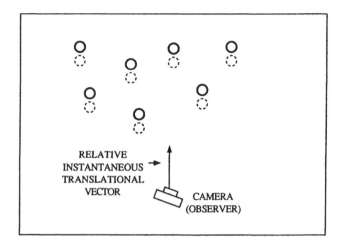

Figure 25. Relative motion between a camera and 3-D objects.

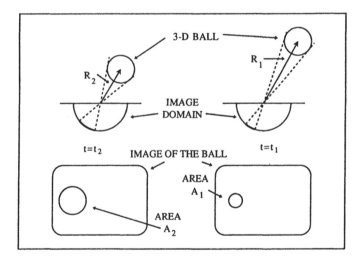

Figure 26. Projections in the image of a 2-D ball at two time instants.
The closer the ball, the bigger the size of the projected ball.

Lee and his colleagues [12, 13, 16, 14, 15, 17] showed how to quantitatively measure the "time to contact" from optical flow for an observer who undergoes only translation when the optical axis coincides with the motion vector. Extensions of the time-to-contact concept were recently reported in [26, 3]. Our definition of looming is related to, but different from, the time to contact. The time to contact according to [12] is the time it takes for an observer to hit a specific *plane* perpendicular to the direction of motion, i.e., it deals with the relative change of the *depth* (as opposed to *range*).

We now introduce a mathematical definition of looming, and a way for measuring looming, using expansion of the projection of objects on the retina [20].

6.3. MATHEMATICAL DEFINITION OF LOOMING

Let a camera and an object (e.g., a ball) move arbitrarily in a 3-D environment (Figure 26). Then at two different time instants they may be in different relative locations. The distance (range) from the center of the ball to the pinhole point of the camera may change, thus resulting in different sizes of projected images. The looming effect is caused by the expansion of the projected ball. Intuitively, the relative rate of expansion, i.e., the relative change of the projection of the ball $\frac{A_2-A_1}{A_1}$ over the period of time $t_2 - t_1$ in which the change takes place, is highly related to the relative change of the range $\frac{R_1-R_2}{R_1}$ during the same period of time. (In fact, for objects that are small relative to their range from the observer, they are proportional, i.e., differ by a scale factor.) Thus one can define looming in terms of the relative change in range instead of relative change in the object's projection.

In order to mathematically define looming and suggest ways to measure it we shall consider infinitesimally small 3-D balls. Let the relative distance between the observer and a point P (the center of the infinitesimally small ball) at time instant t_1 be R_1 and at time instant t_2 be R_2 (Figure 27). Then, we define looming L as the *negative* value of the time derivative of the relative distance between the observer and the point P, divided by the relative distance R, i.e.,

$$L = - \lim_{\Delta t \to 0} \frac{\frac{(R_2-R_1)}{\Delta t}}{R_1} \tag{23}$$

where $\Delta t = t_2 - t_1$. Or

$$L = -\frac{\dot{R}}{R} \tag{24}$$

where dot denotes derivative with respect to time. The reason for the *negative sign* in Equations (23) and (24) is to associate image *expansion* with *positive* looming.

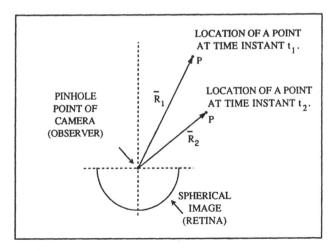

Figure 27. The concept of "looming of a point."

This definition allows the use of the term "looming of a point" for describing the value of L of a point.

6.4. DIRECT CALCULATIONS OF LOOMING

This approach deals with relative motion between the camera and the object. It is based on measuring the looming at the image-region (or object) level, rather than at the pixel level. Techniques for measuring looming at the pixel level are provided in [20].

The 3-D ball scenario

The concept of measuring looming from the relative rate of expansion can be explained using a 3-D ball example. Figure 28 shows an observer moving relative to a 3-D ball. As a result, the projection of the ball on the retina may be different in size at two different time instants t_1 and t_2. Let the relative speed along the ball-observer direction be $|\mathbf{t}|$, the radius of the ball r, and the distance from the center of the ball to the observer R. At $t = t_1$

$$\sin \beta = \frac{r}{R} \tag{25}$$

After $\Delta t = t_2 - t_1$, i.e., at $t = t_2$:

$$\sin(\beta + \Delta\beta) = \frac{r}{R - |\mathbf{t}|\Delta t} \tag{26}$$

For infinitesimally small Δt and by using $\lim_{x \to 0} \frac{1}{1-x} = 1 + x$ the last equation becomes

$$\sin(\beta + \Delta\beta) = \frac{r}{R}(1 + \frac{|\mathbf{t}|}{R}\Delta t) \tag{27}$$

By subtracting Equation (25) from Equation (27), then dividing by Δt, and letting $\Delta t \to 0$, we obtain:

$$\frac{d\sin\beta}{dt} = \frac{r|\mathbf{t}|}{R^2} \tag{28}$$

Using the relations $\frac{r}{R} = \sin\beta$, $\frac{|\mathbf{t}|}{R} = -\frac{\frac{dR}{dt}}{R}$ and $\frac{d\sin\beta}{dt} = \cos\beta\frac{d\beta}{dt}$ in Equation (28) we obtain:

$$\frac{\frac{dR}{dt}}{R} = -\frac{\frac{d\beta}{dt}}{\tan\beta} \tag{29}$$

and the expression for looming becomes:

$$L = -\frac{\dot{R}}{R} = \frac{\dot{\beta}}{\tan\beta} = \frac{d}{dt}ln(\sin\beta) \tag{30}$$

where dot denotes derivative with respect to time.

This means that the looming can be measured using β and $\dot{\beta}$ relative to the center of the ball. $\frac{\dot{\beta}}{\tan\beta}$ contains the information on the relative expansion of the projected ball during fixation at the center of the ball. This also means (see [20]) that a retina that is constructed in a logarithmic fashion, i.e., where the pixel length $\Delta\beta$ is proportional to $\tan\beta$, will measure looming in a linear fashion independently of the size of the object (as long as the retina fixates at the center of the object).

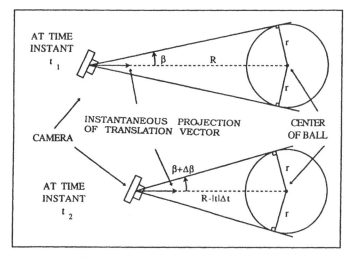

Figure 28. Looming computations.

The above derivation of looming is based on a 2-D angle measurement of a projection of a ball. However, the extension to the projected area of the ball is simple. Relative change of area is also proportional to looming. We shall show next that

$$\frac{\frac{dA}{dt}}{2A} \approx -\frac{\frac{dR}{dt}}{R} = L \tag{31}$$

where A is the projected area of the ball on the spherical image.

The area occupied by a projected ball on a spherical image is $A = 4\pi \sin^2(\frac{\beta}{2}) r_1^2$ where β is as defined in Figure 28, and r_1 is the radius of the sphere of the retina. r_1 is constant. By computing $\frac{\frac{dA}{dt}}{2A}$, which is the relative change of the projected area (divided by 2), we obtain

$$\frac{\frac{dA}{dt}}{2A} = \frac{\frac{d\beta}{dt}}{2\tan\frac{\beta}{2}}$$

For small β,

$$\frac{\frac{d\beta}{dt}}{2\tan\frac{\beta}{2}} \approx \frac{\frac{d\beta}{dt}}{\tan\beta}$$

which has been shown (Equation (30)) to be the expression for looming. Thus the relative change of the projected area can be used to approximate looming values using Equation (31).

6.5. LOOMING AND THE TIME TO CONTACT

As mentioned earlier, looming is different from the time to contact. It is related more to the "two dimensional" time-to-contact concept [24]. According to Lee [12] any point that lies on a plane that is perpendicular to the instantaneous translational motion direction of the camera will produce the same value of "time to contact" T_c (assuming that the optical axis coincides with the direction of motion). This means that the time to contact deals with *depth*. The derivation in [12] is valid only for rectilinear motion (with no rotation) of the camera. Only recently has it been extended to more general motion of the camera [3, 26].

One problem with the time to contact approach is that points which lie on a single perpendicular plane but are located far away from, or close to, the camera produce the same value of T_c even though they are not equally relevant to making vision-based behavioral decisions. The looming value of a point is related to *range* rather than depth.

Figures 29 and 30 illustrate the main difference between the time-to-contact value of a point and its looming value. All points that lie on a plane perpendicular to the camera translation direction will have the same time-to-contact value. However, points on a sphere in front of the camera produce the same looming value. Points 1, 2, and 3 in Figure 30 have the same looming value but different "time to contact" values. Points 2 and 4 have the same time-to-contact value but different looming values. Points 4 and 5 have the same time-to-contact values and the same looming values.

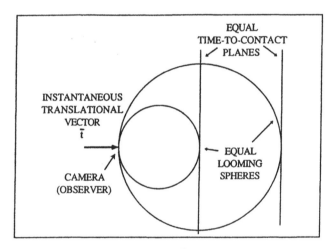

Figure 29. Looming and time to contact.

7. SERVOING AND PASSIVE RANGING FROM MOTION

Passive ranging from motion involves converting image velocities to range values using the known velocity of the camera relative to the objects of interest. Our 2-D based approach is very closely related to passive ranging since we use information about the velocity of features in the image. For a stationary environment the range to a point is a function of the image velocity of that point.

Many of the primitive navigation behaviors can be achieved using only range. However, our approach does not compute range, but involves working directly with position and motion of image features. In principle, the two approaches are similar. However, as explained earlier, they are quite different from the point of view of computation and robustness.

The image *position* of a feature indicates what direction and magnitude to servo the heading vector, e.g., whether to servo left or right, and by how many degrees.

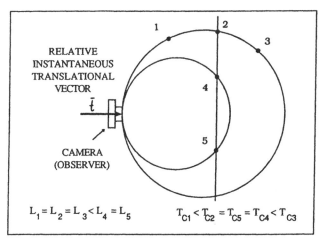

Figure 30. Looming and time to contact.

For example, in road following using the inner road edge, we have shown that for a two-wheeled vehicle following along a circular road, the following constraint holds (Equation (14)):

$$\beta = \sin^{-1}\left[\frac{m}{s}(1 - \sin\theta)\right]$$

where θ is the measured angle (i.e., image position) of the tangent line relative to the x-axis, s is the desired distance of the vehicle from the inner road edge, $2m$ is the distance between the front and rear wheels of the vehicle, and the variable β is the steering angle. The value of the steering angle is directly related to the change in the heading direction.

The image *velocity* of the feature indicates how fast the feature is being approached. This velocity is used to control (a) the rate at which the heading direction is servoed, and (b) the speed of the vehicle. For example, in road following we have shown that the following constraint holds (Equation (13)):

$$\dot{\beta} = \dot{\theta}\tan\beta\cot\theta$$

where β is the current steering angle, θ is the current angle (i.e., image position) of the tangent line relative to the x-axis, and $\dot{\theta}$ is the image velocity of the tangent point. All of these inputs can be measured. The variable being computed is the rate of change of the steering angle, $\dot{\beta}$, which is directly related to the rate at which the heading direction changes.

We have also shown that the value of visual looming is closely related to the time to contact to an object. The time to contact indicates how fast an object is being approached. Knowledge of this value therefore provides us with information to control the speed of the vehicle. Visual looming is measured as the relative rate of expansion of an object, which is related to the image velocity of points on the boundary of the object.

8. Conclusions

In this chapter, we have demonstrated how some visual servoing behaviors can be achieved using direct 2-D image cues (both spatial and temporal). These cues serve as inputs to the motion control algorithms. In such cases, an explicit reconstruction of the scene is not required. We have also demonstrated that each particular behavior will, in general, need different relevant information from the imagery.

For road following the position of a single road edge point in the image (the tangent point for inner road edges or the gaze point for outer road edges) and its image velocity can be used directly as control signals to control the steering. For autonomous landing the runway vanishing point and its image velocity can be used to control the pointing direction of the camera so as to achieve fixation. This can be used to measure the pitch and yaw of the aircraft during landing.

Visual looming—the relative rate of expansion of an object's size in the image— can be used to generate control signals for controlling the speed of the vehicle for obstacle avoidance or for approaching an object without collision.

The advantages of this 2-D based approach are that it is simple, fast and robust. There is no need for 3-D reconstruction. It results in a tight perception–action loop to directly generate action commands from image cues. This chapter represents the initial developments for a theory of image-based control and subsequent work will concentrate on the use of normal flow as a description of image motion [1].

References

1. J. Aloimonos "Purposive and qualitative active vision," In *Proc. Image Understanding Workshop*, 1990, 816–828.

2. J. Aloimonos, I. Weiss, and A. Bandopadhay, "Active vision," *Int'l. J. Computer Vision* **2**, 1988, 333–356.

3. P. Balasubramanyan and M.A. Snyder, "The P-field: A computational model for binocular motion processing," In *Proc. IEEE Conf. on Computer Vision and Pattern Recognition*, 1991.

4. D.H. Ballard, "Animate vision," *Artificial Intelligence* **48**, 1991, 57–86.

5. P.J. Beek, "Perception-action coupling in the young infant: An appraisal of von Hofsten's research programme," In M.G. Wade and H.T.A. Whiting (Eds.), *Motor Development in Children: Aspects of Coordination and Control*, Dordrecht, The Netherlands: Martinus-Nijhoff, 1986, 187–196.

6. R.J. Bootsma, *The Timing of Rapid Interceptive Actions*, Amsterdam: Free University Press, 1988.

7. T.G.R. Bower, J.M. Broughton and M.K. Moore, "The coordination of visual and tactual input in infants," *Perception and Psychophysics* **8**, 1970, 51–53.

8. E. Dickmans and V. Grafe, "Applications of dynamic monocular machine vision," *Machine Vision and Applications* **1**, 1988.

9. E. Dickmans and V. Grafe, "Dynamic monocular machine vision," *Machine Vision and Applications* **1**, 1988.

10. J.J. Gibson, *The Ecological Approach to Visual Perception*, Lawrence Erlbaum Associates, 1986.

11. B.K.P. Horn, *Robot Vision*, McGraw Hill, NY, 1986.

12. D.N. Lee, "A theory of visual control of braking based on information about time to collision," *Perception* **5**, 1976, 437–459.

13. D.N. Lee, "Visuo-motor coordination in space-time," In G.E. Stelmach and J. Requin (Eds.), *Tutorials in Motor Behavior*, Amsterdam: North-Holland, 1980, 281–293.

14. D.N. Lee and D.E. Reddish, "Plummeting gannets: A paradigm of ecological optics," *Nature* **293**, 1981, 293–294.

15. D. N. Lee and D.S. Young, "Visual timing of interceptive actions," In D.J. Ingle, M. Jeannerod, and D.N. Lee (Eds.), *Brain Mechanisms and Spatial Vision*, Dordrecht, The Netherlands: Martinus Nijhoff, 1985, 1–30.

16. D.N. Lee, J.R. Lishman, and J.A. Thomson, "Regulation of gait in long jumping," *J. Experimental Psychology: Human Perception and Performance* **8**, 1982, 448–459.

17. D.N. Lee, D.S. Young, D.E. Reddish, S. Lough and T.M.H. Clayton, "Visual timing in hitting an accelerating ball," *Quarterly J. Experimental Psychology* **35A**, 1983, 333–346.

18. D. Raviv, "Extraction of the 'time to contact' from real visual data," In *Proc. SPIE Symposium on Advances in Intelligent Robotics Systems*, 1989.

19. D. Raviv, "A quantitative approach to camera fixation," In *Proc. IEEE Conf. on Computer Vision and Pattern Recognition*, 1991.

20. D. Raviv, "A Quantitative Approach to Looming," NIST Internal Report, NIST-IR-4808, 1992.

21. D. Raviv and M. Herman, "Towards an understanding of camera fixation," In *Proc. IEEE Int'l. Conf. on Robotics and Automation*, 1990, 28–33.

22. D. Raviv and M. Herman, "A new approach to vision and control for road following," *IEEE Workshop on Visual Motion*, 1991.

23. W. Schiff, J.A. Caviness and J.J. Gibson, "Persistent fear responses in rhesus monkeys to the optical stimulus of 'looming' ," *Science* **136**, 1962, 982–983.

24. W. Schiff and M.L. Detweiler, "Information used in judging impending collision," *Perception* **8**, 1979, 647–658.

25. C. Thorpe, M. Hebert, T. Kanade and S. Shafer, "Vision and navigation for the Carnegie-Mellon Navlab," *IEEE Trans. Pattern Analysis and Machine Intelligence* **10**(3), 1988.

26. M. Tistarelli, E. Grosso and G. Sandini, "Dynamic stereo in visual navigation," In *Proc. IEEE Conf. on Computer Vision and Pattern Recognition*, 1991.

27. M. Turk, D. Morgenthaler, K. Gremban and M. Marra, "VITS—A vision system for autonomous land vehicle navigation," *IEEE Trans. PAMI*, 1988.

28. A. Waxman, J. LeMoigne, L. Davis and T. Siddalingalah, "A visual navigation system for autonomous land vehicle," *IEEE J. Robotics and Automation* **3**, 1987, 124–141.

29. H.H. Yakali and D. Raviv, "A vision-based method for autonomous landing," *SPIE Conf. on Intelligent Robots and Computer Vision*, 1991.

6 | COMPUTATIONAL MODELLING OF HAND–EYE COORDINATION

Andrew Blake
University of Oxford

ABSTRACT

We are developing a visually guided robot arm that is able to grasp and transport objects across an obstacle-strewn environment. Recent work has shown how analysis of moving image contours can provide estimates of the shape of curved surfaces. This forms the basis of the robot's capabilities which we are seeking to elaborate in three respects. First a computational model—the "Dynamic Contour"—is being developed for real-time visual tracking, based on simulated Lagrangian dynamics. Second, we are developing a $2\frac{1}{2}$-D system for incremental, active exploration of free-space. Third, a computational theory of the visual planning of two-fingered grasps has been developed which can be coupled to the Dynamic Contour model. This chapter concentrates on the third of these topics. A qualitative theory for classification of grasps is described and demonstrated. Optimal finger positions are obtained from the mutual intersection of the local symmetry and antisymmetry sets, and of a third set, the *critical set of the grasp map*. These three sets themselves form boundaries in a natural partition of the set of all grasps (the configuration space). The partition corresponds to a classification of possible grasps according to their stability properties.

1. INTRODUCTION

This chapter outlines a model for planning grasping actions. This is done in the context of a robot system driven by *Active Vision* [1, 2]. We are attempting to build a system that links perception with action in real time. The last ten years has seen a

---

The financial support of the SERC and the EEC is gratefully acknowledged. Discussions with M. Brady, H.H. Bülthoff, A. Glennerster, H.C.Longuet-Higgins, M. Taylor, P. Winder and A. Zisserman were most valuable. Thanks to F. Blake for proofreading.

gradual movement away from the Marrian view of vision [25] as a static, information-gathering process. The earlier view of Gibson [19] of vision directly linked to action is attractive, particularly for certain low-level perceptual tasks such as catching, and moving around obstacles. This partial retrenchment is encouraged by practical advances in computing, especially in parallel computing. As the power of parallel processors has increased, the demands on them by vision processes, linked more and more directly to action, has decreased. The result has been the emergence of practical visually driven robots [8, 13, 15, 27, 28].

We are currently building visually guided grasping expertise into a robot that can reach around obstacles. A CCD camera is mounted on the wrist of an ADEPT robot and a computer continually monitors visual signals. Deliberate, exploratory motions are coordinated with visual computation so as to explore the shape of 3-D curved obstacles [5, 11, 18]. The visual computation itself is based on *Dynamic Contours* [12, 21] which are strongly focussed onto obstacle silhouettes and hence efficient. They are computed in parallel. The combination of focussed attention and parallelism leads to real-time performance. This in turn allows integration of perception with control systems for action (Figure 1). Coordinated, sequenced perception and action drives the robot to reach around obstacles toward a goal [4, 6], as in Figure 2. Currently, the robot is able to reach around obstacles and retrieve objects. Equipped with a suction gripper, it is able to grasp only relatively flat objects. For instance, it can locate a hidden box and remove its lid. For more flexible grasping it would be desirable to use a gripper with fingers. Complex, anthropomorphic hands have been built [30] but, for control purposes, the simplest gripper is a two-fingered one. The fingers may open and close either with parallel motion or with hinged motion. They may be either plates or thin cylinders. Of course the human hand has a wide repertoire of grasps [14]. The assumptions of our model are probably closest to the *index roll*, a grip between thumb and index finger.

In this chapter we outline a theory for relating the control of a two-fingered gripper to the information available directly from visual contours. We build on the notable work of Faverjon and Ponce [16], extending it to obtain *qualitative rules* for equilibrium and stability of grasp based on contour shape. The result is a computational procedure for obtaining *seed grasps*, locally optimal finger positions which seem to be intuitive grasps in many cases. The classification of seed grasps is based on an elementary use of differential analysis, of the kind used by Bruce and Giblin in their taxonomy of symmetry sets [9]. Indeed the classification of grasps turns out to be closely coupled to symmetry properties.

Results of a practical computer algorithm based on this analysis of seed grasps indicates their value as qualitative predictors of grasp stability. Figures 3 and 4 show object outlines procured from our active contour tracker.

The robot directs the camera's gaze toward the object to be grasped and the dynamic contour is allowed to lock onto the outline. Then the qualitative analysis of grasp is applied to the contour and distinguished grasp points—the seed grasps—are marked. They can be classified Type 1 and Type 2. Type 1 seeds remain in equilibrium as the coefficient of friction tends to zero, whereas Type 2 require some minimum degree of friction for equilibrium. In the case of Type 1 points, a measure

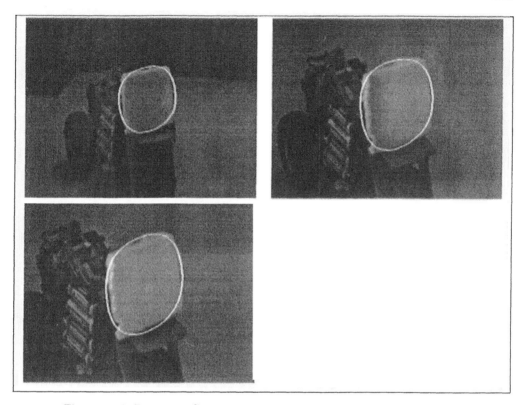

Figure 1. A Dynamic Contour visual tracker follows the motion of a model vehicle. The camera is mounted on the wrist of an ADEPT robot which rotates the camera to maintain the contour in the center of the image. The contour, a computed B-spline, is shown in white, overlaid on the images. (Figure by courtesy of R. Curwen).

of stability can also be computed. A reasonable grasping strategy is to try the most stable grasps first. The remainder of the chapter explains how a theory of two-fingered grasps can be constructed which leads to computational results like those just shown.

2. EQUILIBRIUM OF GRASPS

We assume in this chapter that a thin, planar object bounded by a closed curve is to be grasped by a two-fingered gripper. Only the 2-D problem in which the object rests on a plane will be considered. It is to be gripped by fingers that move only in that plane. Gravitational effects are not considered. The question is simply whether, when gripped, the object remains static. Imagine grasping a coin resting on a highly polished table: How can the coin be gripped in two fingers without it shooting across the table?

In order to study grasps that are in equilibrium in this sense, a mathematical condition for equilibrium is needed. It is standard to use the "force-closure" property [22], which is a sufficient condition for equilibrium. A set of contact points on

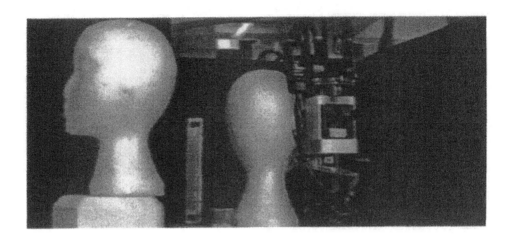

Figure 2. The robot directs the camera's gaze toward one of two obstacles, attempting to plan a path between them. The goal object is marked by the vertical white column in the distance. (Figure by courtesy of A. Zisserman.)

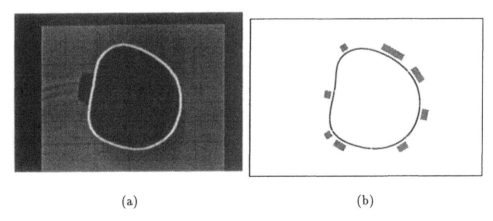

(a)   (b)

Figure 3. (a) An electrical plug, as seen by an ADEPT robot's wrist-mounted camera. Its outline is captured by a "Dynamic Contour" tracker. Once captured, the contour is frozen and analyzed for grip. (b) Seed grips shown here are all of "Type 1," grips that remain in equilibrium as the coefficient of friction approaches zero. They are parallel grips, in which the two fingers (depicted by rectangles) are placed at opposing points on the contour. Four such grips are shown here. The length of each rectangle depicts a measure of stability for one finger in a two-fingered grasp.

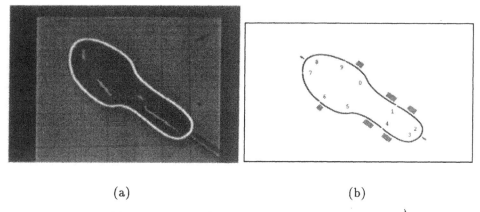

(a) (b)

Figure 4. (a) A screwdriver, as seen by the robot's camera, with a Dynamic Contour locked onto the outline of its handle. (b) There are four seed grasps of Type 1 (see Figure 3), the most stable of which are the natural grasps across the handle. The other, much less stable but still feasible, is longitudinal.

a body satisfies the closure condition if any given force and couple on the body can be achieved by some set of positive normal forces at the contacts. In this chapter we consider conditions for force-closure with frictional fingers. In the case of a 2-D polyhedral body, Markenscoff et al. [24] showed that three such fingers are always sufficient for force-closure. This assumes that vertices are to be considered ungraspable—an appropriate assumption for thin fingers but unduly conservative when the fingers are plates, as in the parallel-jaw gripper or when grasping a smooth curve.

Given that we are using B-splines to represent visual contours, it is more natural to consider 2-D bodies as being bounded by a smooth contour, rather than as a polyhedron. Then, it transpires, every contour has at least one force-closure grasp with just two contact points. Following Nguyen [26] and Faverjon and Ponce [16], the force-closure of a two-fingered grasp can be established by a simple geometric test, expressed in the notation of Figure 5. The contour itself is denoted $\mathbf{r}(s)$ where s is a parameter that will usually be taken to be true arc-length. Grasp points are at $s = s_1, s_2$. Friction angles α_1, α_2 are defined at the two points. Given a coefficient of friction μ, the test is passed whenever

$$|\tan \alpha_1| < \mu \text{ and } |\tan \alpha_2| < \mu \tag{1}$$

For a given coefficient of friction μ, these conditions define a region in "C-space" (configuration space for a two-fingered grasp of the curve $\mathbf{r}(s)$), as in Figure 6. Grasps within a region are in equilibrium at the given μ. Each region is bounded by the four curves

$$\tan \alpha_i = \pm \mu, \quad i = 1, 2 \tag{2}$$

Faverjon and Ponce [16] give an efficient procedure for computing them. What is clear from the figure is that there are just a few distinct regions, each corresponding to natural grips on the contour. Note the symmetry of the diagram about the $s_1 = s_2$

line arising because force closure is invariant to a direct swap of finger positions. The diagram is also periodic over 2π both in s_1 and s_2 because the contour $\mathbf{r}(s)$ is closed. Thus the diagram is topologically toroidal with the upper pair of edges identified and similarly the left and right edges. Allowing for periodicity and the symmetry there are in fact only five distinct regions in the diagram and hence there are five qualitatively distinct grasps.

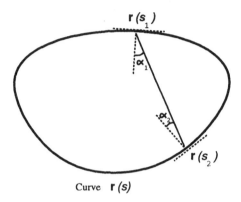

Curve $\mathbf{r}(s)$

Figure 5. We consider a two-fingered grip of a smooth contour (usually closed) $\mathbf{r}(s)$, placing the fingers at $s = s_1, s_2$, respectively. The line joining the two fingers makes angles α_1, α_2 with the normals at $s = s_1, s_2$ respectively.

A weakness of the model so far is the requirement to specify a level of friction μ. It is attractive to replace this requirement by the much weaker assumption that the two fingers merely have the same coefficient of friction. In that case regions in C-space must be replaced by the "C-space diagram"—a contour map showing the regions as a function of μ. Such a diagram is shown in Figure 7, a contour plot of the "friction function"

$$S(s_1, s_2) = \max(|\tan \alpha_1|, |\tan \alpha_2|) \tag{3}$$

so that grasp regions for a given μ are simply those contained in the set

$$\{s_1, s_2 : S(s_1, s_2) < \mu\}$$

The diagram contains, in principle, complete information about the structure of C-space but, given its complexity, it is compelling to seek a concise set of qualitative features conveying the essential structure. A natural candidate is the set of *minima* of the diagram which represent locally optimal grasps— termed *seed grasps*. Such a grasp is optimal in the sense that any perturbation of finger positions causes an increase in $S(s_1, s_2)$. Hence any perturbation of a seed grasp requires a higher level of friction to be in equilibrium. It is clear from the C-space diagram that there can only be a few seed grasps in the case illustrated. Note that each of the five distinct regions in Figure 6b is accounted for by minima in the C-space map.

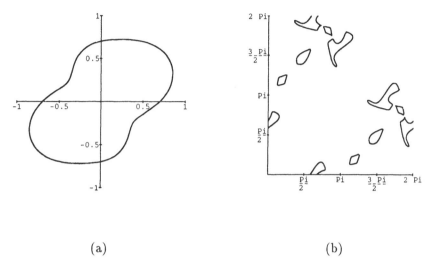

(a)   (b)

Figure 6. Two-fingered equilibrium grasps of the contour $\mathbf{r}(s)$ in (a) can be represented as regions in *C-space*. This is shown in (b) for the case where the coefficient of friction is $\mu = \frac{1}{3}$. Each axis represents the position s_i, $i = 1, 2$ of the ith finger along the closed curve $\mathbf{r}(s)$. (In this case s is not arc-length but polar angle relative to the origin.) Note that equilibrium grasps are organized into just a few discrete regions.

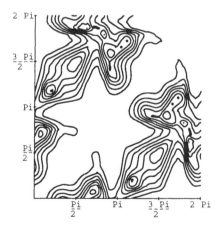

Figure 7. The full structure of C-space is given by this *C-space diagram*. It reproduces regions like those in Figure 6b for all levels of friction. It is a contour plot of the function $S(s_1, s_2)$ (see text).

It seems that the seed grasps may afford a succinct representation of the structure of grasp C-space. A reasonable grasping strategy would be to try to grasp at or near a seed grasp. The next two sections explain how seed grasps can be efficiently located and their relationship to the geometry of the contour $\mathbf{r}(s)$.

3. PRIMARY GRASP STRUCTURE

Seed grasps have been defined as local minima of the friction function S in (3) and could occur as either of two types:

Type 1: A grasp for which $\alpha_1 = \alpha_2 = 0$ so that, from (3), $S = 0$. Since generally $S \geq 0$, the case $S = 0$ is a minimum, representing a grasp that is in equilibrium right down to zero friction.

Type 2: A grasp for which S is minimal but $S \neq 0$. Such a grasp is locally optimal (any nearby perturbation of it increases the friction needed to guarantee stability) but is not in equilibrium down to zero friction.

A natural question concerns the existence of Type 1 and Type 2 grasps. Since S is positive[1] it must achieve a minimum in C-space, at least once. So either Type 1 seeds or Type 2 seeds must exist, but not necessarily both.

In fact it is easy to see that any smooth contour $\mathbf{r}(s)$ must have at least one Type 1 seed and this is illustrated in Figure 8. First, in the case of a convex contour, imagine applying a caliper to the contour to measure its diameter in a particular direction. Then, with the caliper applied, rotate the object so that the caliper opens and closes as the object rotates. There must be at least one position of maximum diameter and one minimum. Each is a Type 1 seed grasp because the line joining the fingers is perpendicular to the curve tangents at each finger (Figure 8a). Hence every convex contour has at least two Type 1 seeds. Indeed, generically there will be an *even* number of Type 1 seeds on a convex contour, corresponding to the maxima and minima of caliper diameter.

In the nonconvex case (Figure 8b) we can construct the convex hull of the contour which, being convex, must have at least two Type 1 seeds. For the one corresponding to the *maximum* diameter, both fingers must also lie on the original contour (Figure 8), hence the contour has at least one Type 1 seed. Moreover, that seed is *accessible* in the sense that it lies on the contour's convex hull so that it can be reached not only by a thin fingered gripper but also by a parallel-jaw gripper whose fingers are plate-shaped.

We have seen that at least one seed grasp must exist on every smooth contour but also that there must exist at least one Type 1 seed. Is it then possible that all seeds are in fact of Type 1 and that the Type 2 seeds never occur? This possibility is attractive because it would mean that the C-space map would be entirely characterized by grasp properties at zero friction. Increasing friction would increase the size of C-space regions (Figure 6b) but no new regions would arise. This is somewhat reminiscent of the "structure-preservation" properties of Witkin's "scale-space diagram" [31], Yuille and Poggio [32] in which all structure in a signal is present

---

[1] and defined on a compact set

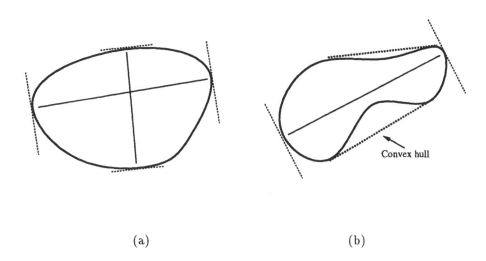

(a)   (b)

Figure 8. (a) Every convex contour has at least two Type 1 (zero-friction) grasps. (b) A nonconvex contour has at least one Type 1 grasp located, moreover, on a part of the convex hull which is in contact with the curve itself. Hence this grasp is guaranteed to be accessible to a parallel-jaw gripper.

at fine scale; no new structure can arise as the scale on which the signal is viewed coarsens.

It turns out that the structure-preservation hypothesis for grasp space does not hold. New regions in C-space *can* be created as friction increases. In fact the C-space map of Figure 7 contains a counterexample to the hypothesis. The minimum of $S(s_1, s_2)$ at $(s_1, s_2) = (\frac{\pi}{2}, \frac{3\pi}{2})$ is at a nonzero value of S, representing a seed grasp requiring greater than zero friction for equilibrium. It is a grasp along the vertical axis on the contour itself (Figure 6a). It can plainly be seen that the vertical axis is not orthogonal to the contour at either intersection with the contour and hence fingers placed at those intersections would require greater-than-zero friction. Yet (and this, admittedly, is less obvious by inspection) that grasp is locally optimal. Any perturbation of the fingers produces a grasp requiring even more friction for equilibrium. Hence it is a Type 2 seed.

A construction for another counterexample is shown in Figure 9 and gives some insight into why Type 2 seeds occur. The contour in Figure 9a is simply a piece of an equilateral triangle; the minimum friction for any grasp to be in equilibrium is clearly $\tan \alpha$, where α is the half-angle at the apex. Now this is not quite what is required because there is no isolated minimum-friction grasp. Rather, minimal-friction grasps form a line in C-space, corresponding to the set of all mirror-symmetrical grasps of the contour. This is nongeneric. However, a perturbation of the contours can cause an isolated minimum-friction grasp to occur as in Figure 9b. This is a Type 2 seed grasp. Note that this counterexample is for the case of a nonparallel grasp—one that would be inaccessible to a parallel-jaw gripper—unlike the previous counterexample.

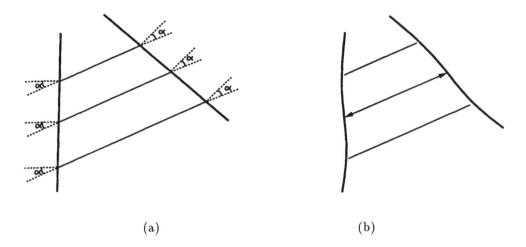

(a)   (b)

Figure 9. This counterexample shows that structure is *not* preserved in grasp-space. (a) Minimum friction ($\mu = |\tan\alpha|$) grasps on this pair of lines form a continuum as shown. (b) A small perturbation introduces a unique minimum friction grasp, shown arrowed. However, the coefficient of friction μ at that minimum is greater than zero. Hence a region appears, at the corresponding point in grasp-space, at a coefficient of friction that is strictly greater than zero.

4. FURTHER STRUCTURE: SYMMETRY SETS AND CRITICAL SETS

The qualitative structure of the C-space map can be represented in terms of the Type 1 and Type 2 seed grasps. The Type 2 grasps occur in one of two forms: antisymmetric (2a) and symmetric (2s). Figure 10 shows that each form is a configuration of local symmetry, as determined by the matching of angles α_1, α_2. The symmetric case (Type 2s) is a "local symmetry" in the sense defined by Brady and Asada [7], and formalized as the "symmetry set" by Bruce and Giblin [10]. The antisymmetric case (Type 2a) is similar to the local rotational symmetry explored by Fleck [17]. Some effort has been applied to the problem of depicting the symmetry set as a set of image curves, overlaid on the contour $\mathbf{r}(s)$. Brady and Asada [7], Bruce and Giblin [10] and Leyton [23] each propose somewhat different solutions. That debate is irrelevant here, however, as the symmetry set is to be viewed in C-space where the operational semantics of grasp are naturally represented, rather than pictorially. Then there is no latitude for alternative definitions. A symmetry (antisymmetry) point in C-space is simply a point (s_1, s_2) for which $\tan\alpha_1 = -\tan\alpha_2$ ($\tan\alpha_1 = \tan\alpha_2$). This is shown for the case of an ellipse in Figure 11a,b. A further simplification is that symmetry sets in C-space are generically smooth, whereas when projected onto image-space they had special points—cusps, free ends and triple-crossings [10].

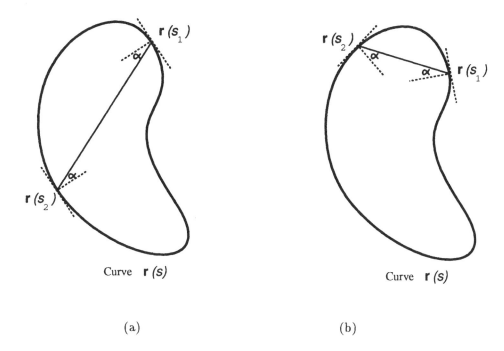

Figure 10. Local symmetries occur in one of two configurations. (a) Anti-symmetry (rotational symmetry) in which $\tan \alpha_1 = \tan \alpha_2$ in Figure 5. (b) Symmetry (mirror symmetry) in which $\tan \alpha_1 = -\tan \alpha_2$.

Seed grasps are points in C-space; the symmetry sets are lines. Now *Type 1 seeds are simply the intersections of the symmetry set with the antisymmetry set.* This is clear since, at such an intersection, both $\tan \alpha_1 = \tan \alpha_2$ (antisymmetry) and $\tan \alpha_1 = -\tan \alpha_2$ (symmetry) so that $\tan \alpha_1 = \tan \alpha_2 = 0$.

Type 2 seeds lie on the respective symmetry sets but are distinguished points on those sets. We require a further condition to localize them. It can be shown that Type 2a and 2s seeds are points of intersection of the antisymmetry and symmetry sets respectively with a third set: the *critical set* of the *grasp map*. This critical set can be defined algebraically by defining the "grasp map." Rather than do that here, an equivalent geometrical construction in terms of osculating circles is given in Figure 12. The construction is a test that can be applied to any pair of points s_1, s_2 on a contour $r(s)$. Generically, the set of points passing the test will form smooth curves in C-space.

To summarize, all seed points are found as intersections of the three sets, as follows:

Type 1: Intersections of the symmetry set and the antisymmetry set.
Type 2s: Intersections of the symmetry set and the critical set.
Type 2a: Intersections of the antisymmetry set and the critical set.

This is illustrated for the elliptical case in Figure 11c,d. Note however that, in the case of Type 2 seeds, these intersection conditions are necessary but not sufficient.

For Type 2s, it is also necessary, generically, that the two fingers are on convex points of the contour. For Type 2a, one must be at a convex point, the other at a concave point. That is sufficient to guarantee *extremality* of the friction function S, that is, either a saddle-point, maximum or minimum of friction. Minimal-friction grasps are what were sought. Maximal-friction grasps are also interesting being locally pessimal, indicating areas of C-space to avoid.

5. GRASP STABILITY

The qualitative description of C-space can be expanded by going beyond mere equilibrium (force-closure) to include stability. Given that a grasp is in equilibrium, a *stable* grasp is one for which equilibrium is maintained even when a perturbation has been applied. Various definitions of stability are useful: both for a thin-fingered gripper and for a parallel-jaw gripper, both dynamic and static stability. In all cases, stability properties are related to the critical set defined geometrically in Figure 12.

Whereas the thin-fingered gripper has the 2-D (s_1, s_2) C-space that we have been using so far, C-space for the parallel-jaw gripper must be a 1-D projection of (s_1, s_2) space. It has only one degree of freedom, namely θ the orientation of the jaws relative to object coordinates. In fact, C-space for the parallel-jaw gripper is simply the antisymmetry set itself (see, for example, Figure 11b). General perturbations in C-space for the thin-fingered gripper are simply projected onto the antisymmetry set. Thus any grasp (s_1, s_2) that is stable for a thin-fingered gripper must also be stable for a parallel-jaw gripper.

The distinction between dynamic and static stability is important. It depends on what *type* of perturbation is to be considered. Dynamic stability covers the case of perturbation of object position, whereas static stability applies to a perturbation of the coefficient of friction.

Dynamic stability is more intuitive and this is probably because it is the more relevant sense for humans, whose eyes and hands are well separated. Any stable perturbations of the gripped object are acceptable because the eyes can monitor them continuously and keep track of the object's position. It is also the appropriate sense of stability for a "frictionless" parallel-jaw gripper [20], one of whose jaws is free to slide longitudinally. A robot like the one pictured in Figure 2, however, suffers from hypermetropia. It cannot see its own hand and in fact it cannot see anything closer than about $\frac{1}{10}$ of the diameter of the workspace. Static stability is then more important. The part is visible *before* it is picked up. Once it is gripped it must not move relative to the fingers; any such motion would be unseen and the precise positioning of the part would be lost.

Statically, one perfectly stable grip is across the diameter of a circle. This corresponds to a point in two-fingered C-space at which the symmetry set, the antisymmetry set and the critical set all meet. Stability then decreases as the centers of osculating circles move apart (Figure 13). Separate stability measures can be computed for each finger and are displayed for the contours of real parts shown in Figures 3 and 4. Finger positions for Type 1 seed grasps are indicated there by rectangles whose length is a measure of stability of the finger. The rectangle indicates the safe range of movement of the finger when the coefficient of friction is 0.05 (perturbed, that is, from a value of 0.0).

Dynamic stability is defined by imagining the fingers to be connected by a spring and computing the potential energy $P(s_1, s_2)$ in the region of the equilibrium point. The equilibrium may be stable, conditionally stable or unstable according to whether P is at a minimum, a saddle or a maximum. Again, it is the osculating circles that determine stability, but in a way that is somewhat independent of the static notion of stability, as Figure 13 shows.

Dynamic stability can be measured for any grasp, not just for a Type 1 seed. In this more general case, transitions between the three types of stability occur exactly on the critical set in C-space. Hence C-space is partitioned by the critical set into regions according to the type of stability. In the case of Figure 11c, regions of conditional stability (e.g., grasping the minor axis) alternate, in C-space, with regions of instability (e.g., grasping the major axis). Furthermore, the symmetry and antisymmetry sets also mark qualitative transitions of stability, namely, a transition of finger dominance. As a symmetry set is crossed, the finger that is dominant, in the sense of requiring less friction for equilibrium, ceases to be dominant; the nondominant finger becomes the dominant one.

6. COMMENTS AND CONCLUSIONS

Implementation of the theory so far covers the cases of Type 1 and Type 2a seed grasps. This is because a reasonably efficient algorithm is available for recovery of the antisymmetry set from spline curves. Type 1 and Type 2a seeds can be recovered by tracking along the antisymmetry set in C-space, testing for intersections with the symmetry set and the critical set, respectively. To recover Type 2s seeds it would be necessary to track along either the symmetry set or the critical set. An approximate algorithm for tracking along the symmetry set of a B-spline curve has been devised by Rom and Medioni [29]. However it is not yet clear whether such an approximation is close enough for our purpose.

An unexpected but pleasing outcome of this study has been the relationship between local symmetry and grasping. Previously, local symmetries have been seen as a descriptive tool, as a simplifying process for shape descriptors. Consideration of grasping, however, forces an *operational description* of shape. This has the effect of both confirming the descriptive value of local symmetry and modifying it. The most significant modification is to view symmetry *in configuration space*, rather than in image-space. This has the additional benefit of removing the mathematically fascinating but practically annoying problem of singularity that occurs in the image-space representation.

It is a matter for speculation whether human performance in visual grasping could be modelled using the ideas of seed grasps and grasp stability. Of course the theory here is 2-D. An extension to 3-D, that may require different machinery than the one described here, is yet to be fully worked out. However 2-D grasping is a significant subproblem that is convenient for psychophysical experimentation. There is psychophysical evidence [3] that the human vision system is highly efficient at recovering symmetry, even with exposure times as brief as 100ms. An appealing hypothesis, then, is that our ability to judge stable grasp may be fed directly by the symmetry perception mechanism without recourse to cognitive mechanisms involving symbolic coding of shape.

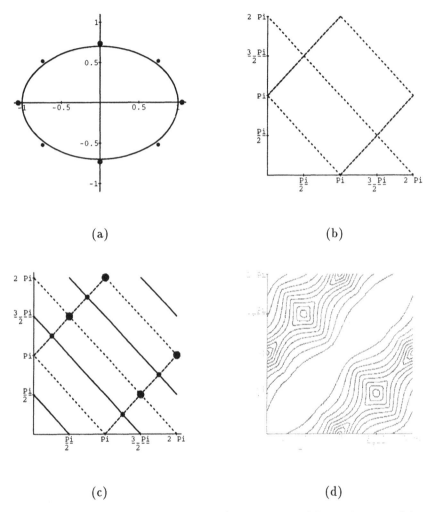

Figure 11. Symmetry sets for the ellipse in figure (a) are shown in (b)—short dashes: symmetry set; long dashes: antisymmetry set. In (c) the critical set (solid line) is also marked. Intersections of these sets correspond the extrema of the C-space map which is shown in (d). Large blobs in (c) are Type 1 extrema, small blobs are Type 2a. There are no Type 2s extrema on this particular contour. The extrema are also illustrated as grasps on the contour $\mathbf{r}(s)$ in (a), involving pairs of opposing finger positions.

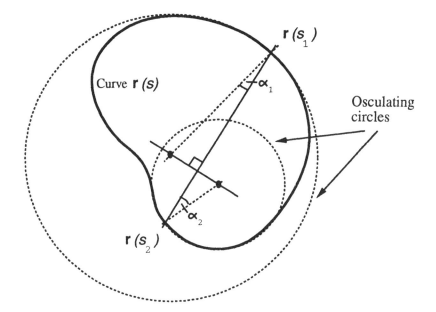

Figure 12. Critical points in grasp space occur under the geometrical condition illustrated; the line joining the finger positions $\mathbf{r}(s_1), \mathbf{r}(s_2)$ is orthogonal to the line joining the centers of osculating circles. (The osculating circle at a point on a curve is defined to be tangent to the curve there and also to have the same radius of curvature.)

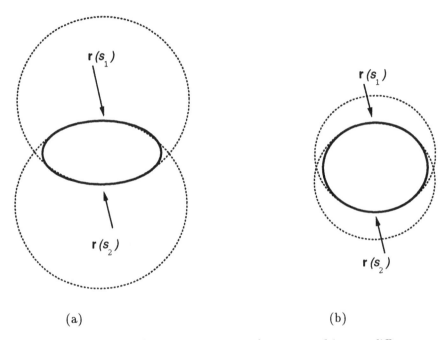

(a)   (b)

Figure 13. Stability of Type 1 grasps can be measured in two different senses, static and dynamic. In either case the measure depends on the vector between the two finger positions and on the centers of the two osculating circles. The grasp in (a) is stable in the static sense and (conditionally) in the dynamic sense. The grasp in (b) is dynamically *less* stable but statically *more* stable than the one in (a).

REFERENCES

1. J.Y. Aloimonos, I. Weiss, and A. Bandyopadhyay, "Active vision," *Int'l. J. Computer Vision* **2**, 1988, 333–356.

2. D.H. Ballard, "Animate vision," *Artificial Intelligence* **48**, 1991, 57–86.

3. H.B. Barlow, "The absolute efficiency of perceptual decisions," *Phil. Trans. Roy. Soc. B* **290**, 1980, 71–82.

4. A. Blake, J.M. Brady, R. Cipolla, Z. Xie, and A. Zisserman, "Visual navigation around curved obstacles," In *Proc. IEEE Int'l. Conf. Robotics and Automation*, 1991, 2490–2499.

5. A. Blake and R.C. Cipolla, "Robust estimation of surface curvature from deformation of apparent contours," In O. Faugeras (Ed.) *Proc. European Conf. on Computer Vision*, 1990, 465–474.

6. A. Blake, A. Zisserman, and R.C. Cipolla, "Dynamic contours: Real-time active splines," In A. Blake and A. Yuille (Eds.) *Active Vision*, MIT Press, 1992, 45–58.

7. J.M. Brady and H. Asada, "Smooth local symmetries and their implementation," *Int'l. J. Robotics Research* **3**, 1984.

8. J.M. Brady, S. Cameron, H. Durrant-Whyte, M. Fleck, D. Forsyth, A. Noble, and I. Page, "Progress towards a system that can acquire pallets and clean warehouses," In *Proc. Int'l. Symp. Robotics Research*, 1987.

9. J.W. Bruce, "Seeing—the mathematical viewpoint," *The Mathematical Intelligencer* **6**, 1984, 18–25.

10. J.W. Bruce and P.J. Giblin, *Curves and Singularities*, Cambridge, 1984.

11. R. Cipolla and A. Blake, "The dynamic analysis of apparent contours," In *Proc. Int'l. Conf. on Computer Vision*, 1990, 616–625.

12. R. Curwen and A. Blake, "Dynamic contours," In A. Blake and A.. Yuille (Eds.) *Active Vision*, MIT Press, 1992, 67–79.

13. E.D. Dickmanns and V. Graefe, "Applications of dynamic monocular machine vision," *Machine Vision and Applications* **1**, 1988, 241–261.

14. J.M. Elliot and K.J. Connelly, "A classification of manipulative hand movements," *Developmental medicine and child neurology* **26**, 1984, 283–296.

15. O.D. Faugeras and M. Hebert, "The representation, recognition, and locating of 3d objects," *Int'l. J. Robotics Research* **5**, 1986, 27–52.

16. B. Faverjon and J. Ponce, "On computing two-finger force-closure grasps of curved 2d objects," In *Proc. IEEE Int'l. Conf. Robotics and Automation*, 1991, 424–429.

17. M. Fleck, "Local rotational symmetries," In *Proc. IEEE CVPR*, 1986, 332–337.

18. P. Giblin and R. Weiss, "Reconstruction of surfaces from profiles," In *Proc. Int'l. Conf. on Computer Vision*, 1987, 136–144.

19. J.J. Gibson, *The Ecological Approach to Visual Perception*, Houghton Mifflin, 1979.

20. K.Y. Goldberg and M.T.. Mason, "Generating stochastic plans for a programmable parts feeder," In *Proc. IEEE Robotics and Automation*, 1991, 352–359.

21. M. Kass, A. Witkin, and D. Terzopoulos, "Snakes:active contour models," In *Proc. Int'l. Conf. on Computer Vision*, 1987, 259–268.

22. J.-C. Latombe, *Robot Motion Planning*, Kluwer, 1991.

23. M. Leyton, "A process grammar for shape," *Artificial Intelligence* **34**, 1991, 213–247.

24. X. Markenscoff, L. Ni, and C.H. Papadimitriou, "Optimum grip of a polygon," *Int'l. J. Robotics Research* **8**, 1988, 61–74.

25. D. Marr, *Vision*, Freeman, San Francisco, 1982.

26. V.D. Nguyen, "Constructing force-closure grasps," *Int'l. J. Robotics Research* **7**, 1988, 3–16.

27. J-M. Pichon, C. Blanes, and N. Franceschini, "Visual guidance of a mobile robot equpped with a network of self-motion sensors," *SPIE* **1195**, 1989, 44–53.

28. R. Rimey and C.M. Brown, "Task-oriented vision with multiple bayes nets," In A. Blake and A. Yuille (Eds.) *Active Vision*. MIT, 1992.

29. H. Rom and G. Medioni, "Hierarchical decomposition and axial representation of shape," *IEEE Trans. PAMI*, 1992.

30. J.K. Salisbury and B. Roth, "Kinematic and force analysis of articulated mechanical hands," *ASME J. Mechanisms, Transmissions Automation in Design* **105**, 1983, 35–41.

31. A.P. Witkin, "Space-scale filtering," In *Proc. IJCAI*, 1983, 1019–1022.

32. A.L. Yuille and T. Poggio, "Fingerprint theorems," In *Proc. AAAI*, 1984, 362–365.

Dana H. Ballard and Christopher M. Brown
University of Rochester

ABSTRACT

Vision theories can be categorized in terms of the amount of explicit representation postulated in the perceiver. Gibson's precomputational theory eschewed any explicit representation. In contrast, Marr used layers of explicit representation, hoping to simplify vision computations. Current technological advances in robotic hardware and computer architectures have allowed the building of anthropomorphic devices that capture important technical features of human vision. Experience with these devices suggests that cooperative gaze-control behaviors can reduce the need for explicit representation. This view is captured in the notion of "animate vision," which is a framework for sequential decision making and visual learning.

1. COMPUTATIONAL THEORIES OF VISION

Vision is the most elaborate sense, and as such has challenged philosophers over many centuries to explain the mystery of its functioning. The advent of the digital computer allowed the development of computational theories that give accounts of the information extracted from the image, and of how it is extracted, processed, and used. One of the last and most influential precomputational theories is that of Gibson [25, 26, 27], which posits direct perception. The crux of this theory is that the environment, by itself, is the repository for information necessary to act. This information is expressed in terms of invariants that are implicitly contained in the optical array. The best known example is that of optic flow, the velocity patterns induced on the optic array by motion of the observer. For instance, if an observer translates in the direction of gaze, the optic flow contains information about

This material is based on work supported by the National Science Foundation under Grants numbered IRI-8920771, IRI-8903582, and CDA-8822724, and by contract MDA972-92-J-1012. The government has certain rights in this material.

significant events such as the time to collision with surfaces. In Gibson's theory the following two components are most important.

1. The world is the repository of the information needed to act. Information is present exterior to the observer, and by implication need not be represented internally in some mental state that exists separately from the stimulus.
2. The information needed to act is computed directly (direct perception).

In the light of later work that meticulously counts the computational overhead of vision, the second tenet seems a controversial claim. However, it is likely that Gibson was not denying an underlying computational theory, but trying to distinguish between the sequential computational model advocated for logical reasoning and the computation involved in perception [30]. Today, part of the credibility of computational theories hinges on the cost of computing invariants.

Marr [36] articulated a comprehensive vision theory in computational terms — an enormous contribution with many different aspects. His emphasis was on the internal representations needed to support an information extraction process. Marr's theory defines vision as the problem of determining "what is where," with the "what" being defined as object-centered representations. Object-centered descriptions are (usefully) invariant with respect to the viewer. However, computing object centered descriptions from the viewer-centered representations of objects on the retina is generally agreed to be a very difficult task that can only be done in stages. Likewise the "where" question is difficult to answer except in viewer-centered coordinates. A series of representations is needed, each with the objective of facilitating the computation of object-centered descriptions. The series is summarized in Table 1.

Table 1.

Data Structure	Index	Type
image	retinotopic	photometric features
primal sketch	retinotopic	photometric features
2 1/2 D sketch	retinotopic	physical properties
object-centered representations	object-centered	physical properties

This first computational theory of vision was quite valuable in defining the principal issues. One of its salient points was to emphasize the role of intrinsic images [9] (such as the "2 $\frac{1}{2}$-dimensional sketch," or surface normal map) for use in what became known as "early vision." Support for such representations has been found in the retinotopic maps of early vision (optic flow, texture, color, disparity) that have been observed in monkey cortex.

Despite the major contributions of Marr's theory, it left some major issues unaddressed [4]. The most important may have been the exclusion of the effects of the perceiver's behavior: The theory was essentially about passive vision. Another thing Marr did not include were special features of human vision, such as the fovea, with its greatly enhanced resolution near the optical axis, and the associated elaborate gaze control system. Absent was the idea of using the world as its own representation, accessed by real-time vision. Finally, there was no role for learning algorithms.

Such omissions have proved important, as their inclusion greatly reduces the need for complete representations postulated by Marr's theory.

2. INTERACTIVE BEHAVIORAL THEORIES

The new school of computational behaviorism is interactionist: The world and the perceiver participate jointly in the computation. Neither is complete without the other. The motivation is performance, since vastly more computationally efficient algorithms can be designed if the world is exploited as a peripheral memory device [6, 11]. The argument is that one needs very little representation when behaviors are taken to be the fundamental primitive. Brooks' robotic platforms demonstrate that simple, real-time behaviors can be built with minimal representations of the world.

In vision, behavior initially influenced visual theories in rather minor ways. The most important has been in the computation of the intrinsic image representations of early vision. Without behavior the computation of optic flow, surface orientation and depth are underconstrained. Computing these quantities can be made well-posed with the addition of smoothness constraints, but the resulting iterative algorithms are slow. In contrast, the incorporation of behavioral assumptions has been used to make these problems well-posed in a way that allows the computations to be performed in constant time. For example in the case of depth cues computed from motion parallax, or "kinetic depth" (a lateral-motion behavior), together with the self-knowledge of its extent, is sufficient to make depth cues easily computable. Table 2 summarizes some of the other computations that have been simplified by behavioral assumptions.

Table 2. Computations Simplified by Behavioral Assumptions

Agent's Behavior	Behavioral Assumption
Shape from Shading	Light source not directly behind viewer [45]
Time to Adjacency	Rectilinear motion; gaze in the direction of motion [33]
Kinetic Depth	Lateral head motion while fixating a point in a stationary world [8]
Color Homing	Target object is distinguished by its color spectrum [66]
Optic Flow	Texture-rich environment [28]
Stereo Depth	System can fixate environmental points [68]
Edge Homing	Target position can be described by approximate directions from texture in its surround [42]
Object Tracking	Vergence can be used to improve tracking performance [19]

However, in retrospect these are relatively minor contributions compared to the major part of the revolution of behavioral interactionism, which is to recast completely the role of vision in terms of larger processes that are geared to the goals of the robot or human. In the first place, it has to be acknowledged that general purpose vision is a chimera; there are too many ways in which image information can be combined, too much that can be known about the world for vision to construct a task-independent description. If the visual world is not always rerepresented internally, then what is vision? The first crucial observation is that vision does not function in isolation, but as part of a complex behaving system that interacts in highly specific ways with the physical world. In fact, directed interaction with the world can permit information that is not readily available from static imagery to be obtained efficiently: For example, moving the head can reveal objects that are occluded in a single view. A second crucial point is that vision is dynamic; it does not compute all things at all times, but only what it needs. Fast vision (fast enough to keep up with the pace of the world) implies the world can serve as its own database, with the system "paging in" relevant parts by directing gaze or attention. A final point is that vision must be adaptive; the functional characteristics of the system may change through interaction with the world. There is no way a programmer can anticipate these developments. Thus a vision system must have the capability of adapting to these changes autonomously.

3. ANIMATE VISION

Work on the human visual system suggests the intuitively appealing notion that the human visual system is a complex repository of technical insights on how to use vision in the course of answering a huge repertoire of questions about the world. The term *animate vision* refers to this notion of visual behavior and capabilities [7].

The human eye is distinguished from current commercial electronic cameras by virtue of having much better resolution near the optical axis. It has a high-resolution fovea where over a one-degree range the resolution is better by an order of magnitude than that in the periphery. One feature of this design is the simultaneous representation of a large field of view and high acuity in the fovea. With the small fovea at a premium in a large visual field, it is not surprising that the human visual system has special fast mechanisms (saccades) for moving the fovea to different spatial targets.

It is instructive to examine the structure and function of saccadic eye movements in the process of solving complex tasks. The first systematic study of saccadic eye movements in the context of behavior was done by Yarbus [67]. When subjects were given the task of remembering the position of the people and the objects in the room the eye movement traces showed a specialized signature for this task that was not similar to other signatures, say for the one elicited for "give the ages of the people in the picture." These findings suggest that representing large amounts of categorical data about the visual world is not done routinely. Instead, the visual system may be used to subserve problem-solving behaviors that may or may not require an elaborate model of the world in the traditional sense of remembering positions of people and objects in a room.

The visual categories an organism uses, and thus the algorithms it uses to derive them and the meaning of symbols representing categories, is in part determined by the physiology of the organism doing the categorization [32]. This is the notion of embodiment of categories. In the interactionist theory, categories are also determined by world structure. Humans and primates are distinguished by their foveal vision, which implies an ability and necessity to scan the world, which then acts as an external "tape" (in a Turing machine analogy). The algorithms (fixation, grouping) that implement the embodiment are intimately related not just to categories (cognitive, abstract) levels but also to the implementational substrate (neural, hardware) levels of a system. Following are some observations about the embodiment of vision.

1. The world obeys physical laws and has predictable structure, and the organism has an essential relationship with the world that depends on its regularity.
2. The visual system is not completely general, nor does it have an arbitrary set of capabilities: It is a particular embodiment of the relationship of the organism to the world.
3. The world can function as an external memory that is interpreted by sequential eye movements and modified by effectors. (On these first three points, see also [12].)
4. At the implementation level, the coupling of the organism to the world can be modeled in terms of a reduced instruction set of possible perceptions and actions.
5. These instructions are referred to the center of gaze, thus requiring extensive gaze control mechanisms.
6. To capture the variability in the world, the possible behavioral programs must be learned over the course of behaving in similar situations.
7. The reduced instruction set induces equivalence classes on situations that allow learned programs to apply in similar situations.

To summarize, the fovea imposes an essential sequentialization of visual activity, which is the first principle of animate vision (Figure 1). Sequentialization has a natural set of primitive instructions described in terms of eye and head movements that are often discrete (saccades).

The second principle partly follows from the first. Gaze control is necessary given a fovea and self-movement, and elaborate continuous and discrete gaze control algorithms exist as embodiment-level phenomena that are major determiners of how and what we see. In particular, gaze control can mediate nongeometric representations, which have the advantage that they can avoid calibration problems and can be invariant to object pose and observer position.

Finally, there is no way, either genetically (with humans) or with a priori programming (in robots) to anticipate the variability in the world. Thus mechanisms must be in place to discover how to modify existing behaviors to account for the particular variations that occur in behavioral instances. That is, there must be at least a localized sort of learning that adapts the existing behavioral repertoire. The claim of animate vision is that learning should be at the embodiment level, since learning abstract, machine-independent categories is too hard. Learning algorithms can exploit various routine repetitive behaviors that remain constant despite novel features of each behavioral instance.

The study of fast visual behaviors can be greatly aided with a system capable of interacting with the real world in real time. Bajcsy [6] developed the first computer-controlled camera platform with extensive anthropomorphic features. She also advocated the integration of vision with behavior, in particular touch sensing. Recent

ANIMATE VISION PRINCIPLES

- Much visual seqentialization is necessary to simplify visual tasks.

- Gaze control is necessary to compensate for animate motion.

- Learning is necessary to compensate for the world's unpredictability.

Figure 1. Animate Vision Principles

revolutionary developments in computer image processing hardware and robotic hardware have brought the needed functionality to the marketplace. The advent of video-rate pipeline image processing computers increased the speed available to a factor of 100 over the fastest workstations and for the first time allowed extensive real-time processing capabilities. At the same time inexpensive microprocessors and lightweight motors allowed the design of many different kinds of mobile platforms. The Rochester laboratory is described in Section 7.

4. SEQUENTIALIZATION

Although some visual phenomena are preattentive, in that the result "pops out" immediately [59], in practice this kind of popout is rare. In fact, most complex tasks have to be performed by the sequential application of simple primitive operations. Such decompositions greatly reduce the combinatorics of the computation. This simplification can be understood with reference to the problem of relating internal models to the world. The general problem of associating many models to many parts of the image simultaneously, as generally advocated in "image understanding," may be too difficult to be performed in real time (Table 3). In order to make the computation tractable within a single fixation it has to be simplified, either into one of location (one internal model) or identification (one world object). A location task is to find the image coordinates of a single model in the presence of many alternatives. In this task the image periphery must be searched and one can assume that the model has been chosen a priori. An identification task is to associate the foveated part of the image with one of many possible models. In this task one can assume that the location of the material to be identified is at the fixation point. This dichotomy is exactly equivalent to the "where and what" dichotomy seen in the parietal and infero-temporal areas of visual cortex [38]. The implication of the "what and where" dichotomy is that a complex visual task may efficiently be implemented as a sequence of these more primitive functions.

In an application of the what–where distinction in the domain of colored objects, Swain [56, 58] has shown that both the identification and location behaviors are much simpler than their combination in image understanding (Section 4.1).

In a visual domain governed by rules and expectations, it is possible to devise visual strategies that optimize some performance index. Such visual strategies were first formalized by Garvey, who implemented them as trees with nodes denoting the AND, the OR, or the SEQUENCE of a set of visual actions [24]. His system used

Table 3. Trying to match a large number of image segments to a large number of models at once may be too difficult.

		Object to Match Against	
		One	Many
Image Portions	One		Identification: trying to identify an object whose location can be fixated
	Many	Location: trying to find a known object	Image interpretation: too hard?

this tree to try to solve the visual task it encoded. However, Garvey's model was developed in the context of passive vision, and had hard-coded strategies. Recent work (Section 4.2) explores how to use Bayes nets as a knowledge representation to develop maximum expected utility plans for sequential visual behavior that integrate run-time information. Extending Garvey's ideas to active vision results in the "object search" problem, where an object being sought may not be in the field of view. Section 4.3 develops models that handle this case.

The what–where distinction is also explicit in recent work on the control of eye movements (continuous paths and sequences of saccades) [49]. This work exploits the what and where dichotomy in the context of the acquisition of visual skills, and is described in Section 6.1. Behavior can be learned either in a "where" mode, in which (say) specific visual locations are foveated in sequence, or in a "what" mode, which sequentially foveates a desired sequence of features in the image, regardless of their location. Further, the output of the "where" and "what" systems each can be fed back to the other system, in order to train the system to output a sequence of desired features or objects in their expected locations in the image.

4.1. OBJECT LOCATION DOES NOT REQUIRE POSE

If internal representations do not keep track of detailed geometrical information, how can the gaze be directed to a target in view? One way to do this is to "backproject" features that have been extracted from the image onto their retinal locations. If this process is successful the resultant locations can specify a gaze shift. To see how this might be done, consider color features as represented by a color histogram. A histogram backprojection algorithm [58] answers the question "Where are the colors in the image that belong to the object being looked for (the *target*)?" The algorithm deemphasizes colors that appear in other objects having different histograms, so that they are less likely to distract the search mechanism. Experiments show that the technique works for objects in cluttered scenes under realistic conditions.

In *Histogram Backprojection* the model (target) and the image are represented by their multidimensional color histograms M and I. A *ratio histogram* R, defined as

$$R_i = \frac{M_i}{I_i}$$

is computed from the model and image histograms. The R histogram is backprojected onto the image, that is, the image values are replaced by the values of R that they index. The backprojected image is then convolved with a mask, which for compact objects of unknown orientation could be a circle with the same area as the expected area subtended by the object. The peak in the convolved image is the maximum likelihood location for the target.

More precisely, let $h(c)$ be the histogram function that maps a color c (a 3-D value) to a histogram bin (another 3-D value). Let D^r be a disk of radius r:

$$D^r_{x,y} = \begin{cases} 1 \text{ if } \sqrt{x^2 + y^2} < r \\ 0 \text{ otherwise} \end{cases}$$

Define the *loc* function to return a pixel (x, y) with the value of its argument, and let the $*$ symbol denote convolution. Then the histogram backprojection algorithm can be written:

1. Compute the ratio histogram
   for each i, j, k, do

$$R(i, j, k) := \frac{M(i, j, k)}{I(i, j, k)}$$

2. Backproject the ratio histogram; each location is rated as to how helpful it is
   for each x, y, do
$$c_{x,y} := \min(R(h(c_{x,y})), 1)$$

3. Blur the saliency image $c := D^r * c$
4. Locate the maximum $(x_t, y_t) := \text{loc}(\max_{x,y} c_{x,y})$

This strategy depends on the colors for the object being colocated in a clump that is more conspicuous than the surround. Surprisingly, experiments with multicolored objects have shown that this is a very useful strategy. Figure 2 shows the backprojected "saliency image" $C(x, y)$ (Step 2 in the algorithm), where a striped shirt has been selected as the target object.

4.2. VISUAL DECISION MAKING CAN BE FORMALIZED

The use of color suggests a mechanism for the control of large-scale changes of gaze, but does not address the issue of which particular sequences of gaze changes are best for a given task.

A task-oriented system is one that performs the minimum effort necessary to solve a specified task from a variety of possible tasks. A visual question-answering system is presented here to illustrate techniques, but a system for navigation or manipulation could be based on the same principles. Depending on the task, the system decides which information to gather, which operators to use at which resolution, and where to apply them. Table 4.2. summarizes the key differences between the standard passive, reconstructionist (or Marrian) vision paradigm and the task-oriented approach.

Figure 2. The response of the full resolution back-projection algorithm with striped shirt as target. Blurring over expected size of shirt accumulates evidence in peak at shirt location.

The technical approach has as background a large amount of research into visual attention, classical work in eye movements, and recent advances in active vision, including camera movements and foveal-peripheral sensors. Specifically, the tools are decision theory, utility theory, and Bayesian probabilistic models [10, 17, 22, 24]. Two recent key developments are Bayes nets [44], and influence diagrams [44, 53]. Applications using these new techniques are beginning to appear. The first large experimental system that applied Bayes nets to computer vision is by Levitt [34]. The formulation of that system using influence diagram techniques is discussed in [2]. A sensor/control problem involving a real milling machine is solved using influence diagram techniques in [1]. A special kind of influence diagram, called a temporal belief network, is discussed in [20], and is being studied for an application in sensor based mobile robot control.

A task-oriented computer vision system, called TEA, uses Bayes nets and a maximum expected utility decision rule [48, 50, 51, 52].

The TEA system

The goal is to support many different visual tasks efficiently. Figure 3 shows a scene from TEA's task domain. In TEA, a task is to answer a question about the scene:

Table 4. Key differences between passive vision and task-oriented vision.

Passive vision	Task-oriented vision
use all vision modules	use only some vision modules
process entire image	process areas of the image
maximal detail	sufficient detail
extract representation first	ask question first
answer question from representation data	answer question from scene data
unlimited resources	resource limitations

Where is the butter? Is this breakfast, lunch, dinner, or dessert? More qualitative tasks are also interesting: Is this an informal or fancy meal? How far has the eating progressed? Is this table messy?

Figure 3. An example scene in the application domain.

The TEA system gathers evidence visually and incorporates it into a Bayes net until the question can be answered to a desired degree of confidence. The TEA system runs by iteratively selecting the evidence gathering action that maximizes an expected utility criterion involving the cost of the action and its benefits of increased certainties in the net.

Adhering to the embodiment of vision using a spatially varying sensor makes the "where to look next" question even more central. In the TEA system the peripheral image is a low-resolution image of the entire field of view from one camera angle, and the fovea is a small high-resolution image (i.e., window) that can be selectively moved within the field of view.

TEA can not view the entire scene at once. Often a camera movement must be made to an area of the scene that has not been viewed before. The target location of such a camera movement must be determined via relations with other portions of the scene for which image data is (or previously has been) available. Following a camera movement the fovea is centered in the field of view, but afterward the system can move the fovea within the field of view. The target location for a fovea movement is always within the field of view so it can be determined either from peripheral image data or by relations with other portions of the scene.

Bayes nets

A Bayes net is a way of representing the joint probability distribution of a set of variables in a way that is especially useful for knowledge representation. Nodes in the net represent variables with (usually) a discrete set of labels (e.g., a *utensil* node could have labels (*knife, fork, spoon*)). Links in the net represent (via tables) conditional probabilities that a node has a particular label given that an adjacent node has a particular label [21, 29, 40, 44, 46, 54].

The Bayes net formalism also includes a form of inference. Formally, belief in the values for node X is defined as $BEL(x) = P(x \mid \mathbf{e})$, where $\mathbf{e}$ is the combination of all evidence present in the net. Elegant solutions have been developed [17, 44] for incorporating a single piece of evidence into the net and for propagating its effect to all other nodes in the net.

TEA-1 uses four kinds of knowledge structured into separate networks. As in previous vision systems, TEA has a PART-OF net [34] and an IS-A tree [17, 34]. Its *expected area* net and *task* net; are new, as is the composite net that results from linking the four.

A PART-OF net models the physical structure of the scene. All nodes in this net have the same set of possible values: *present* and *not present*. The conditional probability on each network link indicates the likelihood that a subpart exists.

Geometric relations between objects are modeled by the *expected area* net, used in combination with the PART-OF net. The two networks have the same structure: A node in the PART-OF net identifies a particular object within the sub-part structure of the scene, and the corresponding node in the *expected area* net identifies the area in the scene in which that object is expected to be located. TEA-1 assumes a fixed camera origin, and the location of an object in the scene is specified by the two camera angles (pan and tilt) that will cause the object to be centered in the visual field. The cost of a visual operation is often proportional to the area over which it must be applied. The expected area of a node X can be used to scale the cost of visual operators by the ratio r_X^l of expected to scene areas.

A taxonomic IS-A hierarchy models *one* random variable that can have many mutually exclusive values, where the possible values can be organized into subsets forming a tree hierarchy. The full hierarchy of subsets can be represented as a tree structured graph. A special version of a Bayes net has been developed to incorporate the mutual-exclusivity constraint [44, 17].

Task-specific knowledge is contained in a *task* Bayes net (for example, Figure 4). One feature of task knowledge is that subtask nodes can be shared by several tasks. Questions such as "Is this a fancy meal?" may be answered using a range of image clues. Some simple tasks, such as "Where is the butter?" do not require a task net since they only involve one particular node in a net. Details on the task net are provided in [51]. The four nets are organized as shown in Figure 5.

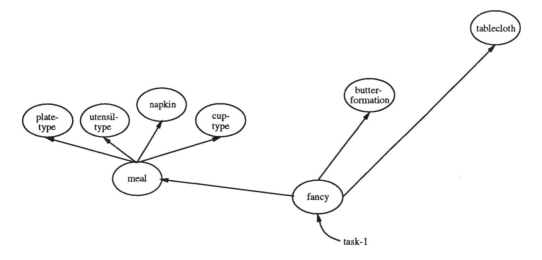

Figure 4. A *task* Bayes net.

Actions in a Bayes net

All actions in the TEA system are visual, and are constructed from one or more low-level *vision modules*. In TEA, each module can operate on either a foveal image or a peripheral image. The primary goal is to develop a framework in which any module with quantifiable performance can be incorporated, not to fashion optimal (or necessarily good) special purpose operators.

Examples of some low-level vision modules are: (a) histogram matching to locate and identify objects by color; (b) grayscale template matching using Sobel edge information to find instances of known objects by correlation detection; (c) Hough transform for circle detection; and (d) matching object representations built of straight lines by geometric hashing or relational structure matching.

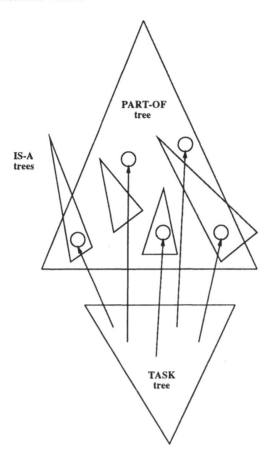

Figure 5. The organization of a large Bayes net used by TEA.

One or more vision modules may be used in a *visual action*. Each kind of object usually has several actions associated with it. TEA-0 had 11 visual actions related to 5 objects. TEA-1 currently has 20 actions. For example, `Per-detect-template-plate` uses a model grayscale template to detect the presence of a plate in the peripheral image and save its location. `Per-detect-hough-plate` uses a Hough transform for plate-sized circles for the same purpose. For `per-classify-plate`, a precondition is that the plate location must have been determined previously. A color histogram is used to classify the plate as paper (blue) or ceramic (green), using a window centered on the plate in the peripheral image. `Fov-classify-plate` moves the fovea to the plate and proceeds as for `per-classify-plate` but with foveal data. Similar actions exist for other kinds of objects. TEA-1 also contains a special table-finding action, since knowing the exact location and extent of the table is very useful. The `table` action assumes that the camera initially views some portion of the table top. It then scans the camera to the left until a large vertical line, the edge of the table, is located. The process is repeated for the other edges of the table.

An action node that is connected to a Bayes net node X represents a random variable that is a visual action's "evidence report." An action in a system that uses a composite net generally can post evidence reports to several different nets. The *expected area* net also handles evidence by the same mechanism. Action nodes can not be used in an IS-A tree. Instead, evidence is injected into the tree via the weight W_i associated with each leaf node h_i. If it is necessary to estimate the expected impact of an evidence report, it is always possible to use some kind of expected value for the λ values used to compute W_i. The *task* net handles evidence as above, but actions generally should not post evidence directly to the *task* tree, since such actions would be task-specific.

Calculating an action's utility

The utility of visual actions is an area of current research. The utility $U(\alpha)$ of an action α is of the form

$$U(\alpha) = \frac{V(\alpha)}{C(\alpha)}.$$

$C(\alpha) = r_A^l C_0(\alpha)$ is the cost of executing the action. $C_0(\alpha)$ is the execution time of action α on the entire peripheral image (or the foveal image, if α is a foveal action). r_A^l is the fraction of the image covered by the expected area of the object A associated with the action, when a confidence level of l is used. Before any actions have been executed, no objects have been located, and so all r_A^l values are close to 1.0. Over time, as other objects in the scene are located and as more and tighter relations are established, the value of r_A^l will approach zero.

$V(\alpha)$ is meant to be the value of the action, how useful it is for achieving the task's goal. All actions in TEA are *information gathering* actions; it uses a fundamental measure of information, Shannon's measure of average mutual information (see, e.g. [47, 44]): $I(x, y) = log_2 \frac{P(x|y)}{P(x)}$. I describes the information content about the event x that is provided by the occurrence of the event y (and vice versa).

When a composite net is used there are some subtleties in how quantities like $I(target, \alpha)$ are calculated. First, the action α may post several evidence reports, one to each net. Second, the *target* node and the action's evidence reports are normally in different Bayes nets.

The problem is made more difficult for a static utility calculation by the fact that it is important to "look ahead" at the future impact of executing an action. TEA-1 uses the following "lookahead" utility function for action α.

$$U(\alpha) = \frac{V(\alpha) + V(\beta)}{C(\alpha) + C(\beta)} + H \sum_{X \in Net} \Delta U(X) \qquad (1)$$

where

$$\beta = argmax_{\gamma \in LocPre(\alpha)} \frac{V(\gamma)}{C(\gamma)}$$

The first term in Equation (1) accounts for the future value of establishing the location of an object. $LocPre(\alpha)$ is the set of actions that have a precondition satisfied by executing action α. Let β be the "best" of the actions in that set. The new utility of action α is an average over both α and β, more specifically an average of the value and cost of the two actions α and β.

The second term in Equation (1) accounts for the future impact of making expected areas smaller. Each node in the expected area network contributes a term $\Delta U(X)$ to the utility:

$$\Delta U(X) = \max_{\gamma \in Actions(X)} [\frac{V(\gamma)}{s_X^l C_0(\gamma)} - \frac{V(\gamma)}{r_X^l C_0(\gamma)}]$$

$$= [\frac{r_X^l}{s_X^l} - 1] \max_{\gamma \in Actions(X)} U(\gamma)$$

This term is the increase in utility of the best action that affects X.

Experimental example

This section presents experimental results using the TEA-1 system to decide whether a table is set for either a fancy meal or an informal meal. The scene laid out on the table is a "fancy" meal.

The sequence of actions executed by TEA-1 is summarized in Table 5. The a priori belief of the table setting being fancy is 0.590, compared with 0.410 that it is informal. As the system executes actions to gather specific information about the scene, the belief that the setting is a fancy one approaches 0.974. The following text discusses a few important points in the sequence of executed actions. The system begins at time step 0 with the a priori belief values mentioned above (i.e., for informal and fancy). One line in Table 5 represents one cycle in the decision loop of the system.

Table 5. The sequence of actions selected and executed by TEA-1. The belief values shown are those after incorporating the results from each action.

time	$U(\alpha)$	α, an action	$BEL(informal)$	$BEL(fancy)$
0		a priori	0.410	0.590
1	10.000	table	0.400	0.600
2	10.505	per-detect-hough-cup	0.263	0.737
3	42.839	per-classify-cup	0.343	0.657
4	11.374	per-detect-hough-plate	0.340	0.660
5	11.917	per-classify-plate	0.041	0.959
6	20.982	per-detect-utensil	0.041	0.959
7	58.810	per-classify-utensil	0.033	0.967
8	4.320	per-detect-napkin	0.026	0.974
9	3.342	fov-classify-cup	0.026	0.974
10	2.405	fov-classify-plate	0.026	0.974
11	1.759	per-detect-hough-bowl	0.026	0.974
12	0.687	per-detect-butter	0.026	0.974
13	0.486	fov-verify-butter	0.026	0.974

E.g., at time step 2 the per-detect-hough-cup action is executed. This action moves the camera to the center of the cup's expected area and then tries (successfully) to detect a cup. The per-detect-napkin action uses a color histogram to detect a (red) napkin. When the action is executed at time step 8, the expected area of the napkin is small enough that it doesn't cover the pink creamer container located just above the napkin, thus avoiding falsely detecting the creamer as the napkin.

As TEA-1 runs, it moves the camera around in the scene, placing its fovea over increasingly constrained areas. Foveal actions are another way to limit processing to smaller contextual areas in the scene. For example, the action at time step 10 only takes data from the center of the plate. Camera/fovea movements and expected areas are very useful for limiting the portion of a scene or image that an action processes. As more objects are located via actions, the expected areas for the remaining objects (not yet located by actions) get narrower.

4.3. SEARCHING FOR OBJECTS CAN USE PROCEDURAL MEMORY

With the advent of active systems, the object location problem becomes transformed in important ways. If the agent is in control of placing as well as locating objects, then the agent can impose order and rules upon an environment that is not structured according to prior rules. In the larger behavioral context of object search, objects are often searched for repeatedly, so that algorithms can be developed that amortize the cost of search over many trials.

A major problem is that objects may be required that are not in the field of view. The 3-D nature of the world, together with its projection onto the image plane combine to make this problem very different from searching a static image, since moving the camera in 3D creates very different images.

Small objects can be very difficult to find. Luckily, manufactured objects come in a variety of scales, and human environments are organized so that the bewildering array of small objects can be located. An office is filled with the clutter of many small objects, but only contains room for a few large objects that are used to organize the small ones.

Combining these ideas, Wixson [64, 65] is studying the learning of behaviors to find objects under the assumptions that size relationships are used to organize the world and that larger objects are inherently easier to locate. The central thesis is that large objects are convenient indexes to use to record the location of small objects, which can be found by indirectly searching for them by finding the big easier-to-find objects first. A simple model allows quantification of the trade-offs between direct and indirect search. Discrete objects of different sizes in a 3-D world can be used to compute the difficulty of finding the small object, expressed as an expected cost sensitive to the relative sizes of the sought and intermediate objects. Figure 6 shows the most important result, that the speedup in object search in 3D is over an order of magnitude with indirect search through easily found objects.

A more complex simulation [65] incorporates a more realistic model of imaging and objects; it substantiates the predictions based on simpler representations. Figure 7 shows a representative case of searching for an orange cup in a panoramic (360° × 66°) scene.

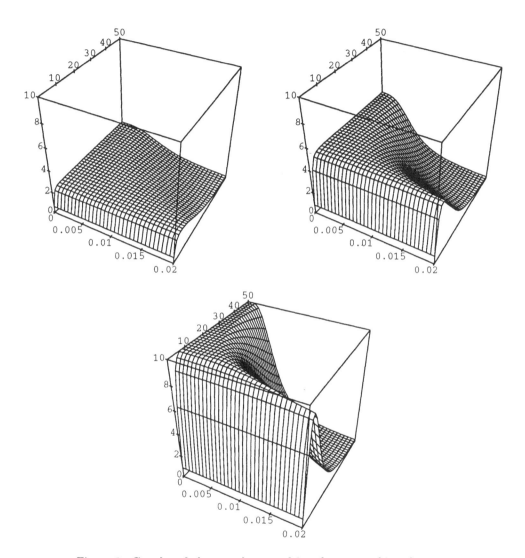

Figure 6. Graphs of the speedup resulting from searching for a target
that is $1/a$ times less wide than the world, using an intermediate object
I that is b times as wide as the target T. Graph at upper left was created
with P(I is present) = P(T near I) = .75. Graph at upper right was
created with P(I is present) = P(T near I) = .90. Graph at bottom was
created with P(I is present) = P(T near I) = .95.

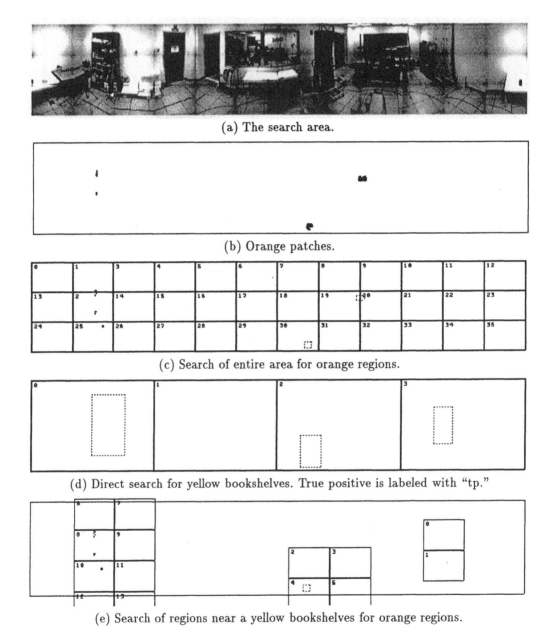

(a) The search area.

(b) Orange patches.

(c) Search of entire area for orange regions.

(d) Direct search for yellow bookshelves. True positive is labeled with "tp."

(e) Search of regions near a yellow bookshelves for orange regions.

Figure 7. Searching for an orange cup.

5. GAZE CONTROL

A hallmark of human vision is the ability to direct the control of gaze, both in changing gaze rapidly and discretely to new targets, as seen in the saccadic eye movements, and in maintaining gaze on a chosen target. It can be safely argued that humans have the most sophisticated gaze control systems of any member of the animal kingdom. This capability is so important that gaze control is one of the defining characteristics of animate vision.

Gaze control is needed for several reasons.

1. *Multiresolution vision*: Photo-sensors are being tested that have varying spatio-temporal resolution. These sensors usually have a central high-resolution area or fovea, and a concentric arrangement of cells implementing a log-polar transform. If the object of interest is not imaged on the fovea, low sensor resolution degrades the performance.

2. *Motion Blur*: If the visual field is not stabilized on the (human or CCD) retina, motion blur degrades the performance of the imaging system and hence performance on quantitative or even qualitative vision algorithms. Fixating a moving object can blur, and thus deemphasize, objects not of interest moving at other velocities.

3. *Mathematical simplification*: Fixating an object of interest puts points on the object near the optic axes of both eyes, allowing an orthographic projection model and simplifying many computations [60].

4. *Facilitating Stereo Fusion*: Since the fixation point has a stereoscopic disparity of zero, points nearby will generally have small disparities. This makes it possible to use stereo algorithms that accept only a limited range of disparities. Such systems can be very fast, and are amenable to hardware implementation.

5. *Active Vision*: There is a whole species of "active" vision algorithms that cooperatively use observer motion and vision (e.g., [5, 8]).

6. *Fixation-relative behaviors*: A fixation point defined by the system's gaze defines a coordinate system that is related as much to the object being observed as it is to the observer. This fixation frame enables the use of fixation-relative behaviors, such as servoing to a fixated target in final phases of reaching for a moving object.

7. *Expanding field of view*: If the object of interest is not in the image, gaze control is needed to put it there.

8. *Implementing sequential allocation of visual resources*: The sequentialization mentioned in Section 4 requires active control of the sensor.

5.1. GAZE CONTROL MECHANISMS MUST COOPERATE

Humans have several interacting control systems that stabilize gaze against ego motion and follow moving targets. What cues should be used in a robotic gaze holding system, and how should they be combined [19]? The adaptive and flexible nature of the visual controls poses a difficult problem for traditional control theory. The visual system seems to build models that allow for zero-latency tracking using prediction. It is also able to select its error-computation mechanisms appropriately:

For instance, in acquiring and tracking a moving object, the optic flow of the object of interest is the error signal, but not the optic flow of the background. Foveating a moving object requires matching both position and velocity, but positional and velocity error signals cannot be simultaneously eliminated.

Gaze control studies have been carried out in simulation and with the Rochester head (Section 7). Techniques of coping with the mutual interaction of several human-like gaze controls, and with the effects of delay in the system were investigated, and are reported in [14, 15, 16]. To cope with delays, the control system was enhanced with a Smith prediction technique, supplemented with optimal (variance minimizing, Kalman) filters to predict target locations. This combination of techniques is an alternative to signal synthesis adaptive control [37] for zero-latency tracking. The predictive filters anticipate object and image states, allowing zero-latency tracking.

Several different inputs can participate in keeping the gaze of a moving agent fixed on a moving target. Target tracking can use visual inputs, and also can proceed open-loop using "proprioceptive" input. In the open-loop case, The six numbers defining the Puma's head position (a 3-space origin and three Euler angles) are read back to the controller at approximately 40Hz, and used with the coordinates of the target (which may be a function of time) to compute the values of pan and tilt that point the camera at the target. Differencing these values gives an approximation to the velocities necessary for smooth tracking. An inverse Jacobian calculation can also be used to compute the required pan and tilt velocities directly [55].

Only rarely is the target's position and trajectory accurately known, and so visual cues are usually necessary to stabilize gaze. Interestingly, neither the biological literature on gaze control and vision nor the robotic vision literature has identified exactly what visual processing is necessary to hold gaze on a visual target. For instance, retinal slip error signals (velocity and acceleration of the target's image) seem to be dominant in the monkey smooth pursuit system, and are surely sufficient to stabilize the target. However, a contribution from position error can achieve foveation as well as stabilization, and seems to play some part.

The vergence system can provide gaze control with useful input. Vergence would result if both eyes independently tracked a target, but independent trackers could easily begin tracking different targets. It is assumed here that vergence is independent from tracking, and that its control takes binocular input and constructs a robust error signal. Ideally, vergence should be driven by image and 3-D cues, including a representation of the 3-D fixation point, visual disparity (here computed over a large area of the visual field), and focusing information (which should in turn be affected by vergence).

Coombs' system implements wide-field vergence using autocorrelationlike techniques between subsampled left and right images. It currently uses only image data to control vergence. The best results have been obtained with the cepstral filter, a nonlinear process akin to phase correlation, to find the best global shift to match left and right hand subsampled images [19, 43]. Its advantage over "optimal" (Wiener filter, matched filter) techniques is that it effectively incorporates its own "interest operator," and pays attention only to broad-band signals with good autocorrelation properties. The output of the filter is a 2-D (horizontal vs. vertical) "disparity image," with peaks for the most common disparities. For gross vergence the largest peak corresponds to the "best" disparity match, and vergence control simply brings the peak to zero horizontal disparity by verging the cameras. A less reflexive and more selective control strategy could "lock on" to an arbitrary peak, bring it to zero disparity, and control vergence to keep it there. On the MaxVideo hardware using a digital signal processing chip, two 32×32 windows are processed at about 10 Hz, and provide the input signal to a PD controller that controls the camera pan motor velocities to achieve smooth performance.

5.2. GAZE CONTROL AIDS FIGURE-GROUND SEGMENTATION

The most severe chicken-and-egg problem of static computer vision is the segmentation problem. It is difficult to separate figure from ground without recognizing objects, and it is difficult to recognize objects if they are not separated from the background and other objects. In contrast, gaze-control behaviors can help a system separate figure from ground precategorically, that is without recognition. Stabilizing one point in a scene that is moving relative to the observer induces target "popout" due to motion blur induced in the nonstabilized parts of the scene, as shown in Figure 8.

A dramatic pop-out can be implemented that uses the organism's expectations about optic flow in the scene given its own motions and a static world. Objects that violate the expectations (that move with respect to the static 3-D world) induce flows that can be detected. Nelson [41] has produced a 30Hz, full-resolution implementation that flags image points where scene motion occurs that is incompatible with the observer's own motion and a static world.

Binocularity can help isolate figure from ground by actively verging gaze control. If only features having zero disparity are passed through a filter, then vergence implements a disparity-based filter that restricts attention to the "horopter," or 3-D locus of points that have zero disparity at the current vergence. Thus disparity filtering can separate a spatially coherent target from foreground and background distractors. Used with a fovea or window filter that limits visual information to a particular solid angle, disparity filtering limits visual information to a small volume of space (Figure 9).

The horopter and foveal constraints are used in a tracking system that pursues a moving object through a field of distractors [18]. A central window acts as a fovea, and the cepstral filter vergence control takes the grayscale image in the window as input. The output of the zero disparity filter is all the zero-disparity vertical edges in the scene. With both constraints, the input to the tracker is limited to edges in the horopter and window. When one or another of the constraints is loosened, tracking performance declines (Figure 10).

Active figure-ground segmentation techniques can cooperate and help each other. Visual tracking with vergence reduces the volume of space considered and also reduces blur in the target (making a stronger input to the tracker), and increases it in the distractors (further reducing their influence).

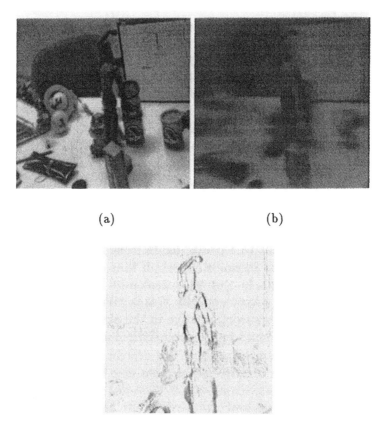

(a)   (b)

Figure 8. Illustration of fixation segmentation: Image (b) shows the weighted average of a temporal sequence of images acquired while moving the head and stabilizing gaze on the doll in scene (a). Image (c) is the result of applying an edge operator to (b).

5.3. FIXATION CREATES AN OBJECT-CENTERED REFERENCE FRAME

The most important visual behavior in humans is gaze-holding, or fixing a target on the fovea. This ability has a number of beneficial effects in low-level vision. At a higher level, the ability has a profound effect on the original "what is where" formulation of vision proposed by Marr. Technically, the ability to fixate means that the human can use an external frame of reference centered at that point, leading to great simplifications in algorithmic complexity [7]. This is a very different assertion than that of Marr, who emphasized that vision calculations were initially in viewer-centered coordinates. The fixation frame allows for closed loop behavioral strategies that do not require very precise 3-D information. For example, grasping an object can proceed by first fixating the object and then directing the hand to the center of

Binocular Fixation Segmentation

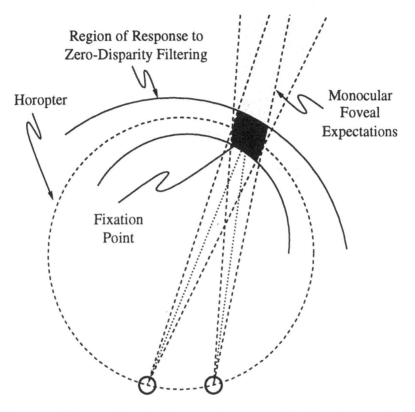

Figure 9. The zero-disparity horopter interacts with a foveal constraint to limit visual input to a small volume of space.

the retinal coordinate system. In depth the hand can be controlled relative to the plane of fixation. This behavior is called a "fixation point" strategy (Figure 11).

One way a fixation point strategy can be used is to generate useful intrinsic images, such as such as depth maps, that are relative to the fixation point [8]. Such maps do not contain absolute depth in egocentric coordinates, but still are useful in behaviors like grasping.

Another way the fixation point can be used, in conjunction with the figure-ground techniques in the previous section, is to serve as a pooled location for view-invariant features [35]. Such features are of vital importance for the indexing or identification of an object from a large memory. To see how such features would work, consider the features represented in a color histogram. The fixation point strategy allows the use of the color histogram of the "figure" image in an accurate matching strategy. Such a strategy intersects this histogram with memory histograms. The memory histogram with the largest overlap is identified as the object in the figure [57].

Given a pair of histograms, I and M, each containing n buckets, the intersection

Results of Ablation on Camera Pan Angle

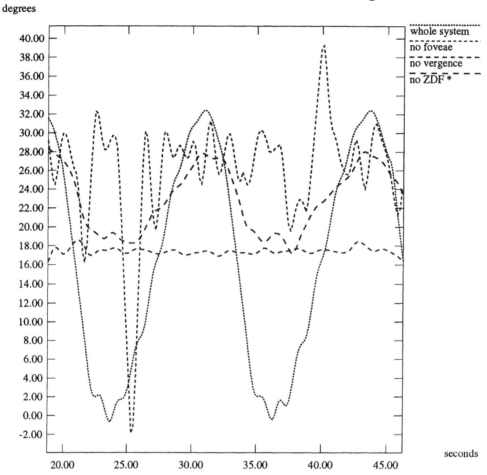

Figure 10. The performance of the cooperative verging and tracking system. The "whole system" trace shows the tracking of a target undergoing approximate harmonic motion—the performance is good except for some ringing at one point in the target's cycle. Without the foveae, tracking the centroid of the entire dynamic image leads to chaotic performance. The third trace results from disabling the vergence control and thus fixing the vergence angle. The fourth trace shows the result of eliminating the disparity filter and using instead the edge energy of one image to drive pursuit. (The large step inputs that resulted make the system unstable, so foveal reduction was also eliminated for this experiment.)

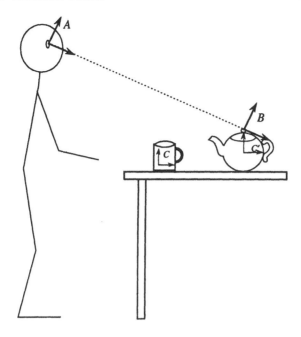

Figure 11. Much previous work in computational vision has assumed that the vision system is passive and computations are performed in a viewer-centered frame (A). Instead, biological and psychophysical data argue for a world-centered frame (B). This frame is selected by the observer to suit information-gathering goals and is centered at the fixation point. The task of the observer is to relate information in the fixation point frame to object-centered frames (C).

of the histograms is defined to be

$$\sum_{j=1}^{n} \min(I_j, M_j)$$

The result of the intersection of a model histogram with an image histogram is the number of pixels from the model that have corresponding pixels of the same color in the image. To obtain a fractional match value between 0 and 1 the intersection is normalized by the number of pixels in the model histogram. The match value is then

$$\frac{\sum_{j=1}^{n} \min(I_j, M_j)}{\sum_{j=1}^{n} M_j}.$$

This basic matching algorithm runs in time linear in the number of items in the database. Ingenious use of selected features and a preindexing of the catalog of objects allows the matching to take place in constant time (for up to 75 objects).

The normalized histogram intersection match value is a metric in feature-space, and so can be used for nearest neighbor classification. It has the useful property that it is not reduced by distracting pixels in the background. The histogram intersection match value is only increased by a pixel in the background if

- the pixel has the same color as one of the colors in the model, and
- the number of pixels of that color in the object is less than the number of pixels of that color in the model.

This match metric has been used in a matching algorithm that matches color histograms of images that contain predominantly one multicolored object with similar histograms of objects in a database of seventy objects. In the experiments the lighting was controlled but no other controls were necessary. Real time performance was achieved: The correct match was always in the 99th percentile of all the matches. Figure 12 shows the two main properties of the match metric. The first shows the view invariance: The match score stays above 0.8 for a given pattern over a considerable range in viewing angle. Comparing Figure 12(a) with Figure 12(b), it is easily seen that the match score when the incorrect model is used is almost always below 0.6, and thus there is considerable separation between the correct match score and the scores of false matches. This separation is the key to the algorithm's performance.

Although geometric features vary with the imaging geometry and hence viewpoint, invariant measures (such as moments), features (such as conics), and representations (such as invariant representations of planar curves) can be derived. They have the potential to provide the capability of recognition without explicit pose determination. Recent work in geometric (affine and projective) invariants [23, 39] shows some promise of discovering feature-extraction processes for planar and 3-D features that yield results not affected by perspective distortion. However considerable technical problems must be overcome before these invariants have the facility of color features, or of invariants to simpler (say affine) visual transformations.

6. LEARNING

Learning is necessary to cope with the world's unpredictability. Without learning, we are committed to programming based on an engineering assessment of the problem. This engineering assessment must anticipate the full extent of environments in which the visual system must operate, which limits the scope and generality of the result. Artificial Intelligence researchers have made great strides recently in the newest attack on the problem of learning. Since some representations used to support vision and manipulation are complex (e.g., Bayes nets, relational structures, kinematic and dynamic information), there is great value in being able to acquire them automatically. In our laboratory we have studied reinforcement learning for block stacking tasks in which foveation provides a "marker" that can be used to simplify and structure visual learning (Section 6.2). Furthermore we have shown that the performance of this algorithm can be greatly improved with the addition of a teacher (Section 6.3). We have learned (and generated) gaze paths and sequences of saccadic eye movements with hidden Markov models (Section 6.1). The object search strategies described in Section 4.3. can be learned.

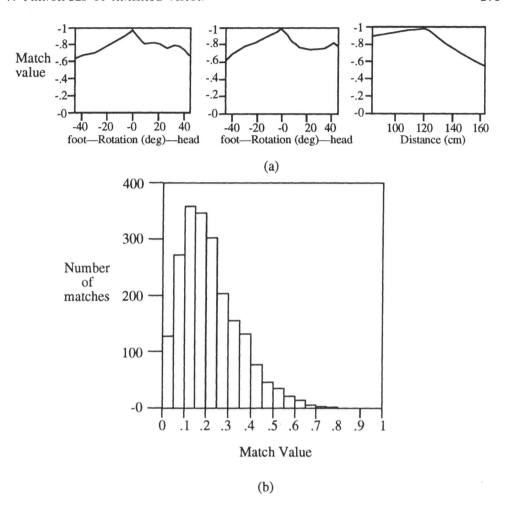

(a)

(b)

Figure 12. (a) Match values based on color histogram stay high despite various transformations of viewpoint. (b) The number of matches drops off violently as the match value increases.

6.1. LEARNING TO CONTROL SACCADES

Augmented (or adaptive) hidden Markov models (AHMMs) can learn graph structures representing either action sequences, adjacency and connectivity information about objects, or even control structures of observed algorithms [49]. The models are augmented in the sense that they can, at run-time, modify their output based on scene information. Their learning capabilities allow them to adapt to slowly varying scene characteristics. They are used in a generative mode to output learned behavior. Behavior can be learned either in a *where* mode, in which (say) specific visual locations are foveated in sequence, or in a *what* mode, which sequentially foveates a desired sequence of features in the image, regardless of their location. The training can come from an instructor, or from another program that is producing the behavior as the result of a cognitive process. The latter case is like learning a skill, in that a visuo-motor skill structure can be developed that does not have to repeat the reasoning process, and thus can run more efficiently.

Using the augmentation feature of the hidden Markov model, the output of the *where* and *what* systems each can be fed back to the other system, in order to train the system to output a sequence of desired features or objects in their expected locations in the image. The system also incorporates the adaptive visual feedback cues and a control scheme for verifying expectations using foveal image data.

The what-where-AHMM has a *what* part, a *where* part, and an output combiner (Figure 13). The *what* part contains two stages. The first stage is an AHMM whose output symbols, called *what-symbols*, are feature vectors intended to describe an object or characteristics of objects. Such feature vectors are assumed to have been computed for each pixel in the (peripheral) image. The second stage of the *what* part performs a "what-to-where" mapping, meaning that it maps a feature vector into a set of camera movement commands, called *where-symbols*, that would cause those locations to be foveated (centered in the image).

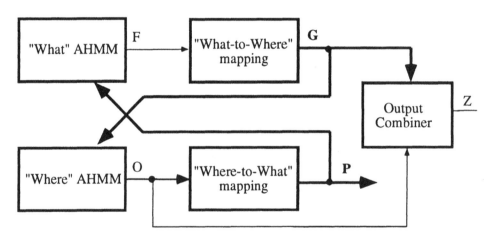

Figure 13. The "what-where" version of the AHMM. A Darker signal path denotes a set rather than a single signal value.

If the set of movement commands has only one member, the output sequence will fixate the desired objects in the scene. However, in general it does not, so some method must be developed to select among the choices. One option is to use a *where*-AHMM to help pick among the choices. In fact, the *what*-AHMM can be made to help the where-AHMM with its *own* choices.

The where-part contains two stages, similar to those in the *what* part. First it has an AHMM, which outputs a sequence of where-symbols. Secondly it has a "where-to-what" mapping that determines for each where-symbol the location in the current (peripheral) image it corresponds to, and outputs a set of feature vectors in that local area of the image. The module in the where-part uses as feedback a sequence of sets of where-symbols, which is the output of the *what* part.

Finally, the output combiner determines the overall output of the what-where-AHMM. The overall output at any time is a where-symbol (i.e., a camera movement command), selected as the element of the set that has the smallest distance to the current what symbol.

The what-where-AHMM operates as follows. At each time step, each of the two parts produces a set of feedback symbols that reflects its own preference for action. Each then updates its own preferences, taking the other's into account, and then generates its own final preference for action at that time step. The set of final preferences is reduced to a single output symbol by the output combiner.

6.2. LEARNING TO PERFORM SIMPLE TASKS

Current reinforcement learning techniques are only practical when the amount of state to be represented is small (less than 100 bits, say). One way to reduce the burden of representation to just that essential for the task is to use markers, temporary variables that record partial computational results. This notion of markers was introduced as a general method of object-centered computation [3]. The notion was that markers provide a local context to resolve reference ambiguity. Agre and Chapman's focus was routine activity. They sought to model behavior in terms of ongoing activity. Responses to the activity were in the form of rules that were activated by local context. The key points were that in routine activity, long causal chains were not necessary. It turns out that the fixation point strategy can be thought of as a kind of marker that has the right kind of transfer for learning many tasks.

A simulated block-stacking system at Rochester provides an example [62, 63]. On each trial, the system is presented with a pile of colored blocks. A pile consists of any number of blocks arbitrarily arranged. Each block is uniformly colored either red, green, or blue. The system can manipulate the pile by picking and placing objects. When the system arranges the blocks into a successful configuration, it receives a positive reward and the trial ends. For example, one extremely simple block stacking task is for the system to learn to pick up a green block. In this case, the successful configurations consist only of those states where the system is holding a green object (see Figure 14) [63]. The system learns to arrange arbitrary configurations of blocks into successful configurations. One key point is that the marker encoding obviates the need for explicit coordinates. However, the main point is that the system learns to build a reduced model of the world together with a behavior that uses only the primitives needed to solve the task. Figure 14 shows the performance on one example problem after the system has learned to solve the task.

6.3. EFFICIENT LEARNING REQUIRES A TEACHER

A very efficient way of extending the blocks learning task is to use a teacher that shows the robot system the task being performed. The teaching process provides vital cues to the relevant actions, the right order of actions, and the relevant objects [31]. If the teaching takes place through vision, the learning system sees the features of the environment in the relevant setting. This means that special-purpose feature encoding techniques can be used that may not generalize well but are vastly more effective.

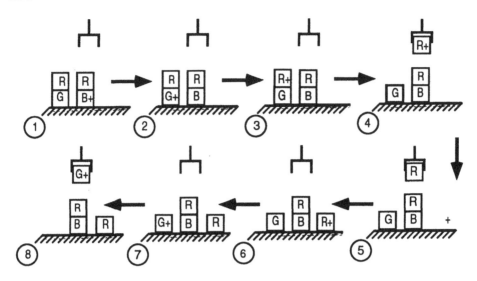

Figure 14. A sequence of world states in a typical learned solution path for the block manipulation task. The (+) shows the course of the fixation frame.

To study the effects of learning in the abstract, Whitehead [61] uses a general state space model and studies the effects of teaching as hints in a reinforcement learning paradigm. In particular, the model studies the effect of the probability of heading in a direction that is closer to the goal on the time to find the goal. The effect of this probability is dramatic and is shown plotted in Figure 15. If the probability of not heading in a helpful direction exceeds 0.5 then the problem becomes infeasible, whereas if this probability is less than 0.5, the problem is sublinear. This significant effect shows the value of a teacher, who could provide helpful information, and also shows that the information need only be vaguely helpful.

7. The Computational Hardware Environment

The Rochester Computer Science Department's Robotics and Vision Laboratory is designed to support research on anthropomorphic systems and is increasingly becoming instrumented to obtain psychophysical data [13] (Figure 16). It currently consists of seven key components: a binocular head containing movable cameras for visual input; a 16 degree of freedom Utah dextrous manipulator, or hand; a robot arm that supports and moves the hand or the head; an eye-tracking device; a special-purpose parallel processor for high-bandwidth, low-level vision processing; a Dataglove for digitizing hand movements (human and robotic); and general-purpose MIMD parallel computation for a wide range of computationally intensive jobs, from high-level vision and planning to hand and gaze control. Our MIMD computers include Transputers, the Butterfly Parallel Processor, and a Silicon Graphics multicomputer.

The head has two movable gray-scale CCD television cameras and a fixed color camera providing input to a MaxVideo pipelined image-processing system. One mo-

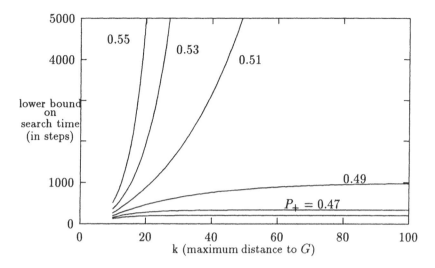

Figure 15. A teacher can influence the probability of making a right move, thus improving performance from infeasible to sublinear.

tor controls the tilt angle of the two-eye platform, and separate motors control each camera's pan angle, providing independent vergence control. The controllers allow both velocity and position commands and data read-back. The main feature of the camera controllers is their speed. Camera movements of 400 degrees per second can be achieved, approximating the 700 degrees per second speed of human eye movements.

The Utah Hand is a four-fingered, 16-DOF, tendon-driven, pneumatically actuated manipulator that allows us to do sophisticated manipulation. It is driven either by the SPARC station or the Transputer array. The Dataglove and Polhemus sensor allow computer readout 3-D position and orientation of a human hand and of certain of its joint positions. We have related the various coordinate systems of these sensors and actuators and can teleoperate the Puma and the Utah Hand via the Dataglove and Polhemus. The eye-tracker is part of a growing laboratory (funded by NIH) in which sophisticated stimuli will be produced by computer graphics and whole-head, arm, and eye responses will be monitored electronically. The basic goal is to extend psychophysics experiments beyond their current reductionist state.

The hand is maneuvered by a PUMA761 six degree-of-freedom arm with a two meter radius workspace and a top speed of about one meter per second. It is controlled by a dedicated LSI-11 computer implementing the proprietary VAL execution monitor and programming interface. We are upgrading the controller to the public-domain RCCL controller and acquiring a second manipulator so that coordinated head and hand movements will be possible. The hand and head are shown in Figure 17.

The MaxVideo pipelined image processing system consists of several independent boards that can be cabled together to achieve a wide range of frame-rate image analysis capabilities. The MaxVideo boards are all register programmable and are

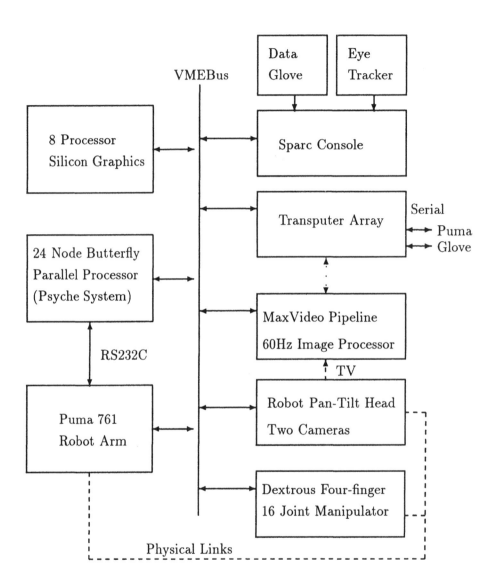

Figure 16. The Rochester Robotics and Vision Laboratory.

Figure 17. The Rochester Head and the Utah Hand.

controlled by the Butterfly or Sun via VME bus. The ZEBRA and ZED programming systems, developed at Rochester, make this hardware easily and interactively programmable.

An important feature of our laboratory is the capability to use a multiprocessor as the central computing resource and host. As more intimate connection is made between frame-rate computations in special hardware and the memory of general purpose computers, the visual computations that can be performed in real time grow more complex. Our Butterfly Plus Parallel Processor is a modest resource by today's standards. It has 24 nodes, each consisting of an MC68020 processor, MC68851 MMU, MC68881 FPU, and 4 MBytes of memory. It has a VME bus connection that mounts in the same card cage as the MaxVideo and motor controller boards. In addition, the Butterfly has a serial port on each board: We use the port to communicate directly with the VAL robot control software. The Silicon Graphics computer is a modern resource with eight 40 MHz MIPS chips. The Transputer array consists of eight 4MByte T805 TRAMS and a smart VME interface that lets the Transputers directly read and write VME memory and hence control the MaxVideo, Puma, eye motors, and hand. The KiwiVision product will allow Transputers to access the MaxBus directly, speeding higher-level visual processing. A Sun4/330 workstation acts as a host terminal system.

8. CONCLUSIONS

The ability to interact with the world and to do vision at high speeds has led to computational models of animate vision, in which the job of vision is not to build a complete internal explicit representation of the world, but rather to exhibit problem-solving behaviors [4]. These models explicitly include the mechanics of the perceiver and substitute behaviors for explicit representation. Development of the models is proceeding formally, in simulations, and in implementations. In particular, to implement these models, we have built an extensive laboratory and are incorporating hardware and software to support animate vision for applications in gaze control, learning, navigation, and manipulation.

We believe that these models collectively circumscribe a theory of vision whose tenets we outlined in Section 3. The theory described by animate vision may be seen as fundamentally different from the theories of Gibson and Marr in that it is cast at a lower level of abstraction, which relies on an essential description of the embodiment of the perceiver. This chapter has attempted to demonstrate how the particular characteristics of this embodiment, particularly the human eye movement system, lead to simplified algorithms for the traditionally knotty problems of computer vision. The resulting animate vision systems have the promise of delivering more accurate and robust visual performance and the theory may be a basis for explaining aspects of our visual experience such as the compelling sensation of a 3-D stable world.

REFERENCES

1. A.M. Agogino and K. Ramamurthi, "Real time influence diagrams for monitoring and controlling mechanical systems," In R.M. Oliver and J.Q. Smith (Eds.), *Influence Diagrams, Belief Nets and Decision Analysis*, John Wiley and Sons, 1990, 199–228.

2. J.M. Agosta, "The structure of Bayes networks for visual recognition," In *Uncertainty in AI*, North-Holland, 1990, 397–405.

3. P.E. Agre and D. Chapman, "Pengi: An implementation of a theory of activity," In *Proc. AAAI*, 1987, 268–272.

4. J.Y. Aloimonos, "Purposive and qualitative active vision," In *Proc. Image Understanding Workshop*, 1990, 816–828.

5. J. Aloimonos, I. Weiss and A. Bandyopadhyay, "Active vision," *Int'l. J. Computer Vision* 1, 1988, 333–356.

6. R. Bajcsy and P. Allen, "Sensing strategies," In *Proc. U.S.-France Robotics Workshop*, 1984.

7. D.H. Ballard, "Animate vision," *Artificial Intelligence* 48, 1991, 57–86.

8. D.H. Ballard and A. Ozcandarli, "Real-time kinetic depth," In *Proc. Int'l. Conf. on Computer Vision*, 1988, 524–531.

9. H.G. Barrow and J.M. Tenenbaum, "Recovering intrinsic scene characteristics from images," In A.R. Hanson and E.M. Riseman (Eds.), *Computer Vision Systems*, Academic Press, 1978, 3–26.

10. R.C. Bolles, "Verification vision for programmable assembly," In *Proc. Int'l. Joint Conf. on Artificial Intelligence*, 1977, 569–575.

11. R. Brooks, "Intelligence without representation," In *Proc. Workshop on the Foundations of Artificial Intelligence*, 1987.

12. R. Brooks, "Intelligence without reason," In *Proc. Int'l. Joint Conf. on Artificial Intelligence*, 1991.

13. C.M. Brown, "The Rochester Robot," Technical Report 257, Department of Computer Science, University of Rochester, 1988.

14. C.M. Brown, "Gaze controls with interactions and delays," *IEEE Trans. Systems, Man, Cybernetics* **20**, 1990.

15. C.M. Brown, "Prediction and cooperation in gaze control," *Biological Cybernetics* **63**, 1990, 61–70.

16. C.M. Brown and D.J. Coombs, "Notes on Control with Delay," Technical Report TR 387, Department of Computer Science, University of Rochester, 1991.

17. P.B. Chou and C.M. Brown, "The Theory and practice of Bayesian image labeling," *Int'l. J. Computer Vision* **4**, 1990, 185–210.

18. D.J. Coombs, *Real-Time Gaze Holding in Binocular Robot Vision*, Ph.D. thesis, University of Rochester, 1991.

19. D.J. Coombs and C. Brown, "Cooperative gaze holding in binocular vision," *IEEE Trans. Control Systems* **11**, 1991, 24–33.

20. T. Dean, T. Camus, and J. Kirman, "Sequential decision making for active perception," In *Proc. Image Understanding Workshop*, 1990, 889–894.

21. T.L. Dean and M.P. Wellman, *Planning and Control*, Morgan Kaufmann, 1991.

22. J. Feldman and R. Sproull, "Decision theory and artificial intelligence II: The hungry monkey," *Cognitive Science* **1**, 1977, 158–192.

23. D. Forsyth, J.L. Mundy, A. Zisserman, and C. Brown, "Projectively invariant representations using implicit algebraic curves," In *Proc. First European Conf. on Computer Vision* (revised version in *Proc. of Int'l. Conf. Computer Vision*), 1990.

24. T. Garvey, "Perceptual Strategies for Purposive Vision," Technical Report 117, SRI AI Center, 1976.

25. J.J. Gibson, *The Perception of the Visual World*, Houghton-Mifflin, Boston, 1950.

26. J.J. Gibson, *The Senses Considered as Perceptual Systems*, Houghton-Mifflin, Boston, 1966.

27. J.J. Gibson, *The Ecological Approach to Visual Perception*, Houghton-Mifflin, Boston, 1979.

28. D.J. Heeger, "Optical flow from spatiotemporal filters," In *Proc. 1st Int'l. Conf. on Computer Vision*, 1987, 181–190.

29. M. Henrion, "An Introduction to algorithms for inference in belief nets," In *Uncertainty in AI*, North-Holland, 1990, 129–138.

30. G.E. Hinton, "Commentary on 'Against direct perception'," *Behavioral and Brain Sciences* **3**, 1980.

31. Y. Kuniyoshi, H. Inoue, and M. Inaba, "Design and implementation of a system that generates assembly programs from visual recognition of human action sequences," In *Proc. IEEE Int'l. Workshop on Intelligent Robots and Systems*, 1990, 567–574.

32. G. Lakoff, *Women, Fire, and Dangerous Things: What Categories Reveal About the Mind*, University of Chicago Press, 1987.

33. D.N. Lee and J.R. Lishman, "Visual control of locomotion," *Scand. J. Psych.* **18**, 1977, 224–230.

34. T. Levitt, T. Binford, G. Ettinger, and P. Gelband, "Probability-based control for computer vision," In *Proc. Image Understanding Workshop*, 1989, 355–369.

35. D. Lowe, *Perceptual Organization and Visual Recognition*, Kluwer Academic Publishers, 1985.

36. D.C. Marr, *Vision*, W.H. Freeman and Co., Oxford, 1982.

37. J.D. McDonald and A.T. Bahill, "Zero-latency tracking of predictable targets by time-delay systems," *Int'l. J. Control* **38**,1983, 881–893.

38. M. Mishkin, L.G. Ungerleider, and K.A. Macko, "Object vision and spatial vision: Two cortical pathways," *Trends Neuroscience* **6**, 1983, 414–417.

39. J.L. Mundy and A. Zisserman (Eds.), *Geometric Invariants in Computer Vision*, MIT Press, 1992.

40. R.E. Neapolitan, *Probabilistic Reasoning in Expert Systems: Theory and Algorithms*, John Wiley and Sons, 1990.

41. R.C. Nelson, "Quantitative motion detection from a moving observer," *Int'l. J. Comp. Vision*, 1991.

42. R.C. Nelson and J. Aloimonos, "Obstacle avoidance using flow field divergence," *IEEE Trans. Pattern Anal. Mach. Intell.* **11**, 1989, 1102–1106.

43. T.J. Olson and D.J. Coombs, "Real-time Vergence Control for Binocular Robots," Technical Report 348, Department of Computer Science, University of Rochester, June 1990.

44. J. Pearl, *Probabilistic Reasoning in Intelligent Systems: Networks of Plausible Inference*, Morgan Kaufman, 1988.

45. A. Pentland, "Shape from shading: A theory of human perception," In *Proc. Int'l. Conf. on Computer Vision*, 1988.

46. M.A. Peot and R.D. Shachter, "Fusion and propagation with multiple observations in belief networks," *Artificial Intelligence* **48**, 1991, 299–318.

47. J.G. Proakis, *Digital Communications*, McGraw-Hill, Inc., 1983.

48. R.D. Rimey, "Where to look next using a Bayes net: An overview," In *Proc. Image Understanding Workshop*, 1992, 927–932.

49. R.D. Rimey and C.M. Brown, "Controlling eye movements with hidden Markov models," *Int'l. J. Computer Vision* **7**, 1991, 47–66.

50. R.D. Rimey and C.M. Brown, "Task-oriented vision with multiple Bayes nets," In A. Blake and A. Yuille (Eds.), *Active Vision*, MIT Press, 1992, 151–172.

51. R.D. Rimey and C.M. Brown, "Task-specific utilities in a general Bayes net vision system," In *Proc. IEEE Conf. on Computer Vision and Pattern Recognition*, 1992, 142–147.

52. R.D. Rimey and C.M. Brown, "Where to look next using a Bayes net: Incorporating geometric relations," In *Proc. European Conf. on Computer Vision*, 1992, 542–550.

53. R.D. Schachter, "Evaluating influence diagrams," *Operations Research* **34**, 1986, 871–882.

54. G. Shafer and J. Pearl (Eds.), *Readings in Uncertain Reasoning*, Morgan Kaufmann, 1990.

55. J. Soong and C.M. Brown, "Inverse Kinematics and Gaze Stabilization for the Rochester Robot Head," Technical Report 394, Department of Computer Science, University of Rochester, 1991.

56. M.J. Swain, *Color Indexing*, Ph.D. thesis, Department of Computer Science, University of Rochester, 1990.

57. M.J. Swain and D.H. Ballard, "Indexing via color histograms," In *Proc. NATO Workshop on Computer Vision*, 1989.

58. M.J. Swain and D.H. Ballard, "Indexing via color histograms," In *Proc. Int'l. Conf. on Computer Vision*, 1990.

59. A. Treisman, "Features and objects: The fourteenth Bartlett memorial lecture," *The Quarterly J. Experimental Psychology* **40**, 1988, 201–237.

60. A.M. Waxman, "An image flow paradigm," In *Proc. IEEE Workshop on Computer Vision, Representation, and Control*, 1984, 49–55.

61. S.D. Whitehead, "Complexity and cooperation in reinforcement learning," In *Proc. Nat'l. Conf. on Artificial Intelligence*, 1991. (Also appeared in the *8th Machine Learning Workshop*, 1991; a longer version appeared as TR 365, Computer Sci. Dept., U. Rochester, 1991).

62. S.D. Whitehead and D.H. Ballard, "A Computational Model of Activity Control in Autonomous Robots," Internal report, Department of Computer Science, University of Rochester, 1988.

63. S.D. Whitehead and D.H. Ballard, "Active perception and reinforcement learning," In *Proc. Int'l. Conf. on Machine Learning*, 1990.

64. L.E. Wixson, "Searching for Objects with a Mobile Camera," Technical report, Department of Computer Science, University of Rochester, 1991.

65. L. Wixson, "Exploiting World Structure to Search for Objects Efficiently," Technical Report, Department of Computer Science, University of Rochester, 1992.

66. L.E. Wixson and D.H. Ballard, "Real-time detection of multi-colored objects," In P.S. Schenker (Ed.), *Sensor Fusion II: Human and Machine Strategies* (*Proc. SPIE Symp. on Advances in Intelligent Robotics Systems*), 1990, 435–446.

67. A.L. Yarbus, *Eye Movements and Vision*, Plenum Press, 1967.

68. Y. Yeshurun and E.L. Schwartz, "Cepstral filtering on a columnar image architecture: A fast Algorithm for Binocular Stereo Segmentation," Technical Report TR 286, Courant Institute, New York, 1987.

Y

Z